Fodor's **Up CLOSE**

IRELAND

the complete guide, thoroughly up-to-date

SAVVY TRAVELING: WHERE TO SPEND, HOW TO SAVE

packed with details that will make your trip

CULTURAL TIPS: ESSENTIAL LOCAL DO'S AND TABOOS

must-see sights, on and off the beaten path

INSIDER SECRETS: WHAT'S HIP AND WHAT TO SKIP

the buzz on restaurants, the lowdown on lodgings

FIND YOUR WAY WITH CLEAR AND EASY-TO-USE MAPS

Previously published as part of *The Berkeley Guide to Great Britain & Ireland*

FODOR'S TRAVEL PUBLICATIONS, INC.

NEW YORK • TORONTO • LONDON • SYDNEY • AUCKLAND

www.fodors.com/

COPYRIGHT

FODOR'S UPCLOSE™ IRELAND

Editor: Anto Howard

Editorial Contributors: Laurence Belgrave, David Brown, Fionn Davenport, M. T. Schwartzman, Cale Siler

Editorial Production: Tracy Patruno

Maps: David Lindroth Inc.; Eureka Cartography, *cartographer*; Robert Blake, *map editor*

Design: Fabrizio La Rocca, *creative director*; Allison Saltzman, *cover and text design*; Jolie Novak, *photo editor*

Production/Manufacturing: Robert B. Shields

Cover Art: ©Pratt-Pries/DIAF

CONTENTS

5. THE SOUTHWEST 70

6. CORK CITY 89

7. THE WEST 98

8. THE NORTHWEST 115

9. NORTHERN IRELAND 126

PORTRAITS OF IRELAND

INDEX 166

TRAVELING UPCLOSE

G o to a festival. Commune with nature. Memorize the symphony of the streets. And if you want to experience the heart and soul of Ireland, whatever you do, don't spend too much money. The deep and rich experience of Ireland that every true traveler yearns for is one of the things in life that money can't buy. In fact, if you have it, don't use it. Traveling lavishly is the surest way to turn yourself into a sideline traveler. Restaurants with white-glove service are great—sometimes—but they're usually not the best place to find the perfect beef and barley stew. Doormen at plush hotels have their place, but not when your look-alike room could be anywhere from Dusseldorf to Detroit. Better to stay in a more intimate place that truly gives you the atmosphere you traveled so far to experience. Don't just stand and watch—jump into the spirit of what's around you.

If you want to see Ireland up close and savor the essence of the country and its people in all their charming glory, this book is for you. We'll show you the local culture, the offbeat sights, the bars and cafés where tourists rarely tread, and the B&Bs and other hostelries where you'll meet fellow travelers—places where the locals would send their friends. And because you'll probably want to see the famous places if you haven't already been there, we give you tips on losing the crowds, plus the quirky and obscure facts you want as well as the basics everyone needs.

OUR GANG

Who's are we? We're artists and poets, slackers and straight arrows, and travel writers and journalists, who in our less hedonistic moments report on local news and spin out an occasional opinion piece. What we share is a certain footloose spirit and a passion for the land of saints and scholars that we celebrate in this guidebook. Shamelessly, we've revealed all of our favorite places and our deepest, darkest travel secrets, all so that you can learn from our past mistakes and experience the best part of Ireland to the fullest. If you can't take your best friend on the road or if your best friend is hopeless with directions, stick with us.

LAURENCE BELGRAVE • Determined to breathe real air again after a winter spent editing his new short film, director and writer Laurence Belgrave leapt at the chance to roam about Ireland writing for the *Upclose Ireland* guide. English by birth, Laurence attended Trinity College Dublin as a literature major and fell head over heels for his adopted country.

ANTO HOWARD • Northside Dublin native Anto Howard (christened Anthony; Dubliners have a bad habit of abbreviating perfectly good names) studied at Trinity College before acquiring his green card in a lottery and moving to New York, where he works as a travel writer and editor and a playwright.

CALE SILER • Highlights of Cale Siler's assignment to Ireland and Northern Ireland included: two spectacular mountain bike crashes on the Beara Peninsula, writing Belfast manuscript at a Dublin Sinn Féin rally, sea kayaking with three-time national kayaking champion Jim Kennedy, and participating in both Dublin and Galway Gay Pride marches. To top off his tour of Northern Ireland, Cale was unwillingly swept into Derry's Catholic Bogside district by rioting nationalists and some very angry members of the British army. Cale eventually returned to the tranquility of his native California.

A SEND-OFF

Always call ahead. We knock ourselves out to check all the facts, but everything changes all the time, in ways that none of us can ever fully anticipate. Whenever you're making a special trip to a special place, as opposed to merely wandering, always call ahead. Trust us on this.

And then, if something doesn't go quite right—as inevitably happens with even the best-laid plans—stay cool. Missed your train? Stuck in the airport? Use the time to study the people. Strike up a conversation with a stranger. Study the newsstands or flip through the local press. Take a walk. Find the silver lining in the clouds, whatever it is. And do send us a postcard to tell us what went wrong and what went right. You can e-mail us at editors@fodors.com (specify the name of the book on the subject line), or write the Ireland editor at Fodor's upCLOSE, 201 East 50th Street, New York, NY 10022. We'll put your ideas to good use and let other travelers benefit from your experiences. In the mean time, bon voyage!

INTRODUCTION

U ntil Columbus stumbled upon the not-so-New World in 1492, Ireland was on the very edge of the European universe. To the merchants and explorers who chanced upon this storm-battered isle, Ireland was a wild, indomitable place, mysterious and brooding; a land that, viewed from afar, appeared to rise in defiance from the water. To the medieval mind, Ireland was only a short sail away from oblivion.

Though an island has the barrier of the sea to protect it from enemies, the history of Ireland really is the history of its many conquerors, be they the Celts, Vikings, Anglo-Normans, or British. According to myth, Ireland was first conquered by the Fir Bolg, a brawny race of giants who are credited in folklore for building Northern Ireland's Giant's Causeway, a bridge hewn from raw stone, which supposedly once connected Ireland with Scotland. The Fir Bolg "invasion" and the shreds of oral history that document it most likely reflect the coming of the Celts, a Continental tribe of warriors who arrived in Ireland during the 6th century BC. This was an age of glory in Ireland, a time of Druidic learning and bardic poetry, a time when ferocious warriors roamed in search of honor, glory, and of course heads (head-hunting was a common Celtic practice). To judge by the tales that survive, poetry and philosophy were highly developed by the early Celts. So, too, were silver working, wood and stone carving, and weapon making.

The next wave of conquerors, the Christians, under the guidance of St. Patrick himself, appeared around the 4th century AD. While continental Europe languished in the so-called Dark Ages, Ireland, basking in its golden age, became a beacon of enlightenment. Some say Christianity has left a deep scar on the country; others contend it's a sign from God that the Irish are among the chosen. In any case, Christianity and the Catholic Church are pervasive forces in Ireland. If you're in doubt, travel to the small village of Knock in County Mayo. Ever since the Virgin Mary was seen on a church wall in 1879, Knock has been inundated with pilgrims. Even today, they can be seen gathered outside the glass-encased shrine 24 hours a day, 365 days a year. But a spate of shock revelations concerning sexual abuse by priests, followed by the admission by one of Ireland's premier bishops that he had fathered a child shook the church's hold on the national psyche. A serious anticlerical backlash across the country has seen the introduction of limited abortion rights and divorce.

The most serious threat to the early Christians was the Vikings, who began their conquest of the coast around 800, establishing settlements in Wexford, Cork, and Dublin. The country's religious orders generally received protection from God-fearing Irish kings, but neither was able to withstand the Vikings'

FORGET TO PACK ENOUGH MONEY?

MoneyGram℠ can help you, NOW!

- Your money arrives in just minutes to any of our 3,300 locations throughout Europe

- Customer Service Representatives available 24 hours a day who can inform you where the closest MoneyGram℠ money transfer location is.

So, if the money you need to see Europe has seen its last days, call us and we'll direct you to a MoneyGram℠ Agent close to you.

Ireland
1-800-55-9372

MONEY IN MINUTES WORLDWIDE℠

ruthless onslaught. Ireland had a short reprieve following the Battle of Clontarf in 1014, when Irish king Brian Boru defeated a troop of Viking raiders off the coast near Dublin. But Boru's subsequent murder signaled the end of an era: Following 1014, Ireland would never again be a Christian or Celtic kingdom. Conquered and subdued, Celtic Ireland would slowly fade into oblivion, its culture and traditions relegated to the imagination, myth, and fairy tale.

It was in this context that, in 1155, English-born Pope Adrian IV boldly granted dominion over Ireland to his fellow Englishman, King Henry II. In retrospect, the move seems presumptuous when you consider that England previously had hardly bothered with Irish affairs; to the Irish, such arrogance simply tells the whole tangled story of Anglo-Irish relations, or the lack thereof. The Irish resisted as best they could, but the disciplined British troops overpowered them. By the time the last of Ireland's Gaelic kings—the O'Neills and O'Donnells—had their remaining land confiscated by the British in 1603, Ireland had become a servile colony where English nobles lorded over an adopted homeland.

Following English King Henry VIII's conversion to Protestantism in 1534, Ireland was divided not only along political lines but also along religious ones. Just over a century later, the religious schism became the focus of renewed animosity in the aftermath of the English Civil War, when the pro-Catholic Charles I was deposed by the vigorously Protestant Oliver Cromwell. Cromwell came to Ireland in 1649, intent on making it a Protestant country, and unleashed his troops, beginning a campaign of persecution against the already bitter Irish Catholics.

Worse was still to come in the wake of Cromwell's Act of Settlement (1652). It called for the forced migration of all Catholics west of the River Shannon. If they removed themselves from the Anglicized and increasingly commercialized east, the Gaels were welcome to relocate, in Cromwell's words, either "to Hell or Connaught." To this day, many in Ireland feel bitter animosity toward the British, whom they blame for more than one grim chapter in their country's history. In the mid-19th century, such feelings led to the rise of an Irish nationalist movement. Known variously as both the Fenians and the Irish Republic Brotherhood, these nationalists agitated for equal rights for Catholics, land reform, and the revival of Ireland's Gaelic heritage—not to mention the expulsion of all Brits from Éire.

Much of this hatred stems from the Great Famine of the 1840s and '50s. Throughout the early 19th century, poverty was endemic and disease was a simple fact of life. Irish peasants worked for absentee British landlords and either paid exorbitant rents for land that had probably belonged to their parents or grandparents or simply starved. The system was harsh and unjust, but somehow the bulk of Ireland survived the lean years prior to 1845. Within a year, however, potato blight ruined crops throughout the country. By 1857, after repeated crop failures, the population of Ireland had decreased from 8 million to 3 million. Starvation was largely to blame for the decline, but this period also marks the first large-scale emigration to America, Australia, and Canada—a draining and disruptive phenomenon that haunted Ireland until very recently. In 1848, nearly a quarter million people were emigrating annually; today, at last, more people are returning that leaving.

The other great victim of the famine was Irish culture. Whole areas of the island were depopulated, and many villages became ghost towns (even today you'll see abandoned famine-era cottages dotting the countryside). As the soul of a centuries-old way of life slipped into oblivion, the English language became the de facto replacement for a people who no longer knew their heritage. The Irish poet Mac Marcus wrote the following in the 17th century, but his words aptly describe the state of post-famine Ireland: "Without laughter at the antics of children; music censored; and Gaelic banned."

But Ireland has effected its own sweetly subtle form of revenge: the development of an identity that is rooted in shared suffering, the subtle twist of a phrase, rural backwardness and poverty, and—perhaps most important of all—in the realization that time and an unhurried lifestyle are the luxuries of the vanquished. In the words of Oliver Goldsmith, another of Ireland's great Anglo-Irish authors: "The natives are peculiarly remarkable for their gaiety . . . and levity; English transplanted here lose their serious melancholy and become gay and thoughtless, more fond of pleasure and less addicted to reason." From an Irish perspective, these are the highest of compliments.

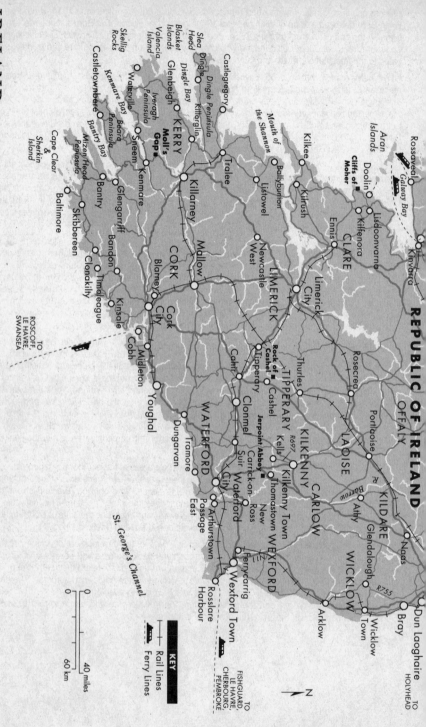

IRELAND

REPUBLIC OF IRELAND

KEY

Rail Lines
Ferry Lines

St. George's Channel

0 40 miles
0 60 km

x

IRELAND

BASICS

contacts and savvy tips to make your trip hassle-free

I f you've ever traveled with anyone before, you know that there are two types of people in the world—the planners and the nonplanners. Travel brings out the worst in both groups. Left to their own devices, the planners will have you goose-stepping from attraction to attraction on a cultural blitzkrieg, while the nonplanners will invariably miss the flight, the bus, and maybe even the point. This chapter offers you a middle ground; we hope it provides enough information to help you plan your trip to Ireland without nailing you down. Keep flexible, and remember that the most hair-pulling situations turn into the best travel stories back home.

AIR TRAVEL

AIRPORTS

The major gateways to the Republic of Ireland are Shannon Airport on the west coast, 25½ km (16 mi) west of Limerick City, and Dublin Airport, 10 km (6 mi) north of the city center. Two airports serve Belfast: Belfast International Airport at Aldergove, 24 km (15 mi) from the city, handles all international traffic; Belfast Harbour Airport, 6½ km (4 mi) from the city, handles local and U.K. flights only. In addition, Eglinton, Derry's airport, receives flights from Manchester and Glasgow in the United Kingdom (Loganair).

AIRPORT INFORMATION • Shannon Airport (tel. 011–353–61/471666). **Dublin Airport** (tel. 011–353–1/844–4900). **Belfast International Airport at Aldergove** (tel. 011–44–1849/422888). **Belfast Harbour Airport** (tel. 011–44–1849/57754).

MAJOR AIRLINE OR LOW-COST CARRIER?

Most people choose a flight based on price. Yet there are other issues to consider. Major airlines offer the greatest number of departures; smaller airlines—including regional, low-cost and no-frill airlines—usually have a more limited number of flights daily. Major airlines have frequent-flyer partners, which allow you to credit mileage earned on one airline to your account with another. Low-cost airlines offer a definite price advantage and fewer restrictions, such as advance-purchase requirements. Safety-wise, low-cost carriers as a group have a good history, but **check the safety record before booking** any low-cost carrier; call the Federal Aviation Administration's Consumer Hotline (*see* Airline Complaints, *below*).

MAJOR AIRLINES • From the U.S. and Canada: Aer Lingus (tel. 212/557–1110 or 800/223–6537). **Delta** (tel. 800/241–4141). From the U.K.: **Aer Lingus** (tel. 0181/899–4747). **Ryanair** (tel. 0171/435–

7101). **British Airways** (tel. 800/AIRWAYS in the U.S.; 1345/222–1111 in the U.K.) and **British Midland** (tel. 0171/589–5599) have regular schedules to Belfast airport. From Down Under: **Qantas** (tel. 800/227–4500 in the U.S.; 02/957–0111 toll-free in Sydney; 0800/808–767 outside Auckland; 09/379–0306 in Auckland).

DON'T STOP UNLESS YOU MUST

When you book, **look for nonstop flights** and **remember that "direct" flights stop at least once.** International flights on a country's flag carrier are almost always nonstop; U.S. airlines often fly direct. Try to **avoid connecting flights,** which require a change of plane. Two airlines may jointly operate a connecting flight, so ask if your airline operates every segment—you may find that your preferred carrier flies you only part of the way.

USE AN AGENT

Travel agents, especially those who specialize in finding the lowest fares (*see* Discounts & Deals, *below*), can be especially helpful when booking a plane ticket. When you're quoted a price, **ask your agent if the price is likely to get any lower.** Good agents know the seasonal fluctuations of airfares and can usually anticipate a sale or fare war. However, waiting can be risky: The fare could go *up* as seats become scarce, and you may wait so long that your preferred flight sells out. A wait-and-see strategy works best if your plans are flexible, but if you must arrive and depart on certain dates, don't delay.

GET THE LOWEST FARE

The least expensive airfares to Ireland are priced for round-trip travel. Major airlines usually require that you **book in advance and buy the ticket within 24 hours,** and you may have to stay over a Saturday night. It's smart to **call a number of airlines, and when you are quoted a good price, book it on the spot**—the same fare may not be available on the same flight the next day. Airlines generally allow you to change your return date for a fee of $25–$50. If you don't use your ticket, you can apply the cost toward the purchase of a new ticket, again for a small charge. However, most low-fare tickets are nonrefundable. To get the lowest airfare, **check different routings.** If your destination or home city has more than one gateway, compare prices to and from different airports. Flexibility is the key to getting a serious bargain on airfare. If you can play around with your departure date, destination, and return date, you will probably save money. Ask which days of the week are the cheapest to fly on—weekends are often the most expensive. Even the time of day you fly can make a big difference in the cost of your ticket. Also look into discounts available through student- and budget-travel organizations (*see* Students, *below*).

CHECK WITH CONSOLIDATORS

Consolidators, also sometimes known as bucket shops, buy tickets for scheduled flights at reduced rates from the airlines then sell them at prices that beat the best fare available directly from the airlines, usually without advance restrictions. Sometimes you can even get your money back if you need to return the ticket. Carefully read the fine print detailing penalties for changes and cancellations, **confirm your consolidator reservation with the airline,** and be sure to check restrictions, refund possibilities, and payment conditions.

CONSOLIDATORS • **Airfare Busters** (5100 Westheimer, Suite 550, Houston, TX 77056, tel. 713/961–5109 or 800/232–8783, fax 713/961–3385). **Globe Travel** (507 5th Ave., Suite 606, New York, NY 10017, tel. 212/843–9885 or 800/969–4562, fax 212/843–9889). **United States Air Consolidators Association** (925 L St., Suite 220, Sacramento, CA 95814, tel. 916/441–4166, fax 916/441–3520). **UniTravel** (1177 N. Warson Rd., St. Louis, MO 63132, tel. 314/569–2501 or 800/325–2222, fax 314/569–2503). **Up & Away Travel** (347 5th Ave., Suite 202, New York, NY 10016, tel. 212/889–2345 or 800/275–8001, fax 212/889–2350).

CONSIDER A CHARTER

Charters usually have the lowest fares but are not dependable. Departures are infrequent and seldom on time, check-in can be chaos, schedules are often weird, and flights can be delayed for up to 48 hours or can be canceled for any reason up to 10 days before you're scheduled to leave. Moreover, itineraries and prices can change after you've booked your flight, so you must **be very careful to choose a legitimate charter carrier.** Don't commit to a charter operator that doesn't follow proper booking procedures. Be especially careful when buying a charter ticket. Read the fine print regarding refund policies. If you can't pay with a credit card, **make your check payable to a charter carrier's escrow account** (unless you're dealing with a travel agent, in which case his or her check should be made payable to the escrow account). The name of the bank should be in the charter contract.

CHARTER CARRIERS • **DER Tours** (tel. 800/782–2424). **MartinAir** (tel. 800/627–8462). **Tower Air** (tel. 800/34–TOWER). **Travel CUTS** (tel. 416/979–2406). **Council Travel** and **STA** (*see* Students, *below*) also offer exclusively negotiated discount airfares on scheduled airlines.

GO AS A COURIER

Courier flights are simple: You sign a contract with a courier service to babysit their packages (often without ever laying eyes on them, let alone hands), and the courier company pays at least half of your airfare. On the day of departure, you arrive at the airport a few hours early, meet someone who hands you a ticket and customs forms, and off you go. After you land, you simply clear customs with the courier luggage and deliver it to a waiting agent.

It's cheap and easy, but there are restrictions: Flights are usually booked only a week or two in advance—often only a few days in advance—and you are allowed carry-on luggage only, because the courier uses your checked luggage allowance to transport the shipment. You must return within one to four weeks, and times and destinations are limited. If you plan to travel with a companion, you'll probably have to travel a day apart. And you may be asked to pay a deposit, to be refunded after you have completed your assignment.

COURIER CONTACTS • **Discount Travel International** (169 W. 81st St., New York, NY 10024, tel. 212/362–3636, fax 212/362–3236). **Now Voyager** (tel. 212/431–1616, fax 212/334–5243).

AVOID GETTING BUMPED

Airlines routinely overbook planes, knowing that not everyone with a ticket will show up, but sometimes everyone does. When that happens, airlines ask for volunteers to give up their seats. In return, these volunteers usually get a certificate for a free flight and are rebooked on the next flight out. If there are not enough volunteers, the airline must choose who will be denied boarding. The first to get bumped are passengers who checked in late and those flying on discounted tickets, so **get to the gate and check in as early as possible,** especially during peak periods.

Always **bring a photo ID to the airport.** You may be asked to show it before you are allowed to check in.

ENJOY THE FLIGHT

For more legroom, **request an emergency-aisle seat**; don't, however, sit in the row in front of the emergency aisle or in front of a bulkhead, where seats may not recline.

If you don't like airline food, **ask for special meals when booking.** These can be vegetarian, low-cholesterol, or kosher, for example.

To avoid jet lag try to maintain a normal routine while traveling. At night **get some sleep.** By day **eat light meals, drink water (not alcohol), and move about the cabin** to stretch your legs.

Some carriers have prohibited smoking throughout their systems; others allow smoking only on certain routes or even certain departures from that route, so **contact your carrier regarding its smoking policy.**

COMPLAIN IF NECESSARY

If your baggage goes astray or your flight goes awry, complain right away. Most carriers require that you file a claim immediately.

AIRLINE COMPLAINTS • U.S. Department of Transportation **Aviation Consumer Protection Division** (C-75, Washington, DC 20590, tel. 202/366–2220). **Federal Aviation Administration (FAA) Consumer Hotline** (tel. 800/322–7873).

BICYCLING

Ireland is a cyclist's paradise. The scenery is phenomenal, the roads are flat and uncrowded, and the distance from one village to the next is rarely more than 10 miles. On the downside, foul weather and rough roads are all too common, so rain gear and spare parts are a must. Although most large and mid-size towns have some sort of bike shop, if you break down in the country, you're very much on your own. Most ferries will transport your bicycle across the Irish Sea for free, and if there is room bikes can be transported on Irish Rail and Irish Bus for a small fee.

There are plenty of shops offering bike rentals scattered throughout Ireland. Most offer some version of the Raleigh Rent-A-Bike scheme, which consists of a 12- or 18-speed mountain bike with index gears, rear carriers, and heavy-duty pannier bags for about £7 per day or £30 per week. A refundable deposit of £40 is often required. For a £12 fee, you can often rent a bike in one location and drop it off in another.

RALEIGH RENT-A-BIKE DEALERS • Contact any Bord Fáilte tourist desk or **Raleigh Ireland Ltd.** (tel. 01/626–1333).

BUS TRAVEL

Bus Éireann provides reasonably priced, comfortable service to nearly every town in Ireland. Expressway routes are listed in yellow in the Bus Éireann timetable (80p), available at any depot or at its Dublin office. A Travelsave stamp (*see* Transportation, *below*) will reduce your bus tickets by 10%–30%. Bus Éireann also issues Rambler tickets (*see below*) for unlimited travel. Be aware that bus travel in Ireland is severely curtailed on Sunday (especially in rural areas) and that winter bus service is less frequent and comprehensive than summer service.

DISCOUNT PASSES

Bus Éireann has a series of passes that allow unlimited intercity bus travel in both the Republic and Northern Ireland. The Irish Rambler Bus Only pass is valid in the Republic of Ireland for either 3 days ($43), 8 days ($105), or 15 days ($152) of travel in any one month. The Irish Rover Bus Only pass is good for travel in all 32 counties of Ireland: 3 days ($56), 8 days ($132), and 15 days ($201). All the above passes are also valid on city services in Cork, Limerick, Galway, Waterford, and Belfast—but not in Dublin. Eurail Pass holders get discounts of up to 20% on the purchase of these passes. Bus Éireann also offers bus and rail passes that are great value for anyone planning extensive travel in more rural parts of the island where trains may not go: the Irish Explorer Rail and Bus covers the Republic only and costs ($140) for 8 days. The Emerald Card allows unlimited use of buses and trains in both the Republic and Northern Ireland and comes in increments of 8 days out of 15 ($163) and 15 days out of 30 ($279).

BUS INFORMATION • **Bus Éireann** (Busáras, Store St., Dublin, tel. 01/836–6111).

BUSINESS HOURS

Standard business hours are Monday–Saturday 9–5. Until recently, it was a no-no (thanks to the church) for stores to remain open on Sunday, but plenty of businesses now do. In small villages, many shops also close for lunch. Pubs are usually open Monday–Saturday 11–11 and Sunday noon–10:30; in summertime they stay open until 11:30. Most banks are open 9:30–noon and 1–3:30; some have extended hours on Thursday evening.

CAR RENTAL

If you are renting a car in the Irish Republic and intend to visit Northern Ireland, make this clear when you get your car. Similarly, if you rent in Northern Ireland and cross the border, make sure the rental insurance applies.

Rates in Dublin begin at $41 a day and $151 a week for an economy car with air-conditioning, a manual transmission, and unlimited mileage. This does not include tax on car rentals, which is 12.5%.

CUT COSTS

To get the best deal, **book through a travel agent who is willing to shop around.**

Be sure to **look into wholesalers,** companies that do not own fleets but rent in bulk from those that do and often offer better rates than traditional car-rental operations. Prices are best during off-peak periods. Rentals booked through wholesalers must be paid for before you leave the United States.

Also **ask your travel agent about a company's customer-service record.** How has it responded to late plane arrivals and vehicle mishaps? Are there often lines at the rental counter, and, if you're traveling during a holiday period, does a confirmed reservation guarantee you a car?

No matter who you rent from, remember to ask about required deposits, cancellation penalties, and drop-off charges if you're planning to pick up the car in one city and leave it in another.

MAJOR AGENCIES • **Alamo** (tel. 800/522–9696, 0800/272–2000 in the U.K.). **Avis** (tel. 800/331–1084, 800/879–2847 in Canada). **Budget** (tel. 800/527–0700, 0800/181181 in the U.K.). **Dollar** (tel.

800/800–4000; 0990/565656 in the U.K., where it is known as Eurodollar). **Hertz** (tel. 800/654–3001, 800/263–0600 in Canada, 0345/555888 in the U.K.). **National InterRent** (tel. 800/227–3876; 0345/222525 in the U.K., where it is known as Europcar InterRent).

LOCAL COMPANIES • Argus (tel. 01/490–4444). **Dan Dooley** (tel. 01/6772723). **ECL Chauffeur Drive** (tel. 01/704–4062) rent Mercedes Saloons and minicoaches on a journey or daily rate.

RENTAL WHOLESALERS • Auto Europe (tel. 207/842–2000 or 800/223–5555, fax 800–235–6321). **DER Travel Services** (9501 W. Devon Ave., Rosemont, IL 60018, tel. 800/782–2424, fax 800/282–7474 for information or 800/860–9944 for brochures). The **Kemwel Group** (tel. 914/835–5555 or 800/678–0678, fax 914/835–5126).

NEED INSURANCE?

The car may not be yours, but you are generally responsible for any damage to or loss of a rental vehicle. Before you rent, **see what coverage you already have** under the terms of your personal auto-insurance policy and credit cards.

Collision policies that car-rental companies sell for European rentals typically do not cover stolen vehicles. Before you buy additional coverage for theft, find out if your credit card or personal auto insurance will cover the loss.

BEWARE SURCHARGES

Before you pick up a car in one city and leave it in another, **ask about drop-off charges or one-way service fees,** which can be substantial. Note, too, that some rental agencies charge extra if you return the car before the time specified on your contract. To avoid a hefty refueling fee, **fill the tank just before you turn in the car,** but be aware that gas stations near the rental outlet may overcharge.

MEET THE REQUIREMENTS

In Ireland your own driver's license is acceptable. An International Driver's Permit is a good idea; it's available from the American or Canadian automobile association or, in the United Kingdom, from the Automobile Association or Royal Automobile Club.

CONSUMER PROTECTION

Whenever possible, **pay with a major credit card** so you can cancel payment if there's a problem and you can provide documentation. This is a good idea whether you're buying travel arrangements before your trip or shopping at your destination.

If you're doing business with a particular company for the first time, **contact your local Better Business Bureau and the attorney general's offices** in your state and the company's home state as well. Have any complaints been filed?

Finally, if you're buying a package, always **consider travel insurance** that includes default coverage (*see* Insurance, *below*).

LOCAL BBBS • Council of Better Business Bureaus (4200 Wilson Blvd., Suite 800, Arlington, VA 22203, tel. 703/276–0100, fax 703/525–8277).

CUSTOMS & DUTIES

When shopping, **keep receipts** for all of your purchases. Upon reentering the country, **be ready to show customs officials what you've bought.** It's best to have everything in one easily accessible place—and don't wrap gifts. If you feel a duty is incorrect, appeal the assessment. If you object to the way your clearance was handled, get the inspector's badge number. In either case, first ask to see a supervisor, then write to the port director at the address listed on your receipt. Send a copy of the receipt and other appropriate documentation. If you still don't get satisfaction, you can take your case to customs headquarters in Washington.

ENTERING IRELAND

Two categories of duty-free allowance exist for travelers entering Ireland: one for goods obtained outside the European Union (EU), on a ship or aircraft, or in a duty-free store within the EU; and the other for goods bought in the EU, with duty and tax paid.

Of the first category, you may import duty-free: (1) 200 cigarettes or 100 cigarillos or 50 cigars or 250 grams of smoking tobacco; (2) 2 liters of wine and either 1 liter of alcoholic drink over 22% volume or 2 liters of alcoholic drink under 22% volume (sparkling or fortified wine included); (3) 50 grams of perfume and ¼ liter of toilet water; and (4) other goods to a value of £142 per person (£73 per person for travelers under 15 years of age).

Of the second category, you may import duty-free a considerable amount of liquor and tobacco—800 cigarettes, 400 cigarillos, 200 cigars, 1 kilogram of pipe tobacco, 10 liters of spirits, 45 liters of wine, 25 liters of port/sherry, and 55 liters of beer. You'll need a truck!

Goods that cannot be freely imported to the Irish Republic include firearms, ammunition, explosives, illegal drugs, indecent or obscene books and pictures, oral smokeless tobacco products, meat and meat products, poultry and poultry products, plants and plant products (including shrubs, vegetables, fruit, bulbs, and seeds), domestic cats and dogs from outside the United Kingdom, and live animals from outside Northern Ireland.

No animals or pets of any kind may be brought into Northern Ireland without a six-month quarantine. Other items that may not be imported include fresh meats, plants and vegetables, controlled drugs, and firearms and ammunition.

ENTERING AUSTRALIA

If you're 18 or older, you may bring back A$400 worth of souvenirs and gifts, including jewelry. Your duty-free allowance also includes 250 cigarettes or 250 grams of tobacco and 1,125 milliliters of alcohol, including wine, beer, or spirits. Residents under age 18 may bring back A$200 worth of goods.

RESOURCES • Australian Customs Service (Regional Director, Box 8, Sydney, NSW 2001, tel. 02/9213–2000, fax 02/9213–4000).

ENTERING CANADA

If you've been out of Canada for at least seven days, you may bring in C$500 worth of goods duty-free. If you've been away for fewer than seven days but more than 48 hours, the duty-free allowance drops to C$200; if your trip lasts 24–48 hours, the allowance is C$50. You may not pool allowances with family members. Goods claimed under the C$500 exemption may follow you by mail; those claimed under the lesser exemptions must accompany you.

Alcohol and tobacco products may be included in the seven-day and 48-hour exemptions but not in the 24-hour exemption. If you meet the age requirements of the province or territory through which you reenter Canada, you may bring in duty-free 1.14 liters (40 imperial ounces) of wine or liquor *or* 24 12-ounce cans or bottles of beer or ale. If you are 16 or older, you may bring in duty-free 200 cigarettes and 50 cigars; these items must accompany you.

You may send an unlimited number of gifts worth up to C$60 each duty-free to Canada. Label the package UNSOLICITED GIFT—VALUE UNDER $60. Alcohol and tobacco are excluded.

INFORMATION • Revenue Canada (2265 St. Laurent Blvd. S, Ottawa, Ontario K1G 4K3, tel. 613/993–0534, 800/461–9999 in Canada).

ENTERING NEW ZEALAND

Although greeted with a "Haere Mai" ("Welcome to New Zealand"), homeward-bound travelers with goods to declare must present themselves for inspection. If you're 17 or older, you may bring back NZ$700 worth of souvenirs and gifts. Your duty-free allowance also includes 200 cigarettes or 250 grams of tobacco or 50 cigars or a combo of all three up to 250 grams, 4.5 liters of wine or beer, and one 1,125-milliliter bottle of spirits.

RESOURCES • New Zealand Customs (Custom House, 50 Anzac Ave., Box 29, Auckland, New Zealand, tel. 09/359–6655, fax 09/309–2978).

ENTERING THE U.K.

If your journey was wholly within European Union (EU) countries, you needn't pass through customs when you return to the United Kingdom. If you plan to bring back large quantities of alcohol or tobacco, **check on EU limits beforehand.**

INFORMATION • HM Customs and Excise (Dorset House, Stamford St., London SE1 9NG, tel. 0171/202–4227).

ENTERING THE U.S.

Like most government organizations, the U.S. Customs Service enforces a number of mysterious rules. These are as follows: When you return to the United States, you must declare all items you bought abroad, but you won't have to pay duty unless you come home with more than $400 worth of foreign goods—as long as you've been out of the country for at least 48 hours and haven't already used the $400 allowance or any part of it in the past 30 days. For purchases between $400 and $1,000, you have to pay a 10% duty. You also have to pay tax if you exceed your duty-free allowances: 1 liter of alcohol or wine (if you're at least 21), 100 non-Cuban cigars (sorry, Fidel) or 200 cigarettes or 2 kilograms of tobacco, and one bottle of perfume. Prohibited are meat products, seeds, plants, and fruits. At press time, a federal rule restricting tobacco access to persons 18 years and older did not apply to importation. Antiques, which the U.S. Customs Service defines as objects more than 100 years old, enter duty-free, as do original works of art done entirely by hand, including paintings, drawings, and sculptures.

You may also send packages home duty-free: up to $200 worth of goods for your own use, with a limit of one parcel per addressee per day (and no alcohol or tobacco products or perfume worth more than $5); label the package PERSONAL USE, and attach a list of its contents and their retail value. Do not label the package UNSOLICITED GIFT, or your duty-free exemption will drop to $100. Mailed items do not affect your duty-free allowance on your return.

INFORMATION • U.S. Customs Service inquiries (Box 7407, Washington, DC 20044, tel. 202/927–6724); complaints (Commissioner's Office, 1301 Constitution Ave. NW, Washington, DC 20229); registration of equipment (Resource Management, 1301 Constitution Ave. NW, Washington DC, 20229, tel. 202/927–0540).

The shandy, a mix of lager and lemonade, is a good option if you want to enjoy a few drinks without losing the run of yourself, as the natives might say, and nobody will know the difference because it looks just like a real pint.

DINING

Rumor has it there has been somewhat of a culinary revolution in Ireland over the last ten years. In higher-priced restaurants, the soggy vegetables and over cooked meat that once characterized Irish cuisine has become increasingly obsolete. A new generation of imaginative chefs has begun to capitalize on what are some of the best raw materials in the world for gourmet cooking. Ireland is famous the world over for its dairy products (just look at the color and texture of the butter on your table), its meat (especially beef and lamb), its seafood, and its river salmon and trout.

At the truly budget end of the scale, things have also changed for the better. In Dublin and the other major cities a slew of reasonably priced, ethnic restaurants have sprung up with Indian and Chinese establishments a particular strength. Vegetarian eateries, so difficult to find a decade ago, are commonplace, and most restaurants will have at least one vegetarian dish. The ubiquitous chipshop (known as the "chipper") is still a deep-fried standard of the post-pub crowd.

The restaurant price categories used in this book are loosely based on the assumption that you're going to chow down a main course and a drink, and they include an appropriate service charge. Legions of antacids, copious extra pints of stout, and humongous desserts are extra.

ENJOY PUBS

Ireland's social life is—for good and bad (mostly for good)—synonymous with the pub and the pint of plain, as they like to call their beloved stout. Going to Ireland without venturing into a pub for a Guinness or a Murphys is equivalent to a trip to Italy without eating out or a trip to Egypt without checking out the pyramids. The public house is the quintessential Irish experience, where people gather to chat, listen, learn, argue, and gossip about literally any topic under the sun, from horse racing to philosophy. Here, in large, inclusive circles about big round tables, the infamous caustic wit of the Irish is honed and perfected. You don't have to drink to enjoy the atmosphere of "the local," but it certainly helps.

The beer of choice among the Irish is definitely stout, a thick, pitch-black brew with a creamy white head that is flatter than that of regular beer. Ireland produces three brands of it: Murphys and Beamish in Cork and the king of them all, Guinness, in Dublin. Lagers, most familiar to American drinkers, are light-color carbonated drinks that are very popular among younger tipplers, and Guinness-made Harp is the favorite domestic brand. American, Mexican, and European imports have made a big impact on the Irish market over the last decade, to the head-shaking disdain of old time purists. The British staple, cider, made from apples, can be found in most establishments and is the perfect thirst quencher on warm summer evenings; Bulmers and Strong Bow are names to watch for. Finally the truly delicious and aesthetically pleasing "black and tan" is a blend of stout and ale sardonically named after the distinctive uniforms worn by hated British irregulars in Ireland in the early part of the century. If poured properly, the dark stout sits majestically atop the amber ale, and the two don't mix until after your first sip.

DISABILITIES & ACCESSIBILITY

ACCESS IN IRELAND

The good news is that many big tourist sights and entertainment venues in Ireland are wheelchair accessible. Some museums and parks even have special attractions like touch tours for the blind and interpreted events for the deaf.

GETTING AROUND

In Ireland, not all train stations are accessible. Irish Rail suggests you **call the station a day or two ahead** to guarantee assistance getting on and off trains. Bus Éireann, Ireland's national bus company, will assist travelers with disabilities getting on and off the coach, but none of its buses is equipped with wheelchair lifts. **Give notice when booking if you will need extra help.**

TIPS & HINTS

When discussing accessibility with an operator or reservationist, **ask hard questions.** Are there any stairs, inside *or* out? Are there grab bars next to the toilet *and* in the shower/tub? How wide is the doorway to the room? To the bathroom? When possible, **opt for newer accommodations,** which are more likely to have been designed with access in mind. Older buildings may offer more limited facilities. Be sure to **discuss your needs before booking.**

COMPLAINTS • Disability Rights Section (U.S. Department of Justice, Box 66738, Washington, DC 20035–6738, tel. 202/514–0301 or 800/514–0301, fax 202/307–1198, TTY 202/514–0383 or 800/514–0383) for general complaints. **Aviation Consumer Protection Division** (*see* Air Travel, *above*) for airline-related problems. **Civil Rights Office** (U.S. Department of Transportation, Departmental Office of Civil Rights, S-30, 400 7th St. SW, Room 10215, Washington, DC, 20590, tel. 202/366–4648) for problems with surface transportation.

TRAVEL AGENCIES

Some agencies specialize in travel arrangements for individuals with disabilities.

BEST BETS • Access Adventures (206 Chestnut Ridge Rd., Rochester, NY 14624, tel. 716/889–9096), run by a former physical-rehabilitation counselor. **Hinsdale Travel Service** (201 E. Ogden Ave., Suite 100, Hinsdale, IL 60521, tel. 630/325–1335), which offers advice from wheelchair traveler Janice Perkins. **Wheelchair Journeys** (16979 Redmond Way, Redmond, WA 98052, tel. 206/885–2210 or 800/313–4751), for general travel arrangements.

DISCOUNTS & DEALS

While your travel plans are still in the fantasy stage, start studying the travel sections of major Sunday newspapers: You'll often find listings for good packages and incredibly cheap flights. Surfing on the Internet can also give you some good ideas. Travel agents are another obvious resource; the computer networks to which they have access show the lowest fares before they're even advertised. Agencies on or near college campuses, accustomed to dealing with budget travelers, can be especially helpful.

Always **compare all your options before making a choice.** A plane ticket bought with a promotional coupon may not be cheaper than the least expensive fare from a discount ticket agency (for more on getting a deal on airfares, *see* Air Travel, *above*). When evaluating a package, keep in mind that what you get is just as important as what you save. Just because something is cheap doesn't mean it's a bargain.

CREDIT CARDS & AUTO CLUBS

When you use your credit card to make travel purchases you may get free travel-accident insurance, collision-damage insurance, and medical or legal help, depending on the card and the bank that issued it. So get a copy of your credit card's travel-benefits policy. If you are a member of the American Automobile Association (AAA) or an oil-company-sponsored road-assistance plan, always **ask hotel or car-rental reservationists about auto-club discounts.** Some clubs offer additional discounts on admission to attractions. And don't forget that auto-club membership entitles you to free maps and trip-planning services.

DISCOUNTS BY PHONE

Don't be afraid to **check out "1-800" discount reservations services,** which use their buying power to get a better price on hotels, airline tickets, even car rentals. When booking a room, always **call the hotel's local toll-free number** (if one is available) rather than the central reservations number—you'll often get a better price. Always ask about special packages. When shopping for the best-deal car rentals, **look for guaranteed exchange rates,** which protect you against a falling dollar. With your rate locked in, you won't pay more even if the price goes up in the local currency.

CHEAP AIRLINE TICKETS • Tel. **800/FLY–4–LESS.**

CHEAP HOTELS • **Hotels Plus** (tel. 800/235–0909). **Steigenberger Reservation Service** (tel. 800/223–5652).

SAVE ON COMBOS

Packages and guided tours can both save you money, but don't confuse the two. When you buy a package your travel remains independent, just as though you had planned and booked the trip yourself. Fly/drive packages, which combine airfare and car rental, are often a good deal. If you **buy a rail/drive pass** you'll save on train tickets and car rentals. All Eurail- and Europass holders get a discount on Eurostar fares through the Channel Tunnel.

DRIVING

The disadvantages of driving in Ireland include getting used to driving on the left and other unfamiliar rules, the very high price of gas, the high price of rentals, and the abundance of winding, treacherous roads (which some Irish drivers like to fly along like crazed rally cross drivers). A recent spate of road building has relieved the last problem, and all of Ireland's major towns, North and South, are connected with good quality roads.

AUTO CLUBS • AAA affiliated **Irish Automobile Association** (IAA; 23 Suffolk St., Rockhill, Blackrock, Co. Dublin, tel. 01/677–9481; 800/667–788 for free roadside service) charges a small fee for maps and travel publications. In the U.S., **American Automobile Association** (tel. 800/564–6222). In the U.K., **Automobile Association** (AA; tel. 0990/500–600), **Royal Automobile Club** (RAC; tel. 0990/722–722 for membership, 0345/121–345 for insurance).

ELECTRICITY

Before tossing a blow-dryer into your bag, consider that European electrical outlets pump out 220 volts, enough to fry American appliances. So you'll want a converter that matches the outlet's current and the wattage of your hair dryer (which still may blow). You'll also want an adapter to plug it in; wall outlets in Ireland take Continental-type plugs, with two round prongs.

You can get by with just the adapter if you bring a dual-voltage appliance, available from travel gear catalogs (*see* Travel Gear, *below*). Don't use 110-volt outlets, marked FOR SHAVERS ONLY, for high-wattage appliances (like your blow-dryer). Most laptops operate equally well on 110 and 220 volts and need only an adapter.

EMBASSIES & EMERGENCIES

For **emergencies** dial 999.

EMBASSIES • **Australia** (Fitzwilton House, Wilton Terr., Dublin, tel. 01/676–1517), open Monday–Thursday 9–1 and 2–5:30, Friday 8–1. **United Kingdom** (31 Merrion Rd., Dublin, tel. 01/269–5211), open weekdays 9–5. **Canada** (65 St. Stephen's Green, Dublin, tel. 01/478–1988), open Monday–Wednesday 8:30–12:30 and 1:30–4, Thursday–Friday 8:30–12:30. **United States** (42 Elgin Rd., Ballsbridge, Dublin, tel. 01/668–8777), open weekdays 8:30–5.

FERRY TRAVEL

Irish Ferries and Stena Sealink are the main carriers between Ireland and Wales. Irish Ferries travel from Holyhead to Dublin and from Pembroke to Rosslare. Stena sails from Fishguard to Rosslare and from Holyhead to Dún Laoghaire (just south of Dublin). Both charge between £20 and £35, and the trip takes from two to three hours. Irish Ferries gives a 25% discount to students and a 50% discount to those with a Travelsave stamp. Stena offers a meager 10% discount to ISIC cardholders. Irish ferries gives no discounts to EurailPass holders, while Stena takes a more schizophrenic approach: some agents give discounts while others don't. Good luck.

Only Irish Ferries serves routes to France. It sails from Cork and Rosslare to the French cities of Le Havre and Roscoff, as well as between Cork and Cherbourg. The trip to France lasts a grueling 22–24 hours, costs £68–£95 single, but is free to EurailPass holders.

If you're heading to Northern Ireland, Stena Sealink ferries travel between Stanraer (Scotland) and Belfast four times per day (eight per day in summer) and P&O ferries between Cairnyarn (also in Scotland) and Larne about six times per day.

FERRY COMPANIES • Irish Ferries (tel. 01/679–7977). **Stena Sealink** (tel. 01/204–7700 in the Republic, 01233/647–047 in Northern Ireland). **P&O** (tel. 0990/980–0888).

GAY & LESBIAN TRAVEL

Although homosexuality is considered "deviant" in many parts of Ireland (and is often met with hostility), there is a huge gay and lesbian subculture. As with most countries, people in more rural areas may have more difficulty accepting gays and lesbians. Many towns have gay/lesbian pubs, bars, or clubs and advertise this fact openly. Gay bashing is a very rare crime in Ireland, but it's always wise to **watch yourself and be careful of public displays of affection.** Dublin, Cork, Galway, and Belfast are the best places to find bars, social events, and publications catering to gays and lesbians. Accommodation-wise, Ireland is not particularly welcoming toward gay travelers—especially if you suggest to a B&B or small hotel owner that you and your significant other would like to share a room.

GAY- AND LESBIAN-FRIENDLY TRAVEL AGENCIES • Advance Damron (1 Greenway Plaza, Suite 800, Houston, TX 77046, tel. 713/682–2002 or 800/695–0880, fax 713/888–1010). **Club Travel** (8739 Santa Monica Blvd., West Hollywood, CA 90069, tel. 310/358–2200 or 800/429–8747, fax 310/358–2222). **Islanders/Kennedy Travel** (183 W. 10th St., New York, NY 10014, tel. 212/242–3222 or 800/988–1181, fax 212/929–8530). **Now Voyager** (4406 18th St., San Francisco, CA 94114, tel. 415/626–1169 or 800/255–6951, fax 415/626–8626). **Yellowbrick Road** (1500 W. Balmoral Ave., Chicago, IL 60640, tel. 773/561–1800 or 800/642–2488, fax 773/561–4497). **Skylink Women's Travel** (3577 Moorland Ave., Santa Rosa, CA 95407, tel. 707/585–8355 or 800/225–5759, fax 707/584–5637), serving lesbian travelers.

HOLIDAYS

Banks, shops, and most everything you depend on in the Republic close on the following national holidays: New Year's Day (January 1); St. Patrick's Day (March 17); Good Friday (the Friday before Easter); Easter Sunday; Easter Monday (Monday after Easter); May Day (the first Monday in May); Summer Bank Holidays (the first Monday in June and August); Autumn Bank Holiday (the last Monday in October); Christmas (December 25); and St. Stephen's Day (December 26). Sunday can also pose problems for travelers, especially in smaller towns: Not only do many shops and restaurants close but also bus and train service becomes less frequent or nonexistent.

Holidays in the North are the same as in the Republic except: Summer Bank Holidays (last Monday of May and August) and July 12, which celebrates the Protestant victory at the Battle of the Boyne.

INSURANCE

Many private health-insurance policies do not cover you outside the United States. If yours is among them, **consider buying supplemental medical coverage,** available through several private organizations. It's worth noting that organizations such as STA Travel and the Council on International Educational Exchange (*see* Students, *below*) include health-and-accident coverage when you acquire a student ID.

Citizens of the United Kingdom can buy an annual travel-insurance policy valid for most vacations during the year in which it's purchased. If you are pregnant or have a preexisting medical condition, make sure you're covered. According to the Association of British Insurers, a trade association representing 450 insurance companies, it's wise to buy extra medical coverage when you visit the United States.

TRAVEL INSURERS • In the U.S., **Access America** (6600 W. Broad St., Richmond, VA 23230, tel. 804/285–3300 or 800/284–8300), **Carefree Travel Insurance** (Box 9366, 100 Garden City Plaza, Garden City, NY 11530, tel. 516/294–0220 or 800/323–3149), **Travel Guard International** (1145 Clark St., Stevens Point, WI 54481, tel. 715/345–0505 or 800/826–1300), **Travel Insured International** (Box 280568, East Hartford, CT 06128–0568, tel. 860/528–7663 or 800/243–3174). In Canada, **Mutual of Omaha** (Travel Division, 500 University Ave., Toronto, Ontario M5G 1V8, tel. 416/598–4083, 800/268–8825 in Canada). In the U.K., **Association of British Insurers** (51 Gresham St., London EC2V 7HQ, tel. 0171/600–3333).

LODGING

Major Irish hotels charge £30–£60 per person. Other, cheaper options include hostels or, for about an extra £9, cozy B&Bs and guest houses. There are also campgrounds scattered throughout the country, many within walking or cycling distance of urban centers; rates are about £3–£5 per tent site and 20p–£1 for each additional person. Most campgrounds are only open from April through September or October. If you plan to do a lot of camping, pick up the handy "Caravan and Camping in Ireland 1997" guide (£1.50) from a tourist office; it is chock-full of maps and information on all registered campgrounds. **During the summer tourist season, reserve as far in advance as possible** for all types of accommodation.

BED-AND-BREAKFASTS & GUEST HOUSES

B&Bs and guest houses are everywhere, from Dublin's city center to County Donegal's most remote reaches. The typical B&B is a family home with a few rooms given over to visitors. The standard rate is about £15–£18 per person, and most B&Bs accept reservations; any Irish tourist office will make one for you for a £1–£2 fee. Breakfast (generally consisting of coffee or tea, cereal, toast, fried eggs, sausages, and a healthy layer of grease) is nearly always included in the price, and some B&Bs will provide dinner for a small additional charge. If B&Bs will be your primary lodging, consider picking up one a nationwide B&B books (£2) at tourist offices. Guest houses are really small, informal hotels with 10–30 rooms; they tend to be less friendly than B&Bs but offer more privacy.

HOSTELS

It is important to remember that almost all hostels in Ireland are open to travellers of all ages; they are not student-only domains. The crowd tends to be a pleasant and exciting mix of university students, professionals with a taste for down-to-earth travel, and older, hardened budget travelers who sometimes come with the whole family. Hostels offer the cheapest beds in the country—generally £5–£9. In more remote areas the local hostel may be one of your only options for affordable accomodation. Non-HI members must purchase a "welcome stamp" (£1.25) to stay in An Óige hostels; however, after staying six nights—thereby accruing six welcome stamps—you're granted full membership and thereafter only pay the standard £4.50–£9 rate. Except for larger cities like Dublin, Cork, and Killarney, most An Óige hostels have an 11 PM–midnight curfew, daytime bedroom lockouts, check-in times between 8–11 AM and 5–8 PM only, and checkout by 10:30 AM. Óige accommodations sometimes can be a little spartan, consisting of sex-segregated dorm rooms with 4–20 beds, standard shower facilities, and self-service kitchens. You must bring your own sleep sheet or sleeping bag or rent bedclothes (85p).

A better bet are hostels overseen by Independent Holiday Hostels (IHH), a friendly organization with nearly 90 hostels throughout Ireland. The good news: no IHH membership fee, no curfews or daytime lockouts, and check-in at any time of day. Accommodations generally include small, 6- to 10-bed coed dorm rooms, self-service kitchens, and showers. Singles and doubles are usually an option. Many also have camping facilities. The bad news: IHH is so popular that its hostels are often booked solid during summer, especially in places like Dublin, Cork, and Galway. Conveniently, it now has a book-ahead system that allows you to reserve a bed at another IHH hostel for 50p, plus a £5.50 deposit on your bed (the remainder, if any, to be paid when you arrive). Some hostels accept phone reservations, so call ahead whenever possible. The main office in Dublin or any member hostel can provide you with an IHH map or information book. A handy, free guide to IHH hostels throughout the country is also available at most tourist offices. There is also a growing number of unaffiliated hostels springing up throughout the country.

Also see Students, *below.*

INFORMATION • Independent Holiday Hostels (IHH; 21 Store St., Dublin, tel. 01/836–4700).

MAIL

The Irish mail service is known as An Post. Post offices and smaller substations (generally housed in the back of shops or newsagents) are located in every town in Ireland. All offices sell stamps: 52p per letter and 38p per postcard for international destinations, 32p per letter and 28p per postcard for domestic and EU destinations. Larger offices offer competitive currency exchange and are usually open Monday–Saturday 9–1 and 2:15–5:30 (some offices are only open 9–1 on Saturday).

RECEIVING MAIL

You can receive those precious letters from home via "Poste Restante" at any post office (or, if you have an AmEx card, at one of their offices). Here's what you do: Figure out where you'll be in 10 days, then tell the folks back home the address, town, and (most importantly) the postal code of the post (or AmEx) office where they'll be sending the package. Tell them to write POSTE RESTANTE and HOLD FOR 30 DAYS in the upper left corner of the envelope. You will need to show ID (and/or your American Express card) to pick up this mail.

MONEY

$1 = 64p and £1 = $1.55. The Irish currency technically is known as the punt, but nearly everyone calls it the Irish pound. Its notes, each color-coded and of a different size, come in denominations of £5, £10, £20, £50, and £100. Coins, also distinguished by their size and shape, come in denominations of 1p, 2p, 5p, 10p, 20p, 50p, and £1. **Remember that Irish and English pounds are NOT equivalent or interchangeable**; Irish pounds are only good in the Republic. Pounds sterling are used in Northern Ireland and likewise cannot be used in the Republic.

Northern Ireland uses the English pound ($1 = 60p and £1 = $1.65) as its main currency, which means you don't have to exchange money if you're coming from England or Scotland. Some Northern Irish banks do issue their own notes, recognized by an odd size and color scheme and because they bear the name of the issuing bank. In any case, both are legal tender here. Do note, however, that while English pounds are accepted in Northern Ireland, the same does not hold true in reverse. **Change your money into English pounds, or be sure to spend any Northern Irish currency before you leave the country—**it's difficult to exchange notes back and nearly impossible to exchange coins. Also remember that Republic of Ireland currency is not accepted in the north. The similarly shaped 5p and 50p coins will fool a machine (even a pay phone), but Irish pound notes and coins are universally scorned in Ulster.

You can usually change money weekdays and Saturday mornings at either the post office or the tourist office in all but the smallest towns (*see* Currency Exchange, *below*).

ATMS

To increase your chances of happy encounters with cash machines in Ireland, before leaving home, **make sure that your card has been programmed for ATM use there**—ATMs in Ireland accept PINs of four or fewer digits only; if your PIN is longer, ask about changing it. If you know your PIN as a word, learn the numerical equivalent since most Irish ATM keypads show numbers only, no letters. You should also have your credit card programmed for ATM use (note that Discover is accepted mostly in the United States); a Visa or MasterCard can also be used to access cash through certain ATMs, although fees may be steep and the charge may begin to accrue interest immediately even if your monthly bills are paid up. Local bank cards may not work overseas; **ask your bank about a MasterCard/Cirrus or Visa debit card,** which works like a bank card but can be used at any ATM displaying a MasterCard/Cirrus or Visa logo.

ATM LOCATIONS • Cirrus (tel. 800/424–7787). A list of **Plus** locations is available at your local bank.

COSTS

Ireland is no longer the cheap destination it once was. For travelers with American dollars, prices for many items in Ireland are more than 1½ times what they are in the United States. It's more than just a bad exchange rate; a booming economy has pushed up prices dramatically, especially in Dublin and other major cities. Even if you stay in hostels or B&Bs and eat only pub grub and cheap chipshop food, be prepared to drop $40 a day. If you plan to stay in hotels and eat in restaurants, your daily bill could top $100 per person.

To add insult to injury, the Irish government slaps a whopping 12%–21% Value Added Tax (VAT) on almost everything. The VAT is usually included in prices, but not always—be sure to ask. VAT refunds are available to all non-EU residents. Look for stores displaying a CASHBACK sticker, where you will receive a voucher with your purchase. Present this voucher at the Cashback desk in the Dublin or Shannon airport for your refund.

In Northern Ireland things cost about the same as in the South, perhaps a little more, except for alcohol and cigarettes. Many southerners who travel north will return with bags full of smuggled cheap beer and cigarettes tucked under their car seat. To obtain a VAT refund for purchases made in Northern Ireland, you'll need to ask the shopkeeper for the appropriate form and get customs officials to stamp it at the airport; finally, after you've arrived home you can send the form and a self-addressed Northern Irish–stamped envelope to the shopkeeper, who will then send you a refund.

In Ireland, **tip generously only if the service is excellent,** and it often is. Standard practice is to tip 10%–15% in taxis and restaurants (unless service is included). Bartenders are almost never tipped, except around Christmas time, when you can tell them to "have one yourself," which translates as tipping them the price of a pint.

Lodging will be your greatest expense in Ireland. Expect to pay about £5–£8 for basic hostel accommodations. Prices for bed-and-breakfasts (B&Bs) vary widely, but you can usually find something for £10–£15 per person. Hotels are expensive throughout Ireland (£40 and up) and often lack the friendliness of B&Bs. You can camp for as little as £3, though fully equipped campgrounds may charge as much as £8 per site.

CURRENCY EXCHANGE

You'll get a better deal if you buy pounds in Ireland rather than at home. Nonetheless, it's a good idea to **exchange a bit of money into pounds before you arrive in Ireland** in case the exchange booth at the train station or airport at which you arrive is closed or has a long line. At other times, for the most favorable rates **change money at banks.** Although fees charged for ATM transactions may be higher abroad than at home, Cirrus and Plus exchange rates are excellent because they are based on wholesale rates offered only by major banks. You won't do as well at exchange booths in airports, rail and bus stations, hotels, restaurants, or stores, although you may find their hours more convenient.

Since tourism is such an important industry, nearly every backwater town throughout Ireland has a Bank of Ireland, an Allied Irish Bank (AIB), or an Ulster Bank branch, making it easy to exchange money. In larger cities, you'll find dozens of banks in the city center. Banks usually take a 1%–3% commission for currency exchanges. In general, Irish banks are open weekdays 10–12:30 and 1:30–3. For weekend exchanges, you generally have two choices: either a gift shop that extorts a large commission or, in larger towns, a post office.

Also, you can often withdraw money with a Visa, MasterCard, or AmEx card. It's better to do so through an ATM machine than through a bank since banks generally charge a £3 commission. Some (apparently randomly selected) AIB, Bank of Ireland, and Ulster Bank ATMs are now linked to the Cirrus and Plus systems, so you can also retrieve money with your bank card if your card is so linked. There will usually be at least one such ATM in towns with populations greater than 10,000, but you may have to hunt for it. Of course, before you leave home, you must get a PIN number (access code) of no more than four digits to use your credit card or bank card at any ATM in Ireland. *See* ATMs, *above.*

EXCHANGE SERVICES • International Currency Express (tel. 888/842–0880 on the East Coast or 888/278–6628 on the West Coast for telephone orders). **Thomas Cook Currency Services** (tel. 800/287–7362 for telephone orders and retail locations).

TRAVELER'S CHECKS

Whether you buy traveler's checks depends on where you are headed. You should **take cash if your trip includes rural areas** and small towns, traveler's checks to cities. If a thief makes off with your checks, you can usually have them replaced within 24 hours. Always pay for your checks yourself—don't delegate—or there may be problems if you need a refund later on.

PACKING FOR IRELAND

You've heard it a million times, and now you'll hear it once again: Pack light. The heaviness of your luggage is always directly proportional to how many days you've been carrying it around. Bring an extra pair of eyeglasses or contact lenses in your carry-on luggage, and if you have a health problem **pack enough** medication to last the entire trip or have your doctor write you a prescription using the drug's generic name because brand names vary from country to country. It's important that you **don't put prescription drugs, your passport, or other valuables in luggage to be checked** since such bags may go astray. To avoid problems with customs officials, carry medications in the original packaging. Use containers that seal tightly, and pack them in a separate waterproof bag; the pressure on airplanes can cause lids to pop off and create instant moisturizer slicks inside your luggage. Also, don't forget to pack the addresses of offices that handle refunds of lost traveler's checks. And note that hostels require you use a sleep sheet; some include them, some don't.

Other stuff you might not think to take but will be glad to have: a miniature flashlight, good in dark places; a pocket knife for cutting fruit, spreading cheese, and opening wine bottles; a water bottle; sunglasses; several large zip-type plastic bags, useful for wet swimsuits, leaky bottles, and rancid socks; a travel alarm clock; a needle and a small spool of thread; extra batteries; a good book; and a day pack.

LUGGAGE

In general, you are entitled to check two bags on flights within the United States and on international flights leaving the United States. A third piece may be brought on board, but it must fit easily under the seat in front of you or in an overhead compartment. If you are flying between two foreign destinations, note that baggage allowances may be determined not by piece but by weight—generally 88 pounds (40 kilograms) in first class, 66 pounds (30 kilograms) in business class, and 44 pounds (20 kilograms) in economy. If your flight between two cities abroad *connects* with your transatlantic or transpacific flight, the piece method still applies. Note to overpackers: If your carry-on bag is too porky, be prepared for the humiliation of rejection and a last-minute baggage check.

Airline liability for baggage is limited to $1,250 per person on flights within the United States. On international flights it amounts to $9.07 per pound or $20 per kilogram for checked baggage (roughly $640 per 70-pound bag) and $400 per passenger for unchecked baggage. Insurance for losses exceeding these amounts can be bought from the airline at check-in for about $10 per $1,000 of coverage; note that this coverage excludes a rather extensive list of items, which is shown on your airline ticket.

At check-in, **make sure that each bag is correctly tagged** with the destination airport's three-letter code. If your bags arrive damaged or don't arrive at all, file a written report with the airline before leaving the airport. If you're traveling with a pack, tie all loose straps to each other or onto the pack itself so they don't get caught in luggage conveyer belts.

PASSPORTS & VISAS

Once your travel plans are confirmed, **check the expiration date of your passport.** If you lose your documents on the road, it's a nuisance to get new ones. It's a good idea to **make photocopies of the data page**; leave one copy with someone at home and keep another with you, separate from your passport. If you lose your passport, promptly call the nearest embassy or consulate and the local police; having a copy of the data page can speed replacement.

AUSTRALIAN CITIZENS

Citizens of Australia need only a valid passport to enter Ireland for stays of up to 90 days.

INFORMATION • Passport Information Service (tel. 008/131–232).

CANADIANS

You need only a valid passport to enter Ireland for stays of up to 90 days.

INFORMATION • Passport Office (tel. 819/994–3500 or 800/567–6868).

NEW ZEALAND CITIZENS

Citizens of New Zealand need only a valid passport to enter Ireland for stays of up to 90 days.

INFORMATION • Passport Office (Internal Affrains Depattment, tel. 04/494–0700).

U.K. CITIZENS

Citizens of the United Kingdom do not need a passport to enter Ireland.

U.S. CITIZENS

All U.S. citizens, even infants, need only a valid passport to enter Ireland for stays of up to 90 days.

INFORMATION • Office of Passport Services (tel. 202/647–0518).

SAFETY

Money belts may be dorky and bulky, but it's better to be embarrassed than broke. You'd be wise to carry all cash, traveler's checks, credit cards, and your passport there or in some other inaccessible place: a front or inner pocket or a bag that fits underneath your clothes. Keep a copy of your passport somewhere else. Waist packs are safe if you keep the pack part in front of your body. Keep your bag attached to you if you plan on napping on the train. And **never leave your belongings unguarded,** even if you're planning to be gone for only a minute.

STUDENTS

To save money, **look into deals available through student-oriented travel agencies** and the various other organizations involved in helping student and budget travelers. Typically you'll find discounted airfares, rail passes, tours, lodgings, or other travel arrangements, and you don't necessarily have to be a student to qualify.

The big names in the field are STA Travel, with some 100 offices worldwide and a useful website (www.sta-travel.com), and the Council on International Educational Exchange (CIEE or "Council" for short), a private, nonprofit organization that administers work, volunteer, academic, and professional programs worldwide and sells travel arrangements through its own specialist travel agency, Council Travel. Travel CUTS, strictly a travel agency, sells discounted airline tickets to Canadian students from offices on or near college campuses. The Educational Travel Center (ETC) books low-cost flights to destinations within the continental United States and around the world. And Student Flights, Inc., specializes in student and faculty airfares.

Most of these organizations also issue student identity cards, which entitle bearers to special fares on local transportation and discounts at museums, theaters, sports events, and other attractions, as well as to a handful of other benefits, which are listed in the handbook that most provide to their cardholders. Major cards include the International Student Identity Card (ISIC) and Go 25: International Youth Travel Card (GO25), available to non-students as well as students age 25 and under; the ISIC, when purchased in the United States, comes with $3,000 in emergency medical coverage and a few related benefits. Both the ISIC and Go 25 are issued by Council Travel or STA in the United States, by Travel CUTS in Canada, and at student unions and student-travel companies in the United Kingdom, Australia, and New Zealand. The International Student Exchange Card (ISE), issued by Student Flights, Inc., is available to faculty members as well as students, and the International Teacher Identity Card (ITIC), issued by Travel CUTS, provides similar benefits to teachers in all grade levels, from kindergarten through graduate school. All student ID cards cost between $10 and $20.

STUDENT IDS AND SERVICES • Council on International Educational Exchange (CIEE; 205 E. 42nd St., 14th floor, New York, NY 10017, tel. 212/822–2600 or 888/268–6245, fax 212/822–2699), for mail orders only, in the United States.

Council Travel in the U.S.: Arizona (Tempe, tel. 602/966–3544). California (Berkeley, tel. 510/848–8604; Davis, tel. 916/752–2285; La Jolla, tel. 619/452–0630; Long Beach, tel. 310/598–3338; Los Angeles, tel. 310/208–3551; Palo Alto, tel. 415/325–3888; San Diego, tel. 619/270–6401, San Francisco, tel. 415/421–3473 or 415/566–6222; Santa Barbara, tel. 805/562–8080). Colorado (Boulder, tel. 303/447–8101; Denver, tel. 303/571–0630). Connecticut (New Haven, tel. 203/562–5335). Florida (Miami, tel. 305/670–9261). Georgia (Atlanta, tel. 404/377–9997). Illinois (Chicago, tel. 312/951–0585; Evanston, tel. 847/475–5070). Indiana (Bloomington, tel. 812/330–1600). Iowa (Ames, tel. 515/296–2326). Kansas (Lawrence, tel. 913/749–3900). Louisiana (New Orleans, tel. 504/866–1767). Maryland (College Park, tel. 301/779–1172). Massachusetts (Amherst, tel. 413/256–1261; Boston, tel. 617/266–1926; Cambridge, tel. 617/497–1497 or 617/225–2555). Michigan (Ann Arbor, tel. 313/998–0200). Minnesota (Minneapolis, tel. 612/379–2323). New York (New York, tel. 212/822–2700, 212/666–4177, or 212/254–2525). North Carolina (Chapel Hill, tel. 919/942–2334). Ohio (Columbus, tel. 614/294–8696). Oregon (Portland, tel. 503/228–1900). Pennsylvania (Philadelphia, tel. 215/382–0343; Pittsburgh, tel. 412/683–1881). Rhode Island (Providence, tel. 401/331–5810). Tennessee (Knoxville, tel. 423/523–9900). Texas (Austin, tel. 512/472–4931; Dallas, tel. 214/363–9941). Utah (Salt Lake City, tel. 801/582–5840). Washington (Seattle, tel. 206/632–2448 or 206/329–4567). Washington, D.C.(tel. 202/337–6464).

STA in the U.S.: California (Berkeley, tel. 510/642–3000; Los Angeles, tel. 213/934–8722; San Francisco, tel. 415/391–8407; Santa Monica, tel. 310/394–5126; Westwood, tel. 310/824–1574). Florida

(Miami, tel. 305/461–3444; University of Florida, tel. 352/338–0068). Illinois (Chicago, tel. 312/786–9050). Massachusetts (Boston, tel. 617/266–6014; Cambridge, tel. 617/576–4623). New York (Columbia University, tel. 212/865–2700; West Village, tel. 212/627–3111). Pennsylvania (Philadelphia, tel. 215/382–2928). Washington (Seattle, tel. 206/633–5000). Washington, D.C. (tel. 202/887–0912).

STA elsewhere: Australia (Adelaide, tel. 08/223–2434; Brisbane tel. 73/229–2499; Cairns, tel. 70/31–41-99; Canberra, tel. 06/247–8633; Darwin, tel. 89/41–29–55; Melbourne, tel. 39/349–2411; Perth, tel. 09/227–7569; Sydney, tel. 29/368–1111 or 29/212–1255). Canada (Calgary, tel. 403/282–7687; Edmonton, tel. 403/492–2592; Montreal, tel. 514/284–1368; Toronto, tel. 416/977–5228; Vancouver, tel. 604/681–9136).

Student Flights (5010 E. Shea Blvd., Suite A104, Scottsdale, AZ 85254, tel. 602/951–1177 or 800/255–8000). **Travel Cuts** (187 College St., Toronto, Ontario M5T 1P7, tel. 416/979–2406 or 800/667–2887) in Canada.

HOSTELS

If you want to scrimp on lodging, **look into hostels.** In some 5,000 locations in more than 70 countries around the world, Hostelling International (HI), the umbrella group for a number of national youth hostel associations, offers single-sex, dorm-style beds, and, at many hostels, "couples" rooms and family accommodations. Membership in any HI national hostel association, open to travelers of all ages, allows you to stay in HI-affiliated hostels at member rates (one-year membership about $25 for adults; hostels about $10–$25 per night). Members also have priority if the hostel is full; they're eligible for discounts around the world, even on rail and bus travel in some countries. There are also two international hostel directories ($13.95 each): one for Europe and the Mediterranean, the other covering Africa, the Americas, Asia, and the Pacific.

ORGANIZATIONS • An Óige (61 Mountjoy St., Dublin 2, tel. 01/830–4555), the HI affiliate. **Hostelling International–American Youth Hostels** (HI–AYH; 733 15th St. NW, Suite 840, Washington, DC 20005, tel. 202/783–6161, fax 202/783–6171). **Hostelling International–Canada** (HI–C; 400-205 Catherine St., Ottawa, Ontario K2P 1C3, tel. 613/237–7884, fax 613/237–7868). **Youth Hostel Association of England and Wales** (YHA; Trevelyan House, 8 St. Stephen's Hill, St. Albans, Hertfordshire AL1 2DY, tel. 01727/855215 or 01727/845047, fax 01727/844126). **Australian Youth Hostels Association** (YHA; Level 3, 10 Mallett St., Camperdown, New South Wales 2050, tel. 02/565–1699). **Youth Hostels Association of New Zealand** (YHA; Box 436, Christchurch 1, tel. 3/379–9970).

TELEPHONES

The country code for Ireland is 353. Within Ireland, the cost of a three-minute local call is 20p. Older phones accept 5p, 10p, and 50p coins. Newer phones will accept all coins except for 5p, but either way there should be a sign stating which coins a particular phone accepts. You'll hear a series of beeps when you need to insert more money.

To cope with card phones, you'll need to **buy a Telecom Eireann card,** available from post offices, Telecom Eireann (the national phone company), or any store displaying the yellow-and-blue CALLCARD sign. Each unit on the card is equivalent to 20p, and cards come in 10-unit (£2), 20-unit (£3.50), 50-unit (£8), and 100-unit (£16) denominations. If you're having any trouble, dial 10 (free) to speak to an operator.

When calling a given Irish city from abroad, drop the "0" from the area code. For example, Dublin's prefix is 01 if you're calling from within Ireland, 1 if calling from the United States or the United Kingdom. AT&T, MCI, and Sprint can place collect and credit-card calls to North America from any phone. Otherwise, dial 114 (in Dublin) or 10 (outside Dublin) and place your international call through an Irish operator—a more expensive (to whomever is paying) and time-consuming task. International direct-dial calls can be made from most pay phones. Bring along a phone card or a barrelful of £1 coins because the average international rate is 60p per minute.

CALLING THE U.S.

AT&T, MCI, and Sprint long-distance services make calling home relatively convenient, but you may find the local access number blocked in many hotel rooms. First ask the hotel operator to connect you. If the hotel operator balks, ask for an international operator, or dial the international operator yourself. One way to improve your odds of getting connected to your long-distance carrier is to **travel with more than one company's calling card** (a hotel may block Sprint, for example, but not MCI). If all else fails, call your phone company in the United States collect, or make your call from a pay phone in the hotel lobby.

PHONE SERVICES • **AT&T** (tel. 800/550–000). **MCI** (tel. 800/551–001). **Sprint** (tel. 800/552–001).

OPERATORS & INFORMATION

For directory assistance in Ireland and Northern Ireland, dial 1190 (free from public phones). Telecom Eireann cards are not good in the north.

TOUR OPERATORS

Buying a vacation package can make your trip to Ireland less expensive. The tour operators who put them together may handle several hundred thousand travelers per year and can use their purchasing power to give you a good price. Their high volume may also indicate financial stability. But some small companies provide more personalized service; because they tend to specialize, they may also be more knowledgeable about a given area.

A GOOD DEAL?

The more your package includes, the better you can predict the ultimate cost of your vacation. Make sure you know exactly what is covered, and **beware of hidden costs.** Are taxes, tips, and service charges included? Transfers and baggage handling? Entertainment and excursions? These add up.

If the package you are considering is priced lower than in your wildest dreams, **be skeptical.** Ask about the hotel's location, room size, beds, and whether it has a pool, room service, or programs for children, if you care.

BUYER BEWARE

Each year consumers are stranded or lose their money when tour operators—even large ones with excellent reputations—go out of business. So **check out the operator.** Find out how long the company has been in business, and ask for references that you can check. And **don't book unless the firm has a consumer-protection program.**

Members of the National Tour Association and United States Tour Operators Association are required to set aside funds to cover your payments and travel arrangements in case the company defaults. Non-members may carry insurance instead. Look for the details, and for the name of an underwriter with a solid reputation, in the operator's brochure. And when it comes to tour operators, **don't trust escrow accounts.** Although there are laws governing charter-flight operators, no governmental body prevents tour operators from raiding the till. For more information, *see* Consumer Protection, *above.*

TOUR-OPERATOR RECOMMENDATIONS • **National Tour Association** (NTA; 546 E. Main St., Lexington, KY 40508, tel. 606/226–4444 or 800/755–8687). **United States Tour Operators Association** (USTOA; 342 Madison Ave., Suite 1522, New York, NY 10173, tel. 212/599–6599, fax 212/599–6744).

USING AN AGENT

A good travel agent is an excellent resource. When shopping for one, **collect brochures from several sources** and remember that some agents' suggestions may be skewed by promotional relationships with tour and package firms that reward them for volume sales. If you have a special interest, **find an agent with expertise in that area** (*see* Travel Agencies, *below*).

SINGLE TRAVELERS

Remember that prices for vacation packages are usually quoted per person, based on two sharing a room. If traveling solo, you may be required to pay the full double-occupancy rate.

PACKAGES

The companies listed below offer vacation packages in a broad price range.

AIR/HOTEL/CAR • **Abercrombie & Kent** (1520 Kensington Rd., Oak Brook, IL 60521-2141, tel. 630/954–2944 or 800/323–7308, fax 630/954–3324). **Aer Lingus** (tel. 212/557–1110 or 800/ 223–6537). **Brian Moore Tours** (1208 VFW Pkwy., Suite 202, Boston, MA 02132, tel. 617/469–3300 or 800/982–2299). **British Airways Holidays** (tel. 800/247–9297). **Celtic International Tours** (1860 Western Ave., Albany, NY 12203, tel. 518/862–0042 or 800/833–4373). **CIE Tours** (Box 501, 100 Hanover Ave., Cedar Knolls, NJ 07927-0501, tel. 201/292–3899 or 800/243–8687). **Delta Dream Vacations** (tel. 800/872–7786). **DER Tours** (9501 W. Devon St., Rosemont, IL 60018, tel. 800/782–2424 for brochures). **Irish American International Tours** (Box 465, Springfield, PA 19064, tel. 610/543–0785 or 800/633–0505, fax 610/543–0786). **United Vacations** (tel. 800/328–6877).

FLY/DRIVE • **American Airlines Fly AAway Vacations** (tel. 800/321–2121). **Delta Dream Vacations** (*see above*). **United Vacations** (*see above*).

THEME TRIPS
BARGE/RIVER CRUISES • **Le Boat** (10 S. Franklin Turnpike, Suite 204B, Ramsey, NJ 07446, tel. 201/236–2333 or 800/992–0291).

BED-AND-BREAKFASTS • **Brendan Tours** (15137 Califa St., Van Nuys, CA 91411, tel. 818/785–9696 or 800/421–8446, fax 818/902–9876). **Value Holidays** (10224 N. Port Washington Rd., Mequon, WI 53092, tel. 414/241–6373 or 800/558–6850). **Irish Tourist Board** (*see* Visitor Information, *below*). **Northern Ireland Tourist Board** (*see* Visitor Information, *below*).

BICYCLING • **Backroads** (801 Cedar St., Berkeley, CA 94710-1800, tel. 510/527–1555 or 800/462–2848, fax 510/527–1444). **Butterfield & Robinson** (70 Bond St., Toronto, Ontario, Canada M5B 1X3, tel. 416/864–1354 or 800/678–1147, fax 416/864–0541). **Classic Adventures** (Box 153, Hamlin, NY 14464-0153, tel. 716/964–8488 or 800/777–8090, fax 716/964–7297). **Euro-Bike Tours** (Box 990, De Kalb, IL 60115, tel. 800/321–6060, fax 815/758–8851). **Himalayan Travel** (110 Prospect St., Stamford, CT 06901, tel. 203/359–3711 or 800/225–2380, fax 203/359–3669).

CULTURE • **Lynott Tours** (350 5th Ave., #2619, New York, NY 10118-2697, tel. 212/760–0101 or 800/221–2474, fax 212/695–8347).

CUSTOMIZED PACKAGES • **Destinations Ireland & Great Britain** (13 Sterling Pl., Suite 4-A, Brooklyn, NY 11217, tel. 718/622–4717 or 800/832–1848, fax 212/622–4874).

FOOD AND WINE • **Annemarie Victory Organization** (136 E. 64th St., New York, NY 10021, tel. 212/486–0353, fax 212/751–3149).

GOLF • **Abercrombie & Kent** (*see* Packages, *above*). **Aer Lingus** (*see* Packages, *above*). **Francine Atkins' Scotland/Ireland** (2 Ross Ct., Trophy Club, TX 76262, tel. 817/491–1105 or 800/742–0355, fax 817/491–2025). **Golf International** (275 Madison Ave., New York, NY 10016, tel. 212/986–9176 or 800/833–1389, fax 212/986–3720). **Golfpac** (Box 162366, Altamonte Springs, FL 32716-2366, tel. 407/260–2288 or 800/327–0878, fax 407/260–8989). **ITC Golf Tours** (4134 Atlantic Ave., #205, Long Beach, CA 90807, tel. 310/595–6905 or 800/257–4981). **Value Holidays** (*see* Bed-and-Breakfasts, *above*).

HIKING/WALKING • **Abercrombie & Kent** (*see* Packages, *above*). **Backroads** (*see* Bicycling, *above*). **Butterfield & Robinson** (*see* Bicycling, *above*). **Hiking Holidays** (Box 711, Bristol, VT 05443-0711, tel. 802/453–4816 or 800/537–3850, fax 802/453–4806). **Himalayan Travel** (*see* Bicycling, *above*). **Mountain Travel-Sobek** (6420 Fairmount Ave., El Cerrito, CA 94530, tel. 510/527–8100 or 800/227–2384, fax 510/525–7710). **Wilderness Travel** (801 Allston Way, Berkeley, CA 94710, tel. 510/548–0420 or 800/368–2794, fax 510/548–0347).

HORSEBACK RIDING • **Cross Country International Equestrian Vacations** (Box 1170, Millbrook, NY 12545, tel. 914/677–6000 or 800/828–8768, fax 914/677–6077). **Equitour FITS Equestrian** (Box 807, Dubois, WY 82513, tel. 307/455–3363 or 800/545–0019, fax 307/455–2354).

TRAIN TRAVEL

Travel on the state-owned Iarnród Éireann is quick, efficient, and free to all InterRail and EurailPass holders, but expect to pay handsomely if you don't have these passes or aren't eligible for the Travelsave stamp (*see* Transportation, *below*). If you are under 26 but not a student, you can purchase a Fair Card (also known as the "Under 26 card") at most train stations for £8; it gives you discounts of 25%–50% on all rail travel. Trains generally run between 5 AM and midnight. Reservations are not accepted for any route, and your ticket does not guarantee you a seat. **On summer weekends, arrive early** if you plan to travel on the popular Dublin–Cork, Dublin–Wexford, or Dublin–Galway routes.

TIMETABLES • Stop by any depot or the **Dublin office** (35 Lower Abbey St., tel. 01/836–6222).

RAIL PASSES

If you plan to ride the rails, **compare costs for rail passes and individual tickets.** If you plan to cover a lot of ground in a short period, rail passes may be worth your while; they also spare you the time waiting in lines to buy tickets. To price costs for individual tickets of the rail trips you plan, ask a travel agent or call Rail Europe, Railpass Express, or DER Tours. If you're under 26 on your first day of travel, you're eligible for a youth pass, valid for second-class travel only (like Europass Youth, Eurail Youth Flexipass, or Eurail Youthpass). If you're older, you must buy one of the more expensive regular passes, valid for first-

class travel, and it might cost you less to buy individual tickets, especially if your tastes and budget call for second-class travel. Be sure to **buy your rail pass before leaving the United States**; those available elsewhere cost more. Also, if you have firm plans to visit Europe next year, consider buying your pass *this* year. Prices for rail passes generally rise on December 31, and your pass is valid as long as you start traveling within six months of the purchase date. The upshot is that a pass bought on December 30, 1997, can be activated as late as June 30, 1998. Prices listed below are valid through December 30, 1999.

If you decide that you'll **save money with a rail pass,** ask yourself whether you want a EurailPass, an InterRail pass, or a pass issued by Irish Rail (*see below*), the state-owned rail companies. InterRail (*see below*) is a great deal and valid for travel throughout the Ireland, but it's available only to European residents and those who have lived in an EU country for more than six months. Eurail passes are a good deal only if you plan to tackle several European countries.

Last warnings: **Don't assume that your rail pass guarantees you a seat on every train.** Seat reservations are required on some express and overnight trains. Also note that many rail passes entitle you to free or reduced fares on some ferries (though you should still make seat reservations in advance).

The EurailPass is valid for unlimited first-class train travel through 17 countries—Austria, Belgium, Denmark, Finland, France, Germany, Greece, Hungary, Italy, Luxembourg, The Netherlands, Norway, Portugal, Republic of Ireland, Spain, Sweden, and Switzerland. It's available for periods of 15 days, 21 days, one month, two months, and three months. If you're under 26, the Eurail Youthpass is a much better deal.

European citizens and anyone who has lived in the EU for at least six months can purchase an InterRail Pass, valid for one month's travel in Austria, Belgium, Bulgaria, Croatia, the Czech Republic, Denmark, Finland, France, Germany, Great Britain, Greece, Hungary, Italy, Luxembourg, Morocco, the Netherlands, Norway, Poland, Portugal, Republic of Ireland, Romania, Slovakia, Slovenia, Spain, Sweden, Switzerland, and Turkey. The pass works much like Eurail, except that you only get a 50% reduction on train travel in the country where it was purchased. Be prepared to prove EU citizenship or six months of continuous residency. In most cases you'll have to show your passport for proof of age and residency, but sometimes a European university ID will do. To prove residency, old passport entry stamps may do the trick, but be forewarned that each time passes are presented, the ticket controller has the option of looking at passports and confiscating "illegitimate" passes. InterRail passes can only be purchased in Europe at rail stations and some budget travel agencies; try the European branches of STA or Council Travel (*see* Students, *above*).

The Brit-Ireland Pass—valid for travel on trains throughout the United Kingdom *and* Ireland and Sealink ferry service between the two—is available in the following increments: 5 out of 30 days ($299) and 10 out of 30 days ($429). All passes are available from most travel agents and from the BritRail Travel Information Office.

Travel on Iarnród Éireann (Irish Rail), the state-owned rail company, is free to InterRail and Eurail pass holders. In addition, you can purchase two passes in the United States and Ireland. The Irish Explorer rail pass ($93) is valid for any five days in a 15-day period on all trains in the Republic of Ireland. The Irish Rover rail pass ($116) is good for 15 days on trains in the Republic and Northern Ireland.

INFORMATION ON RAIL PASSES • **BritRail Travel Information Office** (1500 Broadway, New York, NY 10036, tel. 800/677–8585). **Irish Rail** (108 Ridgedale Ave., Morristown, NJ 07962, tel. 800/243–7687). **Rail Europe** (tel. 800/438–7245). **Railpass Express** (tel. 800/722–7151). **DER Tours** (tel. 800/782–2424).

TRANSPORTATION

Ireland's rail network, operated by Iarnród Éireann (Irish Rail), is modern and comfortable but only serves major cities. Smaller destinations are served by Bus Éireann, Ireland's comprehensive national bus service, and a number of independent, regional bus companies. Rail travel can be pretty expensive, but bus service is about 10%–60% cheaper (and slower). Luckily there are a few deals that can save you some pounds. If you're under 26 and have a valid ISIC card, *definitely* purchase the invaluable Travelsave stamp (£7), which entitles you to a 30%–50% discount on all rail fares, 10%–30% on bus fares, and a slightly smaller discount on all ferries. The Travelsave stamp is available from major Bus Éireann depots and many tourist offices. Both Iarnród Éireann and Bus Éireann also offer great deals on day-return tickets for their "Expressway" routes: main lines like Dublin to Sligo, Waterford, Rosslare, etc. A number of other train and bus passes are available, but they generally aren't worthwhile.

TRAVEL AGENCIES

A good travel agent puts your needs first. **Look for an agency that specializes in your destination, has been in business at least five years, and emphasizes customer service.** If you're looking for an agency-organized package, choose an agency that's a member of the National Tour Association or the United States Tour Operator's Association (*see* Tour Operators, *above*).

LOCAL AGENT REFERRALS • American Society of Travel Agents (ASTA; 1101 King St., Suite 200, Alexandria, VA 22314, tel. 703/739–2782, fax 703/684–8319). **Alliance of Canadian Travel Associations** (Suite 201, 1729 Bank St., Ottawa, Ontario K1V 7Z5, tel. 613/521–0474, fax 613/521–0805). **Association of British Travel Agents** (55–57 Newman St., London W1P 4AH, tel. 0171/637–2444, fax 0171/637–0713).

U.S. GOVERNMENT

The U.S. government can be an excellent source of inexpensive travel information. When planning your trip, **find out what government materials are available.**

ADVISORIES • U.S. Department of State American Citizens Services Office (Room 4811, Washington, DC 20520); enclose a self-addressed, stamped envelope. **Interactive hot line** (tel. 202/647–5225, fax 202/647–3000). **Computer bulletin board** (tel. 202/647–9225).

PAMPHLETS • Consumer Information Center (Consumer Information Catalogue, Pueblo, CO 81009, tel. 719/948–3334) for a free catalog that includes travel titles.

> *Even in summer, rain is an ever-present threat and layering is de rigueur. Summer also means long, long days—sunrise by 6:30 AM and sunset around 10:30 PM. If you're from the United States, you might be forgiven for thinking the miserly Gods have cheated you of daylight for all these years.*

VISITOR INFORMATION

Bord Fáilte (Irish Tourist Board), the umbrella organization for Ireland's seven regional tourist boards, can book you a room, recommend a restaurant, and fill your pockets with maps, brochures, and pamphlets—including a number of helpful lodging guides. Bord Fáilte has offices in major cities and other heavily touristed spots throughout Ireland. Its main office (Suffolk St., Dublin) also makes lodging reservations for the whole country; call 01/605–7777 in Ireland. Most towns also have some form of a locally run visitor's center where you can pick up brochures and inquire about accommodations.

The Northern Ireland Tourist Board offices supply a full range of information on the six counties of Northern Ireland.

IRISH TOURIST BOARD • U.S. (345 Park Ave., New York, NY 10154, tel. 212/418–0800 or 800/223–6470, fax 212/371–9052). **Canada** (160 Bloor St. E, Suite 1150, Toronto, Ontario M4W 1B9, tel. 416/929–2779, fax 416/929–6783). **U.K.** (Ireland House, 150 New Bond St., London W1Y 0AQ, tel. 0171/493–3201, fax 0171/493–9065). **Australia** (36 Carrington St., 5th floor, Sydney NSW 2000, tel. 02/299–6177). **New Zealand** (Dingwall Bldg., 87 Queen St., Auckland 1, tel. 09/379–3708).

NORTHERN IRELAND TOURIST BOARD (NITB) • U.S. (551 5th Ave., Suite 701, New York, NY 10176, tel. 212/922–0101 or 800/326–0036, fax 212/922–0099). **Canada** (111 Avenue Rd., Suite 450, Toronto, Ontario M5R 3J8, tel. 416/925–6368, fax 416/961–2175). **U.K.** (11 Berkeley St., London W1X 5AD, tel. 0171/355–5040 for written or telephone inquiries only; BTA's Ireland Desk, 4–12 Lower Regent St., London BW1Y 4PQ, tel. 0171/839–8416).

WHEN TO GO

The main tourist season runs from mid-April to mid-October, but the real hordes arrive in June, July, and August. During summer prices predictably go up, and many hostels and cheap hotels stop offering weekly rates. Spring in Ireland can also be pleasant—the daffodils and crocuses are in full bloom, and the crowds of foreign tourists are not yet overwhelming. For a very different view of Ireland, come during autumn or early winter. With the tourists all gone, you're more likely to get an honest—albeit cold and wet—view of Hibernia. The west and northwest are at their most colorful in September and October. Unfortunately, during the off-season many B&Bs, campgrounds, and some youth hostels are closed, tourist offices and major attractions operate on limited schedules, and public transportation in many regions goes into semihibernation.

CLIMATE

Every 10 years, Ireland is blessed with a summer so wonderful that it tides everyone over through the next nine years of gray skies. The east and south coasts are the driest areas, while the west is famous for its eternal rain. Though the temperature in Ireland rarely falls below freezing in winter, the air is very damp and the cold seems to go right to your bones. The weather in spring is incredibly schizophrenic; a bright, sunny morning is no guarantee that you won't see rain or even hail by teatime.

FORECASTS • Weather Channel Connection (tel. 900/932–8437); 95¢ per minute from a Touch-Tone phone.

FESTIVALS

The following list of major festivals only scratches the surface of the thousands of events staged in Ireland. For information about smaller, local fairs, *see* the appropriate chapters.

JANUARY • At least six major **horse race** meetings (the sport is an obsession to many Irish) are held at centers such as Thurles (Co. Tipperary), Naas (Co. Kildare), Leopardstown (Co. Dublin), and Gowran Park (Co. Kilkenny).

FEBRUARY • The **Dublin Film Festival** starts at the end of the month, providing 12 days of the best in world cinema, plus lectures and seminars on all aspects of filmmaking.

MARCH • On **St. Patrick's Day** (March 17), raise a celebratory pint of Guinness with the thousands of other Irish types in pubs throughout the country. The **Belfast Music Festival** sponsors speech, drama, and music competitions for younger performers.

APRIL • The two-day **Irish Grand National** race meeting takes place at Fairyhouse, County Meath, about 19 km (12 mi) from Dublin. About 60 choirs raise their voices in the **Cork International Choral Festival.**

MAY • The **County Wicklow Gardens Festival** includes flower festivals, musical evenings, and garden tours. **Belfast Civic Festival and Lord Mayor's Show** lasts 21 days and includes concerts, competitions, and exhibitions, starting on the second Saturday in May with floats in the streets of Belfast.

JUNE • Listowel Writer's Week provides a mix of user-friendly workshops, readings, lectures, and plays. **Bloomsday,** June 16, is celebrated with great affection in Dublin with a flurry of readings and dramatizations of Joyce's *Ulysses,* preceded by fancy-dress shenanigans over breakfast and pilgrimages around the city.

JULY • The city of the west really swings during the **Galway Arts Festival**—the largest in the country—which includes theater, parades, film, and rock music, as well as international art exhibits. The **Killarney Horse Racing Festival** attracts horse fans from around the country and is the perfect place to study the characters of rural Ireland. **Battle of the Boyne** festivities throughout Northern Ireland celebrate the 17th-century battle in which the Protestant William of Orange defeated the Catholic James II.

AUGUST • The **Yeats International Summer School** in Sligo is the oldest and most famous of the 15 or so summer schools taking place during this month. **Puck Fair** is a robust and jovial happening held mid-month at Killorglin, County Kerry. At the end of the month the same county holds the famous **Rose of Tralee Festival,** a talent show and beauty pageant for women of Irish decent from around the world. Near the end of the month, the **Kilkenny Arts Week** is an internationally renowned classical musical festival.

SEPTEMBER • The **Matchmaking Festival** in Lisdoonvarna, County Clare, is the traditional place for bachelor farmers to seek a wife; you'll spot plenty of yanks who made the trip in hope of finding a partner for life. The **Cork Film Festival,** the **Sligo Arts Week,** and the **Waterford International Festival of Light Opera** all start at the end of the month and run into October.

OCTOBER • The **Dublin Theatre Festival** is a fortnight of concentrated drama from around the globe, with a special focus on homegrown talent. Cork swings and bops on the last weekend in October when every young fan and old beatnik in the country seem to arrive for the **Guinness International Jazz Festival.** The **Wexford Opera Festival** runs for the last two weeks of the month and on into November; directors and performers from all over the world descend on the little city by the sea.

DECEMBER • New Year's Eve (December 31) celebrations are ubiquitous, but the best place to be at midnight is one of the thousands of parties that people throw in their homes.

DUBLIN

CALE SILER AND ANTO HOWARD

I n his celebrated work *Ulysses*, James Joyce provided a detailed map of turn-of-the-century Dublin. Except for a few name and street changes, much of Joyce's Dublin remains virtually intact. The dirty lanes are still here, the soot-covered flats, the dockside slums, and smoky pubs. Dublin is famed for its cobbled streets, its tightly packed rows of Georgian flats, and its dockside warehouses where faded billboards still remind passersby to "Smoke Walnut Plug. It's a Nut!" But as Irish writers like Joyce, O'Brien, Yeats, and O'Casey discovered long ago, people are what make Dublin a great city: portly grandmums complaining about the price of tea in Bewley's café; churlish cart vendors hawking fish and Doc Martens boots with equal ease on Henry and Moore streets; a gruff pub fly soaking himself in stout, triple-checking the horse sheet between cordial hellos and handshakes.

But in recent years, the white heat of progress, fanned by money from the European Union Structural Fund, has swept through the capital, and many exiles returning after a few years abroad are taken aback by the big-city feel of their old beloved Dublin. All the talk is of the "Celtic Tiger," as the new, vibrant Irish economy has been labeled. There's construction on every second street and a rash of new clubs, coffeehouses, juice bars, cyber cafés, and sushi restaurants. The traffic jam has become the favorite national conversational topic, and the dreaded cellular phone (much cheaper to use in Ireland than in the United States) is now ubiquitous among the working young. Classic pubs are being replaced by dance-music-inspired, trendy hangouts, reminiscent of London in the mid-'80s.

The capital of modern Ireland, Dublin was first settled by Celtic traders in the 2nd century AD. They christened it Baile Atha Cliath, or City of the Hurdles, a name that is still used by Gaelic speakers (look for it on buses and billboards throughout the city). At the crossroads of four countrywide trade routes, the settlement eventually became prosperous enough to attract the notice of the Greek geographer Ptolemy, who placed Dublin on the very first map of Ireland.

Dublin also attracted the attention of the Vikings, who sailed en masse in their dreaded longboats up the River Liffey. By 850, Dublin was firmly under Viking control, with a Viking king and a brawny city wall. The Norse gold and jewelry found here indicates the importance of Dublin for the Vikings, who established an outpost on the Liffey's southern bank (notice the excavated longboat overlooking the river near Christ Church; it was unearthed in the 1970s). Viking rule, however, was short-lived, and they were soundly trounced in 1014 by Brian Boru, the king of Ireland. Boru was murdered immediately after the battle, and subsequent power struggles left the island divided and vulnerable. Dublin thus declined politically throughout the 11th and 12th centuries, especially after England's King Henry II, with the

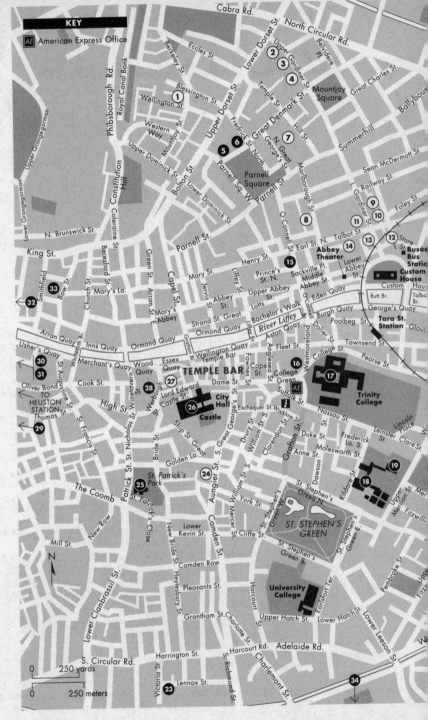

DUBLIN

Cabra Rd.

North Circular Rd.

Eccles St.

Berkeley St.

Blessington St.

Wellington St.

Philbsborough Rd.

Royal Canal Bank

Western Way

Upper Dominick St.

Constitution Hill

Mountjoy St.

Bolton St.

Upper Dorset St.

Lower Dorset St.

Upper Gardiner St.

Temple St.

Great Denmark St.

Belvidere Pl.

Great Charles St.

Mountjoy Square

Ballybour

Hill St.

Summerhill

Sean McDermott St.

Fredrick St. North

N. Great George's St.

Marlborough St.

Railway St.

L. Gardiner St.

Foley St.

Parnell Sq. W.   Parnell Square   Parnell St.

O'Connell St.

Abbey Theater

Lower Abbey St.

Store St.

Busaras
Bus
Station

Custom
House

Parnell St.

N. Brunswick St.

King St.

Smithfield

Bow St.

Church St.

Mary's La.

Green St.

Arran St.

Capel St.

Mary St.

Jervis St.

Abbey St.

Liffey St.

Henry St.

Prince's St. N.

Upper Abbey St.

Middle Abbey St.

Sackville Pl.

Earl St. N.   Talbot St.

Custom House

Talbot Br.

Mary's Abbey

Strand St. Great

Lotts

Bachelor's Walk

Ormond Quay

River Liffey

Aston Quay

Burgh Quay

Eden Quay

Butt Br.

George's Quay

Tara St. Station

Glouc.

Arran Quay

Inns Quay

Whitworth Br.

Merchant's Quay

Ormond Quay

Grattan Br.

Wellington Quay

Temple Bar

Essex Quay

Wood Quay

Fownes St.

Anglesea St.

Westmoreland St.

D'Olier St.

Fleet St.

Poolbeg

Townsend St.

Pearse St.

Usher's Quay

St. Augustine St.

Cook St.

Wineavern St.

High St.

Lord Edward St.

Castle St.

TEMPLE BAR

Dame St.

College Green

Suffolk St.

Nassau St.

Trinity College

Lincoln Pl.

Clare St.

St. Nicholas St.

St. Francis St.

Werburgh St.

Castle   City Hall

Ship St. Great

Exchequer St.

Wicklow St.

Drury St.

William St.

Clarendon St.

Duke St.

Anne St.

Molesworth St.

Dawson St.

Kildare St.

Frederick La. S.

Leinster St.

Upper Mt. St.

Merrion

TO HEUSTON STATION

Oliver Bond St.

Thomas St.

Bride St.

Golden La.

Aungier St.

S. Great George's St.

Grafton St.

St. Stephen's Green N.

Upper Mt. St.

Fitzwi

The Coomb

Patrick St.

St. Patrick's Close

St. Patrick's Park

Bride St.

York St.

S. William St.

S. Mercer St.

Cliffe St.

St. Stephen's Green W.

ST. STEPHEN'S GREEN

St. Stephen's Green E.

Pembroke St.

New Row

Mill St.

New Bride St.

Lower Kevin St.

Camden St.

Camden Row

Pleasants St.

Heytesbury St.

Harcourt St.

St. Stephen's Green S.

University College

Earlsfort Ter.

Upper Hatch St.   Lower Hatch St.

Lower Leeson St.

Lower Clanbrassil St.

Grantham St.   Charlotte St.

Harcourt Rd.

Adelaide Rd.

S. Circular Rd.

Victoria St.

Lennox St.

S. Richmond St.

Charlemont St.

N

① ② ③ ④ ⑤ ⑥ ⑦ ⑧ ⑨ ⑩ ⑪ ⑫ ⑬ ⑭ ⑮ ⑯ ⑰ ⑱ ⑲ ⑳ ㉑ ㉒ ㉓ ㉔ ㉕ ㉖ ㉗ ㉘ ㉙ ㉚ ㉛ ㉜ ㉝ ㉞

0   250 yards

0   250 meters

i

AE

24

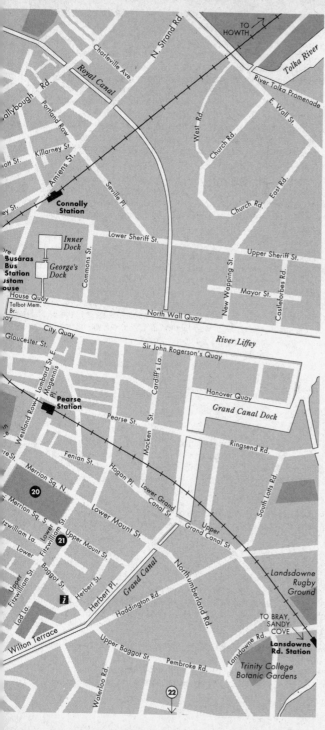

Sights ●

Bank of Ireland, **16**

Chester Beatty Library, **34**

Christ Church Cathedral, **28**

Dublin Castle, **26**

Dublin Writers Museum, **6**

General Post Office, **15**

Guinness Brewery, **29**

Hugh Lane Municipal Gallery of Modern Art, **5**

Irish Jewish Museum, **23**

Irish Museum of Modern Art (Kilmainham Hospital), **31**

Kilmainham Gaol, **30**

Merrion Square, **20**

National Gallery of Ireland, **19**

National Museum of Ireland, **18**

Number 29, **21**

Phoenix Park, **32**

St. Patrick's Cathedral, **25**

Trinity College, **17**

Whiskey Corner, **33**

Lodging ○

Abraham House, **10**

Avalon House (IHH), **24**

Avondale, **11**

Dublin International Hostel (An Óige), **1**

Fatima House, **3**

The Glen, **9**

Globetrotters Tourist Hostel (IHH), **13**

Isaac's, **12**

Kinlay/USIT House (IHH), **27**

Marian Guest House, **4**

Marlborough Hostel (IHH), **8**

Montessori Education Centre (MEC), **7**

Morehampton House, **22**

Stella Maris, **2**

The Talbot, **14**

approval of the pope, landed troops in Counties Wexford and Dublin in 1171, signaling the beginning of the end of Irish home rule for the next seven centuries.

As political ties were strengthened between Ireland and England, Dublin was thoroughly refashioned. Under the rule of the English—who provided the money, artisans, and urban planners—Dublin grew into a modern capital. After Henry II established a secondary court in Dublin in 1173 (mostly to keep a close watch on Ireland's fickle vassal kings), the city was granted a charter, bringing a deluge of skilled immigrants from the Continent. The English influence also led to the creation of Trinity College (1591), a respectable alternative to Cambridge and Oxford for Anglo-Irish Protestants. Politically speaking, the English influence also fueled the much-celebrated Grattan Parliament of 1782, when the English (and Protestant) Henry Grattan demanded Ireland's independence from London. In 1801, the Act of Union brought England and Ireland together in the newly formed United Kingdom. Political power was moved from Dublin to London, and the Irish Parliament was forced and bribed to vote itself out of existence— the only European parliament ever to do so.

One of the first things visitors notice as they wander through the city center—especially on Grafton Street and the Temple Bar area—is the overwhelming preponderance of young people. Statistics put a full quarter of Ireland's population under 25, and with Dublin acting as a magnet for young people looking for jobs, education, dole money, and/or excitement, the effect is staggering. Youthful creativity and progressiveness are evident all over: New magazines pop up all the time, everyone has a friend in a band, and exhibits by new artists are everywhere.

All of this cultural activity may have something to do with the fact that a lot of Dublin's young people have some unwanted time on their hands. In Dublin, which is home to almost half of the country's 3.5 million people, the unemployment rate hovers around 13% (around 40% in some parts) despite the recent economic upswing. Both rural and international immigration are fueling a population growth in the city, bringing to it a certain diversity and urban sophistication along with the problems of overcrowding (pollution, high rents, etc.) that are the scourge of so many other European cities. The pace of the capital is faster than it was 10 years ago, the streets are more crowded, crime is higher, but the underlying gentle magic of Dublin remains in the sanctuary of an out-of-the-way hostelry, in the citizens' unceasing search for a good time, and in their indefatigable sense of humor about themselves and their city. "How do you get from one side of Dublin to another without passing a pub?" the old joke asks, "You go into every one."

BASICS

AMERICAN EXPRESS

This full-service office across from Trinity College changes money, issues and refunds traveler's checks, and holds mail for AmEx cardholders only. There is also a smaller office inside the Dublin Tourism office (see Visitor Information, below). *116 Grafton St., tel. 01/677–2874 or 800/626–000 for after-hours emergency service. Open Mon.–Sat. 9–5; bureau de change also open June–Sept., Sun. 11–4.*

DISCOUNT TRAVEL AGENCIES

CIE Tours. This commission-driven company isn't overly fond of haggard folks looking for cheap deals, but they'll do their best to find you a mid-range plane or ferry ticket. *35 Lower Abbey St., tel. 01/677– 1871. Open weekdays 9–5, Sat. 9–1.*

USIT. This neon-color student agency sells ISIC, HI, and EYC cards and Travelsave stamps, and it can book you on any rail, plane, boat, or rickshaw tour imaginable—usually at half the going rate. The office also has heaps of information on budget travel in Ireland, as well as a bulletin board listing job opportunities, apartments for rent, and people looking for travel companions. USIT is usually packed to the gills, so arrive early to avoid hour-long lines. *19 Aston Quay, west of O'Connell Bridge, tel. 01/677–8117. Open weekdays 9–6 (Thurs. until 8), Sat. 11–4.*

LUGGAGE STORAGE

Most hostels allow you to leave luggage behind for a few hours after checkout, but to be safe, store your bags in a locker. **Busáras** (pronounced bus-*r*-us; *see By Bus in* Coming and Going, *below*) has lockers (£1.50 daily) as well as a left-luggage desk, open Monday–Saturday 8–7:45 and Sunday 10–5:45. Or shove your stuff in the lockers (£1.50–£4 for 24 hours) at **Heuston Station** or **Connolly Station** (*see By Train in* Coming and Going, *below*).

MAIL

Towering over O'Connell Street is the majestic **General Post Office** (GPO), where Patrick Pearse first intoned the Proclamation of the Irish Republic. You can buy stamps, money orders, and phone cards in the main lobby. For currency exchange, turn left and follow the signs. *1 Prince's St., at O'Connell St., tel. 01/705–7000. Open Mon.–Sat. 8–8, Sun. 10–6:30.*

MEDICAL AID

Both **General Medical Service** (tel. 01/834–3644) and **Dental Service** (tel. 01/679–0700) can help foreigners in an emergency. Most hospitals will not charge if your case is minor. The only pharmacy chain in Dublin that stays open past 6 PM is **O'Connell's** (55 Lower O'Connell St., tel. 01/873–0427). You'll find other branches of O'Connell's throughout Dublin, all open daily until 10 PM. Two of the most centrally located are 21 Grafton Street (tel. 01/679–0467) and 6 Henry Street (tel. 01/873–1077).

PUBLICATIONS

For current goings-on in Dublin, pick up the biweekly *Hot Press* (£2) or the weekly *Big Issue* (£1) which gives half of the cover price to the street vendors who sell it. Both have great coverage of the contemporary Irish music scene. Dublin's theater and cinema listings can be found in the *Irish Times* (85p), Ireland's premier national newspaper and major domestic source for the printed daily news. There are also numerous free newspapers, like the *Event Guide*, that have information on current events, festivals, attractions, and entertainment listings.

The Vikings called their colony here Dubh Linn (Black Pool, pronounced dove-linn), and this Norse name has since made its way into both Gaelic and English.

RESOURCES FOR PEOPLE WITH DISABILITIES

The **National Rehabilitation Board** (44 N. Great George's St., tel. 01/874–7503) provides general information for people with disabilities and an access guide to Dublin, which is also available at Dublin Tourism offices.

RESOURCES FOR GAYS AND LESBIANS

Gays and lesbians have steadily increased their visibility in Dublin. The city has a small but vibrant gay scene, which culminates each year in Pride Week (usually in June) with a parade and plenty of cultural events. Both the **National Gay and Lesbian Federation** (Hirschfeld Centre, 10 Upper Fownes St., tel. 01/671–9076) and the **Gay Switchboard Dublin** (tel. 01/872–1055) can give you the scoop on queer happenings. The free monthly *Gay Community News* covers gay and lesbian issues in Ireland and has lists of organizations, restaurants, nightclubs, and pubs that cater to a gay clientele. Most newsagents don't carry this paper; check in the Well Fed Café (*see* Food, *below*) and the Temple Bar Information Centre (*see* Visitor Information, *below*). Lesbians can call **Lesbian Live Dublin** (tel. 01/872–9911) from 7 PM–9 PM on Thursday. The *Big Issue* also has a section on gay and lesbian events.

RESOURCES FOR WOMEN

Well Woman Centre (73 Lower Leeson St., tel. 01/661–0083 or 01/661–0086) provides general information on women's issues, referrals for legal and medical counseling, and options for pregnant women. The Irish government lifted its ban on all abortion-related information in 1995.

VISITOR INFORMATION

An Óige, the Irish Youth Hostel Association, provides maps and listings of its hostels as well as tons of information on sights, tours, transportation, and the like. You can also pick a copy of the invaluable *An Óige Handbook* (£1.50) which lists all affiliated hostels in Ireland. *61 Mountjoy St., tel. 01/830–1766 or 01/830–4555, fax 01/830–5808. Open weekdays 10–5.*

Dublin Tourism has three offices, but the best is their new Suffolk Street location, housed in a former church. You can do almost everything at this tourism nerve center: Gray Line tours, Bus Éireann, AmEx, and Irish Ferries all have offices inside. At any office you can book a room (£1, plus 10% deposit), pick up train and bus schedules, choose from among hundreds of pamphlets on every part of the city and country, and buy walking-tour guides. *2 Suffolk St., tel. 01/605–7777 for reservations or 01/550–112–233 (from Ireland only) for automated 24 hr information (58p per min). Open July–Aug., Mon.–Sat. 9–8:30, Sun. 11–5:30. Other locations: Baggot St. Bridge, facing Grand Canal (open daily 9:15–5:15).*

REJOYCE!

If Joyce fans make one pilgrimage in their lives, let it be to Dublin on June 16 for Bloomsday. June 16, of course, is the day Leopold Bloom toured Dublin in "Ulysses," and commemorative events take place all day long and well into the night. Grown men and women stroll the streets attired in black suits and carrying fresh bars of lemon soap in their pockets, imitating the unassuming hero of what is arguably the 20th century's greatest novel. Dedicated Joyceans can start the day at 6 AM with a Bloomsday breakfast (£8) at the South Bank Restaurant in Sandycove. Here, like Bloom himself, they can enjoy "grilled mutton kidneys which gave to his palate a fine tang of faintly scented urine." While in Sandycove, stop in at the Martello Tower (see Near Dublin, below) for readings and performances by the Dublin Cultural Theatre Group, and general merriment. In Dublin, a number of organized walks retrace Leopold's meanderings. Morning walks leave at 8 AM from the Snug (Dorset St.) and at 9 AM from the Tara Street DART station. You can stop at Davy Byrne's on Duke Street for a midday meal of Gorgonzola cheese sandwiches and red wine. Throughout the day the Balloonatics Theatre Company presents Joycean sketches with a twist—and musical accompaniment—at various locations, including the Dublin Writer's Museum (at noon) and the Ormond Hotel on Ormond Quay (at 4 PM).

Don't despair if you miss Bloomsday, because Dublin swarms with all sorts of Joycean possibilities. The excellent James Joyce Centre (35 N. Great George's St., tel. 01/878-8547), set in an 18th-century town house (former home of Denis Maginni, "professor of dancing, etc."), houses a Joycean archive and library, and hosts readings and lectures. Admission, including a guided tour of the house, is £2.50. Guides—if you're lucky you'll get Ken Monaghan, Joyce's nephew—conduct walking tours from the center for £5.50, including admission to the house; call for times. Tourist offices also sell the "Ulysses Map of Dublin" (£60p), which marks the principal locations of the novel.

Dublin Airport, main terminal (open mid-June–mid-Sept., daily 8 AM–10:30 PM; mid-Sept.–mid-June, daily 8 AM–10 PM). Dún Laoghaire Harbour, Ferry Terminal (open daily 10–9).

Temple Bar Information Centre has the scoop on the ultra-hip Temple Bar area, along the south bank of the Liffey, with a special concentration on the arts scene. They also publish the free bimonthly *Temple Bar Guide*. 18 Eustace St., tel. 01/671-5717. Open June–Sept., weekdays 9–7, Sat. 11–7, Sun. noon–6; Oct.–May, weekdays 9:30–6, Sat. noon–6.

COMING AND GOING

BY BUS

Busáras, Bus Éireann's sole Dublin depot, is just north of the River Liffey and around the corner from the Connolly rail station. You can reach nearly every town in Ireland from here, but Expressway service is offered only to hub cities. Sample destinations from Dublin are: Belfast (7 per day, 3 on Sun., 3 hrs, £10), Galway (8 per day, 4 on Sun., 4 hrs, £8), and Cork (4 per day, 3 on Sun., 4½ hrs, £12). Inside is an **info desk** and a large bulletin board listing the day's departures. *Store St., tel. 01/836–6111. Info desk open daily 8:30–7.*

BY FERRY

Irish Ferries (16 Westmoreland St., tel. 01/679–7977) and **Stena Sealink** (15 Westmoreland St., tel. 01/204–7700) offer regular ferry service between Dublin and Holyhead, Wales. Irish Ferries (2 per day, £20–£25 single) sails directly into Dublin Harbour. Stena (4 per day, £26–£35 single) docks in Dún Laoghaire, 9 ½ km (6 mi) south of the city center. Prices and departure times vary according to season, so call the companies to confirm. Irish Ferries offers 25%–50% fare reductions to those with an ISIC card or Travelsave stamp, while Stena offers a 10% discount to ISIC cardholders. During the summer, reservations are strongly recommended. From Dún Laoghaire, a DART train is the most convenient way to reach the city center; from Dublin Harbour, take a bus (£1.10) or taxi (*see* By Taxi, *below*).

Take a clue from the portly Irish matrons keeping close watch on their kids in the Busáras station, and do the same with your luggage.

BY PLANE

Dublin Airport (tel. 01/844–4900) is 10 km (6½ mi) north of town. Daily flights to and from Britain and the Continent are offered by the Irish carriers **Aer Lingus** (41 Upper O'Connell St., tel. 01/705–6705 for flight info or 01/844–4777 for reservations) and **Ryanair** (3 Dawson St., tel. 01/677–4422). Inside the airport, you'll find car-rental desks, a **bureau de change,** and a **Dublin Tourism** (tel. 01/284–4768) desk, which is open daily 9–8. If you arrive after 11 PM or before 6 AM, most things will be closed and you'll need to take a taxi to reach the city center.

AIRPORT TRANSPORTATION • Airport Express buses (£2.50) make the trip between the airport and the Busáras bus depot every 20 minutes 6 AM–11 PM. You can save some money by taking any bus marked CITY CENTRE or Bus 41 (every 20 min, £1.10), which stop at Eden Quay in the heart of town. If you're traveling to the airport from downtown, catch Bus 41 at Eden Quay (immediately east of O'Connell Bridge, facing the River Liffey) or at the Busáras terminal. There's also a taxi stop outside the airport's main entrance, usually staffed 24 hours a day; expect to pay about £12–£15 to the city center.

BY TRAIN

Dublin has two train stations that receive intercity trains: **Heuston** and **Connolly** are across town from each other but are connected by Bus 90, which runs frequently and costs 90p. Heuston serves routes to Cork (4 per day, 3 on Sun., 3¼ hrs, £16), Galway (4 per day, 2 on Sun., 2½ hrs, £12), Limerick (9 per day, 6 on Sun., 2¾ hrs, £12.50), Tralee (3 per day, 2 on Sun., 4 hrs, £16.75), and Waterford (4 per day, 3 on Sun., 3 hrs, £11.50), while Connolly serves routes to Rosslare (3 per day, 2 on Sun,. 2¾ hrs, £10), Sligo (4 per day, 3 on Sun., 3 hrs, £12), and Belfast (8 per day, 3 on Sun., 2½ hrs, £15). You can buy tickets at either station or at the **Iarnród Éireann** (Irish Rail) office (35 Lower Abbey St., tel. 01/836–6222), which has info on domestic passenger routes and sells a comprehensive timetable (50p).

HEUSTON STATION • Heuston Station, on the River Liffey 3 km (2 mi) west of the city center, is a run-down Victorian relic, lined with rows of arched steel spines that support a massive roof. There are dozens of **lockers** (£1.50–£4 per 24 hrs), a small **information desk** and a **bureau de change.** From downtown, it's not a long walk, but buses leave for the station every 20 minutes from outside USIT on Aston Quay (*see* Discount Travel Agencies *in* Basics, *above*); from the station, take any bus labeled AN LÁR (city center). *St. John's Rd., by Stevens Ln. Call 01/836–6111 weekdays 7:30 AM–10:30 PM, weekends 8 AM–10:30 PM for train info.*

CONNOLLY STATION • Although Connolly Station has an intricate Georgian facade, its interior is a cement-and-steel monstrosity containing a small **information counter** and **lockers** (£1.50–£4 per 24 hrs). A number of hostels are within an easy walk of the station, or you can take any bus marked AN LÁR (city center) to Trinity College or O'Connell Street. If you're walking from the city center, cross the

Liffey at O'Connell Bridge, continue four blocks up O'Connell Street, turn right on Earl Street (which becomes North Talbot Street), and follow the road as it curves left. The walk takes about 15 minutes. *16 N. Amiens St., tel. 01/836–3333. Information counter open Mon.–Sat. 7:30 AM–9 PM, Sun. 4:30 PM–9:30 PM.*

GETTING AROUND

Historically, the heart of Dublin was on the north side of the Liffey, somewhere between **O'Connell Street** and **Mountjoy Square.** This part of town once sheltered the likes of James Joyce and Brendan Behan, and it's also where you'll find the oldest Georgian town houses, grassy city squares, and Dublin's two most important theaters, the Abbey and the Gate. Today, while areas south of the Liffey get a glitzy, often tacky makeover, Dublin's **northside** is still the place to soak up the pure, unadulterated city. O'Connell Street, which abuts the River Liffey at one end and Parnell Street at the other, is the region's main artery, filled to overflowing with cheap tourist shops and neon-color fast-food outlets. **Henry Street** runs off O'Connell Street and leads into one of the city's main shopping districts, including the glorious **Moore Street** markets, where you're sure to hear the peal of a Dublin accent in all its rough splendor. The statue of Parnell (the 19th-century political hero christened by his contemporaries the "uncrowned king of Ireland") marks the beginning of **Parnell Square,** the oldest square in Dublin, now the site of many good-value bed-and-breakfasts. This part of town has a well-deserved reputation for being dangerous, so consider taking a taxi at night or at least walking in a reasonably large group.

Southside Dublin, on the other hand, is where you'll probably want to spend most of your time. Even though it's littered with sweater shops and overpriced restaurants, the southside still has charm, especially around **Merrion Square,** an impressive Georgian masterpiece, and in the **Temple Bar district,** which is filled with old pubs, narrow streets, and lots of cafés. **Trinity College** and the adjacent Bank of Ireland, a block south of the River Liffey from O'Connell Bridge, are Temple Bar's most famous landmarks. **Grafton Street,** just south of Trinity College, is Dublin's most famous pedestrian street and is always awash with good-looking people checking out the upmarket shops and bars. Walking is the best way to get around and experience Dublin; nearly everything of interest is an easy ramble from Trinity's front gate. Street names change often, sometimes every block or so, but they are usually posted on the sides of the corner buildings.

BY BUS

Between 6 AM and 11:30 PM, Dublin's streets rattle with the hum of its green double-deckers—fondly known as vomit-comets once the pubs close. They offer comprehensive service, but you may need a schedule (£1.40), available at the **Bus Atha Cliath** (Dublin Bus) main office, to choose among the 150 or so routes. If you're headed into town, nearly every bus passes Trinity College or O'Connell Bridge; just make sure the sign reads AN LÁR or CITY CENTRE. Fares range between 55p and £1.25, and all drivers give change. There are also late-night buses (£2.50, worth paying just to see young suburban Dubliners letting loose their weekend spirit) that leave from Trinity College and Westmoreland Street on Thursday, Friday, and Saturday at midnight, 1, 2, and 3 AM, but there is no late-night inbound service. Bus stops in Dublin consist of a green pole marked DUBLIN BUS, and many post timetables and route maps. Dublin Bus provides free maps and timetables for all Dublin city bus routes. Call them if you're confused about which bus to take. *59 Upper O'Connell St., tel. 01/873–4222. Open weekdays 9–5:30, Sat. 9–1.*

A number of bus passes are available, but don't bother unless you plan to rely heavily on public transport to get around. The **One Day Travel Wide** (£3.30) allows unlimited travel for one day on buses only. The **One Day Bus/Rail Travel Wide** (£4.50) is valid on the buses, DART, and rail service in the greater Dublin area. **The Four Day Explorer** (£10) is also good on buses, DART, and trains. Insert your pass into the scanner on your right as you get on a bus. The **10 Journey Ticket Books** allow 10 trips of the same price (55p, 80p, £1, £1.10, or £1.25) and can save you up to £2.50. All passes are available from Dublin Bus's main office.

BY DART

The electric DART (Dublin Area Rapid Transport) is a clean, efficient, aboveground train that connects central Dublin with some of the suburbs. Since Dublin is easily navigated by foot, the only times DART comes in handy is for excursions to Sandycove, Dún Laoghaire, Howth, and Bray (*see* Near Dublin, *below*). The only downtown stations are at **Pearse Street** (Westmoreland Row, behind Trinity College), **Tara Street** (off Townsend St., near the Liffey), and **Connolly Station.** DART trains run about every 15 minutes between 6:30 AM and 11:30 PM daily. One-way fares range between 75p and £1.60, and tickets are sold at the station. DART is administered by Irish Rail; all inquiries should be directed to them (*see* Coming and Going, *above*).

BY TAXI

There's no shortage of taxis in Dublin, but at £1 per mile you'll do better to explore the city center on foot. Once the pubs close, though, taxis may look pretty good. In that case, stand in the street and hail anything with an illuminated sign on its roof, or call **Castle Cabs** (tel. 01/831–9000 or 01/831–9947) or **City Cabs** (tel. 01/872–7272). City Cabs accept most credit cards (though not American Express) and can provide wheelchair-accessible cabs. Tipping is optional.

WHERE TO SLEEP

During July and August it's difficult to find even a mediocre bed in a sleazy hole-in-the-wall, especially if you haven't booked in advance. Ditto goes for big rugby- or football-game weekends. Dublin Tourism can tell you when these are, as well as book you a room for a £1 fee. You can also pick up their "Dublin Accommodation Guide 1998" (£3), which lists every approved hotel, B&B, and hostel in Dublin County. Dublin Tourism has also installed **automated reservation kiosks** at the airport and at the Suffolk Street tourist office. With a Visa card, you can choose and book a room at these machines, which will then spit out your confirmation, a map of Dublin, and directions to the lodging.

SMALL HOTELS AND GUEST HOUSES

Forget the big hotels in Dublin, they'll cost you an arm and a leg and most likely one or two more body parts. But if you are up to spending a few pounds, the city at last has a reasonable selection of small hotels and guest houses; prices range from £40–£70 for a double.

Ariel Guest House. This redbrick, 1850 Victorian guest house is a real gem at the heart of the city, just a few steps from a DART stop and a 15-minute walk from Stephen's Green. Rooms (£70 plus for a double) in the main house are lovingly decorated with Victorian and Georgian antiques, Victoriana, and period wallpaper and drapes. Thirteen rooms added to the back of the house in 1991 are more mundane, but all are immaculately kept. A Waterford-crystal chandelier hangs over the comfortable leather and mahogany furniture in the gracious, fireplace-warmed drawing room; you'll swear you're in an old gentleman's club. *52 Lansdowne Rd., Dublin 4, tel. 01/668–5512, fax 01/668–5845. 28 rooms.*

Bewleys at Newlands Cross. On the southwest outskirts of the city, this drab and predictable new four-story hotel is designed for group travelers, especially those planning to head out of the city early to avoid the morning traffic crush. The hotel is emulating the dubious formula recently made popular by Jurys Inns, in which functional rooms—here each have a double bed, a single bed, and a sofa bed—are a flat rate (around £50) for up to three adults or two adults and two children. Breakfast is served in the small café, and there's also a small residents' lounge where you can get a decent pint. *Newlands Cross, Naas Rd., Dublin 22, tel. 01/464–0140, fax 01/464–0900. 126 rooms.*

Jurys Christchurch Inn. Expect few frills at this conveyor-belt budget hotel, part of a new Jurys minichain that offers a low, fixed room rate for up to three adults or two adults and two children for £55. (The Jurys Custom House Inn, Custom House Quay, Dublin 1, tel. 01/607–5000, at the International Financial Services Centre, operates according to the same plan.) The biggest plus: the classy location, facing Christ Church Cathedral and within walking distance of most city center attractions. The rather spartan rooms are decorated in too cutesy pastel colors with ultra utilitarian furniture. A bar offers a pub lunch, and the restaurant serves a mundane breakfast and dinner. *Christchurch Pl., Dublin 8, tel. 01/ 454–0000, fax 01/454–0012. 184 rooms.*

Kilronan House. A five-minute walk from St. Stephen's Green, Deirdre and Noel Comer's guest house is a longstanding favorite with in-the-know travelers—thanks in large measure to the hearty welcome they receive. The large, late-19th-century terraced house, with a white facade, was carefully converted, and the decor and furnishings are updated each year. Richly patterned wallpaper and carpets grace the bedrooms (£45 for a single, £75 double), while orthopedic beds (rare in Dublin hotels, let alone guest houses) help to guarantee a restful night's sleep. Homemade breads are served as part of the full Irish breakfast. If you have a dog back home whom you're pining after, you'll appreciate Homer, the gregarious yellow labrador. *70 Adelaide Rd., Dublin 2, tel. 01/475–5266, fax 01/478–2841. 14 rooms.*

Mount Herbert Guest House. Budget-minded visitors from all over the world flock to this sprawling guest house, made up of a number of large Victorian-era houses knocked into one. The hotel overlooks some of Ballsbridge's fine rear gardens and is right near the capital's main rugby stadium; you can hear the roar of the crowd on match day. The simple rooms (£49 for a single, £79 double) are painted in light shades with little furniture besides the beds, but all of them have bathrooms and 10-channel TVs—true luxury. There is no bar on the premises, but there are plenty of classy hostelries nearby. *7 Herbert Rd., Dublin 4, tel. 01/668–4321, fax 01/660–7077. 195 rooms.*

Number 31. Two Georgian mews strikingly renovated in the early '60s as the private home of Sam Stephenson, Ireland's leading modern architect, are now connected via a small garden to the grand town house they once served. Together they now form a top class guest house, just a short walk from Stephen's Green. Mary and Brian Bennett, the jovial proprietors, serve made-to-order breakfasts at refectory tables in the balcony dining room. The white-tile sunken living room, with its black leather sectional sofa and modern artwork that includes a David Hockney print, might make you think you're in California; but don't fret, it's still Dublin and double rooms are £84. *31 Leeson Close, Dublin 2, tel. 01/ 676–5011, fax 01/676–2929. 18 rooms.*

BED-AND-BREAKFASTS

If you're in the mood for low-cost privacy, take yourself and your money to one of the hundreds of first-rate B&Bs peppered throughout the city center; most cost about £15–£21 per person, including breakfast. The majority lie just north of the River Liffey near the bus station and Parnell Square—Talbot and Gardiner are good streets to try—and south of the River Liffey near Trinity College.

Avondale. Though the plain rooms and pleasantly worn carpets aren't really worth the £20 per person you'd pay on summer weekends, rates are only £17 on weekdays and £13 off-season, and at least there's a shower in every room. *40–41 Lower Gardiner St., tel. 01/874–5200. 30 rooms, none with bath. Reception closes at 11:30 PM.*

Fatima House. For £22 per person (£17.50 off-season), you'll get a simple, comfortable room in a typically plain northside house. Each room comes with a sink and a thickly fried breakfast that can't be beat. *17 Upper Gardiner St., tel. 01/874–5292. 11 rooms, 1 with bath.*

The Glen. If the Marriott hotel chain started renovating Georgian town houses, it would produce this B&B: very nice but bland. Every room has a shower, telephone, and TV, but you'll pay £27.50 per person for them in summer (£18 in winter). *84 Lower Gardiner St., tel. 01/855–1374. 12 rooms.*

Marian Guest House. This clean home is run by a friendly woman who'll ply you with tea and talk your ear off. The rooms (£15 per person) are small, but you'll spend more time chatting in the parlor anyway. *21 Upper Gardiner St., tel. 01/874–4129. 7 rooms, 5 with bath.*

Stella Maris. High ceilings and an oak staircase grace this beautiful old house. The bedrooms (£20 per person, £25 with bath) are airy and bright, and the snug common room is littered with antiques, books, and old family photographs. The owner will accept traveler's checks of any currency. *13 Upper Gardiner St., tel. 01/874–0835. 12 rooms, 8 with bath. Cash only.*

The Talbot. With its brick exterior and lace curtains, this guest house has all the makings of a country retreat (except for the fact that it's in the middle of downtown Dublin). The bright, large, and immaculate rooms cost £33–£35 single, £53–£60 double. *98 Talbot St., tel. 01/874–9202 or 01/874–9205. 48 rooms, 15 with bath.*

HOSTELS

Abraham House. A five-minute walk from the bus station, Abraham House is a good place to crash after a long bus ride. The happy staff of this large but well-kept hostel can sell you bus and Slow Coach tickets and will wash a big bag of laundry for £4. Beds in 10-bed dorms cost £10.50 (£7 off-season), doubles £13.50 (£11), singles £18 (£16), quads £11.50 (£11), and include a decent Continental breakfast, towels, and sheets. Reservations are advised for weekends and July and August. *82–83 Lower Gardiner St., tel. 01/855–0600. 140 beds. Kitchen.*

Avalon House (IHH). Housed in a beautiful Georgian relic two minutes from St. Stephen's Green, the rooms here are bright and cheery, and big plump comforters aid a sound sleep. The Avalon House has dorm beds (£10.50, £7.50 off-season), doubles (£27, £22), and four luxurious singles (£18.50, £17); all rates include breakfast. *55 Aungier St., tel. 01/475–0001. From city center, take Bus 16, 16A, 19, or 22 to the front door. 142 beds. Bureau de change, common room, kitchen, restaurant.*

Dublin International Youth Hostel (An Óige). Housed in the remains of a 19th-century convent, this enormous northside hostel shares the street with working-class flats and is about a 10-minute walk from the city center. The dorm beds (£9, £7.50 off-season) are narrow and cramped, but the dorm rooms are large, and luckily there's no curfew or lockout. Doubles are also available for £24 (£22 off-season). A stained-glass-lined dining room and clean, fully equipped kitchen take the edge off communal living. A Continental breakfast is included in the price. *61 Mountjoy St., tel. 01/830–1766 or 01/830–1396. From O'Connell St., turn left on Parnell St., right on Parnell Sq. W, and continue 4 blocks to Mountjoy St. 420 beds. Bureau de change, laundry (£4), luggage storage (50p), restaurant, sheet rental (£1). Cash only.*

Globetrotters Tourist Hostel (IHH). Globetrotters is a giant step up from many Dublin hostels, with amenities like a pleasant outdoor courtyard; clean, locking dorm rooms with en-suite showers; a turf fire; comfortable bunk beds (with individual lamps for late-night reading); and a delicious, all-you-can-eat breakfast. Plus, you're within walking distance of the city center, one block from the bus station, and two blocks from the train station. Beds cost £12 July–Sept (£10 off-season). They also have a special deal in the off-season: Stay three weeknights for £25. Sharing the building is **The Town House** (tel. 01/878–8808), a cute B&B owned by the same people, with 38 meticulous rooms overlooking the bustling street below. Rooms cost £30–£35 per person (£25–£30 off-season). *46 Lower Gardiner St., near Lower Abbey St., tel. 01/873–5893. 90 beds. Luggage storage.*

Isaac's (IHH). This noisy northside hostel, underneath the DART tracks, has a pleasantly sleazy nightclub feel to it. Dorm beds in large, institutional rooms cost £6.25–£8.50, doubles £31. Besides tea, sandwiches, and vegetarian entrées, Isaac's small café offers live music on an irregular basis, an outdoor patio, and card games and conversation nightly. They have a lockout from 11 AM–5 PM. *2–5 Frenchman's Ln., around corner from Busáras depot, tel. 01/874–9321. 400 beds. Kitchen, luggage storage. Cash only.*

Kinlay/USIT House (IHH). This building, in the heart of southside Dublin, looks like something out of a Dickens novel, with red masonry, wrought-iron fixtures, and tall windows. The six-bed dorm rooms are a bit musty, but you'll survive. You're only 5 minutes from Trinity College and within a stone's throw of Christ Church, St. Patrick's Cathedral, the Guinness Brewery, and the infamous Leo Burdock's (arguably the world's best fish-and-chip shop). Dorm beds start at £9.50, double rooms at £27, singles at £18 including breakfast, and you get a 10% discount with an ISIC card. *2–12 Lord Edward St., tel. 01/679–6644. From Trinity College, walk west on Dame St. (which becomes Lord Edward St.). 150 beds. Bureau de change, kitchen, laundry, luggage storage.*

Marlborough Hostel (IHH). This centrally located hostel, with its brick exterior and rose-tinted walls, is ideal for the traveler who wants hostel prices without the bleak hostel atmosphere. The kitchen is spick-and-span, patrons mind their own business, and the 10-bed rooms are spacious enough that stepping on someone in the dark isn't too big a worry. Beds cost £8.50 (£7.50 off-season), including a small breakfast. *81–82 Marlborough St., tel. 01/874–7629 or 01/874–7812. From O'Connell Bridge, walk north on O'Connell St., turn right on North Earl St., left on Marlborough St. 75 beds. Common room, kitchen, laundry, luggage storage, sheet rental (50p). Cash only.*

Montessori Education Centre (MEC). This enormous, three-story, northside hostel feels like a mansion haunted by friendly ghosts: Rickety steps lead nowhere, apparently purposeless closets appear in strange places, and children's voices emanate faintly from nearby classrooms. The rooms are spacious and clean, however, and the bathrooms are in tip-top shape. Dorm beds are £8.50 (£7 off-season), doubles are £21 (£19), and singles start at £13.50 (£10.50). *42 N. Great George's St., tel. 01/872–6301. From north end of O'Connell St., turn right on Parnell St., left on N. Great George's St. 100 beds. Common room, kitchen, luggage storage (50p), sheet rental (£1). Cash only.*

Morehampton House Tourist Hostel. This hostel's best feature is its location among redbrick Georgian town houses in Donnybrook, an upper-middle-class suburb of Dublin. It's a quick 15-minute bus ride from the city center (80p) or a 25-minute walk. The facilities and dorm rooms (beds £8, £7 off-season) are standard hostel fare, except for the double and triple rooms (£15, £11 off-season), which are abnormally large and well-lit via huge windows. The two drawbacks to this hostel are the moderate noise from the busy street and the management's policy of jacking up prices on all holidays and concert weekends. *78 Morehampton Rd., tel. 01/668–8866. From O'Connell St. or Trinity College take Bus 10, 46A, or 46B. 100 beds. Reception open 24 hrs. Dryer, kitchen, luggage storage.*

STUDENT HOUSING

Trinity College, Dublin City University (DCU), and University College Dublin (UCD) rent dormitory space during the summer holiday (June 17–Sept. 15 in 1998). You won't save any money going this route, but you do get a private or semiprivate room, clean sheets, and modern conveniences. **Trinity Hall** (Dartry Rd., Rathmines, tel. 01/497–1772), 3 km (2 mi) from the city center, has neatly decorated rooms with sinks and shared kitchenettes and baths on each floor. Singles cost £16–£25, doubles £30–£50, including breakfast. **Dublin City University** (DCU, Glasnevin, tel. 01/704–5736) is a couple of miles outside the city center and offers singles in two-room suites for £17. The rooms at **UCD Village** (UCD, Belfield, tel. 01/269–7111) cost £22 per person.

CAMPING

Shankhill Caravan and Camping Park. Sixteen kilometers (10 miles) south of the city center and 3 km (2 mi) north of Bray, this is not exactly a downtown location. Motor homes and caravans share this 7-acre spread with tents, so don't come here with any hopes of Irish countryside. Tent sites are available on a first-come, first-served basis and cost £4.50 (£5 in summer), plus £1 per person. There's a DART stop 1 km (½ mi) away in Shankhill Town. *Shankhill, tel. 01/282–0011. From city center, take Bus 45 or 84 (last bus at 11 PM) to the front gate. Electricity (£1), showers (50p), drinking water.*

North Beach Caravan and Camping Park. What could be a more peaceful way to spend time in Dublin than camping beside the tranquil beach near the little coastal town of Rush? Sites are available on a first-come, first-served basis. They even have indoor beds in case it rains (and it will). *Rush, tel. 01/843–7131 or 01/843–7602. From city center, take Bus 33 or suburban train to Rush. Electricity (£1), water.*

FOOD

Though Dublin's cuisine is dominated by dull sandwiches, bags of greasy chips, eggs and bacon, and Cadbury chocolate, the cosmopolitan spirit sweeping through the city has succeeded in launching a new wave of quality budget eateries. The Temple Bar district in particular has valiantly shaken off the chains of culinary mediocrity and is the place to go for vegetarian, Cajun, Italian, and even Portuguese grub. With a few exceptions the food isn't super cheap, though, so it may be best to adopt the local attitude that Guinness essentially encompasses all four food groups.

Besides local chains like **Abrakebabra** (whose pita pockets are very popular with the aprés-pub crowd) and **Beshoff's** (a fast-food fish place with a popular branch opposite Trinity College), there are innumerable sandwich and tea shops scattered throughout the city center. Another ubiquitous feature of Dublin—and of all Ireland, for that matter—are chippers. These grungy holes-in-the-wall offer deep-fried food at reasonable prices; a burger and chips generally costs around £3, a piece of chicken £2.50, a plate of sausage and eggs around £2.50. If you would rather cook for yourself, stop by the **Moore Street Market** Monday through Saturday 9–6 for great prices on fruit, vegetables, meat, and fish. You can also find a good selection of reasonably priced food at grocery stores like **Dunnes** (50 Henry St., tel. 01/726–8333) and **Quinnsworth** (15 Lower Baggot St., tel. 01/676–1253).

UNDER £5 • Alpha Restaurant. Even if "Irish cuisine" is nothing more than a convenient way to group potatoes and stout under the same heading, the shoe-box-size Alpha is a good place for an authentic Irish meal. The food, drawn mainly from the sinewy-beef and soggy-vegetable food groups, is greasy, heavy, strangely satisfying, and popular with working-class Dubliners who appreciate quantity and fair prices above quality. The staff, a couple of older ladies and their young niece, are about as friendly as it gets. Though it's tricky to find (two floors above a shop with a small neon sign in the window), the Alpha may become your home away from home. *37 Wicklow St., off Grafton St., tel. 01/767–0213. Cash only. Closed Sun.*

Cornucopia. A pioneer among Dublin vegetarian eateries, Cornucopia still serves a menu of fine soups (try the spicy spinach) and sandwiches for £3–£4. The Vegetarian Fry Breakfast includes excellent meatless sausages. The place is a known hangout for some of Dublin's more hippie elements. *19 Wicklow St., tel. 01/677–7583. Cash only. Closed Sun.*

Leo Burdock's. Winner of the "Best in Ireland" award, and touted locally as "The *real* reason the Vikings survived," Leo Burdock's has become a favorite of regulars such as U2, Liam Neeson, Mick Jagger, and Rod Stewart. In fact, so popular has Burdock's become that Leo can occasionally afford to close up shop on a whim and take the day off. For £2.50, try the fresh cod, haddock, whiting, or plaice with a side of tomato and tartar sauce. Dash on the salt and vinegar, wrap it in paper, and you've got yourself a meal.

There is no seating—it's strictly takeout. *2 Wherburgh St., off Lord Edward St., tel. 01/497–3177. Cash only. Closed Sun.*

Marks Brothers. Tasty sandwiches (huge by Dublin standards) and quality salads at a people's price (£1.50–£3), plus a few quiet little nooks hidden away on one of the three floors, act like magnets in drawing the starving Dublin artist and desperate Trinity student to this city-center eatery. The pastries are good, too. *7 S. Great George's St., tel. 01/667–1085. Cash only. Closed Sun.*

Munchies. Thick slabs of freshly baked brown bread come filled with your choice of meat (tandoori chicken, tuna, roast turkey) and various side salads (curried rice, couscous, vegetables). A standard sandwich, filled with as many salads as your taste buds can handle, runs £2.25–£3.50. Watch out for hungry lunchtime office crowds. *Two locations: 146A Lower Baggot St., and 2 South William St., no phone. Cash only.*

Wed Wose Café. Home of Dublin's finest fried breakfast (£3), where the sum is always somehow greater than the parts. Every mundane element (eggs, sausages, bacon, white toast, black-and-white pudding, beans, and fried bread) seems to understand its place in some divine whole. Don't be surprised if the staff engages you in a little lightweight banter, just don't dare try to outdo them. They also serve sandwiches. *Exchequer St., no phone. Cash only. Closed Sun.*

Well Fed Café. This Temple Bar co-op, one of Dublin's most famous vegetarian strongholds, serves a rotating selection of decent, wholesome meat-free and vegan entrées. The school-cafeteria feel (plastic trays and a metallic service counter) is offset by the heartwarming prices—lasagnas and casseroles from £2.70, soups and salads from 60p—and the fact that you can bring your own wine. *6 Crow St., near corner of Dame and S. Great Georges Sts., tel. 01/677–2234. Cash only. Closed Sun.*

> *To blend in with locals, eat only when faint, scorn all fruits and vegetables, and drink plenty of stout.*

UNDER £10 • Bad Ass Café. Sinéad O'Connor used to wait tables at this lively spot in a converted warehouse between the Central Bank and Ha'penny Bridge (a "Rock 'n Stroll" tour plaque notes O'Connor's presence here). Old-fashioned cash shuttles whiz around the ceiling of the barnlike space, which has bare floors and is painted in primary colors inside and out. A wall of glass makes for great people-watching. Although the food—mostly pizzas and burgers—is unexceptional, the Bad Ass experience can be a giggle. *9–11 Crown Alley, tel. 01/671–2596.*

Chameleon. Run by a young couple, Carol Walsh and Vincent Vis, this informal, two-story Indonesian restaurant is on a Temple Bar side street, off the south quays of the Liffey. Coconut and peanut are the dominant flavors in six *rijstafel* ("rice table") menus, with 20 or more items arranged around a large plate of spiced rice. Typical Indonesian dishes include shrimp croquette; chicken satay; Chinese noodles with pork, bean sprouts, ginger, and garlic; and green beans with butter beans in coconut milk. *1 Fownes St. Upper, tel. 01/671–0362. Closed Mon.–Tues. and 1 wk in Nov.*

Clery's Restaurant. The famous Clery's department store on O'Connell Street is a well-kept secret on the Dublin budget food scene. It is home to a third-floor restaurant that serves decent meat-and-two-veg standards; an elegant tearoom with a full lunch menu; and a coffee shop with pastries and sandwiches. It's very popular with the older locals. *O'Connell St., tel. 01/878–6000. Cash only. Closed Sun.*

Elephant & Castle. This is one of Dublin's most accessible upscale restaurants, in the heart of the cobblestone Temple Bar district. E&C is filled daily with wealthy businesspeople and ragged Trinity students alike, both hungry for the huge hamburgers (£7) or Chinese chicken salads (£9.50). A full meal with appetizers and dessert will easily set you back £12, but it's a wonderful place to purge your system of grease and potatoes. *18 Temple Bar, tel. 01/679–3121.*

Il Primo. A few hundred yards from Stephen's Green, this lively two-story Italian restaurant has a bare-bones decor, with bare boards and tables and old-fashioned wooden-armed office chairs. Generous middle-of-the-road Irish-Italian cuisine changes seasonally. Typical offerings include a warm salad of spinach wilted in a balsamic vinegar dressing with shallots and served with Parma ham and new potatoes. Among the main courses, a standout is delicious creamy risotto with chunky chicken breasts, a scattering of chicken livers, and some wild mushrooms. *Montague St., off Harcourt St. tel. 01/478–3373. Closed Sun.*

Juice. A slick vegetarian restaurant? In *Dublin?* It's true: Opened in early 1996, Juice serves upscale vegetarian fare (some of it vegan, or dairy-free, and most of it organic) in a large, deep, airy dining room with brushed stainless steel and dark wine-color lacquer walls. Chef Deb Davis' menu offers a platter of homemade dips and pestos to start—including butter-bean and black olive paté and spinach-pistachio pesto—served with bread and crudités. Main courses include a tasty cannelloni, its fresh pasta filled with spinach, mushroom, hazelnuts, and ricotta cheese, then baked in a creamy tomato and herb sauce. The breads, baked with organic flour, are another treat. *73–83 S. Great George's St., tel. 01/ 475–7856.*

Kilkenny Kitchen. Housed in the Kilkenny Shop, which specializes in superlative (yet sometimes bordering on cheesy) Irish craftsmandhip and overlooks Trinity College, this self-service restaurant showcases wholesome (if sometimes a little bland) home cooking in the traditional Irish style. The menu includes a house quiche (combining Irish bacon, herbs, and fresh vegetables), a good traditional Irish stew, casseroles, and an imaginative selection of salads. Homemade scones, bread, and cakes, as well as Irish farmhouse cheeses are all good bets. Lunchtime is busy; expect to share a table and maybe meet a new friend. *6 Nassau St., tel. 01/677–7066. Closed Sun.*

La Mére Zou. Eric Tydgadt is Belgian and his wife Isabelle is from Paris, so—surprise—their small basement restaurant is Continental in emphasis. The lunch menu includes six king-size plates; one of them, La Belge, has a 6-ounce charcoal-grilled rump steak with french fries and a salad with salami, country ham, chicory, and mayonnaise. In the evening, dishes are more elaborate, such as ragout of venison or medallions of monkfish. *22 St. Stephen's Green, tel. 01/661–6669. Closed Jan. 1–10.*

La Mezza Luna. Good, reasonably priced Italian food is served by a cheerful wait staff in this hip, eclectic setting. Gobble yummy salads (£3–£5) or dazzle your taste buds with a daily special (£8) like chicken stuffed with cottage cheese or pesto on wild-mushroom pasta. The shamelessly rich Death by Chocolate cake (£3) should not be attempted alone. *Temple Ln., corner of Dame and S. Great George's Sts., tel. 01/671–2840.*

Marrakesh. This small spot in Ballsbridge serves authentic food from Morocco—one of the world's most underrated cuisines. Akim Beskri cooks in clay *tagines* (stew pots), the traditional method of desert tribesmen. The tagines' ingredients are a delicate balance of vegetables; meat or poultry; olives, garlic, and preserved lemons; and spices, usually including cumin, ginger, pepper, saffron, and turmeric. There are also a full-blown couscous royale (with beef, lamb, chicken, and spicy sausage), *harira* (a traditional soup with chickpeas), and *mechoui* (a slow-cooked roast side of lamb). *11 Ballsbridge Terr., Ballsbridge tel. 01/660–5539.*

Milano. The open, gleaming stainless-steel kitchen off this well-designed room turns out a tempting array of flashy pizzas. You can expect to find thinner pizza crusts than in the United States, with daring combos like tomato and mozzarella, ham and eggs, Cajun prawns and tabasco, spinach and egg, or ham with anchovies. Last orders are taken at midnight, so keep this joint in mind if you're looking for a late-night bite. *38 Dawson St., tel. 01/670–7744.*

Mitchells Cellars. This perennially popular (with the natives) lunch spot just off Stephen's Green is in the vaulted basement of a posh wine merchant. The quarry-tile floor, whitewashed walls, red-and-white lamp shades above pine tables, and waitresses neatly dressed in navy and white are all virtually unchanged since the early '70s, as is the menu. Still, a bustling crowd continues to pack the place, drawn to its Country French home cooking—fare that includes soups and pâtés, quiche lorraine and salads, beef braised in Guinness, and chocolate-and-brandy meringue. Get here early, or expect a line. *21 Kildare St., tel. 01/662–4724. Closed Sun., Sat. June–Aug.*

Pasta Fresca. This stylish little Italian restaurant and delicatessen somehow squeezes a lot of people into a small area. Antipasto *misto* (assorted sliced Italian meats) makes a good start—or go for a single meat like prosciutto (Italian cured ham) or carpaccio *della casa* (wafer-thin slices of beef fillet, with fresh Parmesan, olive oil, lemon juice, and black pepper). The main courses consist mainly of Pasta Fresca's own very good versions of well-known dishes such as spaghetti *alla bolognese,* cannelloni, and lasagna *al forno.* The pasta is freshly made each day. *3–4 Chatham St., tel. 01/679–2402. Closed Sun.*

Pierre's. Although competition in the area is growing by the day, this spartan, franchised Temple Bar restaurant is holding its own. Its wholesome nutrition makes up for anything it may lack in decor (and that's quite a bit). Enjoy the aromas emanating from the open kitchen, and perhaps start with a homemade soup such as traditional leek-and-barley or a huge bowl of steamed mussels with a rich sauce of melted butter and garlic. *2 Crow St., tel. 01/671–1248.*

Side Door. Style without the pecuniary guilt! The five-star Shelbourne Hotel ably offers a variation on the usual *tres cher* hotel dining room and the uninspired coffee shop. This well-designed budget restaurant has oak floors, cream walls, and art deco wood tables and chairs. You can start off with a bowl of Thai soup, a grilled chicken risotto, or Mediterranean vegetable pizza. Main dishes include supreme of chicken marinated in honey and charcoal-grilled rib eye of beef. Designer beers and a good wine list nicely complement the food. *27 St. Stephen's Green, tel. 01/676–6471.*

Trastevere. Walls of glass and a bright Italianate interior with terra-cotta tiles make this restaurant a stylish place for lunch, dinner, snack time, or simply an espresso. Food ranges from crostini to warm prawn salads, various pastas, and charcoal-grilled chicken. From outside you can watch the chef at work through a large glass window. On a warm summer day you can see and hear the buskers playing away in Temple Bar Square. *Temple Bar Sq., tel. 01/670–8343.*

Yamamori. Ramen noodle bars offer a staple diet for budget travelers to Japan, but this is the first in Ireland. The meals-in-a-bowl offer a splendid slurping experience, and although you will be supplied with a small Chinese-style soup spoon, the best approach is to use the traditional *ohashi* (chopsticks), which allow you to hoist the noodles and leave you to drink the soup (and spill it all down your front). *71 S. Great George's St., tel. 01/475–5001.*

COFFEEHOUSES

Dubliners may spend their evenings in a pub, but a good part of their day is spent at a **Bewley's Café,** the city's oldest coffeehouse chain. Since its founding in 1847, Bewley's has become synonymous with tea sipping and gossip. Bland pastries, sandwiches, and cafeteria-style lunches are served all day at all locations, but most people rightly venture into these 19th-century Georgian masterpieces simply to drink coffee and ponder the newspaper. *Three locations: 78 Grafton St., tel. 01/677–6761. 13 S. Great George's St., tel. 01/679–2078. 12 Westmoreland St., tel. 01/677–6761.*

Café Kylemore (1–2 O'Connell St., at North Earl St., tel. 01/872–2138), smack in the center of town, commands a good view of the teeming streets outside. The coffee is decent at 85p, and you can loiter as long as you like. If you're looking for a hipper, younger crowd, head to **The Globe** (11 S. Great George's St., tel. 01/671–1220), which is a café during the day and a damn good pub at night. Dublin's premier northside coffeehouse is **Winding Stair Café and Bookshop** (40 Lower Ormond Quay, tel. 01/873–3292), which provides a fabulous view of the River Liffey at the base of Ha'penny Bridge. Housed in an ancient, three-story warehouse, the Winding Stair serves tea, pastries, light meals, and outstanding coffee daily.

WORTH SEEING

Dublin Tourism offices offer several snazzy walking guides (£2.50) that highlight particular aspects of the city: "The Dublin Touring Guide" describes five different walking tours, "The Heritage Trails" highlights historical aspects of the city, and "The Rock and Stroll" guide lists pubs, restaurants, and other places frequented by such Irish musicians as Sinead O'Connor and U2.

Historical Walking Tours (tel. 01/845–0241. £4) leads two-hour jaunts covering the history of the city from ancient times to the present. These leave daily at 11, noon, and 3 from the front gate of Trinity College. The guides are top class, including traditional musicians and singers who are liable to belt out a tune on the way. The **Jameson Dublin Literary Pub Crawl** (tel. 01/454–0228), a guided performance tour of pubs with literary associations, is for writers who like to drink and drinkers who like to write. A couple of Dublin bit players act and sing various texts (Beckett's *Waiting for Godot* gets the most laughs) for two hours while everyone gets loopy on Guinness. Tours (£6) set out from the Duke pub on Duke Street nightly at 7:30 PM from Easter to October 21 (Nov.–Mar., Thurs.–Sat. only), and year-round at noon on Sunday. **Gray Line Tours** (tel. 01/605–7705) runs popular, 90-minute bus tours (£7, £5 students) that actually allow you to get off the bus and check out Dublin's main sights. Buses leave from the Suffolk Street tourist office every 30 minutes from 10 AM to 5 PM.

You can choose to save yourself a few bob, as Dubliners like to say (a "bob" was what is now a shilling), and take a self-guided walking tour. The **Old City Trail** begins in front of Trinity and heads up through Temple Bar into the working-class neighborhood called the Liberties. At the other end of the social scale is the **Georgian Heritage Trail,** a southside tour that links many of Dublin's finest homes and streets from the period. The **Cultural Trail** will take you to many of the sights connected with three of Dublin's literary Nobel Prize winners (Shaw, Yeats, and Beckett), as well as Joyce's home, the Dublin Writer's Museum, and the Hugh Lane Municipal Gallery of Modern Art. Information on these trails and others is available from Dublin Tourism.

BANK OF IRELAND

Along with the General Post Office and Trinity College, the Bank of Ireland building is one of Dublin's most recognizable monuments. It was built in 1729 to house an essentially powerless Irish parliament. Under the guidance of Henry Grattan, the predominantly Protestant parliament voted to attain self-government in 1782, though this bloodless rebellion was short-lived. In 1801, Britain passed the Act of Union, legally abolishing home rule for Ireland. In 1803, the historic building was sold to the Bank of Ireland for £40,000. Today, the bank is generally filled with security guards and local customers, but the exquisitely preserved **House of Lords Chamber,** lined with centuries-old tapestries, is definitely worth a long look. Visitors are welcome during normal banking hours, and a short but interesting (and free) guided tour is given every Tuesday at 10:30, 11:30, and 1:45. *2 College Green, tel. 01/677–6801. Admission free. Open weekdays 10–4 (Thurs. until 5).*

CHESTER BEATTY LIBRARY

Bequeathed to the nation in 1956 by Sir Alfred Chester Beatty, the library contains around 22,000 manuscripts, rare books, and objects from mainly Middle and Far Eastern cultures. They have no fewer than 270 versions of the Koran, including some illuminated by master calligraphers from the ancient Arab world. The Japanese and Chinese collections include prints and paintings, a large collection of snuff boxes, and cups made from rhino horn. The library is an important, busy research center and the relatively few exhibits on view to the public change at regular intervals. *20 Shrewsbury Rd., tel. 01/269–2386. Admission free. Open Tue.–Fri. 10 AM–5 PM, Sat. 2 PM–5 PM.*

CHRIST CHURCH CATHEDRAL

Christ Church, the Church of Ireland's flagship, is also Dublin's oldest standing monument, founded in 1038 by the mead-swilling Sitric, king of the Dublin Norsemen. Despite the fact that Christ Church today is surrounded by dilapidated flats and Georgian factories, its squat, gray facade is still captivating, especially the lavishly detailed fenestration, weathered archway chapel, gallery-level carvings, and the famous "leaning wall of Dublin." The interior of Christ Church, filled with a very standard collection of faded murals, tapestries, and men in black robes, is something of a letdown. The **crypt,** which is nearly as large as the church itself, contains some fine religious relics and a set of 17th-century punishment stocks. *Christ Church Pl., tel. 01/677–8099. Off Lord Edward St., 1½ km (1 mi) west of Trinity College; take Bus 21A, 78, 78A, or 50. Admission £1. Open daily 10–5.*

DUBLIN CASTLE

Just off Dame Street behind City Hall, Dublin Castle is one of those sights that's better to look at than to actually visit. Of the original 13th-century Norman castle, only the badly mauled **Record Tower,** an old, weathered stone outcrop, remains. The rest of the site, now used as government offices, is dominated by various 18th- and 19th-century additions, done up nice and fancy to impress dignitaries and a ceaseless flow of EU ministers. Even the sprawling **Great Courtyard,** reputed site of the Black Pool from which Dublin got its name, is lined with stretch limos and security guards. Very few rooms are open to the lowly public, and those that are can be seen only on the guided tours. Viking diehards may enjoy the "Undercroft" exhibit, which displays the remains of a 10th-century Viking fortress excavated on the site. *Dame St., tel. 01/677–7129. Admission £2. Open weekdays 10–5, weekends 2–5.*

DUBLIN WRITERS MUSEUM

In this splendid Georgian-house setting, rare manuscripts, personal diaries, and a rich collection of portraits, publicity posters, and yellowed photographs commemorating the life and works of Ireland's most famous writers all make their home. Ireland's four Nobel Prize winners (Shaw, Yeats, Beckett, and Heaney) are especially well represented, along with the likes of Wilde, O'Casey, Behan, Swift, Joyce, and Synge. The museum is also home to the **Irish Writers Center,** which features periodic readings from local poets and writers, cultural events, and art displays. In the rear is **Books Upstairs** (tel. 01/872–2239), a small bookshop that specializes in Irish-interest titles and rare, out-of-print volumes. All in all, it's a fine place to spend the day. *18 Parnell Sq. N, tel. 01/872–2077. From O'Connell Bridge, walk north on O'Connell St.; or take Bus 10, 11, 12, 13, or 22. Admission £2.90. Open Sept.–May, Mon.–Sat. 10–5, Sun. 11:30–6; June–Aug, weekdays 10–7, Sat. 10–5, Sun. 11:30–6.*

GENERAL POST OFFICE

The GPO is one of the great civic buildings of Dublin's Georgian era, built in 1818 by Francis Johnston. Its fame, however, springs from the role it played during the Easter Rising. It was here, on Easter Monday, 1916, that Republican forces, under the guidance of Patrick Pearse and James Connolly, stormed the building and issued the Proclamation of the Irish Republic. After a week of relentless shelling, both the GPO and the Citizen's Army lay in ruins, and 13 rebels were executed, including Pearse and Connolly. Most of the original building was destroyed in the uprising—the only part that remains is the front facade, in which you can still see bullet holes. This functioning, full-service post office is always packed with customers, but the magnificent central gallery is worth a quick look. *O'Connell St., tel. 01/872–8888. Admission free. Open Mon.–Sat. 8–8, Sun. 10:30–6:30.*

GUINNESS BREWERY

The Guinness Brewery is the most popular tourist destination in town. The brewery itself is off-limits, but the part-museum, part-gift-shop **Hop Store** is open all year. Unfortunately, it's impossible to avoid the "World of Guinness" exhibition, a 10-minute audiovisual show designed to put the brewery into historical context. For all its moving wax figures and silly sound effects, the show merely whets the appetite for what comes next: two free glasses of what's generally considered the best Guinness in the world, poured straight from the adjoining factory. In winter, you can sip your brew leisurely and maybe get a few more out of the servers, but come summer you'll be ushered out of the bar and into the gift shop as quickly as possible. Upstairs from the gift shop is a small but worthwhile art gallery that hosts a rotating collection of local and international art. After the tour, spend some time walking the perimeter of the 65-acre brewery, one of the most Orwellian and genuinely bleak factories in the country. Known as the Liberties, the area is filled with eerie empty streets, ragged brick walls, strange doors, deserted warehouses, and redbrick tenements, which originally housed the Guinness employees and their families. Little has changed since 1759, when Arthur first opened the brewery, and the imposing setting conveys a sense of how austere life must have been for generations of brewers. *Crane St., tel. 01/453–6700. From Trinity College, walk west on Dame St. (which becomes Lord Edward St., High St., and Thomas St.), turn left on Crane St; or take Bus 68A from Fleet St., Bus 123 from O'Connell St., or Bus 8A from Aston Quay. Admission £3. Open Mon.–Sat. 9:30–5, Sun. 10:30–4:30.*

> *It's been said that the pub is the poor man's university. If this is true, Dublin has more than 1,000 opportunities for higher education.*

HUGH LANE MUNICIPAL GALLERY OF MODERN ART

Situated on Parnell Square, this public art gallery is home to many 19th-century Irish and Anglo-Irish works. It also has a good collection of sculptures, contemporary works, and canvases by Jack B. Yeats (W. B. Yeats's brother) and Paul Henry. There's even a small collection of minor European impressionists. *Parnell Sq., tel. 01/874–1903. From O'Connell Bridge, walk north on O'Connell St. Admission free. Open Tues.–Fri. 9:30–6, Sat. 9:30–5, Sun. 11–5.*

IRISH JEWISH MUSEUM

In the land of Liam O'Flahertys and Molly Malones, it's surprising to find a museum dedicated to the Paddy Rosenbergs of Irish history, to the handful of Jews who, fleeing persecution on the Continent, came to Dublin in the early 1800s. Ireland has never boasted a large Jewish population (today it hovers around 5,000), but there is an active synagogue on Adelaide Road (mentioned by the Jewish Leopold Bloom in *Ulysses*) as well as this excellent museum, opened in 1985 by Israeli President Herzog (himself Dublin educated). Inside is a restored synagogue and a display of photographs, letters, and personal memorabilia culled from Dublin's most prominent Jewish families. *3 Walworth Rd., off Victoria St. near S. Circular Rd., tel. 01/676–0737. From city center, take Bus 16, 19, 22. Admission £2. Open May–Aug., Tues., Thurs., and Sun. 11–3:30; Sept.–Apr., Sun. 10:30–2:30.*

IRISH MUSEUM OF MODERN ART (KILMAINHAM HOSPITAL)

The Royal Hospital of Kilmainham, built in 1684 to house retired soldiers in style, is one of the best examples of aristocratic, 17th-century architecture in Dublin. Based loosely on Les Invalides in Paris, with a large stone arcade built around a garden and courtyard, the Royal Hospital was converted into an exhibition annex to handle the National Museum's overflow. In 1991, it was officially transformed into a full-fledged museum and endowed with an excellent collection of works by Rembrandt, Dürer, Manet, and Hogarth, along with temporary exhibits on loan from London and Paris galleries. The gallery frequently rotates its selection, so call to see if the Rembrandts and Manets are out. *Corner of Steven's Ln. and James St., tel. 01/671–8666. Walk west along Liffey, turn left on Steven's Ln. (about 2½ mi); or take Bus 68, 68A, 69, 78A, 79, 90, or 123. Admission free. Open Tues.–Sat. 10–6, Sun. noon–5:30.*

KILMAINHAM GAOL

This squat stone building incarcerated some of the country's foremost revolutionary leaders after the 1789, 1803, 1867, and 1916 uprisings. Both Robert Emmet and Charles Parnell did time here, while

"A PINT OF PLAIN IS YOUR ONLY MAN"

It's said that of the 10 million pints of Guinness produced daily, some six million are consumed in Ireland alone—not bad for a country whose population is 3½ million. You'd start to believe infants must be drinking it in their bottles. When the thick, murky brew was first concocted by Arthur Guinness in 1759, it wasn't known as a "stout" but rather as a "porter," a name derived from a heavy, cheaply made drink popular with working-class porters in London. Over the years, the name "stout" has stuck, and the name aptly describes the formidable heartiness of this thick black brew (and its effects on the human physique). But if you ask for a "stout," you'll get the more bitter bottled brew, so request "Guinness" if you want the smoother draught. Every Dublin drinker has heard the myths about exactly what goes on at night in the Guinness brewery, and God only knows what they cast into the huge turning vats to make the stuff taste so damned good!

Patrick Pearse and James Connolly were executed in Kilmainham's front courtyard (as every Irish school-child can tell you, the wounded Connolly had to be tied to a chair so he could be shot). Modern visitors are gently escorted through the grounds by informative guides and given the chance to watch an excellent audiovisual presentation. A small museum displays relics from the jail's heyday, and there's also an interesting display of pro-Republican placards that explains the history of Ireland's long struggle for home rule. *Corner of Old Kilmainham and S. Circular Rds., tel. 01/453–5984. From city center, take Bus 51, 51B, or 78A. Admission £2. Open May–Sept., daily 10–6; Oct.–Apr., weekdays 1–4, Sun. 1–6.*

MERRION SQUARE

This tranquil Georgian square is one of the few places left in southside Dublin where you can feel what the city must have been like 150 years ago. The square has a pristine public garden buffered by a lovely green. Towering over the square on all four sides are some of Dublin's best-preserved Georgian town houses: brick facades overrun with ivy, sporting sooty clay chimneys and black iron gates, punctuated every few steps by the quintessential Georgian masterpiece, the rounded doorway painted thick green, red, or yellow. Famous former occupants of Merrion Square include Daniel O'Connell, W. B. Yeats, and the Wilde family, all duly commemorated by a series of brass plaques on the east and south sides of the square. *East end of Nassau St. Open daily sunrise–sunset.*

NATIONAL GALLERY OF IRELAND

If for no other reason, visit the National Gallery of Ireland just to take in the building itself—all museums should be this airy and well laid out. The simply perfect south wing has recently been complemented by a brand-spanking-new atrium and a beautifully renovated north wing. Built in 1854, the gallery has grown from an original collection of 150 works to more than 3,000 paintings, watercolors, sculptures, and etchings. It boasts numerous examples of 17th-century Italian, French, Spanish, and Irish schools, in addition to a small collection of Dutch Masters. If a particular piece baffles you, head down to the Multimedia Gallery, where you can use the computers to dissect or learn the artistic highlights of any of the museum's works. *Merrion Sq. W, tel. 01/661–5133. From Trinity College, walk 1 km (½ mi) east on Nassau St., turn right at Merrion Sq. Admission free. Open Mon.–Sat. 10–5:30 (Thurs. until 8:30), Sun. 2–5.*

NATIONAL MUSEUM OF IRELAND

Whenever a work crew unearths the stray Viking tool or Celtic brooch, it gets shipped here for display. As a result, this outstanding museum has the most varied and comprehensive collection of Irish artifacts in the world, culled mostly in the past 50 years. Also on display are the Ardagh Chalice, the Tara Broach, the Cross of Cong, an original Viking longboat, and loads of prehistoric gold jewelry. In the summer of 1997, the museum opened a new branch in Collins Barracks in Smithfield to display its decorative arts and folklife collections. The new museum is on Wolf Tone Quay; take Bus 79 from Aston Quay or Bus 66 or 67 from Abbey Street and ask to be dropped off at the museum. *Kildare St. and Merrion Row, tel. 01/677-7444. Admission free. Open Tues.–Sat. 10–5, Sun. 2–5.*

NUMBER 29

Everything in this exquisite Georgian town house has been meticulously refurbished according to the designs and tastes of the general period from 1790 to 1820. Hand-painted trunks and porcelain dolls lay strewn about the attic; hairbrushes and jewelry sit expectantly on lace-covered mahogany dressers. With every carpet, painting, and bellpull refashioned in exacting detail, Number 29 has a strangely normal feel—as if it were the more eclectic styles of 20th-century Dublin that are unfamiliar and out of place. Arrive early in the morning and you may get one of the museum's super-knowledgeable (and supersweet) guides all to yourself. *29 Lower Fitzwilliam St., tel. 01/702–6627 or 01/702–6165. Opposite Merrion Sq., between Baggot and Upper Mount Sts. Admission £2.50. Open Tues.–Sat. 10–5, Sun. 2–5.*

PHOENIX PARK

Phoenix Park is Europe's largest public park, extending about 5 km (3 mi) along the Liffey's north bank. Laid out in the 1740s by Lord Chesterfield, former lord lieutenant of Ireland, the park is filled with gardens, woods, and lakes. Several monuments punctuate the grounds, including **Phoenix Column,** an obelisk in honor of the Duke of Wellington's defeat of Napoléon, and a great cross to commemorate Pope John Paul's visit in 1979, when one in three Irish people turned out to see him. The park is also home to the **Dublin Zoo** (admission £5.50), the third oldest in the world and one of the few places where lions will breed in captivity. It costs £2 to visit the **visitor center** (tel. 01/677–0095) in the 17th-century Ashtown Castle, which has information about the park's history, flora, and fauna. *Off Parkgate St. From Heuston Station, walk north on Steven's Ln., turn left on Parkgate St. Open weekdays 9:30–6:30.*

St. Stephen's Green, at the south end of Kildare Street, is another magnificent southside park lined by Georgian houses and filled with lakeside paths, gardens, and statues.

ST. PATRICK'S CATHEDRAL

Although the present cathedral seems old by most standards (it was built in 1191), the first church built on this site was consecrated in 450, reputedly in celebration of Patrick's coming to Ireland. Today, St. Patrick's Cathedral is the oldest and most prominent Christian landmark in Ireland—a bristling Gothic structure meant to awaken the fear of God in its visitors. The choir and transepts are plastered with the ragged banners of myriad Irish regiments and long-forgotten orders of knights, while the nave is airy and peaceful, bathed in a dusty amber light. The church's organ is famous for having participated in the world premiere of Handel's *Messiah,* performed here in 1742. Jonathan Swift (1667–1745)—poet, author, wit, and dean of St. Patrick's between 1713 and 1745—is generously remembered with monuments and plaques. Swift's tomb, pulpit, writing table, and death mask are all on display here, along with a memorial to his longtime mistress, Esther Johnson, the poetic "Stella" with whom he had a burning (but supposedly platonic) love affair. *Patrick's Close, tel. 01/475–4817 or 01/453–9472. From Trinity College, walk west 1 km (½ mi) on Dame St. (which becomes Lord Edward and High Sts.), turn left on St. Nicholas St. (which becomes Patrick St.). Admission £1.20. Open Apr.–Oct., weekdays 9–6, Sat. 9–5, Sun. 10–4:30; Nov.–Mar., weekdays 9–6, Sat. 9–4, Sun. 10:30–4:30.*

TRINITY COLLEGE

Trinity College is the oldest university in Ireland, established in 1592 by a grant from England's Queen Elizabeth I. The college was intended to instill Oxbridge fundamentals into Dublin's growing population of well-to-do Anglo-Irish settlers (primarily the sons of the country's Protestant and pro-Brit aristocracy). Even though it occupies some 40 acres in the heart of the city, for more than 300 years Trinity seemed to exist independently of Dublin. Its walls were built thick and tall to keep the riffraff out, while its students spoke with lazy West-Brit accents and drank to the queen's health. As recently as 1966, Irish Catholics faced the threat of excommunication for attending lectures here, even though Trinity itself had opened its doors to all creeds at the turn of the century (today, nearly 70% of its students are Catholic).

Trinity has nurtured an impressive list of graduates over the years, including Dracula creator Bram Stoker, writer and deadly satirist Jonathan Swift, and Nobel Prize winner Samuel Beckett. Although no longer the posh boys' club it once was, Trinity retains some signs of its aristocratic past. Look in the college's **Front Square,** which is accessed via the arches opposite the Bank of Ireland. Here you'll find cobblestone walkways, orderly grass squares, and a few shady maple trees, all dominated by the **Campanile** (1852), or bell tower, which rings for evening meals and exams. Behind the Campanile are the redbrick **Rubrics,** a row of student apartments dating from 1700. The stately building to the left and in front of the Campanile is the **Dining Hall** (open to visitors daily until 6 PM), while across the courtyard is the impressive **Examination Hall,** a lavish rotunda that's also used to host concerts and recitals; check the notice boards under the main arches for listings. Whatever you do, though, don't miss the **Guided Tour of Trinity** (£4.50, £4.25 students, including admission to the Book of Kells) with Joseph, resident fop and wit. He's a County Mayo man with a deadly posh accent, and his hourly tours (May–Sept., daily 10:15–3) are notoriously wry. Meet near the tower in Front Square and keep your eyes peeled for the gentleman sporting tweed and a pocket kerchief.

THE LIBRARY AND BOOK OF KELLS • The *Book of Kells* is generally considered the most striking manuscript ever produced in the Anglo-Saxon world. This 682-page gospel was obsessively illustrated by monks with a penchant for iconographic doodling and frantic spirals. Equally impressive is the smaller and older *Book of Durrow,* essentially a 7th-century coloring book punctuated now and again with religious verse. It has whole pages (known as carpet pages) given over to embellished designs and scribbles, whether a representation of St. Paul with only three fingers or the slithery tendrils of the letter "Q" stretched tightly across an entire page. Both are on permanent display below the library's aptly named **Long Room,** a 210-foot-long exhibition hall that smells heartily of must and old books. Also on display is a wonderful collection of yellowed diaries and old photographs of Dublin, an original copy of the Proclamation of the Irish Republic, and assorted manuscripts of Beckett, Joyce, and Wilde. *Admission: £3.50. Open Mon.–Sat. 9:30–5, Sun. noon–5 (shorter hrs Sept.–May).*

WHISKEY CORNER

Housed in a former distiller's warehouse, this small northside museum offers a detailed look at the making of Irish whiskey. You'll see an antique still, old photographs, and advertising bills, but the best feature of the compulsory guided tour is—you guessed it—the tasting at the end. Everyone gets to sample two Irish whiskeys, but four lucky volunteers get to try three whiskeys and compare them with a scotch and a bourbon. *Bow St., tel. 01/872–5566. Admission: £3. Tours given May–Oct., weekdays at 11, 2:30, and 3:30, Sat. at 2:30 and 3:30, Sun at 3:30; Nov.–Apr., weekdays at 3:30. Reservations advised.*

SHOPPING

Dublin's central shopping area, from O'Connell to Grafton streets, is the top spot in Ireland for concentrated general and specialty shopping; don't expect any great bargains, as prices are competitive with those in most other European countries and that translates to not really very cheap at all. But bargains can be found, and quality, especially when you're buying crafts or clothing, tends to be very high.

Shopping in central Dublin can mean pushing through determined crowds, especially in the afternoons and on weekends. Most large shops and department stores are open Monday–Saturday 9–6. Although nearly all department stores are closed on Sunday, most smaller specialty shops stay open Sunday 10–6. Shops with later closing hours are noted below. Weekday afternoons are the most relaxing times to shop—everyone is just in a better mood.

SHOPPING DISTRICTS

O'Connell Street. The main thoroughfare of the city has been infested with fast-food outlets, but it also has some worthwhile stores. One of Dublin's largest and most famous department stores, Clery's, faces the GPO. On the same side of the street as the post office is Eason's, a large book, magazine, and stationery store.

Henry Street. Running westward from O'Connell Street, this busy street features Arnotts department store and a host of smaller, super-tacky, super-fun, specialty stores selling records, footwear, and cheap fashion. Henry Street's continuation, Mary Street, has a branch of Marks & Spencer, a splendid store for stocking up on good food for a trip.

Grafton Street. Dublin's main shopping street is now closed to vehicles for most of the day. Two substantial, rather swishy department stores face each other here, while the rest of the street is taken up by smaller shops, many of them branches of international chains, such as The Body Shop, Bally Shoes, Next, and Principles. Smaller streets off Grafton Street, especially Duke Street, South Anne Street, and

Chatham Street, have expensive crafts and fashion shops that are good for a browse. Overall, the street can be a little pricey.

SPECIALTY SHOPPING CENTERS

Blackrock (Blackrock, Co. Dublin) is technically outside of Dublin's city center, but it deserves special mention as one of Dublin's first attempts at the mall. It's built on two levels, looking onto an inner courtyard, with the giant Superquinn Center, cafés, restaurants, and the internationally ubiquitous groups of teenage boys and girls hanging out. Blackrock can be reached conveniently on the DART train line.

Ilac Center (Henry St.) was Dublin's first large modern shopping center, with two department stores, specialty shops, and several restaurants. A small public library and ample parking are also available. Good deals are certainly to be found, and there is plenty of variety.

Powerscourt Townhouse (S. William St.), a fashionable town house built in 1771, housed a wholesale textile company for many years until it was updated nearly 15 years ago. The interior courtyard has been thoroughly refurbished and roofed over; on the dais at ground-floor level, live piano music is often heard. Two floors of galleries have a maze of small overpriced crafts shops interspersed with coffee shops and restaurants—a good spot for lunch, but it might be wise to do your purchasing elsewhere.

St. Stephen's Green Centre (NW corner of St. Stephen's Green), Dublin's largest and most ambitious shopping center, resembles a giant greenhouse, with ironwork in a sort-of Victorian style. On three floors overlooked by a vast clock, the 100 mostly small shops sell a variety of crafts, fashions, and household goods. The Dunnes Stores here sells the cheapest groceries in the center of town.

DEPARTMENT STORES

Arnotts (Henry St. and Grafton St.) has a wide variety of relatively mundane clothing, housewares, and sporting goods filling three complete floors; the smaller Grafton Street branch stocks only new fashion and footwear.

Clery's (O'Connell St.) is the city's most famous department store. It has four floors of all types of merchandise, from fashion to home appliances, and it caters to a distinctly modest, traditional sense of style. Shopping for the civilized.

Dunnes Stores (Major city-center stores at St. Stephen's Green Center, Henry St., and Ilac Shopping Center, Mary St.) is Ireland's largest chain of department stores. All stores stock fashion, household, and grocery items and have a reputation for value and variety.

Eason's (Major stores at O'Connell St. and Ilac Shopping Center, Mary St.) is known primarily for its wide variety of books, magazines, and stationery. Recently its biggest outlet on O'Connell Street began to stock music, videos, and other audiovisual goodies.

SPECIALTY SHOPS

An increasing number of Irish-made crafts and souvenir lines reflect an increasing demand by visitors for specifically Irish goods. Some newer specialty shops sell nothing else. Prices can be high, but a little patience usually pays off and you might just find a bargain.

BOOKS • Books make ideal presents from Ireland, land of saints and scholars and all that. With nearly 1,000 titles now published each year in Ireland, the breadth and choice of material is quite impressive. The range of texts is particularly wide in Irish history, fiction, and travel, and the production quality of such titles compares very favorably with books published outside Ireland. **Fred Hanna's** (27 Nassau St.) sells old and new books, with a good choice of books on travel and Ireland. **Greene's** (Clare St.) carries an extensive range of secondhand volumes. **Hodges Figgis** (54 Dawson St.) stocks 1½ million books on three floors. **Waterstone's** (7 Dawson St.), a large branch of a British chain, has two floors featuring a fine selection of Irish and international books. **The Winding Stair** (40 Lower Ormond Quay) sells secondhand books and has a great café that overlooks the River Liffey.

CDS, RECORDS, AND TAPES • An increasing amount of Irish-recorded material, covering traditional folk music, country and western, rock, and even a smattering of classical music, is now available on records, compact discs, and tapes. **Tower Records** (16 Wicklow St.) now has a branch in Dublin. **HMV** (65 Grafton St., tel. 01/679–5334; and 18 Henry St.) is one of the larger record shops in town. **Claddagh Records** (2 Cecilia St.) and **Gael Linn** (26 Merrion Sq.) specialize in traditional Irish music and Irish-language recordings and are a great relief from the megastores that now dominate the market.

OUTDOOR MARKETS

Dublin has a number of open-air markets, selling mostly men's and women's fashions. **Moore Street** is open from Monday to Saturday, 9–6; stalls lining both sides of the street sell fruits and vegetables. The traditional Dublin repartee here is renowned in the city. Other open markets are only open on weekends. A variety of bric-a-brac is sold at the **Liberty Market** on Meath Street, open on Friday and Saturday, 10–6, and Sunday, 12–5:30. The indoor **Christchurch Market,** opposite St. Audeon's Church, is open Saturday and Sunday, 10–5; come here for antiques and bric-a-brac.

AFTER DARK

Dublin offers a wide variety of after-hours pursuits. First and foremost, of course, is drinking. Whether you're in for a staggering pub crawl or a quiet chat over a pint of plain, head to any one of Dublin's 1,000 public houses. A lot of clichés have been uttered about Dublin pubs, but when you've spent a little time in them, wrapped up in the warm energy that radiates through the best of them, where life is on display in all its guises, you'll understand the hyperbole. If your head is still throbbing from last night's throaty sing-along, go to the movies, the theater, or any one of a dozen music pubs in the city center. Be aware that nearly everything here closes by midnight except a couple of new clubs. If you're stuck for inspiration, pick up the weekly magazine *The Big Issue* (£1), which lists nearly every restaurant, pub, music venue, cinema, theater, art gallery, and late-night hot spot in town.

PUBS

As a general rule, the area between Grafton and Great George's streets is a gold mine for classy pubs. Another good bet is the Temple Bar district, sandwiched between Dame Street and the River Liffey. But in recent years both these areas have been overrun with tourists, so try up around Parnell Square for a few real spit-on-the-floor hideaways.

The Brazen Head. Dublin's oldest pub (built in 1198) served as the headquarters for the rebellious United Irishmen during the late 18th century. Loaded with character and friendly drunks, the Brazen Head now has live, traditional music nightly. *20 Lower Bridge St., tel. 01/677–9549.*

Brussels. A disorderly sort of metal dive filled with black leather and greasy longhairs, Brussels features a concert-volume jukebox spewing the likes of Metallica and Soundgarden. *7 Harry St., off Grafton St., tel. 01/677–5362.*

The Crane. A smart place about the size of a shoe box, the Crane has recently been renovated in the "old pub" style (dark oak and buckling hardwood floors). It looked better as it was, but it's a popular stop on the Trinity College weekend pub crawl. A variety of music can be heard in the downstairs lounge. *20 Crane Ln., off Dame St., tel. 01/671–5824.*

The George. Across the street from The Globe (*see below*), this huge gay/lesbian pub is dimly lit, smoky, and laid-back. The crowd—a good mix of locals and out-of-towners of all ages—wraps itself around the long bar. Wednesday–Monday, the upstairs transmogrifies into the dance club "The Block" from 9:30 PM to 2:30 AM; the cover is free Monday and Sunday, otherwise it'll cost you £2–£5. *89 S. Great George's St., tel. 01/478–2983.*

The Globe. It's *the* pub for the young and progressive, with massive oak tables, old posters, and ambient sounds. Trinity students descend on the place after classes. Downstairs is the dance club Rí-Rá, whose atmosphere changes nightly; Thursday is "Funk Off" night, a debauched evening of '70s-style clothes and hair accompanied by heavy bass lines. *11 S. Great George's St., tel. 01/671–1220.*

The Lincoln Inn. The Lincoln is a fine pub in all respects: dark, quiet, sufficiently ancient, and frequented by Trinity students and leathery locals. Standard pub grub is available for less than £4. *19 Lincoln Pl., by Trinity College, tel. 01/676–2978.*

McDaid's. Most nights you'll hear jazz, blues, or Irish folk music in the upstairs lounge of this popular pub. *3 Harry St., off Grafton St., tel. 01/679–4395.*

Mulligan's of Poolbeg Street. Until a few years ago, no women were allowed in Mulligan's. Today, journalists, locals, and students of both genders flock here for what is argued to be "The Best Pint of Guinness on Earth." Allegedly, Mulligan's still uses wooden pipes to bring "Arthur's Nectar" (Guinness) up from the cellar of this ancient pub. Sounds like a fib. *8 Poolbeg St., off Pearse St., next to Evening Press building, tel. 01/677–5582.*

Stag's Head. No visit to Dublin is complete without lunch at the Stag's Head, one of the city's oldest and best-preserved pubs. The Stag's high oak ceilings and beveled windows lend it an open, unstuffy feel. Lunches include a daily special (around £3.50), chicken and peas (£4.50), and soup (£1.20). *1 Dame Ct., 1 block south of Dame St., tel. 01/679–3701.*

Toner's. This is the epitome of a good pub. Built in the early 1800s, Toner's thankfully retains most of its original furnishings and flavor (old men nursing their pints, antique books and bottles on the walls). Toner's also has the distinction of being the only pub ever visited by W. B. Yeats. Cheap pub grub is available daily. *139 Lower Baggot St., tel. 01/676–3090.*

MUSIC AND DANCING

Dublin's music scene is excellent. With more than 120 different clubs and music pubs to choose from, you'll need a copy of *The Big Issue* to get you started. Otherwise, take a walk down Grafton Street and keep your ears open. **International Bar** (23 Wicklow St., tel. 01/677–9250), and a number of other city-center pubs double as independent music venues. Happily, they rarely charge a cover. If you're looking for classical music, the only dependable place in Dublin is the **National Concert Hall** (Earlsfort Terr., tel. 01/671–1888). Their season is extremely limited, so call in advance or thumb through *The Big Issue* for current listings.

Bad Bob's Backstage Bar. In a few words: rock and some country. The lineup may change nightly, but most bands who play here are dependably loud. *35 East Essex St., tel. 01/677–5482. Cover: £2–£8.*

The Baggot Inn. On the fringe of the city center, the Baggot Inn looks like a dull pub from the street, but head inside to the back rooms and you'll find it dark, sweaty, and loud. There's even a full bar. *143 Baggot St., tel. 01/676–1430. Cover: free–£5.*

The only bad thing about Irish pubs is that they close—at 11 PM during winter, at 11:30 PM in summer. When the barman shouts "last call" around 10:55, he means it.

Dublin Arts Club. Held late on weekend nights in the Gaiety Theatre (*see* Theater, *below*), the DA club, as it is affectionately known, is a raucous four floors of hopping live sounds mixed in with some cabaret theater; they even show an old movie. It's the best night out in Dublin. *Gaiety Theatre, South King St., tel. 01/677–1717.*

The Kitchen. Posh subterranean caves stuffed with velvety crimson lounge furniture surround a tiny dance floor in U2's own club (they own the upstairs hotel, too). Although it's open nightly (around 11:30ish), only the super-glam set get in on weekends. *East Essex St., tel. 01/677–6635. Cover: £4–£8.*

Slattery's. Music in this full-service pub varies (mostly rock with the infrequent traditional Irish session). The upstairs (£2–£5 cover) hosts more well-known bands, but the live music on the ground floor is always free. *129 Capel St., tel. 01/873–7971.*

Whelan's. It's a real in spot for up-and-coming bands from Ireland and the U.K. Big crowds descend on the place for most gigs, so get there early. *25 Wexford St., tel. 01/478–0766. Cover £2–£5.*

THEATER

Dublin's theater scene is impressive: Scattered around the city center are no less than 15 established and experimental stages that host a variety of opera, comedy, and tearjerker dramas. Especially popular (with tourists) are the Irish classics staged every summer, whether it's Brian Friel's hit *Dancing at Lughnasa,* Synge's *Playboy of the Western World* (which sparked massive riots when it opened at the Abbey in 1907), or O'Casey's *Plough and the Stars.* Most theaters offer sizable discounts to students with ID, nearly all productions finish by 11 PM, and, like everything else in Dublin, most theaters are dark on Sunday. Check *The Big Issue* for dead-on reviews and comprehensive listings.

If you're in the mood for low-key entertainment with some good-natured song and dance thrown in, **Olympia Theatre's** (73 Dame St., tel. 01/677–7744) "Midnight at the Olympia" program on Friday and Saturday nights is an excellent choice. Shows cost £7–£10. **City Arts Centre** (2325 Moss St., tel. 01/677–0643) also presents experimental works for as little as £2 and hosts a variety of cultural events.

The following theaters offer varied dramatic fare: **Abbey Theatre and Peacock Theatre** (Lower Abbey St., tel. 01/878–7222), **Andrew's Lane Theatre** (9 Andrew's Ln., tel. 01/679–5720), **Focus Theatre** (6 Pembroke Pl., tel. 01/676–3071), **Gaiety Theatre** (S. King St., tel. 01/677–1717), **Gate Theatre** (1 Cavendish Row, tel. 01/874–4045), **Project Arts Centre** (39 Essex St., tel. 01/671–2321), and **The Riverbank** (10 Merchant's Quay, tel. 01/677–3370).

FILM

Most Dublin cinemas offer a standard bag of big-budget Hollywood flicks that were released in the United States ages ago, but Dublin's one offbeat art house, **Irish Film Centre** (6 Eustace St., tel. 01/ 679–3477), does its best to keep your brain from turning to mush. O'Connell and Abbey streets have the highest concentration of movie houses. Admission prices are in the £4–£6 range, and reduced rates (£2.50) are available for students and for most showings before 6 PM. Late shows (10–midnight) are common on weekends only.

NEAR DUBLIN

BRAY

Bray, which lies 16 km (10 mi) south of Dublin, is a trim seaside village known for its sandy beaches and dilapidated summer cottages. When the weather is good, hordes flock to Bray's oceanfront boardwalk to push baby carriages and soak up the sun. The mountains bordering Bray to the south are laced with uncrowded hiking and mountain-bike trails. One of the best is a well-marked trail that leads from the beach to the 10-foot-tall cross that crowns the spiny peak of **Bray Head.** This semi-difficult, one-hour climb affords stunning views of County Wicklow and Dublin Bay and gives a good sense of some very typical Irish countryside.

Bray is connected to Dublin by a ½-hour DART ride (£1.30). From Bray Station, turn left for the beach and for Bray's Main Street, home to a small collection of restaurants, hamburger stands, video arcades, and used-clothing stores. **E. R. Harris & Sons** (87C Greenpark Rd., tel. 01/286–3357) rents bikes through the Raleigh Rent-A-Bike scheme for £7 per day or £30 per week, plus £40 deposit.

SANDYCOVE

Sandycove's claims to fame are its beautiful strand and the squat **Martello Tower,** perched on a rocky headland overlooking Dublin Bay. The tower was built by the British in 1804 in anticipation of a Napoleonic invasion that never materialized. Like most of the 34 Martello towers that ring Ireland's coast, this one was demilitarized in the 1860s. In 1904, it was rented to Oliver St. John Gogarty for the sum of £8 per year. His idea was to create a nurturing environment for writers and would-be literati. To this end, he invited James Joyce to spend a week here in September 1904, leading to a depiction of the tower in *Ulysses*. The small **Joyce Tower** museum exhibits first editions of *Ulysses,* as well as Joyce's piano, guitar, waistcoat, cane, death mask, and a tie he gave to Samuel Beckett (who was Joyce's one-time secretary). *Ulysses* trivia on display includes a Plumtree's Potted Meat tin and the central gun rest that Buck Mulligan mounts in preparation for mass. *Tel. 01/280–9265. Admission: £2.20. Open Apr.–Oct., Mon.–Sat. 10–1 and 2–5, Sun. 2–6; Nov.–Mar. by appointment.*

Adjacent to the tower is the **Forty Foot Pool,** a murky shallow that mostly attracts nude older men. Visitors are welcome to join the old folks for a swim, but be warned that the water is very cold. Women were once banned from the place—an old sign still reads: FORTY FOOT GENTLEMEN ONLY, PLEASE. Nowadays "gentlemen only" is the norm, not the rule. To reach Sandycove, take the DART to Sandycove Station (£1.20 each way).

GLENDALOUGH

Glendalough, one of Ireland's premier monastic sites, is nestled in a lush depression deep in the rugged Wicklow Mountains, set amid trees, lakes, and acres of windswept heather. Glendalough flourished as a monastic center from around 400 until 1398, when English soldiers plundered the site, leaving the ruins that you see today. Its most famous associate was St. Kevin (*Coemghein,* or "fair begotten" in Irish), who founded the monastery in 550. The most impressive feature of Glendalough (aside from the surrounding hills oozing emerald flora) is the perfectly preserved, 100-foot-tall **round tower,** built in the 10th century. The tower was used both to call monks to prayer and as a symbol that could be seen from afar by the many pilgrims to the site. Also notable are **St. Kevin's Kitchen,** which still bears its millennia-old stone roof, the skeletal remains of a 10th-century cathedral (the second largest cathedral in Ireland when it was built), and a gorgeously chaotic graveyard of crumbling Celtic crosses and tombstones.

Sadly, Glendalough swarms with more tourists than you can shake a monogrammed Pierre Cardin camera case at. The problem is compounded by the presence of a luxury hotel (which, on the plus side, has the only pub for miles) and a popular hostel. To make the most of Glendalough, arrive early and/or spend the night. Most everyone goes home around 6 PM, when the monastic site's visitor center closes for the evening. Since the monastic site itself is open 24 hours, you can poke around to your heart's content (exploring the cemetery by moonlight or sunset is particularly cool). Don't leave before you stroll past the monastery along the two pristine lakes that give Glendalough its name, "glen of the two lakes." The visitor center has maps (30p), walking guides, and an audiovisual presentation on monastic Ireland. *Site: Open 24 hrs. Admission free. Visitor center: tel. 0404/45325. Admission: £2. Open June–Aug., daily 9–6:30; mid-Mar.–May and Sept.–mid-Oct., daily 9:30–6; mid-Oct.–mid-Mar., daily 9:30–5.*

COMING AND GOING

Bus Éireann and **Gray Line Tours** (tel. 01/661–9666) organize bus excursions to Glendalough for around £10 including admission. Bus Éireann leaves daily (except Friday) at 10:30 and returns at 5:45. Gray Line's half-day tours leave on Tuesday at 2:30, and Thursday and Saturday at 10. A cheaper option is **St. Kevin's bus service** (tel. 01/281–8119), which departs for Glendalough daily at 11:30 AM and 6 PM from in front of the Royal College of Surgeons on St. Stephen's Green. The cost is £5 single, £8 return. If you're bicycling to Glendalough, consider taking the scenic R755 highway, which passes through the incredible Wicklow Gap.

WHERE TO SLEEP

There are many, many B&B's on the road between the ruins and the nearby town of Laragh. Pick one that intrigues you, or try **Lilac Cottage** (Laragh, tel. 0404/45574), which has three tiny but tasteful rooms for £14 per person (£12 off-season).

Gleann Dá Loch youth hostel is about a 5-minute walk from Glendalough. The dorm beds (£6) are in typically spartan, sex-segregated rooms, but the kitchen facilities are good, it's close to the ruins, and there's often someone interesting to meet in the large common room. *Tel. 0404/45342 or 0404/45143. From visitor center, turn left on main road, walk past the hotel, cross the river and keep straight; the hostel is ½ km (¼ mi) ahead. 120 beds. Midnight curfew, lockout noon–5. Reception open after 3 PM.*

NEWGRANGE

Stonehenge and the pyramids at Giza are spring chickens compared to Newgrange, one of the most fascinating sites near Dublin. Built around 5,200 years ago, Newgrange is a passage tomb—a huge mound of earth with a stone passageway leading to a burial chamber constructed entirely of dry stone (mortar wasn't invented yet). Newgrange was perfectly positioned so that on the winter solstice the rising sun would briefly illuminate the inner chamber—a moment that is dramatically re-enacted on the mandatory guided tour of the inner chamber. The walls of the burial chamber are adorned with mysterious etchings that have baffled archaeologists and beg you to develop your own hypothesis; some think it was a temple for sun-worshipping druids, while others believe it is the vortex of powerful energy lines.

There are three ways to reach Newgrange from Dublin: hitching, taking a bus tour with Gray Line or Bus Éireann, or a bus/hitching combo. To hitch, go to the N1 heading north toward Drogheda, then take the N51 toward Slane and watch for signs. Bus Éireann (tel. 01/836–6111) excursions leave Dublin May–September, every day but Friday at 10 AM (limited service available Oct.–Apr.). Gray Line (tel. 01/661–9666) leaves daily at 2:30. Both return at 5:45, cost £15, and include admission to the site. Alternatively, you can take a standard Bus Éireann bus to Drogheda (hourly, 1 hr, £6) and hitch or hike the remaining 11 km (7 mi) to Newgrange. *Tel. 041/24488. Admission: £3. Open June–Sept. daily 9:30–7, Mar.–Apr. and Oct. daily 10–5, Nov.–Feb. daily 10–4:30.*

THE LAKELANDS

LAURENCE BELGRAVE

I rish schoolchildren were once taught to think of their country as a saucer with mountains around the edge and a dip in the middle. The dip is the Midlands—or the Lakelands, as Bord Fáilte prefers to call it—and this often overlooked region comprises seven counties: Cavan, Laois (pronounced "leash"), Westmeath, Longford, Offaly, Roscommon, and Monaghan, in addition to North Tipperary.

The Lakelands area is usually looked upon with scorn by the Irish as a dull and mundane place (the very worst of offenses in Ireland; better dead than boring). It's a region they drive through to get somewhere else. But as a visitor with a little patience you may uncover a real gem in the rough. It offers you a chance to see Ireland at work, the agricultural-based country of small market towns and viable farms, where citizens can be observed simply getting on with their daily lives. They are friendly, of course, but they are not dependent on the tourist dollar (unlike so many other parts of the country) and so they have not altered their environment to please the big-spending visitors. A town's main hotel is usually the social center, a good place from which to study local life. You might witness a wedding reception (generally a boisterous occasion for all age groups), a First Communion supper, a meeting of the local Lions Club, or a gathering of the neighborhood weight-watchers group.

Appropriately, a fair share of Ireland's 800 bodies of water speckle this lush countryside known as the lakelands. Many of the lakes—formed by glacial action some 10,000 years ago—are quite small, especially in Cavan and Monaghan. Anglers who come to the area boast of having a whole lake to themselves, and many return year after year to practice the sport. The River Shannon, one of the longest rivers in Europe, bisects the Lakelands from north to south piercing a series of loughs (the Irish for lakes): **Lough Allen, Lough Ree,** and **Lough Derg.** The **Royal Canal** and the **Grand Canal** cross the Lakelands from east to west, ending in the Shannon north and south of Lough Ree. Stretches of both canals are now being developed for recreational purposes.

In the countryside around the small, friendly towns, you'll stumble across several well-maintained historic homes with carefully tended gardens, including **Strokestown Park House** and **Birr Castle Gardens.** Examples of the "big house" common in Irish life and literature, including the poetry of Yeats, these mansions were once objects of hate for the local population as they generally housed the big-brother protestant overlord. In times of rebellion it was not unheard of for one of these houses to mysteriously catch fire. You'll also find the impressive monastic remains at **Clonmacnoise,** Boyle, and Fore; excellent fishing and uncrowded parkland golf courses; and numerous lovely country walks along the water.

Dromore
Dungannon
Lower Lough Erne
NORTHERN IRELAND
TYRONE
A4
Ballygawley
Lough Melvin
N16
Enniskillen
Glaslough
Armagh
Manorhamilton
Lough Macnean
A4
FERMANAGH
Monaghan
ARMAGH
Lough Gill
Upper Lough Erne
R189
Clones
N54
Rossmore Forest Park
N2
SLIGO
Lough Allen
Ballyconnell
Annaghmakerrig
MONAGHAN
Castleblaney
Lough Arrow
LEITRIM
Belturbet
Cootehill
N4
Lough Key Forest Park
N3
Killykeen Forest Park
R188
Carrickmacross
Boyle
N4
Carrick-on-Shannon
Lough Oughter
Cavan
R179
Lough Boderg
CAVAN
Lough Bofin
Lough Gowna
N55
Virginia
N3
Strokestown
N61
LONGFORD
Lough Ramor
MEATH
N5
R194
Granard
R195
Longford
N55
Fore
ROSCOMMON
Edgeworthstown
Castlepollard
N60
N63
N4
R395
Navan
Roscommon
Corlea Trackway Exhibition Centre
Lough Derravaragh
R392
WESTMEATH
N61
Ballymahon
Royal Canal
Lough Owel
Crookedwood
Trim
Lough Ree
Moyvore
R392
R390
Mullingar
R363
Lough Ennell
Kinnegad
River Suck
Glasson
R391
Belvedere House Gardens
Enfield
Kilcock
Athlone
Moate
N52
Kilbeggan
N6
N80
OFFALY
Ballinasloe
R357
Clonmacnoise
Grand Canal
Edenderry
N6
N62
Tullamore
GALWAY
Shannonbridge
R420
KILDARE
Banagher
Cloghan
N52
Portarlington
Kildare
Portumna
R439
Birr
R419
Coolbanagher
N7
Terryglass
N62
LAOIS
Portlaoise
Rock of Dunmaise
Borrisokane
N7
Athy
TIPPERARY
Roscrea
N80
Lough Derg
N7
N62
Abbeyleix
Nenagh
Templemore
20 miles
30 km
N

THRILL SEEKERS BEWARE

Quiet and unspectacular, the Lakelands demand thorough and leisurely exploration—the rewards are many, but night owls and thrill-seekers should probably head elsewhere; the wildest thing in these parts is the wind in winter. The towns themselves—including Nenagh, Roscommon, Athlone, Boyle, Mullingar, Tullamore, Longford, and Cavan—are not especially interesting, but they appeal strongly to people hungry for a time when the pace of life was slower and every neighbor's face was familiar.

The main roads from Dublin to the south and the west cross the area, but there is also a network of minor roads linking the more scenic areas. Because of all the water, much of the landscape lies under blanket bog, a fecund ecosystem that's definitely worth closer examination. You'll find more conventionally attractive hill and lake scenery in the forest parks of Killykeen and Lough Key.

One of the best ways to immerse yourself in the Lakelands is to saunter through the region on a bike. Although the area may not offer the spectacular scenery of the more hilly coastal regions, its level, Dutch-like terrain means a less strenuous ride. The twisting roads are generally in good condition (well, good enough), and there are picnic spots in the many state-owned forests just off the main roads. Bord Fáilte recommends two long tours: one of the Athlone-Mullingar-Roscommon area, and another of the Cavan-Monaghan-Mullingar region. Try to avoid the major trunk roads that bisect the region.

Due to the relatively low level of tourist traffic, the lakelands is seriously lacking in budget places to stay and chow down. Bringing a tent and packing some food is a good move.

NORTH TIPPERARY AND THE WEST LAKELANDS

This area includes the western part of the Lakelands, skirting the River Shannon, Lough Derg, Lough Ree, and Lough Key. Between these bodies of water much of the land is bog, a fragile ecosystem that rewards closer investigation. The towns are small and generally undistinguished, with the exceptions of Birr and Strokestown, both of which were laid out by architects and designed to complement the "big houses" that share their names.

NENAGH

WHERE TO SLEEP
The Country House (Thurles Rd., Kilkeary, tel. 067/31193) is not very cheap (£18 for a single, £15 per person for a double) but it's well worth the money. It's actually the home of the Kennedy family, situated about 8 km (5 mi) out of town on a few pleasant acres not too far from Lough Derg. Guests are given the run of the place, including the TV room and the peat-burning hearth, and rooms have coffeemakers and, believe it or not, hair dryers!

WORTH SEEING
Nenagh, 165 km (103 mi) southwest of Dublin, was originally a Norman settlement; it grew to a market town in the 19th century. Standing 31 meters (100 feet) high and 16 meters (53 feet) across the base,

Nenagh Castle Keep is all that remains of the town's original settlement. It stands right in the center of the town and is worth a quick look. The gatehouse and governor's house of Nenagh's old county jail now form the **Nenagh Heritage Centre** (tel. 067/32633). It's open Easter–October, Monday–Saturday 9:30–5, Sunday 2:30–5; November–Easter, weekdays 9:30–5; and you'll get in for £2. It has permanent displays of rural life in the recent past before mechanization, as well as temporary painting and photography exhibits. **Shannon Sailing** (Dromineer, Nenagh, tel. 067/24295) offers cruises of scenic Lough Derg by water bus and also hires out cruisers and sailboards.

ROSCREA

BASICS

There's a **Bank of Ireland** on Castle Street that will change money and has an ATM. **Bus Éireann** from Dublin and Limerick stops three times a day on Castle Street.

WHERE TO SLEEP

Cregganbell (Birr Rd., tel. 0505/21421) is a little bed-and-breakfast of four rooms with showers in a modern bungalow. Rooms cost £18 for singles and £14.50 per person for doubles. **Yellow House B&B** (Main St., tel. 0505/21772) is, surprise, surprise, a yellow house with warm, comfortable rooms (£12.50 per person) and a friendly atmosphere.

The sole purpose of the midlands, people from the rest of Ireland will jest, is to hold the other parts of the island together.

WORTH SEEING

The main road through Roscrea, a town steeped in religious history, cuts through a 7th-century monastery founded by St. Cronan. It also passes the west facade of a 12th-century Romanesque **church** that now forms an entrance gate to a modern Catholic church. Above the structure's round-headed doorway is a hood molding enclosing the figure of a bishop, probably St. Cronan. **Damer House** (tel. 0505/21850) is open mid-May–September, daily 9:30–6 (rest of year, weekends 10–5), and costs £2.50. The building is a superb example of an early 18th-century town house on the grand scale and was used as a barracks during most of the 19th century; it was rescued from decay by the Irish Georgian Society. It was built in 1725 within the curtain walls of a Norman castle. In those days, homes were often constructed beside or attached to the strongholds they replaced. Damer House has a plain, symmetrical facade and a magnificent carved pine staircase inside. The house contains the collection of the Irish Country Furniture Society, supplemented by pieces from the National Museum—a treat for those interested in antiques. In the adjoining building, exhibits take up monastic settlements in the Midlands, the old Irish kitchen, and other local and national themes. The house is home to the **Roscrea Heritage Centre.**

BIRR

BASICS

The **tourist office** (Rose St., tel. 0509/20110) right across from Birr Castle's front entrance is open all summer from 9–5:30. The **AIB** on Emmet Square has an ATM and they will change money. **Bus Éireann** from Dublin and Athlone stops in the middle of town.

WHERE TO SLEEP AND EAT

The relatively new **Spinners Town House** (Castle St., tel. 0509/21673) is a great option for food and lodging right in the center of town. Dorm beds cost £10, singles £17, and doubles £25 including breakfast. If it's raining outside you can amuse yourself with the work of local artists and craft workers that adorns the walls. **Kong Lam** (O'Connell St.) does a mean Chinese takeout; just witness the crowds when the pubs close.

WORTH SEEING

Birr is a quiet, sleepy place with tree-lined malls and modest Georgian houses, where all roads lead to the gates of **Birr Castle Demesne** (tel. 0509/20056), an imposing Gothic castle dating from the early 17th century that is still the home of the earls of Rosse. It isn't open to the common man; however, you can pass a peaceful hour strolling about the surrounding 100 acres of gardens, the oldest of which was planted three centuries ago. The present earl and countess of Rosse continue the adventurous family tradition of undertaking daring botanical expeditions for specimens of rare trees, plants, and shrubs from all over the world. The formal gardens contain the tallest box-hedges in the world (10 meters/32 feet). Spring is the best time to come; you'll see a wonderful display of flowering cherries, magnolias, crab-apple blossoms, and naturalized narcissi. In autumn, the maples, chestnuts, and weeping beeches blaze red and gold. The grounds are laid out around a lake and along the banks of two adjacent rivers; above one of these stands the castle itself. The grounds also contain the remains of a giant (72-inch) reflecting telescope built in 1845, which remained the largest in the world for the next 75 years. Allow at least two hours to see all that's here. Admission is £2.50 and the grounds are open year-round from 9–6 and on until dusk in the summer. Birr is the perfect setting off point for a trip to the Slieve Bloom mountains. The **Slieve Bloom Environmental Display Center** (Railway Rd., tel. 0509/20029) has exhibits on the extensive plant and animal life of the region.

CLONMACNOISE

BASICS
The **tourist office** (tel. 0905/74134) outside the ruins (near the parking area) has information on the site and on the whole region. The **visitors center** (0905/74195) has displays and a surprisingly watchable audiovisual show to educate you about the site.

WHERE TO SLEEP AND EAT
Near the town of Shannonbridge you'll come across **Kajon House** (tel. 0905/74191), with its simple but elegant rooms with bath (£15) and its great views out over the silent bog. Breakfast and dinner—good hearty, starchy stuff—are also available for an extra £5.

WORTH SEEING
Clonmacnoise, from the Irish Cluain Mic Nois (Meadow of the Son of Nos), was once one of Ireland's most important monastic settlements. The remaining buildings are on an esker, or natural gravel ridge, that overlooks a large marshy area beside the River Shannon. When the settlement was founded by St. Ciaran in 545, the Shannon was an important artery of communication, so the site was not as remote as it appears now. Take time to survey the surrounding countryside from the higher parts of Clonmacnoise, and you'll get a good idea of the strategic advantages of its commanding riverside location.

In its long and glorious heyday, Clonmacnoise was the burial place of the mighty kings of Connaught and of Tara. It survived everything thrown at it—raids by feuding Irish tribes, Vikings, and Normans—until 1552, when the English garrison from Athlone ruthlessly reduced it to ruin. Since then it has remained a prestigious burial place; among the ancient stones are many other graves dating from the 17th to the mid-20th century, when a new graveyard was consecrated on adjoining land. The older surviving buildings include the shell of a small **cathedral, two round towers,** the remains of eight smaller churches, and several **high crosses,** the best preserved of these being the **Cross of the Scriptures,** also known as Flann's Cross. the whole place simply reeks of times past. Some of the treasure and manuscripts from Clonmacnoise are now in the National Museum in Dublin. It costs £2.50 to get into Clonmacnoise and it's open year-round.

ATHLONE

Athlone originated as a crossing point of the Shannon, at first as a ford, and it later marked the boundary between the old provinces of Leinster (to the east) and Connaught (to the west). Nowadays it's still a place where folks meet, most likely over a cup of tea in a café after a days hard shopping; Athlone is the commercial hub for the surrounding area, and an important road and rail junction, but it contains little of great interest to the visitor.

BASICS
There is a **tourist office** (tel. 0902/94630) on Church Street with information on the town and the surrounding countryside. There are banks throughout town with ATMs. Bikes can be rented from **M. R. Hardiman** (Irishtown, Co. Westmeath, 0902/78669).

COMING AND GOING
Iarnród Éireann runs trains to Athlone's train and bus depot (tel. 0902/73322) from Dublin and Galway, and **Bus Éireann** has buses to and from Dublin, Galway, and Rosslare.

WHERE TO SLEEP

The **Athlone Holiday Hostel** (Church St., tel. 0902/73399), right next to the train and bus depot, is only two years old. Paintings of Irish myths and legends adorn the common area (TV and pool room). The dorms have 10 beds each (£8) and are always clean and comfortable. Showers, laundry, and sheets are available. **Lough Ree Caravan and Camping Park** (tel. 0902/78561) is a few miles north of town and is the perfect option if the weather holds out. Tent sites go for £2.50 per person and are available from May through September.

FOOD

On Bastion Street in the middle of town, the **Left Bank** is popular with Athlone folk because of the ample size of its sandwiches and salads (£4–£6). If you're vegetarian, or just health-conscious, then seek out the **Crescent Café,** a casual little eatery connected to the Athlone Holiday Hostel (*see above*). The place specializes in meatless pies and pastas at a people's price.

WORTH SEEING

Athlone Castle (Tower Bridge, tel. 0902/94360) was built beside the river Shannon in the 13th century. After their ignoble defeat at the Battle of the Boyne in 1691, the Irish retreated to Athlone and made the river their first line of defense. The castle was extensively renovated in 1991, the 300th anniversary of this rout. It remains an interesting example of a Norman stronghold and houses a small museum of artifacts relating to Athlone's eventful past. Admission (£2.20) includes access to an interpretative center depicting the siege of Athlone in 1691, the flora and fauna of the Shannon, and the life of the famous tenor John McCormack. The castle is open May–September, 10–5. M.V. *Avonree* is a riverboat that travels up the Shannon from the castle to nearby Lough Ree in the summer (tel. 0902/92513); the fare is £4.50.

NEAR ATHLONE

ROSCOMMON

Roscommon is the capital of County Roscommon, where sheep and cattle raising is the main occupation. As you enter this pleasant little town on the southern slopes of a hill, you'll pass the remains of **Roscommon Abbey.** The principal ruin is a church; at the base of the choir stand eight sculpted figures representing gallowglasses, or medieval Irish professional soldiers, a euphemism for ruthless mercenaries. You can roam freely through the ruins. To the north of Roscommon town are the weathered remains of **Roscommon Castle,** a large Norman stronghold dating from the 13th century. Bikes can be rented from **Leo Hunt** (Main St., tel. 0903/26299).

SHANNONBRIDGE

As you pass through the small town of Shannonbridge heading toward **Uisce Dhub,** on either side of the road you'll notice vast stretches of chocolate-brown bog lands and isolated industrial plants for processing this area's natural resource. Not exactly the kind of stuff tourists usually flock to see, but what you're looking at is an ancient industry, long at the heart of the Irish economy. Bog is used in peat-fired electricity-generating stations, compressed into briquettes for domestic hearths, and made into moss peat and plant containers for gardeners. Ireland's liberal use of a resource that is scarce elsewhere in Europe provoked an indignant reaction from botanists and ecologists in the 1980s, which resulted in the setting aside of certain bog areas for conservation. Among these are the **Clara Bog** and **Mongan's Bog** in County Offaly, both relatively untouched, raised pieces of land with unique flora, and the Scragh Bog in County Westmeath. Because of the preservative qualities of peat, it is not unusual to come across bog timber 5,000 years old, or to dig up perfectly preserved domestic implements from more recent times—not to mention the occasional cache of treasure. Deer, badgers, and wild dogs inhabit the bog lands, along with a rich bird and plant life. These areas are being preserved by Bord na Mona, the same government agency that makes commercial use of other bog lands.

If you would like to have a close look at a bog (and who in their right mind wouldn't?), take a ride on **Bord na Mona Bog Rail Tour** (tel. 0905/74114), which leaves from Uisce Dubh. From April to October a small green and yellow diesel locomotive pulls one coach across the bog at an average of 24 km (15 mi) per hour while the driver provides commentary on a landscape unchanged for millennia. There are more than 1,200 km (745 mi) of narrow-gauge bog railway, and the section on the tour, known as the Clonmacnoise and South Offaly Railway, is the only part accessible to the public. The ride costs £3.50.

BOYLE

BASICS

The **tourist office** (tel. 0903/62145) on Main Street opens every day from 9–5 in summer. Also on Main Street is a **Bank of Ireland** branch with an ATM. The train station (tel. 0903/62027) is on the road to Roscommon and has service to Dublin and Sligo. Buses from Dublin, Athlone, and Sligo stop on Bridge Street in the center of town.

WHERE TO SLEEP

Abbey House (Abbeytown Rd., tel. 0903/62385) is luxurious for the price with single rooms for only £15; for £2 extra you get your own bath. The **Lough Key Caravan and Camping Park** (Carrick Rd., tel. 0903/62212), 10 minutes outside Boyle, has tent sites for £8 and is open from April to August.

FOOD

The **Una Bhán** is a restaurant inside the gates of King House offering fried food (chips, fish, etc.) and overcooked vegetables (£3–£5). The breakfast is huge.

WORTH SEEING

Boyle is a grand, old-fashioned town on the Boyle River midway between Lough Gara and Lough Key. The ruins of **Boyle Abbey** (tel. 0903/26100) on the N4, dating from the late 12th and early 13th centuries, still convey an impression of the splendor and religious awe this richly endowed Cistercian foundation must have inspired in all those who saw it in its prime. The nave, choir, and transept of the cruciform church are in surprisingly good condition. Best of all, you can wander about the ruins at your leisure. **King House,** in the center of Boyle, is a magnificent 16th-century house used at one time as a barracks for the famous Connaught Rangers. It was opened to the public in 1994 after extensive restoration and has exhibits on the Connaught Rangers, the Kings of Connaught, and the history of the house. **Lough Key Forest Park** (tel. 079/62214), a popular base for campers and backpackers, is always a big hit with walkers and anglers. The park is 3 km (2 mi) north of Boyle and consists of 840 acres on the shores of the lake, with a bog garden, a deer enclosure, and a cypress grove; boats can be hired on the lake. And they don't charge to get in.

NEAR BOYLE

STROKESTOWN

Like many villages near a "big house," Strokestown was designed to complement the house. The widest main street in Ireland—laid out to rival the Ringstrasse in Vienna—leads to a Gothic arch, the entrance to the grounds of **Strokestown Park House** (tel. 078/33013). As you can see from its facade, this enormous house, seat of the Pakenham Mahon family from 1660 to 1979, has a complicated architectural history. The Palladian wings were added in the 18th century to the original 17th-century block, and the house was extended again in the early 19th century. The interior is full of curiosities, such as the gallery above the kitchen, which allowed the lady of the house to supervise domestic affairs from a safe distance. Menus were dropped from the balcony on Monday mornings with instructions to the cook for the week's meals. One wing houses lavish stables with vaulted ceilings and Tuscan pillars. There is also a distillery and a fully equipped nursery. The gardens, which are undergoing an ambitious restoration plan that will include the widest and longest herbaceous borders in Ireland, opened in 1995. Admission to the house is £3 and it's open 11–5:30, Tuesday–Sunday from April to October. An award-winning **museum** (£2.70) documenting the disastrous Famine (1845–50) opened in 1994.

THE NORTHERN LAKELANDS

Leaving the ancient kingdom of Leinster, you come to two counties of Ulster, **Cavan** and **Monaghan**. Beyond Cavan Town you enter the heart of the northern Lakelands, with lakes both large and small on either side of the road. County Cavan and County Monaghan each have at least 180 lakes. The countryside is distinguished by its drumlins—small, steep hills consisting of boulder clay left behind by the glacial retreat 10,000 years ago. The boulder clay also filled in many of the pre-glacial river valleys, causing the rivers to change course and create shallow lakes, which provide excellent fishing.

LONGFORD

BASICS

You can't miss the little **tourist office** (tel. 043/46566); it's right on Main Street, and it has limited information on the town and the county. Trains from Dublin via Mullingar stop at the **Longford Railway Station** (tel. 043/45208) twice a day. Express Buses from Dublin also stop at the train station, as does a daily bus from Mullingar.

WHERE TO SLEEP

The **Tivoli** (Dublin Rd., tel. 043/46898) is a large B&B run by the amiable and helpful Mrs. O'Donnell out of her own home. The 15 rooms (£13.50) are warm, and some have baths (£3 extra).

FOOD

The locally famous **Peter Clarkes** (Dublin Rd., tel. 043/46478) serves top-notch pub grub and is renowned across three counties for its perfect pint of stout.

WORTH SEEING

Longford, the county seat of County Longford, is a typical little market-town community. The recently opened, £2 million **Corlea Trackway Exhibition Centre** (tel. 043/22386), at the center of a 20-acre site of specially preserved bog land, displays part of an Iron Age timber trackway dating from 147 BC that was found underneath the bog during turf-cutting activities. The history of the bog is explained in reasonably captivating audiovisual and showcase displays. You'll have go 22 km (14 mi) southwest of Longford to visit, you'll pay £2.50 for the privilege, and it's open all through the summer. For a look at gracious country living in 18th-century surroundings, visit **Carriglass Manor** (tel. 043/45165, £2.50). The romantic Tudor-Gothic house was built in 1837 by Thomas Lefroy. His descendants still reside here, and they are proud that as a young man in England, Lefroy was romantically involved with the novelist Jane Austen. Just why they never married is a mystery, but it is believed that she based the character of Mr. Darcy in *Pride and Prejudice* on Mr. Lefroy. The house features some good plasterwork and many of its original mid-19th-century furnishings. For security reasons those wishing to visit the house must book in advance, Thursday–Sunday. A magnificent stable yard belonging to an earlier house on the site dates from 1790. Visitors to the stable yard and gardens also have access to a small **costume museum.**

NEAR LONGFORD

GRANARD

The market town and fishing center of Granard, 18 km (11 miles) east of Longford, stands on high ground near the Longford-Cavan border. The **Motte of Granard** at the southwest end of town was once the site of a fortified Norman castle. In 1932 a statue of St. Patrick was erected here to mark the 15th centenary of his arrival in Ireland. (At least a dozen statues of the patron saint, all virtually identical, were put up that year; see how many others you can spot on your travels.)

CAVAN

Cavan is an undistinguished little town serving the local farming community. **Cavan Crystal** (tel. 049/31800), right in town, is an up-and-coming rival to Waterford in the cut-lead-crystal line; the company offers guided factory tours (free, Mar.–Dec., weekdays 9:30, 10:30, 11:30) and access to their factory shop. If you can't make it to Waterford, this is a good opportunity to watch skilled craftspeople at work.

The **Cavan Folk Museum** (Cornafean, tel. 049/37248, £2) holds what is called with pride "the Pig House Collection": costumes, kitchen and household goods, farmyard tools, machinery, and other bric-a-brac tracing the rural lifestyle from the 1700s to the present. At some quarters in the area, that way of life has changed so little that the "museum pieces" are still in use around the farm—which may be why the locals are so fond of this collection. Its owner-curator describes it as "a one-woman show," hence the request that you phone ahead to make sure she is home.

Travel north from Cavan for 13 km (8 mi) to **Killykeen Forest Park** (tel. 049/32541). Organized within the beautiful mazelike network of lakes called Lough Oughter, this 600-acre park offers a series of planned and signposted walks and nature trails. The park closes in January.

MONAGHAN

BASICS

Walk up Market Street, away from Church Square, to find the **tourist office** (tel. 047/81122). It's open Monday–Saturday 10–5, and Sunday in summer 10–2. **Bus Éireann** buses from Dublin and Belfast stop at the **Monaghan Bus Office** (tel. 047/82377) off Market Square. There are a number of ATMs scattered throughout the town.

WHERE TO SLEEP

Ashleigh House (37 Dublin St., tel. 047/81227) is the cheapest place in town; the simple, unadorned rooms (£15, £19 with bath) come with a massive, fried breakfast. **Willow Bridge Lodge** (Silver Stream, tel. 047/81054) is a super-friendly B&B situated just outside town in an elegantly decorated house with lawns and great views of the countryside. For £15 (£25 for a double) you get a spotlessly clean, warm room and a real home-cooked breakfast with the freshest of ingredients.

FOOD

Supervalu (Church Sq.) shopping center is the best option if you're really low on funds. It's open Monday–Saturday 9–6. **Pizza D'Or** (23 Market St., tel 047/8477) is one of the few quality low-price options in town. Otherwise, if your belly can stand it, stick to one of the numerous chip shops.

WORTH SEEING

Monaghan is an attractive county town built around a central diamond. Monaghan's old market house, dating from 1792, is now the **County Museum** (tel. 047/82928). It's free, and it's display tracing the history of Monaghan from earliest times to the present day is the winner of a European Community Heritage Award. It's open year-round, Tuesday–Saturday, 11–5. On the R189 Newbliss road just outside Monaghan, you'll find **Rossmore Forest Park,** 691 acres of low hills and small lakes with pleasant forest walks and signposted nature trails that are freely accessible. Five kilometers (3 miles) southwest of Newbliss is **Annaghmakerrig,** a small forest park with a lake, and above it Annaghmakerrig House, home of the stage director Sir Tyrone Guthrie until his death in 1971. He left it to the nation as a residential center for writers, artists, and musicians. It is not officially open to the public, but anyone with a special interest in the arts or in its previous owner can ask to be shown around.

NEAR MONAGHAN

COOTEHILL

The little town of **Cootehill** is in the heart of County Cavan. Fans of the songwriter Percy French (1854–1920) will recall the opening lines of his famous song "Come Back, Paddy Reilly, to Ballyjamesduff," which instruct the traveler in search of that little paradise to "turn to the left at the bridge of Finea, and stop when halfway to Cootehill." In fact, as locals will delight in telling you, if you follow these instructions you will not get to Ballyjamesduff at all—you'll get hopelessly lost. Cootehill is one of the most underestimated small towns in Ireland. It has a lovely setting on a wooded hillside, and its wide streets, with their intriguing old shops, are always busy without being congested. Most of its visitors are anglers from Europe, the United Kingdom, and the rest of Ireland. Only pedestrians are allowed through the gates of **Bellamont Forest,** which lead, after about a mile of woodlands, to an exquisite hilltop Palladian villa, small but perfectly proportioned, and virtually unaltered since it was built in 1728. It is now a private home but is occasionally opened to the public. If you are interested, inquire locally or at the Tourist Information Office in Cavan (tel. 049/31942). Walk up the main street of Cootehill to "the top of the town" (past the White Horse Hotel) and you will see the entrance to the forest.

CLONES

Clones is in border country—also known as bandit country—and aimless exploring, especially on roads marked UNAPPROVED ROAD (which lead to unmanned border crossings), is not recommended. In early Christian times, Clones was the site of a monastery founded by St. Tighearnach, who died here in AD 458. An Augustinian abbey replaced the monastery in the 12th century, and its remains can still be seen near the 23-meter (75-foot) **round tower.** In the central diamond of the town stands a 10th-century Celtic high cross, with carved panels representing scriptural scenes. Nowadays Clones, a small agricultural market town, is known chiefly for lace making. A varied selection of lace is on display around the town and can be purchased at the **Clones Lace Centre** (tel. 047/51051), open Monday–Saturday 10–6.

CASTLE LESLIE

If you have time for one more excursion in the area, leave Monaghan on the N12 and follow it for 11 km (7 mi) out of town to Castle Leslie (tel. 047/88109), originally a medieval stronghold, which has been the seat of the Leslie family since 1664. The castle sits on the shores of deep, beautiful **Glaslough,** which means "green lake." The present castle was built in 1870 in a mix of Gothic and Italianate styles. The Leslie family, a mildly eccentric one known for its literary and artistic leanings, has many notable relations by marriage, including the duke of Wellington, who defeated Napoléon at Waterloo, and Sir Winston Churchill. Wellington's death mask is preserved at Castle Leslie, as is Churchill's baby dress, along with an impressive collection of Italian artwork. There are 14 acres of gardens with miniature golf and croquet; home-baked teas are served in the tearoom and conservatory. All summer long they have historical tours of the house (£3) from 2–6 on the hour.

THE EASTERN LAKELANDS

The Eastern Lakelands fan out from the central point of Mullingar. The region incorporates the larger town of Tullamore as well as the ubiquitous small, solid, quiet villages and hamlets of the midlands.

MULLINGAR

BASICS

The **tourist office** (Dublin Rd., tel. 044/48650) is nearly a mile outside of town. It's open weekdays 9–5:30; June–August, Sat. 10–6. Trains and buses arrive at the **train station** (tel. 044/48274) from Dublin, Sligo, and Galway. You'll find a number of ATMs near the center of town. For medical and ambulance service, contact Mullingar's **General Hospital** (tel. 044/40221).

WHERE TO SLEEP

You're never too far from your pint at the **Midland Hotel** (Mount St., tel. 044/48381), which is really a public house with a few, clean, warm rooms above the bar (£15).

FOOD

Greville Arms (Pearse St., tel. 044/48052) is a town-center hotel with an unusual second-floor conservatory overlooking a Victorian patio garden. It is famously associated with James Joyce, who set one of his few scenes outside Dublin in the Greville's bar. Though not exactly adventurous, the menu in the dining room is better than average, relying heavily on grilled or roast beef, pork, and lamb, and the prices are excellent. Dishes prepared with local fish are also offered.

WORTH SEEING

Mullingar is a busy commercial and cattle-trading center on the Royal Canal midway between two large, attractive lakes, Lough Owel and Lough Ennel. This is an area of rich farmland, and the town is known as Ireland's beef capital; farmers all over Ireland describe a good young cow as "beef to the ankle, like a Mullingar heifer." The buildings in Mullingar date mostly from the 19th century.

The large **Catholic Cathedral of Christ the King** was completed in 1939 in the Renaissance style. Finely carved stonework decorates the front of the cathedral, and the spacious interior has mosaics of St. Patrick and St. Anne by the Russian artist Boris Anrep. The **Mullingar Military and Historical Museum** (Columb Barracks, tel. 044/48391) is home to a display of weapons from the two World Wars, boats of oak from the 1st century AD, and uniforms and other articles of the old IRA. You have to call ahead to see the museum. **Belvedere House Gardens** (tel. 044/40861), 5 km (3 mi) south of Mullingar, is remarkable for a beautiful setting on the northeast shore of Lough Ennel. Terraced gardens descend in three stages to the waters of the lake and provide a panoramic view of its islands. The estate also contains a walled garden with many varieties of trees, shrubs, and flowers, and parkland landscaped in the 18th-century style. Admission is £1. **Mullingar Equestrian Centre** (Athlone Rd., tel. 044/48331) offers riding on the shores of Lough Derravaragh and offers lessons at all levels.

NEAR MULLINGAR

KILBEGGAN

Kilbeggan is known mainly for its distillery, which was established in 1757 to produce a traditional Irish malt whiskey. It closed down in 1954 and was re-opened in 1987 by Cooley Distillery. Cooley makes its whiskey in County Louth but brings it to Kilbeggan to be matured in casks. The **Kilbeggan Distillery** (tel. 0506/32134, admission £2) has been restored as a museum of industrial archaeology illustrating the process of Irish pot-whiskey distillation and the social history of the workers' lives. It's open Monday–Saturday, year-round.

TULLAMORE

Tullamore, the county seat of Offaly, is a big country town situated on the Grand Canal. **Charleville Castle** (tel. 0506/21279, admission £2.50), a mile outside of Tullamore on the N52, is a castellated Gothic Revival manor house set on about 30 acres of woodland walks and gardens. This magnificent building dates from 1812 and is a fine example of the work of the architect Francis Johnston, who was responsible for many of Dublin's stately Georgian buildings. Guided tours of the interior are available June–September, daily 11–5.

PORTARLINGTON

If you're turned on by large-scale domestic architecture, drive to Portarlington, a charming Old World town that until quite recently had a sizable bilingual (English/French) population of Huguenot origin. **Emo Court and Gardens** (tel. 0502/26110) was designed by James Gandon, architect of the Custom House and the Four Courts in Dublin, on a similarly grand scale. The domed rotunda, inspired by the Roman Pantheon, is one of the most impressive rooms in Ireland. This vast circular space is lit by a lantern in the coffered dome, which rests on gilded capitals and marble pilasters. The house has been magnificently restored, and it's a wonderful example of living on the grand scale. Emo's owner donated it as a gift to the Irish nation in 1995. The grounds are open daily year-round and also include formal gardens with classical statuary and rare trees and shrubs. The house is open June–September, Friday–Monday 10:30–5:30; admission is £2 to gardens, £2 to the house. **Coolbanagher** (1 km/1 mi south of Emo Court, no phone) is home to the exquisite Church of St. John the Evangelist, which is open daily from 9–6. Gandon's original 1795 plans are on view inside the building, which also has an elaborately carved 15th-century font.

EDGEWORTHSTOWN

Those with literary interests may wish to stop in **Edgeworthstown** (also known as Mostrim). This town was the home of the novelist Maria Edgeworth (1769–1849), whose highly original satirical works, the best known of which is *Castle Rackrent,* were admired by such contemporaries as Sir Walter Scott and William Wordsworth, both of whom visited here. The family residence, Edgeworthstown House, at the eastern end of the village, is now a private nursing home and not open to the public. The Edgeworth family vault, where Maria and her father, Richard Lovell Edgeworth, an author and inventor, are interred, is in the churchyard of St. John's Church.

CASTLEPOLLARD

Castlepollard is an unusually pretty village of multicolor houses laid out around a triangular green. Outside the village (1½ km/1 mi), you'll find **Tullynally Castle and Gardens** (tel. 044/61159) seat of the earls of Longford and the Irish home of the literary Pakenham family, whose members include the prison reformer and antipornography campaigner Frank Pakenham (the current earl of Longford); his wife Elizabeth and his daughter Antonia Fraser, both historical biographers; and his brother Thomas, a historian. The original 18th-century building was extended in the Gothic style in the 19th century, making it the largest castellated house in Ireland, with an elaborate facade of turrets and towers. In addition to a fine collection of portraits and furniture, the house contains many fascinating 19th-century domestic gadgets, as well as an immense kitchen. The grounds also include a landscaped park and formal gardens which, along with the castle itself, are open May–October, daily 10–5; admission is £3.50.

FORE

The simple village of **Fore** is dominated by the remains of **Fore Abbey. St. Fechin's Church,** dating from the 10th century, has a massive cross-inscribed lintel stone. Nearby are the remains of a 13th-century Benedictine abbey, whose imposing square towers and loophole windows resemble a castle rather than an abbey.

THE SOUTHEAST

CALE SILER AND LAURENCE BELGRAVE

With few of Ireland's traditional attractions—no wild romantic coastline or wild bogs, no Irish-speaking communities or thatched farming villages—the Southeast would at first glance appear to have few remarkable assets. One of the main reasons for coming, in fact, is strictly practical. Rosslare Harbour, near Wexford, is one of Ireland's major ferry ports, and it's perhaps the most convenient hub for Eurail and InterRail travelers heading for the Continent. Most people are quickly disappointed by what they find in Rosslare and Wexford, and they take the first train to Galway, Cork, or Dublin, bypassing most of southeastern Ireland.

The Southeast will surprise you if you expect all Irish scenery to be rugged and wild. The coastal counties of Wexford and Waterford are low-lying and relatively flat, with long sandy beaches and low cliffs; inland, Counties Carlow, Kilkenny, and Tipperary consist of lush, undulating pastureland bisected by winding river valleys. This region has the mildest, sunniest, and also the driest weather in Ireland, with as little as 30 inches of rainfall per year—compared with an average of 80 inches on parts of the west coast.

The combination of sunshine and sandy beaches makes the Southeast's coast a popular vacation area with Irish families; it's a great spot to watch the Irish amuse themselves. Except for the resort of Tramore, the area is relatively undeveloped. The Southeast's main attractions remain the natural beauty of its landscape and its small, charming fishing villages.

Both coastal and inland areas have a rich and interesting history. There is evidence of settlements from some 9,000 years ago in the Slaney Valley near Wexford. The Kings of Munster had their ceremonial center on the Rock of Cashel, which in the 7th century became an important monastic center and bishopric. There were other thriving early Christian monasteries at Kilkenny, Ardmore, and Lismore.

The quiet life of early Christian Ireland was disrupted from the 9th century onward by a series of raucous Viking invasions. The Vikings liked what they found here—a pleasant climate; rich, easily cultivated land, and a series of safe, sheltered harbors—so they stayed and founded the towns of Wexford and Waterford. (Waterford's name comes from the Norse Vadrefjord, Wexford's from Waesfjord.) Less than two centuries later, the same cities were conquered by Anglo-Norman barons and turned into walled strongholds. The Anglo-Normans and the Irish chieftains soon started to intermarry, but the process of integration halted with the Statute of Kilkenny in 1366, for the English feared that if such intermingling continued they would lose whatever control over Ireland they had.

The next great crisis was Oliver Cromwell's infamous Irish campaign of 1650, which in attempting to crush Catholic opposition to the English parliament brought widespread slaughter. The ruined or extensively rebuilt condition of most of the region's early churches is a result of Cromwell's desecrations. His outrages are still a vivid part of local folk memory (mention his name in a pub at your peril), but not as vivid as the 1798 Rebellion, an ill-timed and unsuccessful bid for a united Ireland inspired by the French Revolution. The decisive "battle" took place at Vinegar Hill near Enniscorthy, where some 20,000 rebels, armed only with pikes, were cut down by British cannon fire.

Outside the months of July and August, the region is relatively free of traffic, making it ideal for leisurely exploration. Wexford, Waterford, and Kilkenny all have compact town centers best explored on foot, and they also make good touring bases. Wexford's narrow streets are built on one side of a wide estuary, and it has a delightful maritime atmosphere. The new National Heritage Park at nearby Ferrycarrig is well worth a visit, which will contribute enormously to an understanding of Irish history up to the 12th century. Waterford is less immediately attractive than Wexford, but it offers a richer selection of Viking and Norman remains, some good Georgian buildings, and also the famous Waterford Glass Factory, open to visitors. Kilkenny, an important ecclesiastic and political center up to the 17th century, is now a lively market town whose streets still contain many remains from medieval times, most notably the beautiful St. Canice's Cathedral and a magnificent 12th-century castle.

Anglers will scarcely believe the variety of fishing and scenery along the Rivers Barrow, Nore, and Suir, and especially in the Blackwater Valley area. County Tipperary is the location of the Rock of Cashel, ancient seat of the kings of Munster, which can be seen from miles around in all directions; this vast, cathedral-topped rock rising up above the plain is one of Ireland's most impressive sights.

The 1798 rebellion was a prime source of quality rebel songs; "The Rising of the Moon" and "The Croppy Boy" are two favorites still belted out in local bars.

KILKENNY

Dubbed "Ireland's Medieval Capital" by the tourist board, Kilkenny is a 900-year-old Norman citadel 120 km (75 mi) southwest of Dublin. Prior to the 5th century, Kilkenny was a semi-prosperous market town specializing in dyes and woolens, but in the next century St. Canice (a.k.a. "the builder of churches") established a large monastic school here that attracted pupils from as far away as Athens and Istanbul. For this good deed, St. Canice was fondly remembered in the naming of the village, Kil Cainneach (Church of Canice), and his feast day (October 11) is celebrated with zeal. Credit for the city's medieval appearance, however, goes to the anglicized Normans, who fortified the city with a castle, gates, and a brawny wall.

Unfortunately, with a myriad of tourist kitsch and roaring traffic, Kilkenny will not instantly transport you back to the Middle Ages. The town's pride and joy is the gorgeously restored Kilkenny Castle, which is definitely worth a visit. Kilkenny also has a lively pub and traditional music scene. One of the best and more progressive festivals in Ireland is held here during August: **Kilkenny Arts Week,** a showcase for film, theater, and music. This weeklong event, generally held the third and fourth weeks of the month, attracts large crowds and big-name national and international artists; call the Arts Council (tel. 056/63663) or the tourist office for current schedules.

BASICS

MONEY

You can change money at one of the many banks along High Street or in the tourist office on weekends. There is a Bank of Ireland on Parliament Street with an ATM that accepts Visa, Plus, and Cirrus.

VISITOR INFORMATION

The **tourist office** is just a few steps from Kilkenny Castle in the city center, on the south side of the River Nore. *Rose Inn St.; tel. 056/51500. Open Mon.–Sat. 9–6, Sun. 11–1 and 2–5.*

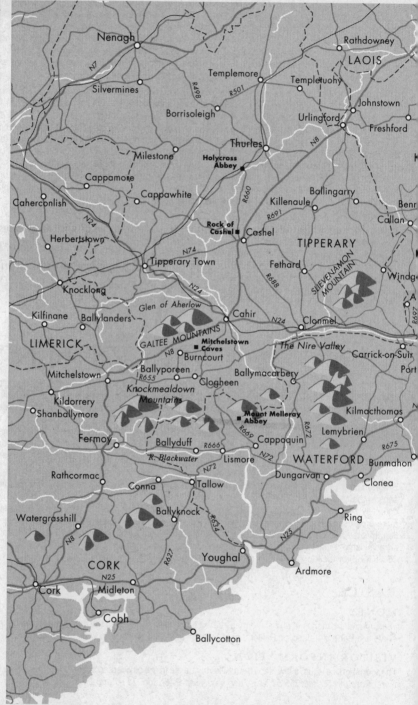

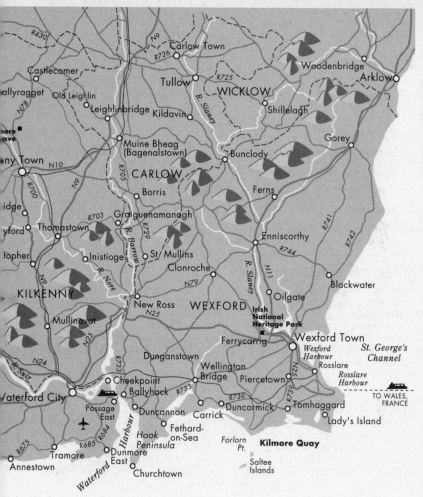

Celtic Sea

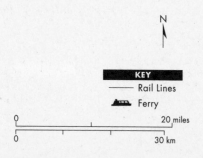

N

KEY
—— Rail Lines
⛴ Ferry

0   20 miles

0   30 km

FROM STAKE TO STEAK

Kyteler's Inn (Kieran St., tel. 056/21064) is famous for having been owned by the notorious Dame Alice Kyteler—a beautiful enchantress who went through four wealthy husbands quicker than you can say "poison." She was finally convicted of sacrificing animals to an evil demon she referred to as "Art." Her behavior aroused suspicion in the superstitious Kilkenny farm folk, and she was charged with witchcraft. Equipped with a quick tongue and a chance to flee to the country, Dame Alice left her poor maid Petronilla to be burned at the stake in her place in 1324. Kyteler's is now a popular pub-restaurant serving excellent traditional meals and good-quality steaks in the £9–£14 range.

COMING AND GOING

McDonagh Station (Dublin Rd., tel. 056/22024 for trains, 051/79000 for buses) serves as both bus and rail terminal and has a staffed information desk open (in theory) Monday–Saturday 8:30–8, Sunday 10–noon, 3–5, and 6–8: The office often closes despite these times and reopens 20 minutes before a train departs. From McDonagh Station, **Bus Éireann** offers twice daily service to Dublin (£7), Waterford (£5), Cork (£9), and Galway (£13). Kilkenny is also on **Irish Rail's** frequently serviced Dublin (Heuston Station)–Waterford line (£10). Transfer in Kildare for all western and northwestern stops. For bike rentals, head to **J. J. Walls** (88 Maudlin St., tel. 056/21236), which offers bikes for £5 per day, £25 per week.

WHERE TO SLEEP

If you're stuck for accommodations, head for Waterford Road (south of Patrick Street), where most of Kilkenny's bed-and-breakfasts are located. Of the B&Bs grouped here, **Beaupre House** (Waterford Rd., tel. 056/21417) and **Ashleigh House** (Waterford Rd., tel. 056/22809) are the nicest—family-run establishments with large, airy rooms (£14–£16 per person) and modern bathrooms. If you'd rather stay in town, the newly renovated **J&K Dempsey B&B** (26 James St., just off High St., tel. 056/21954) has small, frilly rooms (£15 per person) and a cozy breakfast nook.

HOSTELS

Easily the best hostel in town, the **IHH Kilkenny Tourist Hostel** is threadbare, though warm and comfortable. The building has plenty of oak, high ceilings, and a brand-new kitchen that opens into a courtyard. Beds cost £6.50–£7. Best of all, it's in the city center and surrounded by a bunch of good pubs. *35 Parliament St., tel. 056/63541. From McDonagh Station, turn left on John St., cross River Nore, and turn right on Kieran St. 50 beds. Kitchen, laundry, sheet rental (50p).*

FOOD

Most of Kilkenny's restaurants are geared toward big spenders and AmEx-carrying tourists.

Under £5 • Lautrec's. You'll find surprisingly daring fare at Lautrec's, an elegant wine bar and café that serves vegetarian crepes (£3), steak fajitas (£4), and apple burritos with cream (£2.45) among other, higher-priced entrées. They stay open until 12:30 AM. *9 Kieran St., tel. 056/62720. Cash only. Closed Sun.*

Under £10 • Italian Connection. This is a decent low-priced eatery, nothing more, and they serve reasonable lunches (daily noon–3), including pastas (£4), pizzas (£4.50–£7), and grilled entrées in a spiffy, paisley-ensconced dining room. *38 Parliament St., tel. 056/64225. Cash only.*

M. L. Dore. Cluttered and homey, this little café serves coffee (65p), warm fruit scones (50p), and tasty sandwiches (£1.45). There are also dozens of grocers and butchers along nearby High Street, as well as the usual late-night chip shops and kebab stands. *Kieran St., at High St., tel. 056/63374. Cash only.*

WORTH SEEING

The city center is small and, with essentially only three historic sights, can easily be covered in less than three hours. After taking in Kilkenny Castle and the **Riverfront Canal Walk,** an overgrown (and heavily littered) pathway that meanders alongside the castle grounds, mosey down High and Kieran streets. These parallel avenues, considered the historic center of Kilkenny, are connected by a series of horse-cart-wide lanes and are fronted with some of the city's best-preserved pubs and Victorian flats. Both streets eventually merge into Parliament Street. During summer, **Tynan Walking Tours** (tel. 056/52066) organizes excellent guided walks of Kilkenny (£2.50). If you'd rather tour alone, pick up a copy of Joseph O'Carroll's *Historic Kilkenny* (£3), available from the tourist office.

KILKENNY CASTLE

Founded in 1172, Kilkenny Castle has served since 1391 as the seat of the earls and dukes of Ormonde, one of the more powerful clans in Irish history. The Ormondes presented the castle and its 50-acre gardens to the people of Kilkenny in 1967; since then it has undergone countless renovations. Two-thirds of the castle has been meticulously restored—the rest will be completed by 1998. Most impressive is the Long Gallery, a refined, airy hall that contains a collection of family portraits and frayed tapestries. More interesting than the art is the Long Gallery's decorated ceiling, with carved oak beams riddled with Celtic lacework; the roof was designed to look like the inside of a Viking longboat. You can only see the interior of the castle by taking a guided tour. These set out on the half hour and last about 45 minutes. *The Parade, tel. 056/21450. Admission: £3. Open June–Sept., daily 10–7; Oct.–May, daily 10:30–5. (Oct.–Mar., Sun. 11–5).*

Built in 1710 on the site of the St. Francis Abbey, Smithwicks Brewery (tel. 056/51500) is a testament to the fabled brewing skills of Dominican monks; it's open for tasting (June–Sept., daily 3 PM).

ROTHE HOUSE

This typical Tudor-period, middle-class home was built in 1594 by wine merchant John Rothe. Renovations of the structure have recently been completed and the rooms have been restored to their Tudor splendor. Some of the rooms function as a makeshift County Kilkenny museum, with a motley collection of Bronze Age artifacts, smithy tools, ogham stones, and coal-mining gear. *Parliament St., tel. 056/22893. Admission: £2. Open Apr.–Oct., Mon.–Sat. 10:30–5, Sun. 3–5; Nov.–Mar., weekends 3–5.*

ST. CANICE'S CATHEDRAL

Kilkenny's most famous cathedral is also the second longest (212 feet) in Ireland. St. Canice's was founded in 1285 and later used to store volumes of the Irish Annals and other one-of-a-kind religious manuscripts. Cromwell, however, deemed the cathedral better fit for a stable and stationed his 500 steeds within its walls. The smell was so powerful, it's said, that Cromwell's troops were eventually driven to smash open the stained-glass windows. Since then, the cathedral's interior has been blandly restored, and the complex's biggest attraction is the 102-foot **round tower,** built in 847 by King O'Carroll of Ossory. Admission to the tower is 70p and worth it, if only for the thrill of climbing 102 feet on makeshift wooden stairs. The 360° view at the top is tremendous. *Coach Rd., at northern foot of Parliament St., tel. 056/64971. Open June–Sept., Mon.–Sat. 9–1 and 2–6, Sun. 2–6; Oct.–May, Mon.–Sat. 10–1 and 2–4, Sun. 2–4.*

AFTER DARK

If you're craving a pint, there are plenty of pubs to choose from along Parliament and High streets; several of them, including **John Cleare's Pub** (28 Parliament St.), **Widow MacGrath's** (29 Parliament St.), and **Phelans** (30 Parliament St.), also feature traditional music. Among the pubs on nearby John Street, **Langton House** (69 John St., tel. 056/65133), voted "Best Pub of the Year" for the last five years in a row, has four bars and a classy restaurant. If historical pubs turn you on, try **Kyteler's Inn** (*see box, above*). For rock and traditional music sessions and a game of pool, try the hopping **Pump House** (Parliament St., tel. 056/21969), opposite the hostel. Popular **Caisleán Ui Cuain** (High St., opposite Kilkenny Castle, tel. 056/65406) and **Peig's** (John St., tel. 056/63671) also have traditional music during summer. The **Watergate Theatre** (Parliament St., tel. 056/61674) hosts opera, plays, concerts, and comedy for about £6.

ROSSLARE HARBOUR

If you're coming to Ireland from England or the Continent, chances are you'll end up on a ferry bound for Rosslare Harbour, 19 km (12 mi) south of Wexford (not to be confused with Rosslare/Rosslare Strand, an unredeemable resort north of the port), one of Ireland's busiest ferry ports. Rosslare is also one of the dullest places in Ireland, an industrial outcrop that has none of the attributes of a real city despite the presence of a few luxury hotels and acres of summer cottages. If you're stuck, try the **An Óige hostel** (Goulding St., tel. 053/33399), which has beds for £6.50. Reception is open until 10:30 PM.

COMING AND GOING

The **Rosslare Harbour rail depot** (tel. 053/33162), adjacent to the ferry terminal, is serviced by frequent trains to Dublin's Connolly Station (£10) and Cork (change at Limerick Junction, £12). For most other destinations, you have to go back up through Dublin. **Bus Éireann's Rosslare Harbour depot** adjoins the rail station; look for the row of neatly parked Expressway Coaches. Buses go to Dublin (£9), Galway (£16), and Cork (£13), among other places. From Rosslare Harbour, you could also try to catch a ride to Dublin, Cork, or Galway in one of the cars just unloaded from the ferry.

BY FERRY

The two ferry companies serving Rosslare Harbour have small information kiosks in the ultramodern terminal, which also has a **tourist office** (tel. 053/33622), **lockers,** and a sprawling waiting room where you can easily sneak a nap. You can purchase ferry tickets at the terminal, but try to reserve a space in advance at the companies' Cork or Dublin offices to avoid the frequent sellouts, particularly in summer and any time the Irish soccer team is playing in a major tournament abroad. Reservations are also a must if you're traveling by car or motorcycle because onboard parking space is at a premium. ISIC cardholders are (begrudgingly) given discounts on most ferries. The journey from France to Ireland is free for EurailPass holders.

Irish Ferries (tel. 053/33158 or 01/661–0511) makes the 3¾-hour crossing to Pembroke, Wales, twice daily; projected 1998 departures are at 8:30 AM and 8:30 PM. Fares are £25–£30 one-way. Irish Ferries also makes the 22-hour journey to Cherbourg and Le Havre, France, once daily and charges £68–£95 one-way; call for current price and departure times. **Stena Sealink** (tel. 053/33115 or 01/280–8844) sails twice daily to Fishguard, Wales; projected departure times for 1998 are 9 AM and 9:40 PM. The journey takes approximately 3 hours and costs £22–£33 one-way (£20–£28 students).

WATERFORD

Waterford's main claim to fame is its crystal factory (*see box below*), along with its handful of historic sights and its traditional pubs. Built on the banks of the grimly industrialized River Suir, Waterford was founded in the 9th century by Viking raiders who fortified the town against competing waves of Flemish, Gaelic, and French intruders: On Manor Street, near the intersection of John and Parnell streets, are three towers and a crumbling section of the wall that once surrounded the town. The most striking example of Waterford's Viking legacy is **Reginald's Tower** (The Mall, tel. 051/73501), an impressive circular battlement built in 1003 by Reginald the Dane. Around the corner from Reginald's Tower, the **Heritage**

Centre (Greyfriars St., tel. 051/71227) is a one-room museum displaying Viking and medieval artifacts unearthed during excavation of the city center. The collection includes leather work, brooches, and other doodads, such as pewter pilgrim badges worn by medieval folk as proof of their shrine-hopping. Admission to the tower and center costs £1.50, and both are open weekdays 8:30–8:30, weekends 10–5.

These days Waterford is a fairly tourist-oriented city, and shopping opportunities are so abundant that the entire downtown area seems to have sprung up around two malls. The principal shopping district stretches from the River Suir and Barronstrand Street to Broad and Michael streets, where you'll find the bustling **Broad Street Shopping Centre.** But the real action happens a block west, at the intersection of Barronstrand and George streets, where gangs of fashionable Waterford youth hang out between forays to the very modern and chic **City Centre** shopping mall. Waterford's student population (mostly from Waterford Regional College) ensures good weekend pub crowds and gives the town a youthful feel. If you want a sense of Waterford's other life, continue down George Street toward O'Connell and Bridge streets. This undeveloped and seemingly forgotten quarter of town is dominated by gray buildings and crumbling Georgian-era warehouses, evocative of Waterford's industrial past.

BASICS

The **tourist office** (41 The Quay, tel. 051/75788) stocks Irish-interest books and tourist information, including the excellent *Historical Walking Tour of Waterford* (£3), and has a competitive bureau de change. Considering Waterford's bleak choice of accommodations, you may want to book a B&B here for £1. The office is open weekdays 9–6 and Saturdays 9–1 and 2–5. **USIT** (37 Georges St., tel. 051/72601), open weekdays 9:30–5:30 and Saturday 11–4, also has lots of travel info and can book ferry and plane tickets. Mountain bikes (£7 per day, £30 per week) can be rented at **Wright's Cycle Depot** (Henrietta St., off The Quay, tel. 051/74411).

COMING AND GOING

The joint bus and rail depot, **Plunkett Station** (Dock Rd., tel. 051/79000 for bus info or 051/73401 for train info), is on the River Suir's north shore, west of the city center. Turn left out of the station, cross Rice Bridge, and head left on the riverfront quay for the tourist office and Barronstrand Street shops. Inside the station are an info desk, open Monday–Saturday 9–6, and a left-luggage desk (£1) open slightly longer hours. Trains run to Rosslare Harbour (2 per day, £6), Cork (1 per day, £10), and Dublin's Heuston Station (3–4 per day, £11.50). If you're heading to Cork, take the bus. It's cheaper (£8), more frequent (7 daily), and won't backtrack like the train, which heads first to Kilkenny and then on to Cork.

WHERE TO SLEEP

Ask to see your room before booking into one of the many dingy B&Bs in downtown Waterford, so you won't be unpleasantly surprised. Some exceptions are the conveniently located **Beechwood** (7 Cathedral Sq., off Greyfriars, tel. 051/76677), which is right next to Christ Church Cathedral and has lovely rooms for £15 per person, and **Derrynane House** (19 The Mall, tel. 051/75179), with spacious rooms for £13 per person. Waterford also has two good hostels and one hostel to be avoided.

HOSTELS

Bolton House. This unaffiliated hostel is a small, decrepit place with cramped dorm rooms (£6), nappy comforters, and dirty bathrooms. Think twice about staying here—especially if you're a woman traveling alone—or, at the very least, first check with the Waterford tourist office for other suggestions. If the owner approaches you at the train station, don't be afraid to tell him that you have another place to stay. *Bolton St., tel. 051/79870.*

IHH Viking House Holiday Hostel. This friendly hostel is smack in the center of town and has dorm beds in bright, clean rooms for £8, breakfast and sheets included. There's also a beautiful 15th-century stone fireplace in the common room. *Coffee House Ln., off Greyfriars St., tel. 051/853827, fax 051/971730. From Plunkett Station, cross the river, walk left along the riverfront, turn right on Henrietta Street, and make a quick left. Kitchen, laundry.*

ROLLS-ROYCE OF CRYSTAL

Silica sand + potash + litharge = Waterford crystal: It reads like cold science but something magical happens when the craftsmen of Waterford produce arguably the finest crystal on the planet. When the Waterford Glass Factory opened in 1783, it provided English royalty with a regular supply of ornate handcrafted flatware, chandeliers, and decorative knickknacks. Over the years, its clientele has diversified along with its product line, and today the United States is the biggest market for its crystal.

If you're in Waterford, a tour of the nearby factory is a must, even if you can't afford the expensive crystal. From April through October, guided tours (£2.50), which include glassblowing and glass-carving demonstrations, are given daily 8:30–4. The rest of the year, tours operate weekdays 9–3:15. The adjacent crystal gallery is open April–October, daily 8:30–6, November–March, weekdays 9–5; bargains are sometimes available in the adjoining gift store. Both are 1½ km (1 mi) west of Waterford on the N25/Cork Road, an easy walk or hitch from the city center. For information call 051/73311.

Waterford Hostel. Smaller and a pound cheaper than the other hostels in town, the friendly Waterford Hostel serves a Continental breakfast and has free city maps showing which of Waterford's many pubs are having traditional music sessions on any particular night. At the height of the summer season, *definitely* make a point of reserving a bed because rooms fill up quickly. *70 Manor St., tel. 051/50163. Kitchen, laundry.*

FOOD

Expensive restaurants line Waterford's main shopping avenue, but you're better off at **Haricots** (11 O'Connell St., at western foot of Georges St., tel. 051/50828), a small, intimate whole-food restaurant with a warm, wooden interior and cheap meals. Try one of the daily specials (£4), fresh salmon (£4.85), or vegetarian goulash (£4.65). Waterford's most popular Chinese restaurant is **Happy Garden** (53 High St., tel. 051/55640), noted for its prawns (£6.50) and beef chop suey (£4.50), and prized for its late hours (daily until 12:30 AM, Fri.–Sat. until 1 AM). Prices go up 50% if you sit down, so you may want to order your food to go. If you're hankering for atmospheric pub grub, try **The City Arms** (Arundel Sq., tel. 051/72220) or **Lords of Waterford** (6 Arundel Ln., tel. 051/75041).

AFTER DARK

The weekly *Waterford News & Star* (£1) and *Waterford Today* (free) both provide exhaustive accounts of the goings-on in the city. Waterford's large student population results in most city-center pubs, especially the ones on John Street, being packed to capacity seven nights a week. The undeniable favorite is the **Pulpit** (10 John St., tel. 051/79184), a dark, old-style place endowed with a wooden pulpit and a handful of semiprivate snugs. After a pint or two, head next door to **Geoff's** (9 John St., tel. 051/74787), another cavernous pub decorated with large oak tables and antique billboards. For tunes, check out **Old Ground** (The Glen, tel. 051/852283) for Friday-night traditional music or **Fitzgeralds** (High St., tel. 051/875612) for disco and hip-hop.

If your idea of a good time runs more to poetry readings and lectures, head to **Garter Lane Arts Centre** (22A O'Connell St., tel. 051/55038 or 051/77153), which coordinates daytime photography and art exhibits with evening entertainment. **Theatre Royal** (City Hall, The Mall, tel. 051/74402), Waterford's public theater, stages everything from modern Irish and international drama to musicals during its May–September season. Ticket prices vary but are usually between £5 and £10, and student discounts are often available. On the first weekend of August, Waterford hosts the **Spraoi Festival,** the largest "rhythm festival" (lots of percussion and African music) in the country; call the tourist office for details.

CASHEL

Cashel owes its fame to the surrounding **Rock of Cashel,** a ragged outcrop of limestone that, over the centuries, has been endowed with churches, towers, and stone crosses by a successive troop of religious orders. The "Rock," as it's known, stands like an ominous beacon in the middle of a sloped, treeless valley, as if it had been uplifted by some subterranean violence. Set atop the limestone is a completely restored Romanesque church, a complete round tower, the 15th-century Hall of Vicars, a handful of carved stone crosses, and a buttressed medieval cathedral—all in all, a stunningly comprehensive collection of Irish religious architecture. It's also one of the tourist board's prized gems and the favorite of Dublin-bound tourist coaches. The Rock (admission £2.50) is

It was at Cashel that St. Patrick preached the doctrine of the Trinity, using a handy shamrock as an example.

open mid-June–mid-September, daily 9–7:30, mid-March–mid-June, daily 9:30–5:30; the rest of the year it closes at 4:30. Crowds are at their worst after noon, so try to arrive as early as possible. Unfortunately, renovation of the cathedral walls is underway indefinitely, and the scaffolding definitely detracts from the scenic beauty of the Rock. An audiovisual presentation is shown every half hour. Guided tours run less frequently but are wheelchair accessible. For more info, stop by the **tourist office** in the Cashel Heritage Center (Town Hall, Main St., tel. 062/61333).

The easiest way to get to Cashel is from Dublin or Cork. **Bus Éireann** has four departures per day from Cork (£8) and twice-daily service from Dublin (£11 round-trip) and Clonmel (£4.80). It's also possible to reach Cashel from Waterford or Kilkenny, but the trip involves about 3 hours and three transfers. Bus tickets and schedules can be purchased at **Rafferty's Travel** (102 Main St., tel. 062/62121). The closest train station is in Cahir, which can be reached on any of three daily buses (£2.50).

WHERE TO SLEEP AND EAT

Cashel Holiday Hostel (John St., 2 blocks from tourist office, tel. 062/62330) has dorm beds (£6.50–£8.50), double rooms (£16), and amenities like a blazing fire nightly in the common room and 7-foot beds for tall hostelers. Another option is the IHH **Lisakyle Hostel** (tel. 052/41963), 1½ km (1 mi) outside the town of Cahir and 18 km (11 mi) south of Cashel. Free transportation to the hostel is provided from IHH's office across from the post office in central Cahir. Lisakyle charges £6 for a dorm bed, £16–£17 for a double, and £4 for tent spaces. The best B&B in town is **Maryville** (17 Bankplace, tel. 062/61098), a prim guest house with tremendous views of the Rock. It has eight meticulously cleaned and decorated rooms from £14.50. Even better views can be had around the corner at **Rockville House** (Rock Pl., tel. 062/61760), where rooms start at £13.50 and include breakfast in a super-posh dining room. Some of the better places to get cheap eats in Cashel are at **O'Dowds** (103 Main St., tel. 062/62650), **The Royal Oak** (49 Main St., tel. 062/61441), and **The Bakehouse Coffeeshop** (Main St., tel. 062/61680), all of which serve sandwiches and soup for less than £5.

5 THE SOUTHWEST

CALE SILER AND LAURENCE BELGRAVE

A varied coastline, spectacular scenery (especially around the famous lakes of Killarney), and a mild climate have long attracted visitors to this romantic region; the place has become so popular in the last decade that some locals whisper of being a little overwhelmed by the well-intentioned invasion. But the area's most notable attractions are rural and still very much intact: miles and miles of country lanes meandering through rich but sparsely populated farmland. Even in the two main cities the pace of life remains perceptibly slower than in Dublin. To be in a hurry in this region is to verge on demonstrating bad manners. It was probably a Kerryman who first remarked that when God made time, he made plenty of it.

As you look over thick fuchsia hedges at thriving dairy farms or stop off at a wayside restaurant to sample the region's seafood and locally raised meat, it is hard to imagine that some 150 years ago this area was decimated by famine. Thousands perished in the fields and the workhouses, and thousands more took "coffin ships" from Cobh in Cork Harbour to the New World. Between 1846 and 1849 the population of Ireland fell by an estimated 2½ million. Many small villages in the Southwest were wiped clean off the map. The region was battered again in the civil war that was fought with intensity in and around "Rebel Cork" between 1919 and 1921. Economic recovery only began in the late '60s, which led to a boom in hotel construction and renovation—not always, alas, in the style most appropriate to the area's aesthetic.

Outside of crazy Killarney (oh, and it is crazy), tourist development remains fairly low-key. The area is trying to absorb more visitors without losing too much of what attracts them in the first place: uncrowded roads, unpolluted beaches and rivers, easy access to golf and fishing, and unspoiled scenery where wildflowers, untamed animals, and rare birds (which have all but disappeared in more industrialized European countries) still thrive. The jury is still out on their success.

The southwest coast of the region is formed by three peninsulas: the Beara, the Iveragh, and the Dingle; the road known as the Ring of Kerry makes a complete circuit of the Iveragh Peninsula. Killarney's sparkling blue lakes and magnificent sandstone mountains, inland from the peninsulas, have a unique wild splendor, though in July and August the area is packed with and tamed by visitors. Around the Shannon estuary you move into "castle country," littered with ruined castles and abbeys as a result of Elizabeth I's attempt to subdue the old Irish province of Munster in the 16th century. Limerick City, too, bears the scars of history from a different confrontation with the English, the Siege of Limerick, which took place in 1691.

As in the rest of Ireland, social life centers around the pub, and a visit to your local is the best way to find out what's going on. Local residents have not lost their natural curiosity about "strangers," as visitors are called. You will frequently be asked, "Are you enjoying your holiday?" "Yes" is not a good enough answer: What they're really after is your life story, and if you haven't got a good one you might want to make it up.

Tourism reaches a frenzied crescendo, which borders on the ugly, in Killarney, a largish market town and the best base for exploring the adjacent Ring of Kerry. Cape Clear, an island just south of Mizen Head, is another area famed for its rural wonders—a terrain of sea cliffs, thatched cottages, and rolling farmland. North of Killarney, Tralee makes a good base for extended trips into the picturesque Dingle Peninsula. Although Dingle Town itself is becoming a popular stop on the tour-bus circuit, the peninsula's thinly populated Slea Head and Blasket Islands are everything Ireland is meant to be—harsh, rugged, and spectacularly scenic.

BALTIMORE, CAPE CLEAR, AND SHERKIN ISLAND

Despite the look-alike holiday homes that infest the area, the crescent-shape port village of **Baltimore** is beautiful and not touristy. Its well-protected harbor attracts the occasional sailboater during the summer season, along with a handful of Irish and German families on holiday. Baltimore was sacked in 1631 by a band of Algerian sailors, who after razing an abbey on Sherkin Island, kidnapped an Irish fisherman and forced him to pilot their two frigates into the bay. As a result, watchtowers were installed at the harbor mouth to protect the town. Today, you can walk to a modern version of the watchtower—a phallic, whitewashed weather beacon—southwest of the pier; the view is particularly stunning when the fishing trawlers head for port around sunset.

Baltimore's most famous attractions are **Sherkin Island** and **Cape Clear,** both accessible by regular ferry. Sherkin, a mile off the coast and visible from Baltimore's waterfront pubs, receives the bulk of visitors, mainly because it's only 10 minutes away by boat. The island has recently been featured in the popular works of young playwright Sebastian Barry. **Bushe's Bar** (tel. 028/20125) provides info on the **Sherkin Island Ferry Service,** which runs seven boats per day in the summer (three per day off-season) that will drop you at Sherkin's port and collect you later the same day for £4. On the island, you'll find the ruins of **Dun Na Long Castle** and **Sherkin Abbey,** both built around 1470 by the O'Driscolls, a seafaring clan known as the "scourge of the Irish seas." On the island's northwestern shore, stop by the Sherkin Island Marine Station, 1 km (½ mi) from the pier, for nice views.

More impressive by far is **Cape Clear,** a 10 sq km (3 sq mi) island 6 km (4 mi) offshore. The most southerly port in Ireland, Cape Clear's unofficial slogan is "Next Parish: America." With its sparse population (about 200), the island is rugged and unblemished, perfect for hiking. In the 17th century, before the famine, Cape Clear's population was nearly 10 times its present size. Near the pier in North Harbour, the cape's principal port, are the ruins of **St. Chiaran's Church.** It was here in 351 that Ireland's first saint, Chiaran of Clear, was born and taught the gospel of Christianity some 70 years before St. Patrick reached Ireland. The ferry *Naomh Chiaran* (tel. 028/39135) leaves Baltimore harbor for Cape Clear three times per day July–August, twice per day September–June, and four times every Sunday year-round (45 min, £8 round-trip), weather permitting.

BASICS

The waterfront **tourist office** (tel. 028/20226), open Monday–Saturday 9:30–5:30 in summer, can provide bus schedules and book accommodations.

ATLANTIC OCEAN

Ennistymon

CLARE

N67

Kilkee

Kilrush

Killimer
Tarbert

G

Mouth of
the Shannon

Ballybunion

Listowel

R523

Abbeyfeale

N69

Brandon
Bay

Tralee
Bay

Mt. Brandon

Tralee

N21

N21

Ballydavid

Connor
Pass

Kilcummin

R559

Blennerville

Castleisland

DINGLE PENINSULA

Castlemaine

R577

R.

Ballyferriter

Dingle
Town

R561

N70

N22

Dunquin

Ventry

Annascaul

Inch

Killorglin

Killarney

Slea Head

Dunbeg

Rossbeigh

R562

Dingle Bay

Glenbeigh

Kerry

Caragh
Lake

N72

Blasket
Islands

Ring

of

N70

KERRY

Lake
Leane

Muckross

Cahirciveen

IVERAGH PENINSULA

R568

Upper
Lake

KILLARNEY
NATIONAL
PARK

Valentia
Island

N70

R569

Ballinskelligs
Bay

Kerry

Ring

Sneem

Tahilla

N70

Kenmare

R584

Waterville

N70

Parknasilla

R571

Gougane Ba
Forest Park

Skellig
Islands

Caherdaniel

Kenmare River

N71

Glengarriff

BEARA PENINSULA

Garnish
Island

Ballylickey

Dursey
Island

Castletown
Bere

R572

R586

Bantry

Bere Island

Bantry Bay

Durrus

N71

Ballydehob

Skibbereen

Schull

R592

N71

Liss Ar0
Foundation

R596

Mizen Head
Signal Station

Goleen

R595

Castletowns

Crookhaven

Roaring Water Bay

Baltimore

Cape Clear
Island

Sherkin
Island

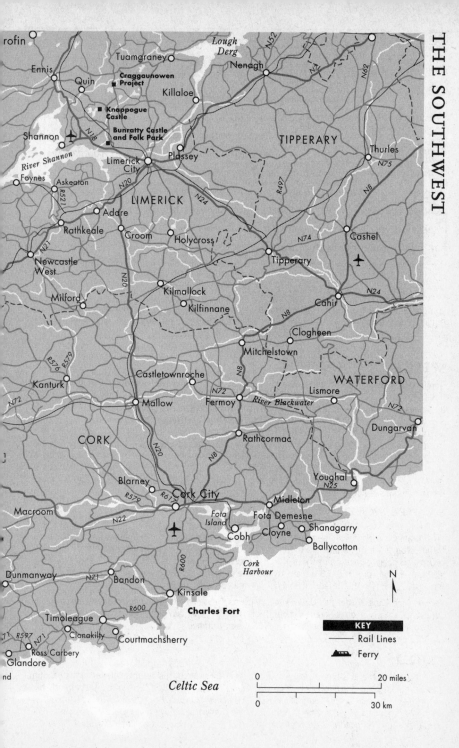

rofin

Lough
Derg

N52

Tuamgraney

Ennis

Craggaunowen
Project

Quin

Killaloe

Nenagh

N7

N62

TIPPERARY

Knappogue
Castle

Bunratty Castle
and Folk Park

N18

Shannon

Plassey

Thurles

River Shannon

Limerick
City

N75

Foynes

Askeaton

R521

N20

N24

N8

Adare

LIMERICK

Rathkeale

N21

Croom

Holycross

N74

Cashel

R497

N20

Tipperary

Milford

Kilmallock

N20

Kilfinnane

N8

Cahir

R576

R579

Clogheen

N24

Kanturk

Castletownroche

N8

Mitchelstown

WATERFORD

N72

Lismore

N72

Mallow

Fermoy

River Blackwater

Dungarvan

CORK

N20

Rathcormac

N72

N8

Blarney

R579

Youghal

Cork City

R617

Midleton

N25

Macroom

Fota Demesne

Fota
Island

Cloyne

Shanagarry

N22

Cobh

Ballycotton

R600

Cork
Harbour

N

Dunmanway

N7

Bandon

Kinsale

R600

Charles Fort

N71

Timoleague

KEY

Rail Lines

7

R597

N71

Clonakilty

Courtmachsherry

Ferry

Ross Carbery

Glandore

0

20 miles

nd

Celtic Sea

0

30 km

COMING AND GOING

To reach Baltimore you will have to change buses in **Skibbereen.** Buses go between Skibbereen and Baltimore four times a day Monday–Saturday (£2.10). Buses run from Cork to Skibbereen (2 per day, £6) and in the summer from Killarney (2 per day, £7.60).

WHERE TO SLEEP

Comfortable bed-and-breakfast rooms from £15 per person are available in Baltimore at **Algiers Inn** (tel. 028/20145), above its adjoining pub and around the corner from the waterfront pubs. If that's full, try the nearby **Sunbury House** (tel. 028/20150), a cozy place that's less atmospheric and lively but also £15 per night. Near the harbor on Cape Clear, **Cluain Mara House** (tel. 028/39153) has a virtual monopoly on the area's B&B business. Fortunately, it doesn't abuse this privilege, and all five of its rooms (£14 per person) are immaculate and endowed with sag-free beds. They also offer a two- to three-person studio for £21. When the weather is fine (June–September), you can camp at **Cuas An Uisce** (tel. 028/31149) in South Harbour, 1½ km (1 mi) from Cape Clear's main ferry port. Its 20 pitches (£2 per person) hug the rocky coast: a beautiful setting on a clear day, miserably damp and dreary when it's raining.

HOSTELS

Baltimore is blessed with the phenomenal IHH **Rolf's Hostel** (tel. 028/20289), ½ km (¼ mi) east of town on a rural farm road (follow the signs). Besides being amazingly friendly and relaxed, Rolf's has stone-faced cottages with pine interiors (dorm beds £6, doubles £20), a welcome change from the dusty-couch-and-peeling-paint category of hostels. Inside is a luxurious common room and self-service kitchen—though for £3.50–£8 you can try their Malaysian and Italian dishes, served nightly in the common room (prices in the restaurant next door are steeper).

The An Óige **Cape Hostel** (tel. 028/39144) on Cape Clear is a well-kept house with 42 beds (£5, £6 June–Sept.) that overlooks South Harbour. It's a mile from the main port (follow the signs), so stock up on food and supplies. The hostel is closed November–March.

FOOD

Baltimore's food scene is pretty dreary, composed mostly of pricey restaurants catering to the yachting crowd. Your best bet is to chow on pub grub at **Bushe's Pub** (tel. 028/20125), grab a burger and chips at a kiosk on the pier, or head to Rolf's Hostel (*see above*). **Cotter's** (tel. 028/20106), across from the pier, sells produce and groceries. On Sherkin Island, **Jolly Roger Tavern** (tel. 028/20379) has decent pub eats and a terrace with incredible views. You can pick up grocery items at **Abbey Store** (tel.

028/20181), which also doubles as the post office. Cape Clear's **The Club** (tel. 028/39184) serves cheap sandwiches during the day.

MIZEN HEAD PENINSULA

Poor Mizen Head. Though still incredibly scenic, it doesn't have jaw-dropping views like the Ring of Kerry or Beara Peninsula. But it *does* have a marked dearth of tourists (which Kerry lacks), accessibility via public transport (Beara's Achilles' heel), and a couple of great hostels, all of which make Mizen Head well worth a couple of days of exploring. The main highlight is the Mizen Head itself, where the peninsula ends in a series of cliffs. The **Mizen Head Signal Station** (tel. 028/35225), admission £2, is perched on one of these cliffs. At the entrance to the station is a narrow bridge that affords dizzying views of the rocks below and access to a lookout point offering an amazing view. The station is open April–October, daily 11–5, and November–March, weekends noon–4.

Small towns dot the peninsula's southern coast. With a great hostel, bike-rental shops, and plenty of pubs, **Schull** makes the best base for exploring the peninsula. It's a cute, little harbor town where you can take scenic walks along the bay. Rent a bike from **McCarthy's Garage** (Main St., £7 per day) and head west along the less-trafficked road along the coast. You'll pass an incredibly remote 16th-century castle (*see box, below*) and a heather-and-cow landscape, which soon begins to include coves and inlets. About 11 km (7 mi) west, you'll reach the tiny town of **Goleen,** where you can grab picnic supplies or lunch. From Goleen, it's another 11 km to Mizen Head. Other spots worthy of exploration are **Barley Cove** (18 km/11 mi from Mizen Head), a sandy beach with craggy rocks on one side and brilliant blue water on the other, and **Crookhaven,** at the end of a smaller peninsula, which has a few markets and a pub.

COMING AND GOING

Bus Éireann buses depart from Skibbereen and Ballydehob and rumble down the peninsula as far as Goleen (£5). Buses leave three times per day in summer (once daily in winter). From Goleen to Barley Cove and the Mizen Head, you'll need to drive, cycle, or hitch a ride with one of the many cars that make that trip.

WHERE TO SLEEP AND EAT

The excellent and outdoorsy **Schull Backpacker's Lodge** (Colla Rd., tel. 028/28681), is a five-minute walk from Schull. Dorm beds are £7, private rooms £10, and tent sites £5. Smack in the center of town is Mrs. McSweeney's **Schull Central B&B** (Main St., tel. 028/28227), with large, plain rooms for £12.50–£14 a head. The place has a well-worn, homey feel—probably because Mrs. McSweeney has lived here her entire life. **The Barley Cove Holiday Park** (Barley Cove, tel. 028/35302) is a campground that overlooks the beach but swarms with RVs and their owners at the height of summer. Tent sites cost £6, plus £1 per person. A far better choice is to camp at the nearby beach for free (and it's even legal).

In Schull, **Bunratty Inn** (Main St., tel. 028/28341), on the main square, serves seafood chowder (£2.50), smoked mackerel salad (£4.50), and sandwiches for less than £2. They also put on frequent, foot-stomping traditional music shows. **Courtyard Bar** (Main St., tel. 028/28209) bakes bread on the premises and serves sandwiches and the like for about £4. In Goleen, **Heron's Cove Restaurant** (Goleen Harbour, tel. 028/35225) serves cheap soup, sandwiches, and fish-and-chips in a secluded courtyard overlooking a cove. You'll find grocery stores in every town.

MULLING OVER
A LITTLE YEATS

A few hundred years ago, the O'Mahony's built a tiny town on an equally minuscule island about 45 minutes off the coast road between Schull and Goleen. These days, you'll probably be the only person enjoying this gorgeously remote bit of Ireland, with lapping waves and wildflower-ensconced views. Unless, of course, Tim Hyde (the occasional inhabitant of the tower) is home. In which case you may (if you ask nicely) receive a personal tour of the tower.

To reach the castle from Schull, bike or hike along the coast road toward Goleen; turn left on the unmarked road across the street from the barn with the red, corrugated-metal door; turn right at the extremely overgrown footpath at the white house (which, incidentally, belongs to Fred Astaire's daughter); then meander across the fields and over several gates (they're meant to stop the cows, not you) until you reach the bridge to the tower. Exercise caution as you hike this "path," as it is overgrown, occasionally strays close to moderately steep cliffs, and is often muddy.

BEARA PENINSULA

The Beara Peninsula (pronounced BAR-a) is one of Ireland's better-kept secrets. Despite its proximity to Killarney and the heavily trod Ring of Kerry, Beara sees only a handful of cyclists and hitchhikers during the summer season, and only locals and sheep during winter. Bus service is very minimal, and hitching may entail standing two hours in the rain waiting for a single car to pass. The rewards, however, are substantial. Much of the road hugs either the coast or the ridge of the Slieve Miskish Mountains and gives phenomenal views. Come nightfall, when the air is pungent with peat smoke and farm smells, the greatest reward may be a small, smoky pub filled with the sort of locals who are actually impressed when they meet foreigners. The 141-km (88-mi) Beara Loop is best explored by a lengthy hike or a few days of cycling between Beara's phenomenal hostels. The loop is accessible via **Kenmare** from the north or west and **Glengarriff** from the south and east. If experiencing Beara's strikingly desolate beauty is your goal, stop in one of these tourist towns to buy a map and rent a bike, then hit the road. If you're hiking, the well-marked **Beara Way** is an excellent way to see the peninsula—it stays off the roads and strays near hundreds of prehistoric monuments sprinkled across Beara. Both the trail and monuments are shown on the superb "Discovery Series Map 84" (£4.20), useful for hikers and bikers alike. Pick one up at post or tourist offices.

Traveling counterclockwise from Kenmare, the first town you'll hit is **Lauragh,** an outcrop of pubs and newsagents surrounded by woods and small lakes stocked with trout and salmon. From here, you can head south via the steep but wildly scenic **Healy Pass** or continue west for the postage-stamp-size town of **Eyeries,** possibly the most beautifully remote settlement on the entire peninsula. Sweeping views and the wonderfully deserted beach fascinate during the day. Come Thursday night the entire town turns out at local pubs for untouristy traditional-music sessions that often lead to dancing in the street. Further west is tiny **Allihies,** from where you can begin the return leg toward Glengarriff or make a 8-km/5-mi (and highly recommended) detour to **Dursey Island.** To reach the island, take a rickety cable car (£2.50 round-trip) from Garnish Point, a trip that involves swinging violently 50 feet above the ocean on a journey that many fear will be their last. The carriage—which can carry six people, two cows, or 10 sheep—

makes crossings year-round, Monday–Saturday 9–11, 2:30–5, and 7–8, with irregular times on Sunday; call 027/73016 or 027/73095 for schedules. Back on the main road, there are hostels (*see below*) in **Cahermore** and **Adrigole**, from where it's 19 km (12 mi), uphill, to Glengarriff.

Castletown (which also appears as Castletownbere or Castletown Bearhaven on some maps) has the distinction of being the most westwardly town on Beara to be served by buses. Near Castletown are the decent **Beara Hostel** (2 mi west, tel. 027/70184), with dorm beds for £6.50, and **Dunboy Castle** (Admission 50p), 3 km (2 mi) southwest. You can rent bikes at **Supervalue** (Main St., tel. 027/70020) for £7 per day. **Glengarriff** lies at the foot of one of Ireland's most scenic roads, the 27-km (17-mi) stretch of N71 that connects Glengarriff with Kenmare. This mountaintop route twists and turns through desolate valleys and 100-year-old, rough-carved rock tunnels—a steep ascent from either side, but a favorite among veteran travelers. Luckily, the bus from Glengarriff to Kenmare keeps to this route, so all is not lost if you don't have a bike. If you do plan to cycle this route, start out early in the day so you can take your time with the killer climbs.

BASICS

Beara has two **tourist offices**: one in Glengarriff (Main St., tel. 027/63084) that's open May–September 9–9, and one in Kenmare (The Square, tel. 027/412331), which is more oriented to Kerry. The local Raleigh Rent-A-Bike agent operates out of **Jem Creations Craft Workshop** (Main St., Glengarriff, tel. 027/63113), where bikes cost £7 per day, plus a £40 deposit. Pick up the excellent "Walking Around Glengarriff" brochure (5p) from the tourist office or Jem Creations Craft Workshop. Castletown's information trailer doesn't have a phone or address; look for it on the road to Dursey, west of the square.

COMING AND GOING

Bus Éireann offers regular daily service from Glengarriff to Cork (3 per day, 1 on Sun., £9) and Dublin (1 per day, £16), and summer-only service to Kenmare (2 per day, £3.50) and Killarney (2 per day, £7.30). All buses stop on Main Road in front of the Harrington's office. Bus Éireann does not operate at all on the peninsula itself, but **O'Donaghue's** (tel. 027/70007) and **Harrington's** (tel. 027/74003) offer service from Glengarriff to Castletown (£3–£4) once a day Monday–Saturday. It is extremely important that you call these companies to find out when they are going through Glengarriff: You must literally flag down the O'Donaghue bus, but the Harrington's bus will pick you up if you call.

WHERE TO SLEEP

GLENGARRIFF

On the main road heading to Bantry, a five-minute walk from town, is **O'Mahony's Hostel** (Main Rd., tel. 027/63033), a family home with largish, plain dorm rooms (beds £5), as well as a kitchen and homey common room. At the east end of Glengarriff's two-block-long center is **Cottage Bar and Restaurant** (Main Rd., tel. 027/63331), which triples as a B&B (£13.50 per person), hostel (beds £7.50), and restaurant. All rooms have en-suite bathrooms, and there's also a small kitchen. There are also two excellent campgrounds outside town on the road to Castletown. **O'Shea's Camping Park** (Castletown Rd., tel. 027/63140) has 30 tent sites peppered throughout a small forest adjacent to Bantry Bay. A stone's throw away is **Dowling's** (Castletown Rd., tel. 027/63154), which is larger (90 sites) and more crowded, thanks to the nearby food shop and the traditional-music pub on the grounds. Both charge £5–£6 per site and are open mid-March–October.

GLANMORE LAKE/HEALY PASS

An Óige's **Glanmore Lake Hostel** (tel. 054/83181) is set on the lake's southeastern shore, parallel to Healy Pass Road and well signposted. With 40 beds (£4, £5.50 June–Sept.), a large kitchen, and a spacious common room, it's popular with cyclists who have exhausted themselves climbing the steep pass. The hostel is closed October–Easter. The nearest food shop is in Lauragh, so stock up on supplies in advance.

CAHERMORE

Adjacent to the Tibetan Buddhist Retreat outside Cahermore is the **Garranes Hotel** (tel. 027/73147), touted as the best hostel on the peninsula. This cliff-side farmhouse—with stunning views of the Atlantic and the peninsula—has 18 beds (£5), but in a pinch, they sometimes allow tent camping. Inquire about free meditation classes at the retreat next door.

ALLIHIES

The charming Amanda runs the An Óige **Allihies Youth Hostel** (tel. 027/73014), which has standard dorm rooms (£5.50) and a relaxed attitude. Smack in the middle of Allihies is the well-kept and mellow **IHH Village Hostel** (Main St., tel. 027/73107), with 14 beds (£6) tucked into small, bright rooms, as well as three doubles (£16) and laundry facilities (£3). The hostel has a common room/kitchen with a wood-burning stove and is closed October–February.

KILLARNEY

Killarney is the most heavily touristed city in southwestern Ireland, so much so that you feel it's on the verge of ceasing to be a town at all and becoming a Celtic theme park instead. Its proximity to Shannon Airport ensures a constant flow of wealthy foreigners, and most coach companies use Killarney as a base for their bus tours. Another reason this prim tourist village is at the top of everyone's must-see list is its location on the eastern fringe of the **Ring of Kerry** (*see below*). If you're planning to explore the Ring by thumb, bicycle, or tourist coach, you will inevitably find yourself in Killarney for at least one night, and that's probably enough.

The impressive **Killarney National Park** (tel. 064/31440), a pristine, 25,000-acre wood whose principal entrance is 1½ km (1 mi) east of the city, is a good reason to visit. Much of the park straddles **Lough Leane** (Lower Lake), a tranquil, windswept lake that's littered with rocky islets and dozens of hard-to-reach (and rarely visited) waterfalls. It would take three or four days and a good map to fully explore the park, but a few good day hikes are signposted at each of the park's entrances. The park's gates are open daily 9–6, but technically the park is accessible 24 hours and admission is free.

BASICS

AMERICAN EXPRESS

East Avenue Rd., tel. 064/35722. Open weekdays 9–9, weekends 10–7.

BIKE RENTAL

The local Raleigh Rent-A-Bike agent is **O'Callaghan's Cycles** (College St., tel. 064/31175). They rent 18-speeds for £5 per day, £30 per week. A half-block toward Main Street, **O'Neill's Cycles** (Plunkett St., tel. 064/31970) also rents 18-speeds for the same price. Your best bet, however, is **O'Sullivans** (High St., tel. 064/31282), which rents 21-speeds with all the extras for £5 per day and a mere £25 per week.

MAIL

Post New St., tel. 064/31288. Open Mon.–Sat. 9–5:30.

VISITOR INFORMATION

The **tourist office** books B&B rooms (£1 fee) and organizes guided tours of the Ring of Kerry through the coach companies that have offices across the street. It's best to visit the tourist office first if you want an objective rundown of Ring tours. *New Town Hall, south end of Main St., tel. 064/31633. Open July–Aug., Mon.–Sat. 9–8, Sun. 10–6; June and Sept., daily 9–6; Oct.–May, Mon.–Sat. 9:15–5:30.*

COMING AND GOING

BY BUS

Killarney's **bus station** is adjacent to the rail depot and the Great Southern Hotel, both of which are off East Avenue Road, east of the city center. Inside the bus annex is an information desk and a listing of daily departures. To reach town, turn left from the depot and follow the main road as it curves right. There are buses to Cork (5 per day, £8.80), Dublin (3 per day, £14), and Tralee (8 per day, £4.40). *East Avenue Rd., tel. 064/34777. Information desk open Mon.–Sat. 8:30–5:45, Sun. 8:30–1 and 1:45–4.*

BY TRAIN

Killarney Station, roughly 30 yards from the bus depot, has a staffed information counter. Killarney is on both the main Tralee–Dublin line and the Tralee–Limerick line, with connections to Cork (sometimes via Mallow). Four trains per day go to both Dublin (£17.50) and Tralee (£5.50). A one-way fare to Cork is £13.50, while a trip to Galway costs £15. *East Avenue Rd., tel. 064/31067. Information counter open Mon.–Sat. 7:30–6, Sun. for train departures.*

WHERE TO SLEEP

Killarney has nine hostels, 35 hotels, and hundreds of B&Bs. The city-center hostels fill up quickly in summer, so unless you relish a long hike or bike ride to the suburbs, reserve in advance whenever possible. The only time you may end up sleeping on the roadside (or on your credit card) is in mid-May or the last weekend in July, when Killarney hosts its biannual horse races. Reservations are a must during this posh extravaganza.

Muckross Road and New Road have the largest selection of B&Bs, but in Killarney nearly one house in three seems to provide accommodations during the summer season. Try **Innisfallen House** (Muckross Rd., tel. 064/34193) or **Killarney View Guest House** (Muckross Rd., tel. 064/33122), both of which charge £16.50–£18 per person. The Killarney House is probably the nicest, decorated in a cutesy grandmotherly style of antiques and flowery wallpaper. **The Arch House** (East Avenue Rd., near train station, tel. 064/32184), has rooms with bath starting at £16 per person. **Gleanntán House** (New Rd., tel. 064/32913) is another fine option, with fluffy comforters and gleaming bathrooms for £15 per person.

Commercialized Killarney feels like a movie set. The day-to-day life of locals has been elbowed out of existence by the needs of tourists, and you'll be lucky to hear an Irish accent on the Babel-like streets.

HOSTELS

Atlas House. This lovely hostel has large, bright, airy rooms and beds with real mattresses. Dorm beds start at £7.50, doubles at £27, including breakfast. The hostel is a 15-minute walk from the bus station and provides wonderful views of the town and mountains. *The Park, tel. 064/36144. From bus station, follow Park Rd. toward Cork, walk under the train bridge, and turn left at the first traffic light. 100 beds. Bike rental (£5), common room, kitchen, laundry, luggage storage.*

Bunrower Hostel (IHH). Owned by The Súgán (*see below*), this stately lodge with high-ceilinged sitting rooms is set in a forest 1½ (1 mi) southwest of Killarney and about a 20-minute walk from the train station. Dorm beds cost £6–£7. Call in advance for a free shuttle from the bus station. *Ross Rd., tel. 064/33914 or 064/33104. From train station, turn left on Muckross Rd., right on Ross Rd. 20 beds. Kitchen, sheet rental (£50p).*

Four Winds (IHH). There's a fire-warmed common room and dorm rooms with new beds (£6–£7) at this large and generally crowded hostel. It's comfortably modern and situated in the heart of Killarney. Doubles are £17 (£23 high-season). *43 New St., tel. 064/33094. From train station, turn left on East Avenue Rd., left on New St. 56 beds. Reception open until midnight (until 3 AM weekends). Common room, kitchen.*

Neptune's. Neptune's is your standard huge hostel, but it's surprisingly quiet for being in the city center. Comfortable 6- to 10-bed dorm rooms (beds £6–£9.50) and a large kitchen help to make up for its rather sterile and vast common room. Singles are also available for £13–£18. *Bishop's Ln., just off New St., tel. 064/35255. 102 beds. Bureau de change, laundry, luggage storage, sheet rental (50p)*

The Súgán (IHH). This hostel, spread throughout a two-story stone cottage, is heavy on character and claustrophobia. Downstairs, an excellent "vegetarianish" restaurant is popular with locals and hostelers alike. Unfortunately, there is only one shower, and the bathrooms are tiny, but this hostel still fills up fast. Dorm beds cost £6–£7. *Lewis Rd., tel. 064/33104. From train station, turn left on Park Rd., right on Lewis Rd. 18 beds. Kitchen, sheet rental (50p).*

CAMPING

The best of the three campgrounds near Killarney is **Whitebridge Camping Park** (tel. 064/31590), a mile east of Killarney on the banks of the River Flesk; take the Cork Road and follow the signs. Its 40 sites (£3–£3.50, plus £2.50 per person) are developed and crowded, although there's good hiking on nearby Lough Leane. Bicycles (£6) can be rented on the premises, and a food shop and pub are nearby. The park is closed November–mid-March. Five kilometers (3 miles) west of Killarney, along St. Margaret's Road (which becomes the N70 just outside of town), is **Beechgrove** (tel. 064/31727), which has 50 sites available from mid-March to mid-October. A little farther is **Fossa Caravan and Camping Park** (Killorglin Rd., tel. 064/31497), open mid-March–October. Neither is particularly scenic, but Fossa has an on-site restaurant and food shop. Beechgrove's rates are £3 per person (£5 July–August). The rates at Fossa are £3–£3.50 per site, plus £2.50 per person.

FOOD

The Súgán (*see* Hostels, *above*) serves delicious three-course meals for £10 (£7 for hostel guests) in its intimate dining room, which features live traditional music on summer weekends. The restaurant is open May–October, Tuesday–Sunday, 6 PM–9:30 PM. Nearby, **Mayflower Chinese Restaurant** (Church Ln., off Plunkett St., tel. 064/32212) serves chow mein (£4–£6), tofu dishes (£5), and inventive chicken concoctions like crispy chicken with plum sauce (£5) daily until midnight (a little later on weekends). Both the food and the ultracozy feel of the vegetarian **An Taelann** (Bridewell Ln., tel. 064/33083), open daily 12:30–4 and 6:30–10, make this place popular with carnivores and veg heads alike. It serves unusual pastas, such as spinach pasta with blue cheese and broccoli (£6). Lunches are a bargain, but the same dishes cost £3 more in the evenings. Do not leave without trying the rhubarb crumble (£2). At the other end of town, **Grunts** (New St., tel. 064/31890) whips up good soups and sandwiches for less than £3. For late-night, post-pub feasts, **Busy B's Bistro** (15 Upper New St., tel. 064/31972) serves all things deep-fried Monday–Saturday until 3 AM. For groceries and such, **Dunnes** (New St., tel. 064/31560) has it all.

AFTER DARK

For information on current Kerry events, pick up the weekly *Killarney Advertiser,* free and available at the tourist office. Most of Killarney's pubs are unabashedly devoted to the tourist trade. **The Laurels** (Main St., tel. 064/31149), a beautiful old-style public house, charges a scandalous £3 cover for the simple privilege of singing "Danny Boy" with a choir of drunken foreigners; however, the front bar isn't too bad and has no cover. **O'Connor's** (High St., tel. 064/31115) is a worn 1960s pub that balances large tourist crowds with solid pints and traditional music on Monday and Thursday nights. A sure bet for traditional acoustic music in the summer is **Fáilte Bar** (College St., tel. 064/31893), which also irregularly hosts rock bands. Stake your claim on a seat by 8 PM or prepare to stand. **Yer Man's Pub/The Strawberry Tree** (Plunkett St., tel. 064/32688) is mobbed by local twentysomethings most nights. At closing time, they move to the adjoining **Rudy's Nightclub,** which stays open until 1:30 AM. The cover charge for Rudy's is free before 10:30 and £2–£4 thereafter. **The Killarney Cineplex,** a brand-new, four-screen cinema opposite Killarney Towers Hotel, might be your only means of escape from the tourist glut.

RING OF KERRY

Running along the perimeter of the Iveragh Peninsula, the 176-km (110-mi) Ring of Kerry can be accessed at any number of places, although Killarney (*see above*) is the traditional—and most practical—starting point. On sunny days, the two-lane highway that handles the bulk of traffic is choked with rental cars, tourist coaches, and cyclists, all engaged in the vain struggle to find the real, rural Ireland promised by the tourist board. Many are disappointed to find that the Ring is one of the country's busiest roads, overflowing with cars, buses, fumes, gift shops, restaurants, and other tourists. Most of the loop is not recommended for serious cyclists or hikers who are looking for beautiful rugged countryside; for that, time could be better spent in the Beara (*see above*) or Dingle (*see below*) peninsulas.

Yet as long as you don't mind sharing the road, you will encounter some incredibly stunning coastal and mountain views. To do the Ring justice, you'll need a minimum of two days on bike, more if you're hitching or traveling by bus. Most prefer to tackle the Ring in a counterclockwise direction, starting from Killarney, then pausing for a night at one of the Ring's numerous hostels in the villages of Glenbeigh, Caherciveen (also spelled Cahersiveen), Valentia Island, Ballinskelligs, Waterville, and Kenmare. You can also begin the loop in Kenmare, but during the winter, it will be difficult to get around in this direction unless you have a car or hitch. The Ring can be explored in as little as a day, either by car or on a guided tour, but most of the Ring's best sites are found on spontaneous detours and winding back roads—the sort of pleasant traps that take time to fall into. Another reason to spend more time here is to do the 36-km (22½-mi) **Skellig Loop,** a short but scenic circuit ignored by most luxury coaches. Touring this smaller loop will add an additional day or two to your itinerary, but it may well be the highlight of your Ring of Kerry tour.

BASICS

Bord Fáilte's only Ring of Kerry tourist desk is in Kenmare's **Courthouse** (The Square, tel. 064/41233), open May–September, daily 9–5:30 (closed Sun. 1–2:15). Most towns on the Ring have numerous pubs, restaurants, food stores, a bureau de change, and street-side triangular billboards crowned with a Bord Fáilte shamrock that contain town maps and a brief list of B&Bs. In Caherciveen, the privately owned **Old Oratory** (Main Rd., tel. 066/72996) stocks regional maps and brochures and changes money. The **post offices** in Kenmare (Bridge St., tel. 064/41490), Killorglin (The Square, tel. 066/61101), and Waterville (Main St., tel. 066/74100) also change money. The post office in Glenbeigh has tourist brochures and free guides to the Ring.

GETTING AROUND

Killarney has four competing companies that offer three nearly identical tours at identical prices: a full-day tour of the Ring of Kerry (£10), a half-day tour of the Ring of Kerry (£7.50), and a boat/bus combo trek through the Gap of Dunloe and the Lakes of Killarney (£13); some companies give a £2 discount to students or hostelers. The companies are **Castle Lough Tours** (High St., tel. 064/32496), **Deros Tours** (Main St., tel. 064/31251), **O'Connors** (Ross Rd., tel. 064/31052), and **Cronin's Tours** (College St., tel. 064/31521).

BY BICYCLE

Though the roads teem with luxury coaches, the 176-km (110-mi) Ring of Kerry is easy to navigate and generally quite flat. Youth hostels and restaurants are found every 32 km (20 mi) or so, making it possible to tackle the loop in a piecemeal fashion. A fast-paced bike tour will take at least two days, but most cyclists prefer to do it in three–four days in order to have time to explore a few unmarked back roads and/or to detour through Valentia Island and the Skellig Loop. No matter where you're headed, however, storms are a year-round threat, so rain gear is a must, as are spare parts and a good map. The most convenient place to rent cycles is in Killarney (*see above*), but a few shops are scattered throughout the area. In Killorglin there's **O'Shea's Cycle Centre** (Lower Bridge St., tel. 066/61919), which rents bikes for £6 per day. In Kenmare, **Finnegan Cycles** (37 Henry St., tel. 064/41083), the local Raleigh Rent-A-Bike agent, rents bikes for £6 per day and £35 per week, with a £40 deposit. Be sure to time your departures so that you miss the cavalcade of coaches that could leave you headfirst in a ditch, bike and all, or worse; keep in mind that the coaches leave Killarney between 9 and 10, stop in Waterville and Sneem for lunch at 12, and then head back to Killarney.

BY BUS

If you're short on time, one of the cheapest ways to see the Ring is on Bus Éireann's **Ring of Kerry** route (tel. 064/34777), which departs Killarney twice daily (less often late September–May), stopping at Killorglin, Glenbeigh, Caherciveen, Waterville, Caherdaniel, Sneem, and Moll's Gap, before returning to Killarney. The entire loop costs £9.70; £12.20 if you want to get off (once) and then continue on in the next bus. At no extra cost, you can extend the loop as far as Tralee. For Valentia Island or Ballinskelligs, take the bus to Caherciveen or Waterville, respectively, and walk or hitch from there.

HITCHING

If you think there are no redeeming qualities to the tourists on the Ring of Kerry rampage, try hitching, and you may change your mind. Although hitching the extensive Ring can be a two- to three-day venture, you'll never be standing too long on the road because the swarms of slow-driving tourists are usually quite good about giving rides.

WHERE TO SLEEP

GLENBEIGH

Unfortunately, there is no hostel in Glenbeigh, so it's not a cheap place to stay. **Breens Diner** and **The Village House** (Main Hwy, 066/68128) are two functional B&Bs run by the same people. Rooms are £16–£20 per person. **Glenbeigh Hotel** (Main Hwy., tel. 066/68333), a country house thick with rural charm and cutesy antiques, has rooms for £25 per person. It's small enough to avoid large tour groups and quite luxurious in its own way. Slightly cheaper (£17.50 per person) is **Ocean Wave House** (tel. 066/68249), closed November–March, a family-run B&B 1 km (½ mi) east of town. Campers should try **Glenross Caravan and Camping Park** (Main Hwy., tel. 064/68456), which is open mid-May–early September and charges £3.50 per person. It is clean and well kept, with showers (50p) and a small laundry for washing and drying (£4.50).

CAHERCIVEEN

The IHH **Sive Hostel** (15 East End, tel. 066/72717) is three blocks from Caherciveen's small square; you can't miss the smart, newly painted yellow-and-blue exterior. Inside it's tidy and comfortable. The hostel charges £6.50 for a bed and £3.50 for a tent site. It also arranges day trips to the Skellig Islands (£20). Paul, who runs the place, is bubbling over with information on local musical events and might even be able to get you invited to play in a session if your talents lie in that direction. The most comfortable B&B in town is in the village center: **Dun An Oir** (New St., tel. 066/72565), a four-room, family-run place that charges £13 per person. If it's full, there's a cluster of dull B&Bs on the road to Valentia Island. From mid-March to mid-October, when the weather is good, **Mannix Point Campground** (tel. 066/72806) has 42 pitches (£3.25 per person) on the waterfront. Nearby is a semi-stocked food shop and a common room with an open fireplace and a 160-year-old piano.

VALENTIA ISLAND

Of the two hostels on the island, both IHH affiliates, the most easily reached is **Ring Lyne Hostel** (Chapeltown, tel. 066/76103), an immensely comfortable place within a stone's throw of Chapeltown's pubs and chippers. Beds cost £6–£7, tent sites £3. More intimate, at least if you opt for a private room, is the **Royal Pier Hostel** (Knightstown, tel. 066/76144), housed in a brooding manor house with a pool table and restaurant. Private rooms are £7.50, dorm beds £6.50, and tent spaces £3 per person. Otherwise, **Mrs. Lyne's B&B** (Knightstown, tel. 066/76171) is well tended and cozy. All of its rooms come equipped with thick comforters and an assortment of religious icons for £13. It's closed October–March.

WATERVILLE

Peter's Place (no phone) is an amazingly mellow town house 300 yards west of town. Some of the rooms have exceptional views out to sea. Beds are £6.50, tent sites £3, but rates are negotiable—Peter's a very laid-back guy and has the lowdown on how best to explore the local area. He can also arrange bike rentals (£5) and trips to The Skelligs (£20). **Waterville Leisure House** (tel. 066/74400) is generally packed with families and school-age tour groups. Dorm beds cost £6.50, singles £8. **Clifford's** (Main St., tel. 066/74283), closed November–February, is a nice B&B with en-suite rooms for £15 per person. **The Ashling House** (Main St., tel. 066/74247) has rooms starting at £14.

CAHERDANIEL

It's not a big stopping-off point for coaches or one-day Ring of Kerry visitors, so Caherdaniel is one of the more pleasant spots for a weary tourist to rest his or her limbs. **The Travellers Rest Hostel** (tel. 066/75175) on the main road is comfortable and clean. Beds are £6–£7, and if no one answers the phone, inquiries should be made across the road at the gas station. Further into the village is **The Caherdaniel Village Hostel** (IHH; Main Rd., tel. 066/75277). Small (only 12 beds) but snug, it's open March to November but is fully booked for much of that time, so be sure to phone in advance. A bed costs £6.50. The hostel is also a recognized PADI diving center, where you can learn to dive in a day for only £30. They also organize full mountaineering courses and sea-angling trips.

KENMARE

Kenmare's IHH **Fáilte Hostel** (Henry St., tel. 064/41083) is a comfy town house with a spacious sitting room and oak-paneled bedrooms. Its rooms, spread over three floors and accessed via a Georgian staircase, are clean, small (six to eight beds), and airy. Private rooms are £9, dorm beds £6.50. If you're looking for B&Bs, there's a large cluster just outside town on the Killarney Road. None is particularly outstanding; the cheapest are **Riverside House** (Killarney Rd., tel. 064/41316), closed November–March, and **Ardmore House** (Killarney Rd., tel. 064/41406), closed December–February; doubles cost £26 and £32–£36 respectively. On the N70, 4 km (2½ mi) west of Kenmare, is **Ring of Kerry Camping Park** (tel. 064/41648), closed January–March. Its 60 sites (£4.50 per person) have good views of Kenmare Bay and the Caha Mountains, and there's a food shop, kitchen, and common room with fireplace.

WORTH SEEING

Traveling west from Killarney, the first major stop on the Ring of Kerry is **Killorglin,** 16 km (10 mi) west, a quiet riverside village on the slope of a gentle hill. The flat and only vaguely scenic road from Killarney to Killorglin disappoints many travelers, but once they regain the rural road west of Killorglin, the flat bog turns into hilly, sylvan pastures. Despite its small size, Killorglin has a handful of budget restaurants and is a popular lunch stop with Ring of Kerry cyclists.

Because Killorglin is so close to Killarney, most travelers prefer to cycle or bus straight through to **Glenbeigh,** 11 km (7 mi) west of Killorglin, where there's a hostel to crash in if your legs have given out. Set on a boggy plateau by the sea, Glenbeigh is one of those block-long towns where everyone knows what everyone else had for breakfast. A detour leads to a long stretch of pristine beach at the end of the R564. Glenbeigh's only other attraction is the **Kerry Bog Village Museum** (tel. 066/69184), a small place with exhibits on bogs and peat and reconstructed 18th-century houses. At £2.50, it's worth a quick look, especially since a mug of Bewley's coffee at the pub next door is half off with admission. The museum is just west of town on the main highway, signposted from the village center. West of Glenbeigh, the highway curves toward the coast, where it ultimately changes into a creeping cliff-side road, battered on one side by the Atlantic and overshadowed by steeply rising mountains on the other.

The next stop is **Caherciveen** (pronounced care-sha-VEEN), 26 km (16 mi) southwest of Glenbeigh. Large by Ring of Kerry standards, Caherciveen is a tiny town with lots of long-standing hardware stores and butcher shops. Refreshingly undeveloped and old fashioned for this part of the country, its bay-side quay has a few weathered storehouses, but its only official attraction is the **Barracks** (tel. 066/72777), which highlights local history and also houses a tourist desk. For a quiet pint, try the worn **Kelly's Pub** or **Anchor Bar;** both are on Main Street and host live music during summer.

Caherciveen marks the Ring's western fringe; from here the road turns south and inland, rejoining the coast at **Waterville,** 13 km (8 mi) south. If you'd rather continue along the coast, 5½ km (3½ mi) south of Caherciveen is the turnoff for **Skellig Loop.** The first 11 km (7 mi) of this 35-km (22-mi), semicircular detour are unimpressive, but at Portmagee you'll find the turnoff for **Valentia Island,** accessed via a two-lane bridge or a shuttle ferry that leaves from Renard point. The fastest route from Caherciveen, the ferry runs April–October, daily from 8:15 AM–9:30 PM, and it costs £1 for foot and bike passengers. The island itself is mostly flat and studded with fields of sheep and cattle. Its two principal villages are Chapeltown and Knightstown. You can easily cycle the 11-km-long (7-mi-long) island in less than two hours. Besides its untouristy roads and ocean views, Valentia's major attraction is the **Skellig Heritage Centre** (tel. 066/76306), open April–September, daily 10–6. Here you'll find a good collection of Skellig Island artifacts and photos, along with a 15-minute audiovisual show that charts Skellig's development as a monastic site. Admission is £3.

South from Portmagee, the Skellig Loop keeps to the coast and passes through the villages of **Ballynahow** and **Killonecaha.** This 26-km (16½-mi) stretch affords unbeatable views of the Atlantic and, on a clear day, the Skellig Islands. If you're in the mood for yet another detour, take any of the rough dirt roads to the short cliffs that guard St. Finan's Bay. Or continue south 4 km (2½ mi) toward **Ballinskelligs,** a small fishing village with an old monastery, a pub, and an **An Óige hostel** (tel. 066/79229) that will give you a fairly gruff and unfriendly reception. Unless you're spending the night, the only reason to stop here is to catch a ferry to the Skellig Islands (see box, below). From Ballinskellig, it's an easy 9½-km (6-mi) ride east (via the R567) to rejoin the main Ring road at Mastergeehy.

Like so many villages on the Ring, **Waterville** has a few restaurants, pubs, and a hostel, but little else. Many people end up calling it a day here, but be warned, there is no bank machine in town. Three kilometers (2 miles) south of Waterville is **Coomakesta Pass.** Its summit gives stunning views of the Kerry coast, but cyclists should be prepared for a long, grueling, 1,014-foot ascent. A rugged, signposted trail by the parking lot atop the pass leads to **Hog's Head.** On foot, it takes 45 minutes to reach the point, which affords a clear view of the offshore Scariff Island and, to the left, the stunning Derrynane National Park with its immaculate white sandy beach and dunes. Your last chance for accommodation before you reach Kenmare is in **Caherdaniel.** This tiny village has two hostels and is a great base from which to walk Derrynane National Park and visit Derrynane House, home of Daniel O'Connell, great patriot, who fought for Catholic emancipation and home rule. Every major city in the south of Ireland, including Dublin, has an O'Connell Street. The house is open May–September, Monday–Saturday 9–6 and Sunday 11–7. Admission is £2. Caherdaniel is also popular with divers (see Where to Sleep, above). Once past Caherdaniel, the road becomes relatively flat and dull for the next 53 km (33 mi), never regaining the rugged splendor of the northern circuit. For tour-bus travelers, this means time for a sweater-shop stop in **Sneem.** For cyclists and hitchers, on the other hand, it means getting to Kenmare as quickly as possible.

Situated slightly inland without a clear view of Kenmare Bay, **Kenmare** is a natural stopover for buses and cyclists, mainly because it's the last large town with a hostel before Killarney, 42 km (26 mi) north. Kenmare is also well served by bus, making it a good first or last stop on the Ring if you're looking to

THE SKELLINGS

Sure, £20 is a lot to spend on a boat ride, but the wet, wonderful ride to Skellig Michael is worth it for adventurers with plenty of Dramamine. During the 1½-hour journey you'll pass the Lesser Skellig, a sanctuary where 40,000 birds careen around the island's jagged spires. Farther out is the phenomenal Skellig Michael: home to an amazing 6th-century village of monastic beehive dwellings and vertigo-inducing views. To get here, book at least one day in advance via Joe Roddy (tel. 066/74268) or Sean Feehan (tel. 066/79182), both of whom leave from Ballinskelligs; or Michael O'Sullivan (tel. 066/74268), who departs from Portmagel or Waterville. Be warned: the pinnacles of this ancient Christian (possibly pagan) center of worship will haunt you for days.

avoid the more touristy Killarney completely. On summer evenings, Kenmare's pub scene is surprisingly lively, boasting frequent music sessions and lots of drunken conversation. Worth visiting is the nearby **Druid Circle,** a 3,000-year-old monument that dates from the early Bronze Age. It consists of 15 large stones arranged in a circle around a center stone. Its precise use is unknown, but it is believed to have served in the rituals of the ancient Druid priests. The beauty of the site is somewhat marred by industrial garbage littering the surrounding area. There's also a worthwhile walk down to the harbor with a great view of Kenmare Bay and boat trips around the bay (£8–£9.50). Call **Sea Fari Cruises** (tel. 064/83171) for times and details.

DINGLE PENINSULA

The Dingle Peninsula stretches for some 48 km (30 mi) between Tralee (pronounced tra-LEE) in the east and Slea Head in the west. It is home to the villages of Castlegregory, Ventry, Inch, Dingle Town, and, just off the coast, the Blasket Islands. Its small size makes it one of Ireland's most accessible and popular summer retreats, especially for cyclists and hitchers who don't have time to cover the larger Beara or Ring of Kerry circuits. Despite its size, the Dingle Peninsula is topographically diverse and brazenly scenic. Driving or cycling over its high mountain passes, in fact, may conjure images of the Alps or Rockies, and the lushly forested mountains along the shore look like they belong on a South Pacific island.

Culturally, however, the Dingle Peninsula is uniquely Irish. It's part of County Kerry's *Gaeltacht* (Irish-speaking region), where Irish is still spoken on a daily basis. You won't come across many locals openly engaged in Irish conversation, but during summer, the region is swamped with school-age children who have enrolled in one of the peninsula's Irish-language courses. Folk customs and handicrafts are still integral to the Dingle lifestyle, especially now that tourism has become its principal industry. A day or two in Dingle Town, and another few busing or hitching the perimeter, are sufficient to behold the peninsula's best sights, particularly if good weather allows a trip to the impressive Great Blasket Island.

BASICS

The town of **Tralee** is not actually on the peninsula but is the main local transportation hub. Tralee also has a **tourist office** (Ashe Memorial Hall, tel. 066/21288) that's generous with brochures and information about the Dingle Peninsula and is open year-round, Monday–Saturday 9–6 (also Sunday July–August). **O'Shea's Tours** (2 Oakpark Dr., tel. 066/27111) runs tours of the Ring of Kerry (£10) from here. They depart Tuesday and Saturday (additional Thursday tours in August). You'll find plenty of banks and bureaux de change around town. The closest to the bus/train station is **AIB** on Denny Street. Tralee's **post office** (Edward St., tel. 066/21013) is open Monday–Saturday 9–5:30.

The peninsula's lone **tourist office** is in Dingle Town (Main St., tel. 066/51241) and is open daily 9–6, mid-April–October only. Grab their handy map of Dingle and the peninsula for £1. Another good source for maps and peninsula-related literature is Dingle's **Café Liteartha** (Dyke Gate Ln., tel. 066/51388), a small bookshop with an intimate, budget-friendly soup and sandwich bar. Along Main Street in Dingle, you will also find a **post office** (tel. 066/51661), open weekdays 9–1 and 2–5:30 and Saturday 9–1, and plenty of bureaux de change.

Most peninsula hostels rent bikes for local day trips, but for long-term rentals try Dingle's **Paddy's Bike Shop** (Dyke Gate Ln., next to the Grapevine Hostel, no phone), which rents the best bikes in town for £5 per day or £25 per week, plus a £5 deposit. Or try **Foxy John Moriarty Bikes** (Main St., tel. 066/51316), the local Raleigh Rent-A-Bike agent, with 18-speeds for £5–£7 per day or £25 per week, plus a £30 deposit.

COMING AND GOING

Gallarus Oratory, 1½ km (1 mi) from Smerwick Harbour, is one of the best-preserved early churches in Ireland. Built by monks in the 7th or 8th century, the corbeled structure is still waterproof today.

Tralee makes a good springboard for exploring the Dingle Peninsula. **Irish Rail** offers daily service to Tralee from Killarney (3 per day, £5.50), Cork (2–4 per day, £17), and Dublin's Heuston Station (3 per day, £16.75). The joint **bus/rail station** is on J. J. Sheehy Road, at Oakpark Road; call 066/23522 for rail information, or 066/23566 for bus information. From Tralee, **Bus Éireann** offers year-round Expressway service to Dingle five times a day, three per day on Sundays. Fares are £5.90 one-way, £8 round-trip. During summer there's also service to Dunquin (direct to youth hostel, 2 per week, £7.70). Buses to Castlegregory (£3.80) leave Tralee on Friday at 8:55 AM and 2 PM. Bus Éireann offers slightly more frequent service to the peninsula's smaller towns and Dingle and Dunquin in the summer; get a schedule at the Tralee bus station.

WHERE TO SLEEP

Because it is the most popular stop on the peninsula, Dingle has the largest selection of cheap accommodations. There are also a few hostels scattered throughout the region, convenient for cyclists and hitchers but too far off the beaten track to be easily reached by bus. One of these is the IHH **Bog View Hostel** (tel. 066/58125), a small place with a modern kitchen, common room with open turf fire, clean doubles (£16), and dorm beds (£6). Open May–October, the Bog View is 8 km (5 mi) southwest of the town of Camp on the N86, on the far side of Caherconree Pass. It is also near Inch Beach, where *Ryan's Daughter* was filmed. Closer to Castlegregory is the IHH **Connor Pass Hostel** (Stradbally, tel. 066/39179), a family-run home with a kitchen, sitting room, and comfortable dorm beds (£6). At the peninsula's opposite end, 3 km (2 mi) from Ballydavid Village, is **Tig An Phóist** (Bothar Bui, tel. 066/55109), which overlooks Smerwick Harbour in the middle of the rugged countryside. The hostel makes a perfect base for exploring nearby ruins like Gallarus Oratory. Dorm beds cost £6.50, and it is open Easter–October.

DINGLE

The incredibly friendly people at **Avondale House** (Corner of Dyke Gate Ln. and Avondale, tel. 066/51120) offer cozy rooms for £15–£16.50 per person, which includes a stunning breakfast. Some rooms have just been renovated and are quite nice, others are just OK—ask to see the room first to ensure you get a good one. **Mrs. Russell** (The Mall, tel. 066/51747) has luxurious, en-suite rooms (£17 per person) in a small but cozy town house. Both the Avondale and Mrs. Russell offer vegetarian breakfasts for those who just can't stomach another drop of grease. **An Dreoilin** (Lower Main St., tel. 066/51824) offers smaller, less comfortable rooms in a standard row house from £13–£15 per person.

There are several hostels in and around Dingle, but many are seasonal, so be sure to call ahead. The best hostel is **Rainbow Hostel** (The Wood, tel. 066/51044), a 15-minute walk from town toward Ventry;

a free shuttle also whisks hostelers to and from the bus stop. Set in a secluded farmhouse on a country lane, it has an awesome kitchen, common room, dorm rooms (beds £6), campsites (£3) and, perhaps best of all, it offers 1½-hour massages (£20) to soothe your weary body. For £6 the owner leads trips to see Fungi the dolphin, a super-friendly aquatic mammal who has made his permanent home just off the coast. The claustrophobic **Grapevine Hostel** (Dyke Gate Ln., tel. 066/51434), in the center of town, has £6 dorm beds, en-suite showers, and musty, pea-green paisley carpets that may drive you insane. On Dingle Bay lies **Marina Hostel** (The Wood, tel. 066/51065), a small, plain house with dorm rooms (£6 beds), private rooms (£8 per person), and camping (£3 per person). The gorgeous bay windows and aristocratic interior of **Ballintaggart House and Equestrian Centre** (Anascaul Rd., tel. 066/51454) reveal the grandeur of its earlier function as the Earl of Cork's hunting lodge. It's a mile outside town, but worth the trip: A frequent shuttle zips hostelers into town, the huge dorm rooms (£6–£7 per bed) have a definite charm, and they rent wet suits (£5) for a "swim with Fungi." They also offer guided two-hour horse treks to a secluded beach (£10), where you can gallop and pretend you're in the classic Irish movie of your choice.

DUNQUIN

Grand-prize winner of Ireland's Most Characterless and Lonely Hostel contest is An Óige's **Dunquin Hostel** (tel. 066/56121). Its location, overlooking the coast and Blasket Islands, is superb, but the room lockout, shower lockout, and strict midnight curfew make this place hard to love. Beds cost £5.50 (£6.50 June–Sept.). The hostel's saving grace is its proximity to **Kruger's Pub** (tel. 066/56127), just down the road. Open as a B&B March–October, Kruger's has comfortable rooms (£14 per person), and the adjacent pub has good views of the frothy Blasket Sound.

TRALEE

Tralee is blessed with three hostels and a slew of B&Bs. Around the corner from the tourist office is the magnificent **Finnegan's Holiday Hostel** (17 Denny St., tel. 066/27610). Most of the rooms of this 19th-century mansion, including the vast kitchen and wood-beamed common room, have been painstakingly restored. Dorm beds are £7.50, private rooms go for £10 per person, and there's a superb (yet pricey) restaurant downstairs. A 10-minute walk from the town center is the large, homey **Lisnagree Hostel** (Ballinorig Rd., tel. 066/27133), which has dorm beds from £6.50 and an inviting kitchen and common room. Farther out is **Collis-Sandes House** (Oakpark, tel. 066/28658), where dorm beds in sunny, spacious rooms cost £6.50. They also have doubles (£16), bike rental (£5 per day), cycle tours, and a nice garden. Call for a free shuttle from the bus/train station.

FOOD

Outside Dingle, your meals will either be pub grub or sandwiches at cafés irregularly sprinkled about the peninsula. Most eating establishments close October–February, so be sure to bring your own food during the winter, or prepare to exist solely on fish-and-chips. There are a few chippers and a grocer in Castlegregory, but head for Dingle Town or Tralee for anything substantial. In Dingle, **Sméara Dubha** (The Wood, tel. 066/51465) serves pricey but satisfying vegetarian cuisine 6 PM–10 PM. Bean and hazelnut bake, and peppers stuffed with fruited couscous both cost £8. Slightly cheaper are **Cois Farraige Café** (Strand St., no phone) and **Nell's Coffee Shop** (Strand St., no phone). Both conjure up soups, sandwiches, and fried things in the £2–£4 range. Near the church is **Cúl an Tí/Café Ceol** (Green St., tel. 066/52083), a wholesome vegetarian café/restaurant tucked into a pretty courtyard. Crepes (£2–£3) filled with goodies like spinach and cheese, sweet-and-sour vegetables, or apples and cinnamon are their specialty. During summer, they host traditional musicians on the weekend. **An Grianán** (Dyke Gate Ln., next to Grapevine Hostel, tel. 066/51910), open weekdays 9–6 (Sat. 10–6), stocks an array of dairy-free foods and organic fruits and vegetables. A mile or two south of Dunquin lies the work of a deranged children's book illustrator—the annoyingly cute **Enchanted Forest Museum and Café** (tel. 066/56234). Inside the pink, teddy-bear-laced facade are cheap sandwiches (£1.50), excellent views, and a toy museum based on pagan Celtic holidays. Really. Between Ballyferriter and Dunquin lies the cozy **Tig Aine** (tel. 066/56214), which serves up a dynamite veggie stir-fry and salad (£5) with the ubiquitous stunning views of the sea.

In Tralee, **Blasket Inn** (Church St., tel. 066/28095) serves filling, standard fare for £4 and is the only pub that serves food on Sundays. **Brats** (18 Milk Market Ln., no phone) whips up vegetarian entrées and salads for £4–£5. For groceries, try **Dunnes** (tel. 066/28333) on North Circular Road.

WORTH SEEING

Dingle Town is a small, lively fishing village that makes an excellent base for exploring the surrounding peninsula. Although many expect Dingle to be a quaint and undeveloped Gaeltacht village, it's popular with tourists and has become a haven for pricey seafood restaurants and a handful of luxury hotels. In many of its music pubs—**O'Flaherty's** (Bridge St., tel. 066/51983) and **The Small Bridge Bar** (Main St., tel. 066/51564) are the best—you'd be hard-pressed to find more than two or three locals among the summer video-camera crowds. That said, Dingle is blessed with a beautiful harbor and encircled by low-lying hills that offer good views of the peninsula. Since 1985, the harbor has been home to a bottle-nosed dolphin named **Fungi,** notorious for playing with swimmers and boaters. Boat trips to visit Fungi are led by a variety of operators and cost about £6; ask at the tourist office or the Rainbow Hostel (*see* Where to Sleep, *above*) for more information. More tactile interaction with marine life can be had at Dingle's **Oceanworld** (Waterside, tel. 066/52111), where you can pet sea rays and ogle sharks from within an underwater tube. It's open daily 9:30–9:30 and charges £4. The local archaeologists at **SCIUIRD** (Holy Ground, tel. 066/51937) lead two- to three-hour walking tours of some of the peninsula's more interesting prehistoric—and more recently created—sites. Dingle's main streets—The Mall, Main and Strand streets, and The Wood—can be covered in less than an hour, so plan to spend most of your time walking the countryside or hitching to Slea Head.

From Dingle, an excellent walk or cycle is to **Ventry,** a small outcrop of pubs and newsagents 3 km (2 mi) west. If you keep to the R559 coast road from Ventry, you'll soon end up on the 32-km (20-mi) **Slea Head Loop,** an incredible circuit that skirts the foot of Mt. Eagle (1,692 feet) and eventually curves north past Dunmore Head, Dunquin, and An Óige's Dunquin Hostel. This road offers views of the coast and Blasket Islands that are unforgettable—two notches above "don't miss."

Dick Mack's pub on Green Lane in Dingle Town appears not to have changed since it opened in 1899. The little snug was where women, not allowed into the pub proper, used to wait for their husbands to get sloshed.

Dunquin itself is a loose collection of sheep fields and isolated, peat-smoke-spouting cottages. Here you can stop for lunch at **Kruger's Pub** (tel. 066/56127) and catch the **Blasket Island Ferry** (Dunquin Pier, tel. 066/56455). During summer (weather permitting), boats leave daily on the hour, starting at 10 AM, for the 20-minute ride (£7) to this desolate island, where you'll find the ruins of 15th- and 16th-century monasteries and dozens of good hiking trails. The beautifully designed **Blasket Centre** (tel. 066/56371), admission £2.50, tastefully highlights the history and surprisingly strong literary tradition of the islands. The center's cafeteria offers good views and moderately priced food. North of Dunquin, the Slea Head Loop continues past Clogher Head and its ragged cliffs—another popular spot for picnics—before veering south toward Dingle and Ventry via the publess and shopless village of Ballynana. To extend the circuit, continue northeast from Dingle over **Connor Pass** (2,020 feet), a steep, rough road that clings to the side of Brandon Mountain as it curves its way toward Castlegregory, 22 km (14 mi) north. Like the Slea Head's southern leg, this high-altitude pass affords incredible views but is dauntingly steep and narrow; it is recommended only for serious cyclists. Over the pass, there's hostel accommodation in **Castlegregory,** a sleepy resort town that sees only a handful of cyclists and foreign families on holiday but attracts a number of windsurfing fanatics.

It used to be that the only good things to come out of **Tralee** (the capital of County Kerry) were the buses shuttling travelers elsewhere. To a certain extent, that is still the case: There are no ruins or quaint architecture. Accordingly, however, there are no tourists, and the local folk (21,000 strong) have slowly but surely been fashioning worthwhile sights (and accommodations) that deserve a look. Aesthetically, Tralee is bland, with a medium-size-town-with-no-character feel to it. **The Kerry Kingdom Museum** (Ashe Memorial Hall, next to tourist office, tel. 066/27777) is Tralee's star attraction. The museum traces human history in Kerry from 5000 BC with artifacts and interactive exhibits (with special sound, lighting, and "odour effects"), such as a streetcar ride through a life-size reconstruction of Tralee in the Middle Ages. Another option is the multimillion-pound **Aquadome** (Princes Quay, tel. 066/28899), with a wave pool, water slides, and an adults-only section to shield you from the evil hordes of shrieking children; admission is £6, £3 off-season. Also in Tralee is **Siamsa Tíre** (Godfrey Pl., tel. 066/23055), the National Folk Theatre of Ireland, which stages dances and plays based on Irish folklore. Shows take place six nights a week during summer and cost £8. At the end of August, Tralee gets down with its annual festival extravaganza: the **Rose of Tralee International Festival.** Essentially a beauty pageant where one lucky gal is crowned "The Rose" and paraded through the streets, the festival includes raucous street entertainment, horse races, fireworks, and lots of drinking. Just outside Tralee, on the N86 toward Dingle, looms the five-story **Blennerville Windmill** (tel. 066/21064). The surrounding buildings have been turned into a visitor center, featuring audiovisual displays, a crafts workshop, and an exhibit on Blennerville's history as County Kerry's main point of emigration during the Great Famine (1846–51). Admission is £2.75. The best pubs in Tralee are **Paddy Macs** on Castle Street and **Baileys,** around the corner on Ashe Street. Both have traditional music sessions on summer nights. Tralee also hosts a folk and blues festival on the last weekend of July.

CORK CITY

CALE SILER AND LAURENCE BELGRAVE

D ublin is home to more than half of Ireland's 3.5 million people. So when you say Cork is Ireland's second-largest city, with a population of only 175,000, you might expect Cork to be small and provincial. This is certainly how Dubliners view Ireland's "second city." For them, a trip to Cork is a trip to the country, a place to come for hurling, Gaelic football, and locally televised plowing contests.

Cork has few "don't miss" attractions, but that's not the point. Unlike so many towns in Ireland, Cork is very much alive. After weathering a severe recession in the grim '80s, the city's economy is beginning to bounce back. It has a formidable pub scene, some of the country's best traditional music, a respected and progressive university, art galleries, and offbeat cafés. Next to Galway, it also has one of the largest communities of hippies, dropouts, artists, musicians, and poets outside Dublin. Cork can be very "Irish" (music pubs, sheep, and peat smoke). But depending on what part of town you're in, Cork can also be distinctly un-Irish—the sort of place where hippies, gays, and conservative farmers drink at the same pubs, and the sort of place where a Catholic church, a motorcycle bar, and a vegetarian café can share the same street without causing too much of a ruckus.

At the heart of it all is Cork's sprawling, partially pedestrian shopping district—though cheaper shopping and meals can be had if you wander down the less-traveled alleys. Cork (or Corcaigh in Irish) means "marshy place" and takes its name from the Great Marsh of Munster, atop which Cork is built. The original 6th-century settlement was spread over 13 small islands in the River Lee, and as late as 1770 Cork's major streets—Grand Parade, Patrick Street, and the South Mall—were submerged (notice the street-level boathouses in the modern city center). Around 1800, the river was partially dammed, nearly tripling the amount of arable land in the city center. As a result, Cork's center grew at a furious but even pace: Cork does have slums and a few bleak warehouse districts, but most of the present city was built in the same style at the same time by the same people, giving Cork a homogeneous feel. Cork also features many bridges and quays that, although initially confusing, add to the unique character of this ancient port town.

Practically speaking, Cork is a good base for touring the southwest of Ireland—particularly the villages and sights that flank the city to the south and west. Cork is well serviced by international ferry, so it's also a logical stop for those headed to or from the Continent. In late summer and early autumn, Cork hosts an incredible range of festivals. At the end of October, the huge **Cork Jazz Festival** draws about 50,000 visitors from around the world. Although you can often buy tickets for music events on the day of the

CORK CITY

Sights ●

Beamish
Brewery, **5**
Bishop Lucey
Park, **6**
Cork Arts and
Theater Club **11**

Cork City Gaol, **1**
Crawford Art
Gallery, **8**
Fitzgerald Park
and Cork
Museum, **2**

Murphy's
Brewery, **12**
St. Fin Barre's
Cathedral, **4**
Shandon Church, **9**
Triskel Arts
Centre, **7**

Lodging ○

Alma Villa, **16**
Campus House
(IHH), **3**
Clon Ross, **18**

Cork City
Independent
Hostel, **20**
Isaac's (IHH), **13**
Kent House, **15**
Kinlay House USIT
(IHH), **10**

Oakland's, **17**
Sheila's Cork
Tourist Hostel, **14**
Tara House, **19**

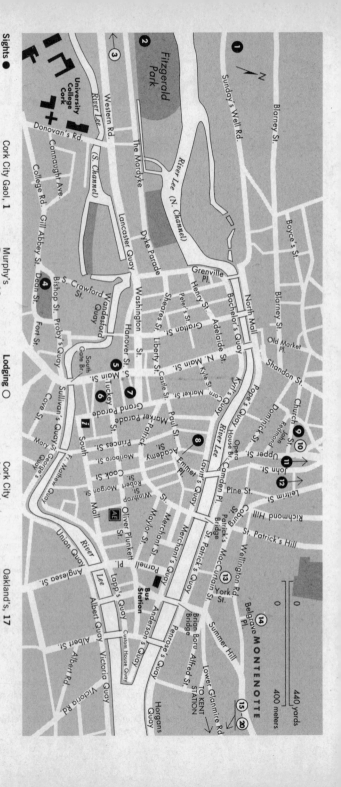

performance, make room reservations at least a month or so in advance or risk spending your nights—all night—in a pub. At the beginning of August, the nearby town of Yougal has its annual **Busking Festival,** which draws street musicians from all over the world, and in early September look for the **Cork Folk Festival.** Cork's **International Film Festival,** held the second week in October, is one of the best in Ireland. Call **Cork Kerry Tourism** (*see* Visitor Information, *below*) to find out the exact dates for 1998.

BASICS

LAUNDRY

If your jeans are standing and you're not in them, lug them over to **Cork City Laundry Service.** Washers cost £1, dryers 50p. *14 MacCurtain St., tel. 021/501–421.*

MAIL

The **General Post Office** has a bureau de change, phone cards, and a stamp kiosk. *Oliver Plunkett St., at Pembroke St., tel. 021/272–000. Open Mon.–Sat. 9–5:30.*

VISITOR INFORMATION

Cork Kerry Tourism has maps, brochures, walking guides, B&B info, and a bureau de change. *Grand Parade, near Washington St., tel. 021/273–251. Open Mon.–Sat. 9:15–5:30.*

USIT. This student-run travel shop, with two Cork locations, offers the best deals on rail, bus, and air tickets. They're also quite skilled at changing return dates on tickets or finding you a cheap connecting flight from Cork to Calcutta, Santiago, and the like. *10–11 Market Parade, tel. 021/270–900. UCC Travel, Boole Library, University College, tel. 021/273–901. Both open weekdays 9:30–5:30, Sat. 10–2.*

Cork's port served as the departure point for 2½ million emigrating Irish, was the chief recipient of the survivors and casualties of the Lusitania (which was torpedoed off the coast), and was the Titanic's last port of call.

COMING AND GOING

Cork's city center can be thought of as an island, surrounded by the River Lee and dominated by a maze of pedestrian shopping alleys impaled upon the crescent-shape Patrick Street; all the sights are easily reached on foot from here. Local buses arrive and depart from Parnell Place Station, though most serve the suburbs rather than the city center.

BY BUS

All **Bus Éireann** buses depart from the city-center **Parnell Place Station** (tel. 021/508–188 or 021/506–066), which faces the water on the south side of the River Lee. The bus station has a bureau de change and a left-luggage desk (£1.30 per day) open weekdays 8:30–6:15, Saturday 9:30–6. The station's information counter is staffed daily 9–6. Buses leave for Galway (£12), Cashel (£11), and Dublin (£12).

BY FERRY

Cork's ferry port is in **Ringaskiddy** (tel. 021/378–401 or 021/378–111), a desolate industrial complex 16 km (10 mi) south of town. Bus Éireann runs nine daily coaches (45 min, £3 one-way) from 7 AM–midnight to the ferry port from Parnell Place Station. **Brittany Ferries** (42 Grand Parade, tel. 021/277–801) sails Saturday at 3:30 PM to Roscoff, France, arriving the next day at 7 AM. One-way fares are £40–£61. Eurail passes are not valid. **Swansea-Cork Ferries** (52 South Mall, tel. 021/271–166) sails every second day except Tuesdays (daily in summer) to Swansea, Wales. Ferries generally leave Cork at 9 AM and arrive in Swansea at 7 PM. Fares are £21–£30. **Irish Ferries** (9 Bridge St., at St. Patrick's Bridge, tel. 021/551–995) offers summer sailings to Le Havre, France. Ferries usually leave Cork at 2:30 PM on Sundays and arrive 22 hours later, but call for current schedules. A one-way trip costs £76–£92, but EurailPass holders are only charged a £5 port tax.

BY PLANE

Cork Airport (Ballygarvan, tel. 021/313–131) is 9½ km (6 mi) south of town. A taxi to or from the airport runs about £6, or you can take the airport shuttle, which runs every 45 minutes from the bus station (£2.50 one-way). **Aer Lingus** (Union Quay, tel. 021/318–121) offers service to London, Paris, Manchester, Frankfurt, and Amsterdam, among other places.

BY TRAIN

Cork is easily reached from all parts of the country. Inside Cork's **Kent Station** (Lower Glanmire Rd., tel. 021/504–777 or 021/506–766), open daily 7 AM–8:30 PM and for all departures and arrivals, are an info counter, bureau de change, and lockers (£1 per day). Destinations from Kent Station include Dublin (7 per day, £16), Tralee (4 per day, 3 on Sun., £17), Killarney (4 per day, 3 on Sun., £13.50), Limerick (4 per day, £13.50), and Waterford (1 per day, £10) and Rosslare (4 per day, 3 on Sun., £13).

WHERE TO SLEEP

With six city-center hostels, a couple of small hotels, and hundreds of good B&Bs, Cork is hardly ever short of cheap beds. Reservations are a good idea if you want a bed near the train station during July and August, and they're absolutely imperative during the October Jazz Festival, when beds are at a premium; try to book at least two months in advance. The rest of the year, competition between the hostels is fierce, and lodging hustlers are often posted at the bus and train stations to collar weary travelers. If you'd rather camp, **Cork Camping Park** (Togher Rd., tel. 021/961–866), 1½ (1 mi) southwest of Cork University, has tent sites for £5 (plus £1 per person) available May–October. The park is accessible by Bus 14 and has a nearby food shop.

SMALL HOTELS AND GUEST HOUSES

Jurys Cork Inn. Opened in 1994, this unexciting budget hotel pursues the same function-over-form policy as its Dublin and Galway counterparts: charging £53 per room, each of which sleeps three adults or two adults and two children. Beside a busy bridge over the River Lee, the inn is a short walk from the city center and bus and rail stations. *Anderson's Quay, Co. Cork, tel. 021/276–444, fax 021/276–144.*

Victoria Lodge. This B&B, originally built in the early 20th century as a Capuchin monastery, is a five-minute drive from the town center; it's also accessible by several bus routes. Breakfast is served in the spacious old refectory, with its intact polished benches and paneled walls; the common room is now a television lounge where you can catch up on old episodes of the best (and worst) American shows. Singles go for £30, doubles £44. *Victoria Cross, Co. Cork, tel. 021/542–233, fax 021/542–572. 30 rooms.*

BED-AND-BREAKFASTS

Cork's B&Bs are mainly clustered around the train station on Lower Glanmire Road (turn right as you leave the train station), near Cork University on Western Road, and on Wellington Road. The cheapest is **Kent House** (47 Lower Glanmire Rd., tel. 021/504–260), which has airy rooms for £12–£15 per person. Three other comfortable B&Bs within a two-block radius are run by the Murray family: **Clon Ross** (85 Lower Glanmire Rd., across from the train station, tel. 021/502–602), **Oakland's** (51 Lower Glanmire Rd., tel. 021/500–578), and **Alma Villa** (50 Lower Glanmire Rd., tel. 021/502–602). At all three the rates are £15–£18 per person. **Tara House** (52 Lower Glanmire Rd., tel. 021/500–294) charges £13.50–£20 per person.

HOSTELS

Campus House (IHH). This hostel, the smallest and most relaxed in town, is popular with cyclists and vagabonds looking to escape institutional, prison-style accommodations. Clean dorm rooms (beds £6.50) have double-glazed windows to keep the noise down. If you're coming from Killarney by bus, the driver will drop you off at the hostel if you ask. *3 Woodland View, Western Rd., tel. 021/343–531. From bus station, take Bus 8 to Brighton Villas (70p). 18 beds. Common room, kitchen, luggage storage, sheet rental (50p).*

Cork City Independent Hostel. Opposite the train station on the north side of Cork, this unaffiliated hostel is an easy 10-minute walk from the pubs and shops. It doesn't look like much, situated among the quay's ramshackle port facilities, but the interior—with brightly painted doors and mismatched furniture—is folksy and fun. Dorm beds are £6, doubles £14. *100 Lower Glanmire Rd., tel. 021/509–089. 30 beds. Bike rental (£5), kitchen, laundry, luggage storage.*

Isaac's (IHH). This is definitely Cork's best-looking hostel (inside and out), and it's close to both the bus and rail stations. Too bad the staff are curt, there's an 11–5 lockout, and the main common room is only open for four hours a day; the rest of the time, two chairs, a table, and a TV constitute the common area. Dorm beds are £6.25–£8.50 and doubles £36. *48 MacCurtain St., tel. 021/500–011. From train station, turn left and continue for ¼ mi. 190 beds. Bike rental (£7), bureau de change, kitchen, luggage storage.*

Kinlay House/USIT. The large and thoroughly modern Kinlay House isn't a true hostel but rather an upscale holiday complex that happens to rent cheapish beds. Kinlay House offers a range of accommodations: singles (£15), doubles (£22), and dorm beds (£7.50), all of which include a Continental breakfast. *Bob and Joan Walk, Shandon, tel. 021/508–966. From bus station, turn left on Merchant's Quay, right on the second bridge (Opera House Bridge), walk north on Upper John St. (past the Northern Infirmary) and look for steps on the left. 126 beds. Bureau de change, common room, kitchen, laundry, luggage storage.*

Sheila's Cork Tourist Hostel. Commanding citywide views from its perch at the top of steep York Street, Sheila's is housed in a big, comfortable, ramshackle building. Dorm beds cost £6.50–7.50, singles £15 (£11 off-season), and doubles £19. The hilly front yard has tables and chairs where you can sip your morning coffee. *Belgrave Pl., Wellington Rd., tel. 021/505–562. From bus station, cross the river on Brian Boru St., turn left on MacCurtain St., right on York St., right on Wellington (which funnels onto Belgrave Pl.). 130 beds. Reception open 8 AM–3:30 AM. Bureau de change, kitchen, laundry, sauna, sheet rental (50p).*

FOOD

Cork has a good collection of upscale restaurants and unpretentious, dirt-cheap cafés. Most are scattered in the city center between the Grand Parade and the River Lee, notably in the network of narrow pedestrian lanes that slice across St. Patrick and Oliver Plunkett streets. For breakfast and afternoon snacks, snag an outdoor table at **Gingerhouse** (10 Paul St., tel. 021/276–411), famous for its authentic cappuccinos and buttery, flaky croissants. Cork's slackers, longhairs, and gays tend to gather at **The Other Side** (South Main St., between Castle and Washington Sts., tel. 021/278–470), where they sip coffee leisurely over newspapers and fill up on cheap salads and vegetarian soups (£1–£3). For pub grub and solid pints, try **The Lobby** (1 Union Quay, tel. 021/319–307), **Dan Lowrey's** (13 MacCurtain St., tel. 021/505–071), or **The Long Valley** (10 Winthrop St., off Oliver Plunkett St., tel. 021/272–144); all famed for their old-style decor and high-quality bar food. Enter the wrought-iron arch opposite Bishop Lucey Park to reach Cork's **City Market,** a pungent indoor bazaar that runs between the Grand Parade and Princes Street. **Natural Foods** (26 Paul St., tel. 021/277–244) has organically grown produce and yummy baked goods. For groceries go to **The English Market,** built in 1881, which houses numerous traditional market stalls selling a range of fresh food. There are entrances on Grand Parade, Patrick Street, Princes Street, and Oliver Plunkett Street. It's open from 9–5:30. **Quinnsworth** (Paul St., tel. 021/270–791) has the biggest selection and best prices of all the supermarkets.

UNDER £5 • Quay Co-op. It's Cork's most happening vegetarian hangout, especially on weekend mornings when the local veg-heads stumble in for coffee and a hand-rolled cigarette. The Co-op's couscous salad, blue-cheese cannelloni, curried eggplant, and broccoli soup make a welcome change from chips and toasted sandwiches. During the afternoon, the second and third floors of this riverside complex open as a self-service café, with dishes starting at £2. Around 6 PM, the second floor is transformed into a semi-posh sit-down restaurant, offering the same foods at slightly inflated prices. *24 Sullivan's Quay, 1 block south and across the river from tourist office, tel. 021/317–660. Cash only. Closed Sun.*

Triskel Arts Café. This quiet tearoom in the top floor of the Triskel Arts Centre serves simple but delicious salads (£3–£4) and hearty soups and sandwiches. Bow down and worship the chocolate-and-pear tart (£1.95). Everything here is made daily from scratch. *South Main St., off Washington St., tel. 021/272–022. Cash only. Closed Sun.*

UNDER £10 • Farmgate Café. On a terrace above the fountain at the Princes Street entrance to Cork's English Market, this simple restaurant-café is one of the best-value lunch spots in town. One side of the terrace is open to the market and operates as self-service; the other is glassed in and served by waiters (reservations advised). A piano player does his stuff at lunchtime most days. Tripe is always on the menu, while daily specials include less challenging but no less traditional Irish dishes such as corned beef with colcannon and loin of smoked bacon with *champ* (potato mashed with scallions or leeks). A large share of the food prepared here comes from the market below. *English Market, Cork, tel. 021/278–134. Closed Sun.*

New Maharajah. It looks shabby, but this family-run restaurant serves the best and cheapest Indian food in Cork. The fixed-price lunch menu (appetizer, tandoori entrée, dessert, and tea) is a steal at £5, or choose from the à la carte tandoori menu (£6.50) for slightly larger portions. *19 Cook St., tel. 021/276–576. Closed Sun.*

Pierre's. This superb restaurant in an old country house is refined and stately, decorated with mahogany panels, an open fire pit, and a beautifully carved high ceiling. Surprisingly, it's also reasonably priced.

The menu changes daily and features a variety of fish, steak, and pasta dishes. Lunch is around £6–£8, dinner £7–£9.50, but even if you're broke, Pierre's is highly recommended for late-night coffee or wine and divine homemade desserts. *17 Church St., tel. 021/278–107.*

WORTH SEEING

Cork's historical sights are spread out and easy to overlook, especially if you're unfamiliar with the city's confusing layout. Consider buying the useful "Tourist Trail Walking Guide" or the "Cork City Area Guide" (£1) from the tourist office. The Walking Guide outlines a three-hour walk covering the city's history and architecture. The tourist office also sponsors free guided tours of historic Cork that depart at 7:30 PM on Tuesdays and Thursdays July–August. **Cork Harbour Cruises** (44 Grand Parade, tel. 021/277–085) also offers pleasant harbor cruises (£5) of the area's many waterside sights and a short day trip to **Cobh** (£10, including admission to the Cobh Heritage Centre).

BEAMISH BREWERY

Beamish has been brewing its mild, fruity stout since the early 19th century. Over the years, it's become the pint of choice and a point of pride for locals. The brewery is a Cork landmark and is easily found by following the smell of boiling hops from the tourist office (or simply head north on Grand Parade, left on Washington Street, and left on South Main Street). Keep your eyes peeled for the brewery's brooding Tudor frontispiece, cupola, and clock. You can take a free tour with tastings Thursdays 10–noon, but only if you write one week in advance to Chris Reynolds (Beamish Inc., S. Main St., Cork, tel. 021/276–841).

BISHOP LUCEY PARK

This park was opened in 1985 in celebration of the 800th anniversary of the town's Norman charter. During excavation for the park, workers unearthed portions of Cork's original fortified walls, now preserved just inside the arched entranceway. Adjacent to the site is the 18th-century **Christ Church,** built on the foundation of an older (1199) Norman church. The building currently houses the city and county archives and is not open to the public. *Grand Parade, tel. 021/277–809. Park open daily sunrise–sunset.*

CRAWFORD ART GALLERY

This is Ireland's most active and respected provincial art gallery. Its permanent collection of second-rate Irish landscapists and portrait painters is completely forgettable, but the Crawford regularly mounts superb exhibitions of modern Irish and foreign work. The building itself was originally the city's custom-house, dating from 1724. *Emmet Pl., tel. 021/273–377. Admission free. Open Mon.–Sat. 10–4:45.*

FITZGERALD PARK AND SUNDAY'S WELL

Cork's largest public green is a mile from the city center, directly behind the Campus House and An Óige hostels. The **Mardyke,** a small footpath along the River Lee, makes for a good afternoon stroll. Near the park's entrance is the free **Cork Museum** (tel. 021/270–679), home to a large collection of Republican memorabilia and local artifacts; particularly good is the glass, silversmith, and coopering section. Across the water is the quiet suburb of **Sunday's Well,** a stately redbrick Victorian district. On the hill across the river (use the footbridge) is the foreboding **Cork City Gaol,** a creepy 19th-century jail that looks like a castle. On view are the prison cells (inhabited now by life-size replicas of some of the jail's most notorious criminals) and two walls of graffiti left by Republican prisoners in the early 20th century. *Park open May–Aug., daily 8 AM–10 PM; Sept.–Apr., daily 8–5. Cork City Gaol, tel. 021/305–022. Open Mar.–Oct., daily 9:30–5; Nov.–Feb., weekends 10–5, weekdays by guided tour only (tours given at 10:30 and 2:30). Admission: £3.50.*

MURPHY'S BREWERY

Murphy's began brewing here in 1856, but the company's purchase by Heineken in 1983 has led diehards to bemoan that the ol' familiar "hasn't been the same since." The brewery isn't open to the public, but you can taste for yourself in the Brewery Tap Pub across the road. **Lady's Well,** the brewery's second name, refers to a celebrated well across the street that's supposedly been blessed by the Virgin Mary herself. *Lady's Well, Leitrim St., tel. 021/503–371. Walk west on MacCurtain St. and follow the road as it veers right.*

ST. FIN BARRE'S CATHEDRAL

Built on the site of the original settlement of 606, this church was designed by Victorian architect William Burgess and completed in 1879. From the looks of it, Will had a lot of fun with the design, sprinkling leering gargoyles in every nook and cranny of the cathedral; there's even one under the book rest on the pulpit. The rich and lofty interior also contains mosaics, wood carvings, stained-glass windows, and a 3,000-pipe organ, which is sunk 15 feet into the floor. *Bishop St., off S. Main St., tel. 021/963–387. Admission free. Open daily 10–5.*

SHANDON CHURCH AND STEEPLE

One of Cork's most famous landmarks, the church of St. Ann Shandon was built in 1722 on the site of a derelict Viking fort (Shandon, or Sean dun, means "old fort" in Irish). The steeple's motley faces of red sandstone and bleached limestone inspired Cork's official city colors—red and white—while the 11-foot-long, salmon-shape weather vane is a tribute to the River Lee and Cork's founder, St. Fin Barre. For 50p, you can make the treacherous climb to the top of the 170-foot tower and ring Shandon's famous bells. *Church St., off Shandon St., tel. 021/505–906. Church admission: £1. Open daily 10–5:30.*

SHOPPING

For general bygones and curiosities, try **O'Regan's Antiques** (27 Lavitt's Quay), where to look around is a pleasure, and who knows?—you might find a bargain hidden away. For inexpensive rainwear (a real necessity in these parts), go to **Penney's** (27 Patrick St.). **Matthews** (Academy St.) has a wide selection of sporting gear. **Great Outdoors** (23 Paul St.) caters to most outdoor-sports needs. **Cash's** (18 Patrick St.) is Cork's leading department store and has a good selection of Waterford glass. Fans of Irish music should visit **The Living Tradition** (40 MacCurtain St.), a specialist Irish music shop. The **Merchant's Quay Shopping Centre** (Merchant's Quay, Cork) is the largest indoor mall in downtown Cork.

> *In a country where accents come in all shapes and sizes, the Cork twang is deemed the thickest of the thick—a blunt and guttural lilt that, in the words of one Dubliner, "reeks of the farm and field."*

AFTER DARK

Like Galway and Dublin, Cork is best appreciated from inside a pub, especially during the chaotic **Jazz Festival** in October. Cork's theaters and art centers also mount a diverse selection of productions year-round, most with substantial student discounts. **Triskell Arts Centre** (Tobin St., just off South Main St., tel. 021/272–022) presents a variety of plays, concerts, performances, films, and even dance lessons throughout the year. Tickets usually cost £2–£6; sometimes, they're free. **Cork Arts and Theatre Club** (7 Knapps Sq., tel. 021/508–398) also presents theater, comedy, and musicals; tickets usually go for £5. For entertainment listings, pick up a copy of the free weekly *What's On* or the extremely useful *Guide to Cork* from the tourist office or the *Evening Echo* (50p) from any newsagent.

PUBS

Cork has some of the best pubs in Ireland, especially for those into loud traditional music and rowdy crowds of college students. Right in the center of town, on Marlboro Street, you'll find **Fanny Adams** (021/272703) friendly and full of students. Connie, who runs it, will give a 15% discount to any traveler who asks; he also has some derring-do stories about windsurfing and lifeboat rescues. At lunchtime you can get large doorstop sandwiches (that is, big enough to act as a doorstop) for £1.60. One of the most popular stops is Union Quay, on the south side of town opposite the South Mall and River Lee. Here three excellent pubs stand side by side: **An Phoenix** (tel. 021/964–275), famed for its old-style decor; **The Lobby** (tel. 021/319–307), a folk/traditional music pub packed with yuppies and middle-age slackers; and **Donkey Ears** (tel. 021/964–846), home to a drunken horde of bikers and youthful fashion slaves. The Lobby has free traditional-music sessions Tuesday and Friday, country and blues on Monday, and a variety of folk and local rock upstairs (for a small cover). Farther down the river, **Callagan's** (24 George's Quay, tel. 021/274–604) is an unpretentious (okay, shabby) pub frequented by professional alcoholics and grandmotherly sorts, but its spur-of-the-moment, untouristy music sessions are not to be missed. Across the river, the popular **An Bodhrán** (42 Oliver Plunkett St., tel. 021/274–544) and **An Spailpín Fánac** (28–29 S. Main St., tel. 021/277–949) host regular traditional music during the summer. The only gay pub in town is **Loafers** (Douglas St., tel. 021/311–612), which is papered with gay and lesbian community info and hot-line numbers. Saturday night at **The Other Side** (*see Food, above*) is gay disco night; the first Friday of each month is lesbian dance night. **An Bros** (72 Oliver Plunkett St., no phone) spins mainstream Top-40 music, and **Mojo's** (George's Quay, tel. 021/311–786) hosts blues bands for a slightly older crowd. Depending on who's playing, these pubs often charge a £1–£3 cover.

THE GIFT OF THE GAB

The word "Blarney" was introduced into the English language by Queen Elizabeth I, who had attempted to force Cormac MacCarthy, Lord of Blarney, to will his castle to the crown. Lord Blarney consistently refused her request with eloquent excuses and soothing compliments. Enraged by his chameleon talk, Queen Elizabeth reportedly exclaimed, "This is all Blarney. What he says he rarely means." The gift of the Blarney is alive and well in present day Ireland.

NEAR CORK CITY

JAMESON HERITAGE CENTRE

At the Jameson whiskey distillery—once fourth-largest in the world—nearly 10,000 gallons of the dry, malty Irish brew known as Uisce Beatha, or Water of Life, was made each day until the 1970s, when production was stopped. The impressive distillery itself, built in 1795 and transformed into a heritage center in 1975, covers 11 acres. Everywhere you turn are stone-faced warehouses, redbrick smokestacks, mills, still houses, and kilns, all interspersed with working waterwheels, whiskey barrels, and a 30,000-gallon, copper-plated pot—still the largest ever built. From March to November, if demand warrants, tours and free tastings are given weekdays 10–4. Even if you miss the tour, it's worth making the trek just to walk the distillery grounds. Inside is an exhibition center, museum, and, of course, gift shop. Bus Éireann runs coaches (17 per day, £4.50 round-trip) here from Cork's Parnell Place Station; take the bus going to Midleton and ask the driver to stop at the gate. *Midleton, tel. 021/631–594. Admission: £3.50. Open Mar.–Nov., daily 9–6.*

BLARNEY CASTLE

Blarney Castle, 8 km (5 mi) northwest of Cork City, is one of Ireland's best-known historic sites. In other words, it's plagued by herds of tourists and nearly impossible to enjoy; try to visit in the very early morning or be prepared to wait in long lines. That said, it's hard to deny the allure of the **Blarney Stone,** set in a wall below the castle's battlements. Tradition holds that all who kiss the Blarney Stone will gain the gift of "the Blarney," meaning eloquence and a crafty tongue. To receive this blessing, you lean backward from the second-story parapet and stick your head through a small opening, grasping an iron rail for support lest you fall into a murky shaft. Despite the difficulty, there's generally a long line of overweight retirees waiting to scale the skeletal remains of Blarney Castle, a strangely derelict edifice in this otherwise neatly groomed setting. *Admission: £3, £5 for combined ticket with Blarney House (see below). Open daily 9–6:30 (slightly shorter hrs in winter and on Sun.).*

The recently restored **Blarney House** (tel. 021/385–252), 200 yards from the castle, is a Scottish baronial mansion graced with a series of asymmetrical spires and stone chimney spouts. Inside are some fine Elizabethan and Victorian antiques showcased alongside period furniture and a handful of dark, ceiling-high portraits. *Admission: £2.50. Open July–Aug., Mon.–Sat. 12:30–5:30.*

BASICS

From Cork's Parnell Place Station, **Bus Éireann** offers 15 daily coaches (30 min, £2.60 round-trip) to Blarney Square, an easy walk from the castle. You can also walk (2 hrs) or hitch from Cork by taking the N8 past the train station and following the signs, or the N20 past Murphy's Brewery on Upper St. John Street. In Blarney itself there's a small **tourist desk** (The Square, tel. 021/381–624) with a bureau de change.

CLONAKILTY

This small but happening seaside village, about 51 km (32 mi) southwest of Cork, has become something of a buzzword in the Cork-area live-music scene. Strung along **Pearse Street,** the main thoroughfare, are a handful of pubs that host excellent traditional, folk, and blues bands almost every night of the week. The locals mingle peaceably with the growing immigrant musician population and are often, in fact, their loudest supporters. This mix makes for a true West Cork experience: hippies clad in Indian cotton sharing a bar with wizened local men, all tapping their feet to the sounds of a visiting folk duo. Popular, cluttered **De Barra's** (Pearse St., tel. 023/33381) usually has the best music lineups. Check their window for the night's entertainment. Other good bets are **Shanley's** (Connolly St., no phone), which hosts everything from blues and jazz to trad and folk seven nights a week in the summer, and **An Teach Beaj** (in O'Donovan's Hotel, Pearse St., tel. 023/33250), which rocks with traditional music every evening. Clonakilty's other draw is the nearby beaches. **Inchydoney** beach, about 5 km (3 mi) south, was once an island and is now a gorgeous stretch of sand connected to the mainland. From Cork, there are two buses a day to Clonakilty (£5.90 one-way, £7.90 round-trip); only one bus is direct, the other is via Skillereen.

THE WEST

CALE SILER AND LAURENCE BELGRAVE

A s even a Jackeen (Dubliner) will tell you, the West is distinctively different from the rest of Ireland. The area embodies, in a concentrated form, all the stereotypes generally associated with the country—whitewashed cottages, sheep, rugged seascapes, misty bog lands, and firelit country pubs, all processed through a filter of Guinness and traditional music.

Within Ireland, the West refers to the region that lies west of the River Shannon; most of this area falls within the old Irish province of Connaught. The coast of this region is situated at the western extremity of Europe, facing its nearest neighbors in North America across 3,200 km (2,000 mi) of Atlantic Ocean. While the East, the Southwest, and the North were influenced by either Norman, Scots, or English settlers, the West escaped systematic resettlement and, with the exception of the walled town of Galway, remained purely Irish in language, social organization, and general outlook for far longer than the rest of the country. The land in the West, predominantly mountains and bogs, did not immediately tempt the conquering barons. Oliver Cromwell was among those who found the place thoroughly unattractive, and he gave the Irish chieftains who would not conform to English rule the choice of going "to Hell or Connaught."

It was not until the late 18th century, when better transport improved communications, that the West started to experience the so-called foreign influences that had already Europeanized the rest of the country. The West was, in effect, dragged out of the 16th century and into the 19th. You will notice that all buildings of interest in the region date either from before the 17th century or from the late 18th century onwards.

Today, the West features the highest concentration of Irish-speaking communities and the best traditional musicians in the Republic. Many residents still live on small farms rather than in towns and villages (towns were unknown in pre-Christian Irish society); especially in winter, the smell of turf fires still pervades the region.

As in the Southwest, the population of the West was decimated by famine in the mid-19th century and by mass emigration from then until the 1950s. A major factor in the region's recovery from economic depression has been the attraction of visitors to its sparsely populated mountain landscape and long, indented coastline with its many lakes and rivers. Tourism's development, however, has been mercifully

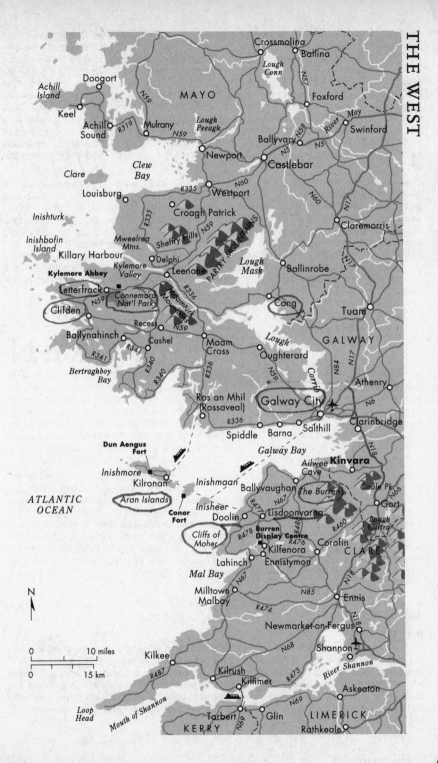

Crossmolina
Ballina
Lough Conn
Foxford
N57
River Moy
N58
Swinford
MAYO
N59
Doogort
Achill Island
Keel
Achill Sound
R319
Mulrany
N59
Newport
Ballyvary
N5
N5
Castlebar
Clew Bay
Clare
Louisburg
R335
Westport
N60
N60
N17
Claremorris
Croagh Patrick
Inishturk
Mweelrea Mtns.
Sheffry Hills
N59
PARTRY MOUNTAINS
Lough Mask
Ballinrobe
N17
Inishbofin Island
Killary Harbour
Delphi
Leenane
Kylemore Abbey
Kylemore Valley
Cong
Tuam
Letterfrack
Connemara Nat'l Park
R336
Lough Corrib
GALWAY
N84
Athenry
Clifden
N59
Maumturk Mountains
R336
N6
Ballynahinch
Recess
N59
Oughterard
R341
Cashel
Maam Cross
N59
R341
R340
R336
Corrib
N17
R340
Bertraghboy Bay
Ros an Mhil (Rossaveal)
R336
Galway City
Clarinbridge
N18
Spiddle
Barna
Salthill
ATLANTIC OCEAN
Dun Aengus Fort
Galway Bay
Ailwee Cave
Kinvara
Coole Pk
N66
Inishmore
Kilronan
Inishmaan
Ballyvaughan
The Burren
Gort
N66
Aran Islands
Inisheer
R477
N67
R460
Lough Cutra
Conor Fort
Doolin
Lisdoonvarna
R478
Cliffs of Moher
R478
Burren Display Centre
R476
Corofin
CLARE
Lahinch
Kilfenora
Ennistymon
N18
Mal Bay
N67
Milltown Malbay
R474
N85
Ennis
N
Newmarket-on-Fergus
N18
0   10 miles
0   15 km
Kilkee
N68
Shannon
Kilrush
Killimer
R473
River Shannon
Askeaton
R487
N69
Loop Head
Mouth of Shannon
Tarbert
Glin
N69
LIMERICK
KERRY
Rathkeale

low-key. Apart from a seaside promenade and fun palace at Salthill, just outside Galway, the area has seen no major investment in public amenities. Instead, additional land has been acquired for the Connemara·National Park. The existence of some of the best angling in Europe on the West's rivers, lakes, and seas accounts for many regular visitors. Most holiday cottages, so often a concrete blight on the Irish landscape, are built according to the model of the traditional thatched cabin. The residents of the West have encouraged the revival of such cottage industries as knitting, weaving, and woodworking; the provision of bed-and-breakfast in existing homes; and informal sessions of traditional music in small bars. The lack of razzmatazz makes the West an ideal destination for travelers on a tight budget. The place comes alive between June and September. April, May, and October are good times for an off-peak visit. Outside these months many places will be closed; nightlife options and restaurant choices become limited. During the winter, weather can be harsh, with gales and rain sweeping in day after day from the Atlantic.

Limerick, Ireland's third-largest city, is a nearby urban center. Northeast of Dingle on the banks of the River Shannon, Limerick is a dull, grimy expanse of parking lots, electronics stores, fast-food joints, and tacky tourist pubs and shops. It's an inevitable stop for those flying into **Shannon Airport,** 24 km (15 mi) west of the city, though once you arrive, you'll probably want to head as quickly as possible to anywhere else in Ireland. Happily, Limerick is well served by Bus Éireann and Irish Rail. Galway, the other big city in western Ireland, is a major bus hub with connections to all surrounding towns. The barren Aran Islands—with their Gaeltacht communities—are serviced by ferries from Galway and nearby Doolin, a tiny village with a huge traditional-music scene. You'll witness western Ireland's beauty from the bus window everywhere you travel, but a stop at the famed Cliffs of Moher or a cycle through the desolate limestone Burren will really bring home the strange beauty of the west.

THE BURREN

The Burren, a limestone escarpment in the western part of County Clare, ranks as one of Ireland's fiercest landscapes. No matter from which direction you approach the Burren, rolling green hills and smooth valleys quickly give way to jagged shelves of green-gray rock, rough and porous and bordered by a series of stark mountains. Even on a sunny day, the Burren seems stuck in mourning, silent except for the pound of the surf or the cry of a seagull scavenging the shore. Because it's so inhospitable, few actually live in the heart of the Burren, a narrow strip that hugs the coast from Black Head in the north to Doolin and the Cliffs of Moher in the south; the few villages you pass seem barely to grip the rugged terrain, grateful to have even a small clutch of earth in this otherwise unaccommodating region.

Like the desert, the Burren nourishes abundant animal and plant life despite the harsh conditions. Volumes have been written on the diverse species of plants and birds that manage to thrive here, and the best way to discover these is on foot. Dozens of signposted walks run through both coastal and inland areas, and most hostels stock topographic maps and organize reasonably priced day trips. The villages of **Lisdoonvarna** and **Doolin** (the unofficial music capital of Ireland) are also good bases for exploring the Burren. Both have comfortable hostels and are regularly serviced by Bus Éireann, though you can easily walk or cycle the short distance from one village to the next when the weather is good. The Burren is no secret, however, and summer crowds are a given, especially in Doolin. Unless you want to pitch a tent on a bed of rock, hostel reservations (even if only one day in advance) are strongly encouraged in July and August.

LISDOONVARNA

BASICS

There is a pointless **tourist office** (tel. 065/74630) outside town in Spa Wells, downhill from the Imperial Hotel. Much better is **Kincora House** (*see below*), which stocks maps and cycling guides and rents sturdy 18-speed bicycles (£6 per day, £30 per week). They also have a good idea of when buses come and go. Expressway buses stop at Lisdoonvarna's village square, once daily (twice in summer) from Dublin (£12) and at least twice daily on summer weekdays from Galway (£7.30), Ennis (£6), and Doolin (£2). Both the **post office** (Church St., tel. 065/74110) and the **Imperial Hotel** (Lisdoonvarna Ave., tel. 065/74042) have a bureau de change.

WHERE TO SLEEP

Cheap beds are not a problem except during September, when the Matchmaking Festival and the World's Barbecue Championship collide in a saucy mélange of chefs and hopeful bachelors. You'd never guess **Kincora House and Burren Holiday Hostel** (tel. 065/74300) only charges £6 (£6.50 July–Sept.)—this 19th-century mansion looks like an upscale hotel, with a bureau de change, a good pub, and a popular restaurant (entrées £4.50–£7). The four- to six-bed rooms are comfortable, the common room is huge and bright, and they rent bikes for £6 per day. Coming from the coast, this resort-style hostel is on your right just before town.

For comfortable B&B accommodations March–November, try the homey, family-run **Ravine House** (The Square, tel. 065/74043) or the classy **O'Loughlin's** (Church St., tel. 665/74038). They and the other 20 or so B&Bs in town have rooms for £13–£15 per person.

FOOD

With its memorabilia-covered walls and rustic charm, **Roadside Tavern** (Coast Rd., no phone) provides some of the best and most affordable pub grub in town. They serve soups (£2), sandwiches (£1.50), and lasagna (£4). **Dolmen Restaurant** (The Square, tel. 065/74760) offers entrées for less than £6. For groceries, **Family Value Supermarket** (The Square, tel. 065/74608) is open daily 7 AM–10 PM.

WORTH SEEING

Lisdoonvarna's location, 8 km (5 mi) inland from the sea and set atop a small hill, is well suited to excursions into the surrounding Burren. Particularly fun is the 6½-km (4-mi) walk or cycle to **Corkscrew Hill**, reputedly the curviest road in Ireland. From the top of this zigzag road there's an incredible view of County Clare, the Burren, and the Aran Islands. In the village of **Kilfenora**, 8 km (5 mi) south of Lisdoonvarna, is the **Burren Centre** (tel. 065/88030), open March–October, daily 10–5 and

> *Surveying the region for Oliver Cromwell in 1651, General P. Ludlow wrote that the "Burren is a country where there is not water enough to drown a man, wood enough to hang one, or earth enough to bury him."*

June–September, daily 9:30–6. For £2.20 you get to see a representative model of the Burren, an extensive display of the region's flora and fauna, and a short audiovisual show that does a good job of explaining the Burren's geology and topography. Adjoining the center is the **Kilfenora Cathedral**, whose graveyard is worth a look for the ruins of six crosses, including the 12th-century **Doorty Cross.** It's possible to camp in the fields behind the churchyard for £5 for two or more people; ask for Dermot Hogan at the shop across from the fields. Summer evenings in Lisdoonvarna are filled with the sounds of excellent traditional music. Weekend nights there are sessions (and dancing) in Lisdoonvarna's hostel, and top-rate music is played nightly at the nearby **Roadside Tavern** (Coast Rd., no phone), one of County Clare's best pubs.

DOOLIN AND THE CLIFFS OF MOHER

BASICS

There's a **tourist office** (tel. 065/81171) at the Cliffs of Moher open Easter–October, daily 10–6, with longer hours in summer. They have maps of the Burren (around £2) and a bureau de change. There's no tourist information office in Doolin, nor is there a bank, so, if you're living off your credit card or ATM card, stock up on quids before arriving. You can exchange cash or buy maps at the front desk in Doolin Hostel (*see below*), which also serves as both the local Raleigh Rent-A-Bike outlet and the **Bus Éireann** depot.

COMING AND GOING

Doolin is shaped like a long hourglass, with the Rainbow Hostel, Aille River Hostel, and McGann's and McDermott's pubs at one end and the Doolin Hostel and O'Connor's pub at the other, ½ km (¼ mi) down the main road. In the summer, Expressway buses run twice daily (once on Sundays) to Dublin (£12), Tralee (£9.70), Killarney, Cork, and the Cliffs of Moher. Buses to Galway (£8.20) and Lisdoonvarna (£1) run four times per day in the summer (twice on Sundays). Much cheaper is the **West Clare Shuttle** (tel. 088/517–963), which operates a daily service to Galway (£5) and Lisdoonvarna (£1) March–October. West Clare will also pick you up from wherever you're staying and transport bikes for £2. Call to see when the shuttle runs and to tell them where to pick you up.

WHERE TO SLEEP

It has finally happened: Doolin now has more B&Bs than residential houses, so pick one that strikes you. For great views of the cliffs, stay at **Atlantic View** (The Pier, tel. 065/74569), which has six clean rooms starting at £12. Of Doolin's three hostels, **Aille River** (tel. 065/74260) is the most comfortable. Its well-equipped kitchen, spacious common room, and free laundry facilities attract a lively crowd. It's open mid-March–early November and has dorm beds (£6.50), campsites (£3.50 per person), and doubles (£15). Farther up the road, **Rainbow Hostel** (tel. 065/74415) has cramped bedrooms with beds that sag (£6.50–£7), but there's a cozy common room, fireplace, and camping (£3). At the other end of town, **Doolin Hostel** (tel. 065/74006) offers £6.50–£7 dorm beds in large, rather characterless surroundings. The hostel also offers free 1½-hour guided walks of the Burren most evenings. The facilities, including a bureau de change, a tiny food shop, and bike rental, are good, but there's not much charm. You can set up camp at **Doolin Camping and Caravan Park** (The Pier, next to the ferry dock, tel. 065/74458) for £4 per tent site, plus £1 per person. The grounds are scenic but summer crowds are a serious problem. It's open May–September, and reservations and earplugs are recommended.

FOOD

Considering its size, Doolin has a staggering number of upscale restaurants. Of these, **Ivy Cottage** (Fisher St., near O'Connor's pub, tel. 065/74244) is the best. Housed in a cozy, candlelighted cottage, it offers a tremendous selection of home-baked breads, fresh seafood, and grilled meats nightly 6–9. A full meal with wine runs £11–£14. For a good mid-range meal, **Doolin Café** (tel. 065/74795) prepares vegetarian and vegan dishes for £4–£7. Doolin's **post office** (opposite Doolin Café, tel. 065/74209) doubles as the village's grocery store.

WORTH SEEING

Although this small village boasts a larger population of sheep than people, Doolin is *the* place to come for traditional music. Its international reputation has attracted many—if not all—big names in Irish music, who spend a summer or two here learning their trade from old-timers and any players who happen to drop in for a pint and a tune. Traditional music greats like Michael Russell, Kevin Griffin, and Sharon Shannon have all played here. Doolin's three pubs—**McGann's, McDermott's,** and **O'Connor's**—host top-rate music sessions nightly throughout the year. Summer, especially, draws crowds of tourists, but the music is unbeatable. Happily, the three pubs also habitually defy the puritanical 11:30 PM closing time by bolting the doors and drawing the curtains, obeying the "be a good man and pour us another pint" law of the country.

Doolin's other main draw is its proximity to both the Cliffs of Moher and the Aran Islands (*see below*), visible off the coast. The preferred way to see the **Cliffs of Moher** is to hike the 4-km (2½-mi) **Burren Way** from Doolin. Known also as the "Old Road," this rugged dirt trail (walk past the Doolin Hostel, cross the riverbed, and continue straight) keeps entirely to the coast, providing great views of the sea and the occasional village of run-down thatched cottages. Best of all, the trail approaches the cliffs from the less-touristed north side, where you can fearlessly walk to the very edge and have a picnic without being disturbed by the putter of tour buses. Be warned: At some points, the only thing separating you from the sea, 700 feet below, is a patch of slippery heather and a jagged overhang that may or may not offer a last-chance handhold. For other walks and a good rundown of the area's history, pick up Martin Breen's *Doolin Guide & Map* (£1.50), available in shops and at the Doolin Hostel.

The Aran Islands are accessible from both Doolin and Galway (*see below*). **Doolin Ferries** (Doolin Pier, tel. 065/74455) makes the 30-minute to two-hour (depending on the weather) trip to the islands of Inisheer (£15 round-trip) and Inishmore (£20 round-trip) daily between mid-April and late September. If demand warrants, they also head to Inishmaan (£18 round-trip). Departure and arrival times are notoriously unpredictable (due largely to the ornery weather in these parts), so be flexible.

GALWAY CITY

Galway, Ireland's fourth-largest and fastest growing city, is a progressive student town with a flair for the hip and offbeat. Despite its block houses and factories, Galway's small city center has the atmosphere of a bustling market town, especially in the streets that lead from the River Corrib to **Eyre Square,** the city's main social hub. Founded by the Normans in 1240 and later fortified and transformed into a prosperous trading outpost by the Lynch clan, Galway has since become western Ireland's most prominent music and arts center. Because of its close relation with the surrounding Gaeltacht (Irish-speaking region), Galway's music scene is happily and predominantly traditional. Lacking a large number of historic sites, Galway seems to cherish its traditional-music pubs with a vengeance, recognizing their importance to the town's cultural (and touristic) appeal. Civic pride also stems from the city's famed academic institution, the University College Galway (UCG). Opened in 1846 to promote the development of local industry and agriculture, UCG today has become a center for Irish-language and Celtic studies, attracting crowds of youthful misfits, buskers, New Age prophets, and wandering hippies. The Galway-based Druid Theatre Company and An Taibhdhearc Theatre also sustain Galway's commitment to Irish culture by staging a variety of raucously celebratory summer festivals. One of these, the **Galway Arts Festival** (tel. 091/583800), held in late July, showcases Irish and international drama in dozens of city-center venues. During the festival, Galway is packed with musicians (and tourists) from all over Ireland, so book a bed in advance and get to the pub early if you want a seat.

Galway also makes a good base for exploring western Ireland, since it's well served by train and bus from most major cities. During the day you can visit the Aran Islands (*see below*), Kinvarra Bay, or, if you're short on time, take in the Burren on a reasonably priced tour, but stay in town for the unbeatable nighttime pub scene. There are no less than nine hostels in Galway, a sure sign that it's neither the "hidden jewel" nor "quiet coastal village" that the tourist brochures would have you believe.

BASICS

LAUNDRY
Take your grubby clothes to **Bubbles Inn Laundry,** in the center of town, for a cheap (£3.50) wash and dry. *Mary St., tel. 091/563–434. Open Mon.–Sat. 8:45–6:15.*

MAIL
Take care of all your postal needs at Galway's main **post office**. *21 Eglinton St., tel. 091/562–051. Open Mon.–Sat. 9–5:30.*

VISITOR INFORMATION
The **tourist office** exchanges money, arranges tours of the city and county, and can book ferry tickets to the Aran Islands. They can also book you in a cheap B&B (£1 fee) or call hostels to check for vacancies. *Victoria Pl., tel. 091/563–081. From station, turn left on Eyre Sq., left on Merchants Rd. Open June–Aug., daily 9–8; Sept.–Apr., weekdays 9–5:45, Sat. 9–12:45.*

USIT, the student-run travel organization, has two offices in Galway. One is on the UCG campus (New Science Building, tel. 091/524–601), open weekdays 9:30–5. The other is directly across from the tourist office on Merchants Road (tel. 091/565–177) and is open weekdays 9:30–5:30, Saturday 10–1 (July–Aug. until 3).

COMING AND GOING

Ceannt Station (tel. 091/562–000 for bus info, 091/561–444 for train info), on the east corner of Eyre Square, doubles as the rail and bus depot. Inside the station is a bureau de change and an information and left-luggage desk. Galway is served by six daily trains from Dublin (£12); for any other destination you'll have to change in Athlone. **Bus Éireann** Expressway buses make daily hauls to Dublin (8 per day, £8), Donegal (3 per day, £10), Sligo (4 per day, £10.50), and Cork (3 per day, £12). To reach the hostels, shops, and pubs from the station, walk to the opposite corner of Eyre Square, turn left down Williamsgate Street, and cross the River Corrib.

If you want to cycle around the area, **Europa Bicycles** (Earl's Island, tel. 091/563–355) rents bikes for £5 per day, £25 per week, plus a £30 deposit. They'll transport you and your bike up to Connemara (or other biking musts) for £6. The local Raleigh Rent-A-Bike agent is **Celtic Cycles** (Queen St., off Victoria Pl., tel. 091/566–606), which rents bikes for £7 per day, £30 per week, with a £40 deposit.

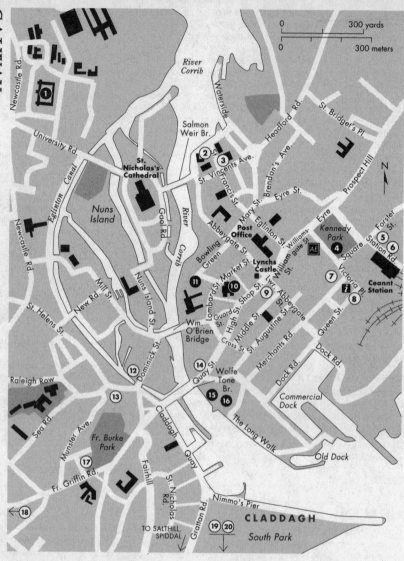

GALWAY

River Corrib

Salmon Weir Br.

Waterside

St. Bridget's Pl.

Headford Rd.

Prospect Hill

Newcastle Rd.

University Rd.

Eglinton Canal

St. Nicholas's Cathedral

St. Vincents Ave.

St. Francis St.

Brendan's Ave.

Eyre St.

Mary St.

Eyre St.

Kennedy Park

Forster St.

Nuns Island

Gaol Rd.

River Corrib

Mary St.

Eglinton St.

Post Office

Williams St.

Eyre Square

Station Rd.

Newcastle Rd.

Mill St.

Nuns Island St.

Bowling Green

Abbeygate St.

Market St.

Lynchs Castle

Williamsgate St.

AE

Victoria Pl.

Ceannt Station

St. Helens St.

New Rd.

Lombard St.

Shop St.

High St.

William St.

Lwr. Abbeygate St.

Queen St.

Guard St.

Cross St.

Middle St.

St. Augustine St.

Merchants Rd.

Dock Rd.

Dock Rd.

Raleigh Row

Dominick St.

Wm. O'Brien Bridge

Quay St.

Wolfe Tone Br.

The Long Walk

Commercial Dock

Sea Rd.

Munster Ave.

Fr. Burke Park

Claddagh Quay

Old Dock

Fr. Griffin Rd.

Fairhill

St. Nicholas Rd.

Grattan Rd.

Nimmo's Pier

CLADDAGH

TO SALTHILL, SPIDDAL

South Park

0 300 yards

0 300 meters

N

Sights ●

Civic Museum, **15**

Collegiate Church of St. Nicholas, **10**

Eyre Square, **4**

Nora Barnacle House, **11**

Spanish Arch, **16**

University, **1**

Lodging ○

Adare Guest House, **17**

Celtic Tourist Hostel, **8**

Corrib Villa, **2**

Galway City Hostel, **12**

Galway Hostel, **5**

Great Western Hostel, **6**

Inishmore Guest House, **18**

Kinlay House, **7**

Knockrea B&B, **19**

Le Chalet, **20**

Lydon House, **9**

Quay Street House, **14**

Salmon Weir Hostel, **3**

West End Hostel, **13**

WHERE TO SLEEP

SMALL HOTELS AND GUEST HOUSES

Cregg Castle. Set on a 165-acre wildlife preserve about 15 km (9 mi) north of Galway, this 17th-century castle is surprisingly informal. The Brodericks, the owners, all play instruments, and traditional sessions often take place around the huge, log-and-turf fire in the Great Hall. The bedrooms (£35 for a single, £60 for a double) vary in shape and size and are mainly decorated with sturdy Victorian bygones. Breakfast is served until noon around an antique dining table that seats 18 people, so be prepared for chatting. *Corrandulla, Co. Galway, tel. and fax 091/791–434. 10 rooms, 5 with bath. Closed Nov.–Feb.*

Jurys Galway Inn. This newly built, four-story hotel offers boring but budget accommodation (£53 per room). The atmosphere unavoidably tends toward anonymous-international, but each room is big enough for three adults or two adults and two children, and Jurys fixed-price policy applies to all of them. Try to get one overlooking the river; they're quieter than those in front. *Quay St., Co. Galway, tel. 091/566–444, fax 091/568–415. 128 rooms.*

Norman Villa. Dee and Mark Keogh's Victorian town house, midway between the city center and the seaside promenade of Salthill, is away from the bustle but within easy walking distance of both places. Brightly painted walls, Victorian brass beds with Irish linen sheets, varnished floorboards, working wooden shutters, and fun, off-beat paintings and artifacts make for lively, pleasant decor. Vegetarians are readily accommodated at breakfast. Double rooms cost £50. *86 Lower Salthill, Galway, tel. and fax 091/521–131. 5 rooms. Cash only. Closed Jan. 10–31.*

BED-AND-BREAKFASTS

Galway has more than 150 B&Bs scattered throughout its suburbs, and there are a few in the city center. One of the most convenient is **Lydon House** (8 Lower Abbeygate St., tel. 091/564–914), a city-center home with cozy doubles (£30) available March–October. Many B&Bs are clustered along Father Griffin Place, a five-minute walk from downtown along Quay Street. Try the very modern **Adare Guest House** (9 Father Griffin Pl., tel. 091/586–421), which has nine rooms with bath starting at £17.50 per person, or the charming **Inishmore Guest House** (109 Father Griffin Pl., tel. 091/582–639), with eight rooms for £16–£18 per person. Prospect Hill, which meets Eyre Square at its north corner, also has a string of look-alike B&Bs near the station. Otherwise, hop on Bus 1, labeled SALTHILL, and head for Lower Salthill Road, where you'll find at least 20 competitively priced B&Bs. **Le Chalet** (60 Lower Salthill, tel. 091/525–880) offers airy rooms with TVs, skylights, and en-suite baths for £16 per person, including a great breakfast. The gorgeous, pine-floored rooms at **Knockrea B&B** (55 Lower Salthill, tel. 081/523–196) are available for a bargain £14–£16 per person.

HOSTELS

Even during the summer, it's not very difficult to find a bed in one of Galway's many hostels. However, if you're planning to be in town during July or August, you should definitely book a bed at least two weeks in advance.

In addition to the hostels reviewed below, the following hostels also have beds for £5.50–£7: **Galway City Hostel** (25–27 Dominick St. tel. 091/566–367), **Galway Hostel** (Frenchville Ln., tel. 091/566–959), and **West End Hostel** (20 Upper Dominick St., tel. 091/583–636).

Celtic Tourist Hostel. Clean and modern with no personality whatsoever, this hostel's metal bunk beds (£5 per person, £7.60 in summer) with mauve comforters pack sterile dorm rooms. Smurf-size doubles are £20 (£22 summer). *Queen St., around the corner from tourist office, tel. 091/566–606. 46 beds. Common room, kitchen, luggage storage.*

Corrib Villa. What this old and dilapidated town house lacks in modernity, it makes up for in character. A clean kitchen, spacious common room, and no-stress management make this one of the better city-center hostels. A bed in a standard 6- to 10-bed room with lots of thick blankets is £6.50 (£7.50 in summer). *4 Waterside, tel. 091/562–892. From Eyre Sq., walk SW on Williamsgate St., turn right on Eglinton St. 24 beds.*

Great Western Hostel. This block-long hostel beckons weary backpackers from its perch directly opposite Ceannt Station. You can stay in an immaculate dorm room (£7.50–£8.50), a four-bed room with bath (£10.50–£12.50), or a double with bath (£28–£31). All rates include a Continental breakfast. They even have a pool table. *Frenchville Ln., tel. 091/561–150. 230 beds. Bureau de change, kitchen, laundry, luggage storage, sauna.*

Kinlay House. Relive your college dorm days at this monstrous, muraled hostel two minutes from Ceannt Station. Sure, it's institutional, but it has everything, including a free Continental breakfast. Dorm beds cost £8, doubles £12–£13. Flash your ISIC card for a 10% discount. *Merchants Rd., across from tourist office, tel. 091/565–244. 150 beds. Bureau de change, common room, kitchen, laundry, luggage/bike storage.*

Quay Street House. This is the serious pub-goer's paradise: It's just across the street from Quays Bar (one of Galway's most popular pubs) and steps away from a slew of great restaurants and coffee shops. Take your pick of a bed in a plain, overfilled dorm (£6.20), a four-bed room with bath (£8), or a double (£22). All prices are £1–£2 higher June–September. The common room rocks until the wee hours, which ensures that the hostel is pretty noisy. *10 Quay St., tel. 091/568–644. From station, head west along Eyre Sq., turn left on Williamsgate St. (which becomes Quay St.). 97 beds. Bureau de change, kitchen, laundry, luggage storage (50p).*

Salmon Weir Hostel. Salmon Weir does what no other Galway hostel can—combine an intimate, homey town house with small but extremely well-kept rooms. The happy staff organizes Monday night pub crawls and Thursday night barbecues (£3). Dorm beds are £5 (£7 in summer), double rooms £20. *3 St. Vincent's Ave., tel. 091/561–133. Head north from station, turn left on Eyre St., right on Eglinton St., right on St. Vincent's Ave. 40 beds. Curfew 3 AM. Kitchen, laundry, luggage storage.*

CAMPING

Grassy sites right on the water go for £3 per person at the **Salthill Caravan and Camping Park** (tel. 091/523–872). It's 1 km (½ mi) west of Salthill, open May–September, and has showers, laundry, and a TV room.

FOOD

Galway has an abundance of cheap and offbeat whole-food restaurants and cafés, most of which are south of Eyre Square between Abbeygate Street and the River Corrib. **Fat Freddy's** (Quay St., tel. 091/567–279) does good pizzas and pastas in the £5–£6 range and is the only cheapish sit-down place that's open on Sundays (daily 10–10). Try their beef-and-Guinness stew for £5.45. For bulk supplies and fresh vegetables, head to one of the many grocers along Shop and High streets. **Evergreen Health Food Store** (High St., tel. 091/564–215) has a good selection of fresh sandwiches, juices, breads, and organic foods, or visit the fruit and vegetable market, held Saturday mornings on Market Street, near St. Nicholas Church.

UNDER £5 • Couch Potatas. Wonderful smells waft from this immensely popular restaurant serving monstrously huge potatoes filled with almost anything you can imagine for £4. The menu also includes delicious brown bread, soups, vegetarian dishes, and homemade pies. *40 Upper Abbeygate St., tel. 091/561–664. Cash only.*

Food for Thought. Homemade soups, sandwiches, and veggie casseroles for less than £3 are indeed food for thought. While this living-room-size café doesn't look like much, it's one of the cheapest and least pretentious places around. *Lower Abbeygate St., no phone. Cash only. Closed Sun.*

The Home Plate. Galway's local youth and visiting backpackers come here in droves for generous portions of excellent home-cooked food. The most popular dish is the chicken or vegetarian pita fajita (£3.25–£4), which comes with a heaping plate of mixed salad, fresh veggies, rice, refried beans, pita bread, and a drink. For breakfast there's all things fried with French bread for £3. *Mary St., off Abbeygate St., tel. 091/561–475. Cash only.*

McDonagh's. Ask any local where to get a cheap meal and they'll steer you to McDonagh's, Galway's most popular chipper. You can tell it's a classy chippy because they actually have tables to eat at while the aquarium-bound lobsters glare at you. *22 Quay St., tel. 091/565–001. Cash only.*

The Round Table. A 15-foot-high stone fireplace makes a splendid centerpiece to this 16th-century dining room. The popular, down-to-earth eatery specializes in hearty pork, beef, and chicken dishes and tasty desserts. The mammoth breakfast is also worth a try. *6 High St., tel. 091/564–542. Cash only.*

Runner Bean. This comfy little place with brightly painted tables and stools has vegetarian dishes like quiche (£3.75) and vegetarian curry (£4). They also offer chicken-and-pineapple sandwiches (£2) and tacos for the carnivorous. *20 Mary St., tel. 091/569–292. Cash only.*

UNDER £10 • Bridge Mills. A 400-year-old former grain mill right beside the River Corrib has been renovated into a minimall (oh no, they're everywhere!), and this restaurant dominates the ground floor. You can sit outside beside a bubbling stream and watch local fishermen pulling salmon out of the river. During the day, the fare includes freshly made salads and sandwiches and hot daily specials, with desserts like fresh fruit tarts and homemade crepes. The evening menu is more substantial: roast rack of lamb with mustard and tarragon, 10-ounce sirloin steaks, and vegetarian specials like the spinach-and-ricotta cannelloni. *O'Brien's Bridge, Galway, tel. 091/566–231.*

House of Bards. Come here for refined, upscale dining in a beautiful 16th-century villa. Surprisingly, this family-run place caters less to the AmEx crowd than to locals looking for candlelighted intimacy and superbly conceived menus. Lunch (£4–£5) and dinner (£5–£14) menus change regularly but generally include a steak, lamb, and fresh-fish course, complemented by homemade soups and desserts. If you're looking to splurge, this is the place. Reservations are recommended on weekends. *1 Market St., tel. 091/568–414. Cash only.*

McDonagh's Seafood Bar. The McDonagh's are one of Galway's most entrepreneurial families, and this spot is a longtime town landmark. It's now partly a fish-and-chips bar and partly a "real" fish restaurant. If you've yet to try fish-and-chips, this is the place to take the plunge: cod, whiting, mackerel, haddock, or hake is deep-fried in a light batter and served with a heap of freshly cooked chips. Or try Galway oysters au naturel or a bowl of mussels steamed in wine and garlic. *22 Quay St., Galway, tel. 091/565–001.*

WORTH SEEING

Your first impression of Galway is bound to be **Eyre Square,** opposite Ceannt Station in the center of town. Formerly a green where livestock and produce were sold, it's not much to look at today, but the park in its center (named Kennedy Park in honor of JFK's 1963 visit to Galway) is a fine place for a picnic or an afternoon snooze. From Eyre Square's west corner, Galway's main shopping artery leads to the River Corrib. Confusingly known at different points as Williamsgate Street, William Street, Shop Street, High Street, and Quay Street, this is where you'll find the best pubs, restaurants, tourist shops, and most of Galway's youth hostels. On nearby Market Street is the **Nora Barnacle House** (4 Bowling Green, Market St., tel. 091/564–743), birthplace of James Joyce's wife. Joyce and Nora Barnacle first met in Dublin on June 16, 1904, a date known to most Joyce fans as Bloomsday because *Ulysses* follows its hero, Leopold Bloom, on that day. Inside the house is a mediocre collection of photographs and letters and a small gift shop. The house is open mid-May–mid-September, Monday–Saturday 10–5, and admission is £1. Also close by is the **Collegiate Church of St. Nicholas** (Market St., tel. 091/564–648), one of the best-preserved medieval churches in Ireland. Built in 1320, the interior is filled with interesting carvings, and rumor has it that Christopher Columbus stopped in here to pray before sailing off to distant lands.

At the opposite end of town are the **Spanish Arch** and **Civic Museum** (tel. 091/567–641), both visible along the river near Quay Street. The arch, built in 1594 to shelter stores of Spanish wine unloaded to the docks, is easily (and often) mistaken for a pile of weathered stones. The museum (admission £1; open daily 10–1 and 2:15–5:15), built into the arch's base, houses an exhibit of old photographs and miscellaneous antiques, from fishing hooks to rusty food tins. Galway's other main draw is the **university,** on the opposite side of the River Corrib from town and clearly visible from the Salmon Weir Bridge. Much of the campus is modern and unfriendly looking; only the Tudor-style courtyard and the administrative block (1845) save it from the aesthetic trash heap. The university library (tel. 091/524–411), open weekdays 9:30–5, has an impressive collection of dusty manuscripts and volumes of Galway's municipal records, mostly penned between 1485 and 1820. **Lynchs Castle,** on the corner of Shop and Abbeygate streets, now houses an AIB bank. The stone work on the outside of the building has some great gargoyles leering down at you. Within the bank foyer (open weekdays 10–4) is a detailed history of the castle, with old prints and drawings displaying its original state and surroundings.

If you want to explore nearby regions in western Ireland, **Western Heritage** (34 Carragh Hill, tel. 091/521–699) offers tours of both the Burren and Connemara for £8–£11. The five-hour Burren tour departs Galway at 11:30 AM daily and includes stops at the Cliffs of Moher, Kinvarra, and Poulnabrone Dolmen. The Connemara tour leaves Galway daily at 1 PM and stops at the Ross Erilly Medieval Friary, the "Quiet Man" village of Cong, and Hen's Castle. **Bus Éireann** (Ceannt Station, tel. 091/562–000) and **Lally's Coach Tours** (19 Shop St., tel. 091/562–905) offer similar tours at basically the same rates, as well as tours of Galway Town for about £4. Lally's tends to focus more on Yeats and The Quiet Man than the others.

SHOPPING

Cobwebs (7 Quay Lane) stocks small antiques and gifts with an accent on nostalgia. Stop at **Claddagh Jewellers** (Eyre Sq.) for jewelry; the store has a wide selection of traditional Claddagh rings. **The Galway Woolen Market** (21–22 High St.) offers good value in sweaters. **Kenny's Bookshop** (High St.) offers five floors of books of Irish interest, mainly secondhand and antiquarian, as well as prints, maps, and a small art gallery. Check out **The Cornstore** (Middle St.), a stylish new shopping mall. **The Eyre Square Shopping Centre** (Eyre Sq.) offers a wide range of midprice clothing and household goods. **Design Ireland Plus** (Unit 14, Eyre St. Shopping Centre, Eyre Sq.) has an excellent range of Irish-made crafts and clothing.

AFTER DARK

Given Galway's great pubs, and live music and theater scenes, there's no lack of options for evening entertainment. Pick up the free *Galway Advertiser,* a weekly newspaper available in stores and at the tourist office, for listings of Galway events.

PUBS AND CLUBS

There are dozens of good pubs scattered throughout Galway's eminently crawlable city center. For traditional music, **Taaffes** (19 Shop St., tel. 091/564066) and **King's Head** (15 High St., tel. 091/566630) are musts, though a recent deluge of video-camera-bearing and green-sweater-wearing folks threatens the authenticity of their summer sessions (winter sessions, however, are still tourist-free). Two underpublicized old-style pubs that have good reputations with local traditional-music fans are **An Púcán** (11 Forster St. tel. 091/561528) and **Crane Bar** (2 Sea Rd., tel. 091/587419). At the other end of the spectrum, **The Snug** (Shop St., tel. 091/564771) is popular with UCG students and classic-rock lovers. **Lisheen Bar** (Bridge St., tel. 091/563804) and **Sally Long's** (33 Upper Abbeygate St., tel. 091/565756) are dependable for jazz and folk. From an aesthetic point of view, **The Quays** (Quay St., tel. 091/568347) is Galway's most impressive pub. The never-ending, wood-paneled, cavernous interior— including a sunken back room—is done in brass and features several long bars.

Galway's postpub nightclub scene is formidable. In the center of town is **Central Park Disco** (36 Upper Abbeygate St., tel. 091/565974), popular with the twentysomething crowd. The cover hovers around £3–£5. Otherwise, most everyone heads to Salthill, a small suburban community 3 km (2 mi) west of Galway. The main road, Upper Salthill, is lined with clubs. Try **Liquid** (tel. 091/722715) for nightly indie and techno music, or **Warwick** (tel. 091/521244, cover £3–£7.50), which plays '70s, '80s, and indie music.

THEATER

Galway's theater scene is nearly world famous, and if either of its two home companies are in town, do not fail to lay your hands on some tickets. **The Druid Theatre Company** (Quay St., tel. 091/568660), which produces lunchtime and evening shows in their **Chapel Lane Theatre** (tel. 091/568617), has built an international reputation with their revivals of Anglo-Irish classics and a slew of Irish-language plays. More touristy, but no less entertaining, **An Taibhdhearc Theatre** (Middle St., tel. 091/562024) is famous for its bilingual productions of lesser-known Irish plays, generally accompanied by live traditional music and bawdy pantomime. Productions are most frequent during summer; stop by their Middle Street theater for performance schedules or inquire at the tourist office. The **Punchbag Co.** (6 Quay Ln., tel. 091/565422) does successful commercial shows (in English) that attract the unpretentious masses. Tickets for performances range from £6 to £10, and student discounts are often available.

NEAR GALWAY

KINVARA

Kinvara is not as striking as the Burren or as lively as Doolin, but it is a picture-perfect seaside village 18 km (11 mi) southeast of Galway that is easily reached by bus or bicycle. Kinvara's most notable attraction is **Dunguaire Castle** (1 km/½ mi west of town, tel. 091/37108), a squat tower set atop a rock on the fringe of Galway Bay. Originally built by merchants between 1450 and 1650, its two previous owners, Oliver St. John Gogarty (surgeon and model for Joyce's Buck Mulligan) and Lady Ampthill, both commissioned modest restorations. Admission to the castle, open May–September, daily 9:30–5, is £2.35.

COMING AND GOING • Bus Éireann sends buses (£5) to Kinvarra from Galway once daily during winter, four times daily in the summer. If you're cycling, avoid the N67 and stick to the coast. Although the coast road adds a good 5 km (3 mi) to the ride, it's less congested and infinitely more scenic.

WHERE TO SLEEP AND EAT • The semi-isolated IHH **Johnston's Hostel** (tel. 091/37164), on Kinvara's main (and only) road, is open June–September and offers comfortable four- to six-bed dorm rooms (beds £6) and tent sites (£3.50 per person). Otherwise, try **Kinvarra House** (tel. 091/37118) or **Cois Cuain** (tel. 091/37119), the village's best moderately priced B&Bs. Both are closed November–February and charge £14–£16 per person.

Kinvara has a solid handful of great pubs (try the Ould Shawl or Winkles), as well as **Café on the Quay** (tel. 091/37654), on the quay overlooking the bay. The café is one of the best restaurants in County Galway. Particularly exceptional are the salmon pasta (£6), Irish stew (£6), and ginger sponge cake (£1.65)—reason enough to visit this sleepy village. The café is open daily 9–9 in summer, irregularly in winter.

ARAN ISLANDS

No one knows for certain when the Aran Islands—Inishmore, Inishmaan, and Inisheer—were first inhabited, but judging from the number of Bronze and Iron Age forts found here (especially on Inishmore), 3000 BC is a safe guess. Why scraggly nomads in deerskin jerkins would be attracted to these barren islets remains a greater mystery, not the least because fresh water and farmable land were (and still are) scarce commodities. Much of the islands' arable land, in fact, is the by-product of centuries of erosion. After clearing as many loose stones as possible (which now form stone walls all over the islands), early farmers carpeted the ground with seaweed and kelp. Years and countless rain showers later, this decomposed to make soil suitable for shallow-rooted crops and grass. Add sheep, horses, and cows, their attendant tons of manure, and a few generations of backbreaking labor, and you have a proven recipe for transforming rocky wasteland into reasonably productive cropland.

During the 1800s, the islands, wracked by famine and mass emigration, were virtually forgotten by mainland Ireland. At the turn of the 20th century, however, they became the focus of renewed attention. Intrigued by the islanders' rugged lifestyle and centuries-old traditions, the playwright J. M. Synge spent four summers on Inishmaan between 1898 and 1902. Both his book, *The Aran Islands,* and his play, *Riders to the Sea,* prompted Gaelic revivalists to study and document this isolated bastion of Irish culture and to work for the islanders' economic development. In 1934, American director Robert Flaherty filmed his classic documentary *Man of Aran* (screened daily in Kilronan town hall on Inishmore), bringing the islands into the world spotlight. Much has changed since the film was made, but the islands continue to preserve a way of life that's all but disappeared on the mainland. This alone is reason enough to make the ferry ride from Galway or Doolin. To appreciate the fierce loneliness of the islands, however, you must spend the night on one. Because all the islands, especially Inishmore, crawl with day-trippers between 11 AM and 6 PM, it's difficult to let the rugged beauty of the islands sink into your soul until around 10 PM, when the sky is dark, the wind howling, and the pubs filled with the acrid smell of peat smoke and Guinness.

COMING AND GOING

BY FERRY • **Island Ferries** (Merchant Rd., next to tourist office, Galway, tel. 091/568903) serves all three islands year-round, departing from Rossaveal, 37 km (23 mi) away. Island Ferries buses depart from the tourist office to meet the three ferries bound for Inishmore, daily April–October at 9:15 AM, 12:15 PM, and 5:15 PM. The ferry journey takes 45 minutes and costs £19 round-trip, including the bus ride. Island Ferries also depart once a day to Inisheer and to Inishmaan at 11:15 AM; catch the 9:15 bus from the tourist office. Ferries from Inishmaan and Inisheer leave for Inishmore around 4 PM daily. The interisland trips cost £6. In the winter, service to Inishmore is reduced to once per day, with additional trips (for any of the three islands) dependent on demand and weather. Reservations at least one day in advance are strongly advised during July and August.

O'Brien Shipping/Doolin Ferries (Victoria Pl. tourist office, Galway, tel. 091/567283) sends ferries once a day June–September from Galway Harbour to all three islands. The trip takes about 90 minutes and costs £15 round-trip. They travel directly to the smaller islands on Wednesday and Thursday in the summer. They also travel to Inishmore every other day in the winter, weather and demand permitting.

INISHMORE

WHERE TO SLEEP

If you want to stay through the witching hour, when dusk turns Inishmore hauntingly barren, be sure to book early into the IHH **Mainistir House** (tel. 099/61169). Located 1 km (½ mi) west of Kilronan's ferry port (walk uphill and follow the main road) and built on a rock plateau overlooking Galway Bay, the Mainistir House offers comfortable B&B-style accommodations for £8.80–£10 per person, including Continental breakfast. In the evening Joel's "vaguely vegetarian" buffet costs £7 (£8 for nonguests) and is highly recommended. Mainistir House also offers an off-season deal with Island Ferries: transportation to the island and one night's accommodation for £21.

Otherwise, **Dun Aengus House** (tel. 099/61318), 6½ km (4 mi) west on the far side of the island, offers dorm beds (£6) April–October. This place is quiet and scenic, but you'll have to depend on their erratic shuttle bus to reach town unless you have a bike and don't mind a long, winding ride through the country. A third hostel right next to the pier is due to open by early 1998. You'll find B&B's along most of the main roads on the island. One of the nicest is **Clai Bán** (tel. 099/61111), open mid-March–September; it's a five-minute, signposted walk from Kilronan's small center, with rooms for £13 per person. Down the road, **An Crugan** (tel. 099/61150), open March–November, is also a safe bet, with rooms for £13.50 per person.

WORTH SEEING

Inishmore (Inis Mór, or Large Island) is the biggest, most popular island of the three. Most people visit only for the day, content to see the island from the window of a minibus before catching the last ferry back to Galway. Once these folks clear out, Inishmore's stunningly fierce and brooding beauty is disturbed only by the "baa" of sheep and the incessant rush of the wind. Even if you only have a few hours to explore Inishmore, spend £5 on a rental bike (available next to the pier) and head straight for **Dun Aengus,** a 4,000-year-old stone fort perched on the edge of a 300-foot cliff, on the far side of the island, 8 km (5 mi) from the port. Along the way, about 5 km (3 mi) from the fort, you'll pass a cluster of religious ruins—a few small churches, a monastery, and some crosses—called **The Seven Churches.** At the southern end of the island, **Black Fort** (Dun Duchathair) is Inishmore's other archaeological treasure, built around 1000 BC into a cleft of razor-sharp rocks. According to military historians, this cliff-top fort was probably the most defensible in Ireland, evident by the fact that it was never overrun in battle. Unfortunately, erosion and landslides have done what military might could not, and sections of the stone battlements have been destroyed. An intriguing history of the islands is provided by the **Aran Heritage Centre** (Kilronan, tel. 099/61355), which is open April–October, daily 10–7. For £2 you'll discover fossils, ingenious farming techniques, a few cheese-ball models, and a cliff rescue cart for saving shipwrecked sailors. Buy the £3.50 combo ticket to watch one of the frequent showings of Robert Flaherty's famous *Man of Aran.*

A number of locals also offer minivan tours of Inishmore. Prices range from £3 to £7 per person, depending on your ability to haggle, and most last two or three hours. The islanders know the ferry timetables by heart and congregate on the pier at the appropriate hours. Several bike shops lie on the harbor and charge £5 per day. Toward sunset a handful of locals pedal their squeaky bicycles down the long road to **Kilronan,** the island's port and largest village. A few pubs share this block-long, harbor-front settlement with a chipper, a grocery store, and a **tourist office** (tel. 099/61263), open late May–mid-September, Monday–Saturday 10–6ish, depending on the weather and crowd. Day-trippers can leave their luggage here (75p) or with one of the bike shops for free if you rent from them. The best two bars in town are **Joe Watty's** (on the main road between Kilronan and Mainistir House, tel. 099/61155) and **Joe Mac's** (right off the pier).

INISHMAAN

WHERE TO SLEEP

Inishmaan's tourist industry is in its infancy, which means that accommodations here are strictly B&B. In fact, there are only two Bord Fáilte-approved B&Bs on the island and, confusingly enough, both are run by a Mrs. Faherty (not related). **Angela Faherty's B&B** (Creigmore, tel. 099/73012) is open April–October and costs £12 per person. Maura Faherty's **Ard Alainn B&B** (West Village, tel. 099/73027) costs £11 per person (£12 in high-season). Reservations are a must. Camping is possible in any one of a hundred rocky fields, but you must obtain permission from the owner in advance.

WORTH SEEING

Inishmaan (Inis Meáin, or Middle Island) is both less touristed and, in many ways, more scenic than Inishmore. Though it doesn't have a wealth of archaeological sites, the ruins of **Dún Conchúir** (*see below*), a 3rd-century stone fort overlooking a valley, and **Cill Cheannannaech** (½ km/¼ mi from the pier), a church from the 8th century, make interesting stops. Inishmaan is surprisingly lush—compared with Inishmore's rock-strewn terrain—and is dominated by smooth patches of heather and pasture. Still, there isn't much arable land, and Inishmaan's 350 residents rely mostly upon fishing for their livelihood, so you're more likely to see people sporting cable-knit sweaters, knee-length boots, and woolen caps here than on the other islands. Around 8 PM on summer nights you can sometimes see the currachs, hide- and tar-covered fishing skiffs, unload the day's catch at beachfront landings all along the shore.

To get a sense of the island's antiquity, head to **Dún Conchúir** (Connor's Fort), the largest of all Aran stone forts. Measuring 225 by 115 feet, with walls 20 feet high, the fort dominates the landscape from its position atop a cliff in the island's center, brooding over a sunken valley. To the east, a small footpath leads to **Cathaoir Synge** (Synge's Chair), one of the playwright's favorite sea-viewing points, carved neatly into the rock. A **tourist desk** (inside An Cora, tel. 099/73092) is open June–September daily 11–6, and has maps and hiking info. For refreshment, pull up a stool at **O'Conghaille's Pub** (tel. 099/73003), a smoky, friendly drinking room that serves sandwiches and soup and often hosts traditional music on summer weekends.

As you pedal around Inishmore, keep your eyes peeled for faded signs pointing the way to the impressive sets of ruins scattered about the island.

INISHEER

Inisheer (Inis Oírr, or Eastern Island) is the smallest island in the Aran chain, but its proximity to Doolin in County Clare 11 km (7 mi) means it's often packed with day-trippers. On the plus side, Inisheer's relative prosperity means you'll find a hostel, a cheapish hotel, numerous B&Bs, pubs, and restaurants near the ferry dock. The island is suitable for an overnight stay, especially since you can (and should) walk its entire length, 3 km (2 mi), in the dark without fear of getting too lost (there are only two roads). By day, you'll want to check out the ruins of **O'Brien Castle,** set inside a stone-ringed fort that's clearly visible from the pier. The castle itself was built in the 15th century by the O'Brien clan, which ruled Inisheer from 1150 to 1585.

At sunset, you'll find most people ambling slowly toward the pier-side village and its pubs. Inisheer's two most popular pubs are attached to hostels. One hundred yards from the pier, **Radharc na Mara** (tel. 099/75024) offers standard dorm-style accommodations (£6) for 40 people. It doesn't look like much, but its cozy common room has a blazing peat fire whenever the weather is gray (i.e., always). Next door is the hostel's excellent pub and restaurant, the latter serving soups, sandwiches, and stews for £3–£5. Nearby, **Ostan Inis Oír** (tel. 099/75020) offers hotel-style accommodations (£15–£17 per person) to herds of well-to-do tourists between mid-April and August. Its restaurant (open to nonguests) is a better deal: Hearty steak and seafood dishes are £5–£10. You can also stay at **Inisheer Hostel** (near the post office, tel. 099/75077), which has 10 beds for £5. **Fisherman's Cottage** (tel. 099/75073) serves fish dishes for lunch in the £3.30–£7 range. Between May and September, you can camp at **Lathair Campala** (tel. 099/75008), 1 km (½ mi) north of the ferry port and well signposted from the docks. The 40 sites (£2) all have good views of the coast.

CONNEMARA

The Connemara region, in the northwest corner of County Galway, is wild and desolate. Its geography—expanses of windswept bog land buffered by mountains, white-sand beaches, and glacial lakes—provides endless fodder for the "rugged and rural" Irish stereotype. Part of Connemara's appeal stems from the extremes of its landscape, noted for such features as the Twelve Pin Mountains, Lough Corrib, and Killary Harbour. Botanists and rangers from the **Connemara National Park Visitor Centre** (tel. 095/

41054; open May–Sept., daily 9:30–6:30), near Letterfrack, lead walking tours at 10:30 AM Mondays, Wednesdays, and Fridays during July and August. The walks highlight the varied features of the park's bog lands, megalithic tombs, and flora and fauna, and cost £2, including admission to the center. Aside from the stunning geography, Connemara is equally popular for its lazy country feel and for the rugged characters who live in the area. Although Connemara is not heavily Irish-speaking, its relative isolation has helped to insulate it from the nastier effects of mass tourism, which in turn has helped to foster a more traditional, some even say a more authentically Irish, style of living. On the downside, Connemara's rugged conditions present certain travel problems, especially for those traveling in winter when Bus Éireann goes into semihibernation.

CONG

BASICS

Cong's **tourist office** (Abbey St., tel. 092/46542), open March–September, daily 10–6, has brochures and maps on Cong and Connemara and a bureau de change. If you plan to hike the area, pick up the booklet "Cong: Sights, Walks, Stories" (£2.50), which details some excellent, scenic walks. Buses go to and from Galway (£5.50) once per day (except Sun.). The stop is in front of Ryan's Hotel on Main Street. Cong's **post office** (Main St., tel. 092/46001) is open weekdays 9–1 and 2–5:30.

WHERE TO SLEEP

Cong theoretically has two hostels, but one is closed most of the year and the other lies a good distance from the village. Both charge £6 per person, have a laundry, are utterly spotless, and show *The Quiet Man* every night at 9 PM. **The Quiet Man Hostel** (Abbey St., tel. 092/46511), a prim town house in the center of town, is the cozier of the two, but is only open June–August. Down the Galway Road (1½ km/1 mi) is An Óige's **Cong Hostel** (Lake Quay Rd., tel. 092/46089), a thoroughly modern and clean place with a huge kitchen and cozy TV room. They also offer a shuttle to town; have flat, grassy camping sites (£3.75 per person); and rent fishing rods (£1) to snag the many trout and salmon in the adjacent and stunningly beautiful Lough Corriband. Neither has a strict lockout or curfew. If you're looking for some privacy, **The White House** (Abbey St., tel. 092/46358) charges £15 per person and is across from the Cong Abbey. Less comfortable is **Rising of the Waters Inn** (Main St., tel. 092/46316), which charges £12 per person and has a run-down pub downstairs with sandwiches under £2. Both are closed for the winter. If all of the above are full or they just don't take your fancy, then head to **Corrnamona** (The Bend in the Bog), a cluster of houses, two pubs, and a good village shop on the road to Maam. Facing the road is the **Corrnamona Hostel** (tel. 092/48002), a very basic accommodation with comfortable beds and a peculiar charm. Beds in a huge dormitory are £5.50, and they have a laundry (£1.50) and rent bikes (£6). You can also hire boats in the village for £12 a day to explore Lough Corrib. The hostel is open from April to September.

WORTH SEEING

Resting on a narrow isthmus between Lough Corrib and Lough Mask on the County Mayo border, Cong is dotted with ivy-covered thatched cottages and dilapidated farmhouses. Just two blocks long, and bisected by the chocolate-brown River Cong, the village is surrounded on all sides by thickly forested hills. Unfortunately there is something a little too refined about the place; perhaps all those film stars left a lot of airs and graces behind. Also nearby is the immensely posh Ashford Castle (tel. 092/46003). Built by the De Burgos family in 1228, the castle was purchased by the Guinness family and transformed into a luxury hotel in the early 1970s. You'll need upward of £200 per person to spend the night here, but visitors are encouraged to walk the castle's grounds (admission £3). If you can manage it, poke your head inside the lobby, which is decorated in period style and oozes aristocratic elegance. An infinitely more romantic way to see the castle is via rowboat, which you can rent (£6 for 2 hours) from the Cong Hostel (*see above*).

Cong's other main attractions are the remains of **Cong Abbey,** built in 1120 by Turlough Mór O'Connor, king of Connaught, and now open (free) to the public. There's not much to this roofless, skeletal ruin, but if you continue past the abbey toward the banks of Lough Corrib, about a mile south, you'll get a clear view of the stupendous natural beauty that surrounds the town. Take a short detour on one of the signposted footpaths that meander through the Cong Hills and you'll end up in dense, old-growth forest. Cong is also surrounded by many caves, stone circles, and burial mounds. The impressive **Pigeon Hole** cave is 1½ km (1 mi) from town on the road to Clonbur, and **Giant's Grave,** one of Ireland's megalithic burial chambers, is 1 km (½ mi) farther. Ask at the tourist office for hiking information and maps.

CLIFDEN

BASICS

Clifden's small **tourist office** (Market St., tel. 095/21163) is open May–September, Monday–Saturday 9–6; also July–August, Sunday noon–4. The office distributes maps and brochures, exchanges money, and organizes day trips to Inishbofin Island (*see below*), starting at £10. The **Bus Éireann** depot is in front of Cullen's on Market Street. Expressway buses from Galway (£7) stop here five times daily July–September, once daily in other months. Other destinations include Cong (1 per day in summer, £7) and Cleggan (2 per week). Pat Lydon's **Mini & Midi Coach Hire** (095/41043) is the local bus company, offering daily trips between Clifden and Westport, stopping in Cleggan along the way, for £7 round-trip. The bus runs twice daily Monday–Saturday in the summer (if there is demand). Michael Nee's **Connemara Bus** (tel. 095/51082) runs between Cleggan and Galway twice daily in the summer (£7 round-trip, £5 one-way) and once a day otherwise. The local Raleigh Rent-A-Bike agent is **Mannion's** (Bridge St., tel. 095/21160), just off Main Street on the east side of town, which rents bikes for £7 per day, £30 per week, plus a £10 deposit. Change your money at **AIB Bank** (The Square, tel. 095/21129), open weekdays 10–12:30 and 1:30–4.

WHERE TO SLEEP

For a town its size, Clifden has more than enough hostels to accommodate the summer rush. The very modern **Clifden Town Hostel** (Market St., ½ block west of the bus stop, tel. 095/21076) has comfy dorm beds (£7–£8) and private rooms (£9). Unfortunately, the staff has more than a little attitude. The IHH **Leo's Hostel** (The Square, tel. 095/21429) commands the best views of any hostel in town: Most rooms (and even one choice toilet) look out over the bay and surrounding mountains. Standard dorm beds cost £7–£8, doubles £12–£14; an excellent campsite with great views out over the bay and full use of the hostel facilities costs £3 per person. The hostel also rents bikes at £5 a day. For loads of authentic Irish hospitality, try the family-run **Brookside Hostel IHH** (Hulk St., off Bridge St., tel. 095/21812), which offers spartan but clean dorm accommodations (beds £7–£8). Proprietor Richard Bartley gives copious advice on the best hiking and biking in the area. Brookside Hostel offers reduced rates for the Inishbofin ferry (£9) and is fully wheelchair accessible. The run down but cozy **Blue Hostel** (across from Leo's, no phone) is really, really small and has 26 dorm beds for £5 apiece. They also have the traveler's holy grail—free laundry facilities in the high season.

There are a dozen good B&Bs huddled together on Bridge Street, east of the square off Main Street. Try **Ben View House** (Bridge St., tel. 095/21256), which has 10 refined rooms with bath from £15 per person, or **Errismore House** (Bridge St., tel. 095/21360), which has five rooms starting at £14 per person. Both are in small, family-inhabited flats—the sorts of places where the fried breakfasts are lovingly steeped in grease and served in huge portions.

WORTH SEEING

During summer, Clifden is painfully overcrowded with snap-happy tourists and luxury coaches from Galway, proof that Clifden is indeed the unrivaled "capital" of Connemara. For the past few years the town has been subject to intense tourist development in the style of Killarney. Although not yet tainted to the same degree as that southern town, some of Clifden's old charm and timelessness have disappeared forever. Despite the crowds, however, its old rural market-town flavor is especially ripe during August's world-famous **Connemara Pony Show**, usually held during the third week of the month. It's worth booking a bed well in advance for this festival, which features horse traders from a dozen countries parading their yearlings and stallions and bartering over a pint or two. Admission to the principal market runs around £3, but there are always a few ponies on parade in the streets or at the nearby beach, which is also the site of informal races when the weather is good.

The town's main attraction for visitors is its location; perched above Clifden Bay on a forested plateau and flanked in the east by the impressive Twelve Ben Mountains (also known as the Twelve Pin Mountains). At the western edge of Connemara, Clifden is regularly serviced by bus in the summer months and easily hitched to, making it a convenient hub for exploring the mountains and nearby coast. To appreciate the scenery, you need to get out of and above Clifden, preferably on one of the small hillocks that form its western border. Here, down Sky Road, you'll find the derelict ruins of **Clifden Castle,** built in 1815 by the town's founder, John D'Arcy. To the west, just below Clifden's main cluster of tourist shops and pubs, the **Owenglin Cascades** are also worth a quick tour. Formed by large limestone boulders jammed into the mouth of the River Owenglin, the steep cascades are believed to have the power of healing. Hikers should head for the **Connemara Walking Centre** (Market St., tel. 095/21379), which has maps, plenty of advice on the best hiking around, and archaeologists who lead half-day (£10) and full-day (£20) hikes. After conquering the Maumturk or Twelve Pin mountains, give your aching muscles the Guinness treatment at **Guy's** (Main St., tel. 095/21130) or **Humpty's** (Market St., tel. 095/21511). Both feature the best of, well, the Clifden live-rock scene.

CLEGGAN, LETTERFRACK, AND INISHBOFIN ISLAND

BASICS

A tourist desk in Cleggan at **Oliver Coyne's Pub** (tel. 095/44640) stocks brochures, maps, and bus info. Between June 22 and August 27, **Bus Éireann** offers one Expressway bus each Monday and Thursday to Letterfrack and Kylemore Abbey from Clifden; local service operates once a day year-round. You can exchange money at the Cleggan **post office** (Main St., tel. 095/44655), open weekdays 9–5:30 and Saturday 9–1.

WORTH SEEING

Northwest Connemara is famous for the rugged barrenness of its land and the harsh beauty of its coast, where desolate bog land and ragged mountains are tempered by the sea. In towns like Clifden, those striking contrasts are often muted or ruthlessly exploited by the tourist board for mass consumption. But you can encounter pure and unblemished Connemara in a village like **Cleggan,** a tiny fishing settlement 9½ km (6 mi) northwest of Clifden. Cleggan has its fair share of tourist shops, along with a well-developed harbor and fishing industry, but its pace is soothingly rural and its scenery stunning. Enveloped by mountains and perched on the cusp of Cleggan Bay, the village is crisscrossed by hundreds of good hiking trails and by the sort of curvy coastal roads that give cyclists a reason to live. The IHH **Master's House Hostel** (tel. 095/44746) has become more of a riding center than a hostel, with riding at £10 an hour. Closed October to May, it offers top-rate dorm accommodations (£7) and private rooms (£8 per person). The hostel is a three-minute walk from the village's minuscule center; just follow the signs.

If Masters House Hostel is full, head for the village of **Letterfrack,** which has a very laid-back and welcoming hostel set behind the church on your right as you come from Clifden. The **Old Monastery Hostel** (095/41132) has beds from £6.50–£9. The price includes a hearty breakfast with home-baked bread. They also do evening meals for £5. Letterfrack itself is really just three pubs, an excellent village shop, and a couple of houses at a crossroads. **Veldons** (095/41046) is a pub and shop in one, with an excellent selection of fresh fish. Traditional musicians gather and play most evenings in the pub. Letterfrack is also a good point from which to visit **Kylemore Abbey** (admission £2) on the road to Westport. Built in the 19th century, the abbey is set alone beside Kylemore Lake in a perfect, postcard setting. It's still in use as a convent boarding school run by nuns, but it's open to the public. There is a serene walk beside the lake, and you can stroll up the hill to the life-size statue of Jesus, usually surrounded by grazing sheep. The view out over the lake is well worth the effort.

Master's House Hostel can arrange summer boat trips (£10 per hosteler) to nearby **Inishbofin Island,** an amazingly laid-back outcrop of rocky farmland 9½ km (6 mi) northwest of Cleggan Harbour. You can also book ferries for yourself at **Coyne's Shop** (tel. 095/44750) and **King's Shop** (tel. 095/44642). Coyne's will book you on *Dun Aengus,* the island's mail boat, while King's sells tickets for *The Queen,* the better and larger boat of the two. Check at the shops for sailing times and prices, both of which vary according to demand and weather. Inishbofin has a deserved reputation for attracting Euro-hippies and unrepentant boozers looking to commune with nature and a pint or two. During the day, the island's protected beaches are littered with longhairs and the strains of Bob Marley; at night, the three pubs overflow with locals and bleary-eyed Guinness-pounders of all nationalities. If you stick around for the strange and wonderful pub scene here, check into the excellent IHH **Inishbofin Island Hostel** (tel. 095/45855), near the island's harbor. Besides its modern kitchen, dorm rooms (£5.50), and double rooms (£16), the hostel has an airy conservatory that's perfect for rainy-day cups of tea and meaningful conversation.

THE NORTHWEST 8

CALE SILER AND LAURENCE BELGRAVE

I n the wild, wet, grass-and-heather hills of Donegal and Sligo, two counties in the remote Northwest, you'll find some of Ireland's most majestic scenery. Cool, clean waters from the roaring Atlantic Ocean slice the landscape into long peninsulas of breeze-swept rocky crests, each one remote from the next. The lower country, at least where it is covered by layers of moist bog, cuts open to reveal dark brown peat underneath; although this area may be thought less pretty than the rest of the region, it has a haunting, lonely appeal.

Tucked into the folds of the Northwest's hills, modest little market towns and unpretentious villages with muddy streets go about their business quietly. In the squelchy peat bogs, cutters working with long shovels pause to watch and wave as you drive past. Remember to drive slowly along the country lanes, for around any corner you may find a whitewashed thatched cottage with children playing outside, a shepherd leading his flock, or a bicycle-riding farmer wobbling along in the middle of the road. Yes, it may sound too cute to be true, but that's just the way it is with Ireland.

Keep in mind, though, that the whole region—and County Donegal in particular—attracts a good share of visitors during July and August; this is a favorite vacation area for people who live in nearby Northern Ireland. To be frank, a few places are quite spoiled by popularity with tourists and careless development; the coast between Sligo Town and Donegal Town, a cheap-and-cheerful family beach resort full of so-called "Irish gift shops" and "amusement arcades," is another place to pass by rather than visit. On the whole, though, the Northwest is big enough, untamed enough, and grand enough to be able to absorb all of its summer (and weekend) tourists without too much harm.

County Donegal has the country's largest Gaeltacht (Irish-speaking area). Drivers in this part of the country, you'll be amused to notice, often end up frustrated whenever they come to a crossroads: Signposts show only the Irish place names, often so unlike the English versions as to be completely unrecognizable. All is not lost, however—maps generally give both the Irish and the English names, and locals are usually more than happy to help out with directions (in English), sometimes with a yarn thrown in. County Donegal was part of the near-indomitable ancient kingdom of Ulster, which was not conquered by the English until the 17th century. By the time they were driven out in the 1920s, the English had still not eradicated rural Donegal's Celtic inheritance.

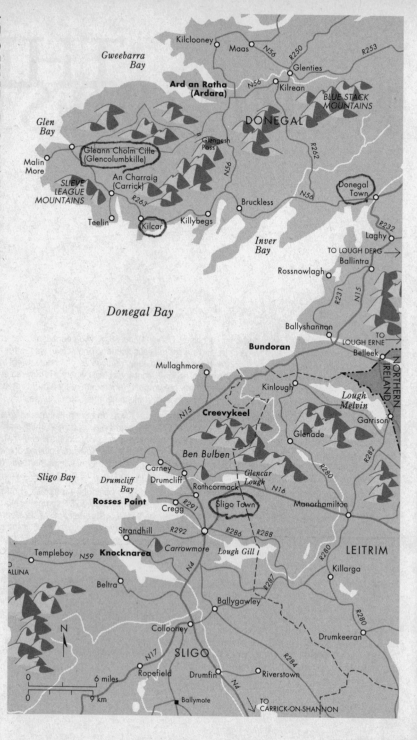

Gweebarra Bay

Kilclooney

Maas

N56

R250

Glenties

N56

Kilrean

R253

Ard an Ratha (Ardara)

BLUE STACK MOUNTAINS

DONEGAL

Glen Bay

Glengesh Pass

Malin More

Gleann Cholm Cille (Glencolumbkille)

An Charraig (Carrick)

N56

R262

SLIEVE LEAGUE MOUNTAINS

R263

Bruckless

N56

Donegal Town

Teelin

Kilcar

Killybegs

R232

Laghy

Inver Bay

TO LOUGH DERG

Ballintra

Rossnowlagh

R231

N15

Donegal Bay

Ballyshannon

TO LOUGH ERNE

Bundoran

Belleek

Mullaghmore

Kinlough

Lough Melvin

N15

Creevykeel

Glenade

Garrison

R282

Ben Bulben

R280

Sligo Bay

Carney

Drumcliff Bay

Drumcliff

Glencar Lough

N16

Rosses Point

Rathcormack

Cregg

R291

Sligo Town

Manorhamilton

Strandhill

R292

R286

R288

R280

LEITRIM

Templeboy

N59

Knocknarea

Carrowmore

Lough Gill

Killarga

ALLINA

Beltra

N4

R287

Col/ooney

N

R280

Drumkeeran

N17

SLIGO

R284

0   6 miles

Ropefield

Drumfin

Riverstown

0   9 km

N4

Ballygawley

Ballymote

TO CARRICK-ON-SHANNON

NORTHERN IRELAND

If the whole of Ireland is a land of seemingly infinite diversity, in the Northwest even the air, the light, and the colors of the countryside change like a kaleidoscope. Look once, and scattered snow-white clouds are flying above tawny-brown slopes. Look again, and suddenly the sun has brilliantly illuminated some magnificent reds and purples in the undergrowth. The inconstant skies brighten and darken at will, bringing out a whole spectrum of subtle shades within the unkempt gorse and heather, the rocky slopes merging into somber peat and grassy meadows of scintillating green.

Not only close to the bracing ocean shore but also farther inland, water in all its forms dominates the Northwest; countless lakes, running streams, and rivers wind through lovely pastoral valleys. Be prepared for plenty of rainfall as well; don't forget to carry a raincoat or umbrella—although, as a kind local may inform you, the "brolly" acts purely as a talisman: "For it's only when you *don't* have it with you that the rain will really come down" is a piece of local wisdom.

With no train and limited bus service, there's no denying that northwestern Ireland is a hard region to traverse. Steep hills and winding roads frighten away all but the hardiest of cyclists, as do the frequent cold weather and rain. Fortunately, hitching is fairly easy here: Even if you get stuck in what seems like the middle of nowhere, odds are some farmer with a thick accent will eventually offer you a lift to the next pub. Besides Bus Éireann, the area is served by **McGeehan Coaches** (tel. 075/46150), which offers competitively priced service to many of the same destinations and covers areas ignored by the national bus company during winter. The same holds true for **Lough Swilly Buses** (tel. 074/22400), a private company with routes between Letterkenny, Derry, and northern County Donegal.

In northwestern Ireland, it's said that sheep outnumber people by roughly 100 to 1.

SLIGO

Considering its location, straddling the mouth of Lough Gill at the foot of Sligo Harbour, Sligo ought to be a picturesque and thoroughly enjoyable market town. The Great Famine of 1846 reduced the town's population by nearly half, but even then Sligo's port and shipping industry profited from the mass emigrations, transporting as many as 400 people per week to America during the 1850s and 1860s. Over the past 20 years, however, Sligo has fallen victim to its own prosperity. Companies from Dublin and the Continent continue to refashion the small city center with bleak, modern shopping malls, giving Sligo an artificial and anonymous look. A few historic buildings survive intact—Hargadon's Pub on O'Connell Street is a good example—but even these look strangely out of place in a city where every second shop blazes in neon.

As the city to which William Butler Yeats was fervently attached, Sligo benefits from the Yeats Museum and Yeats Summer School (*see* Worth Seeing, *below*) and from its proximity to the poet's grave in Drumcliffe. But Sligo remains little more than a functional stopover on the way to somewhere else, preferably County Donegal and its wildly gorgeous coastline. Since Sligo is the last stop on all northbound trains, train travelers headed for County Donegal or Northern Ireland must transfer to a bus or hitch from here—an awkward process that may require you to spend at least one night in town.

BASICS

The **tourist office** (Temple St., tel. 071/61201), open weekdays 9–5 (longer and weekend hours in summer), stocks a full range of maps and brochures, can book you into a bed-and-breakfast for a £1 fee, and houses a competitive bureau de change. From the train and bus depot, walk down Lord Edward Street and turn right on Adelaide Street, then veer left on Temple Street. Both **Gary's Cycles** (Quay St., tel. 071/45418) and **Conway Bros.** (6 High St., tel. 071/61370) rent 15-speed mountain bikes for £7 per day, £30 per week, plus a £40 deposit.

COMING AND GOING

Bus Éireann and Irish Rail offer regular daily service to Sligo, though only Bus Éireann makes the journey northward to County Donegal and Derry. Conveniently, their two depots are right next to each other.

The rail station, **McDiarmada Station** (Lord Edward St., tel. 071/60066 for bus info and 071/69888 or 071/69889 for rail info), is an easy 10-minute walk to the city center (walk downhill and turn left). Inside there's an info desk (open daily year-round) and a left-luggage desk (open weekdays 9–6, Sat. 9:30– 6:30), which will store your luggage for £1 per day. The only major destination served by rail from Sligo is Dublin (4 per day, £12). Even if you're traveling to nearby Galway or Belfast, you must transfer in Dublin first. In other words, take the bus. Bus Éireann destinations include Belfast via Enniskillen (1–3 per day, £12.10), Cork via Galway (1–2 per day, £16), Derry (2–6 per day, £10), and Galway (5 per day, £10.50).

WHERE TO SLEEP

Sligo has five satisfactory youth hostels and a slew of mid-range B&Bs, most of which are on Lower and Upper Pearse roads. Finding a bed isn't usually a problem, but things fill up during August, when the Yeats Summer School draws poets and Yeats fans from around the world. If everything is booked, you can always camp in nearby Rosses Point or along the banks of Sligo Bay. This latter option isn't particularly legal, but people do it anyway. Of the city-center B&Bs, **Parkmore** (32–34 Wolfe Tone St., opposite bus station, tel. 071/60241) has rooms for £14–£16 and **The Anchor Guest House** (Quay St., tel. 071/42904) offers standard rooms and lovely fried breakfasts for £15–£17 per person. **Renate Central House** (Upper John St., tel. 071/62014 or 071/69093), only a short walk from the bus station, is spotlessly clean and homey at £14–£16 per person for a double.

HOSTELS

The Ivy Hostel. The coolest, smallest, and most eclectic hostel in Sligo has three doubles for the low, low price of £6 per person. Wonderfully strange lights are in every nook, wall-imbedded shoes in the front hall provide coat hooks, and laundry is free. *26 Lord Edward St., tel. 071/45165. Common room, kitchen, sheet rental (£1). Closed Sept.–May.*

The White House (IHH). It's the most comfortable of Sligo's hostels, overlooking the river in the heart of the city center. All the rooms are small, but there's a large common room with big, comfortable couches. Beds cost £6.50. *Markievicz Rd., tel. 071/45160. From bus/train station, follow Lord Edward St., cross river, quick left on Markievicz Rd. 40 beds. Key deposit (£1).*

The Yeats County. Clean but boring, this hostel's chief asset is its 50-yard proximity to the bus station. For £6.50 you get a dorm bed with a thicker than average comforter and use of the claustrophobia-inducing showers. *Lord Edward St., tel. 071/46876. 29 beds. Key deposit (£5).*

CAMPING

Greenlands Caravan & Camping Park. Eight kilometers (5 miles) northwest of Sligo at the tip of Rosses Point, the Greenlands has 25 tent sites, all with good views of the bay. Sites cost £5, plus 50p per person. *Rosses Point, off R291 Hwy., tel. 071/77113. From city center, take the Rosses Point bus. Showers. Closed mid-Sept.–mid-May.*

Strandhill Camping Park. More secluded than the Greenlands, the seaside Strandhill is generally filled with no-stress families and goofy dropouts touring the world on £5 a day. It, too, is 8 km (5 mi) outside Sligo Town, and it's the place to come for outstanding ocean views. Sites cost £3.50, plus 50p per person. *Strandhill, off R292 Hwy., tel. 071/68120. From city center, take any bus marked STRANDHILL. 100 sites. Laundry, showers (50p). Closed mid-Sept.–May.*

FOOD

Food in Sligo is like American televangelism: cheesy, shameless, tasteless, and often hard to stomach. One of the few places that defies the Jim Bakker school of cooking is **Bistro Bianconi's** (44 O'Connell St., tel. 071/41744), which serves delicious antipasto platters (£3.75), exotic pizzas (£6–£7), and pastas (£6–£9.50). **Gourmet Parlour** (Bridge St., tel. 071/44617) creates superb, takeout meals baked fresh on the premises and made with mostly organic ingredients. Try the salmon salad (£3.20), wholewheat sandwiches (£1.50), or a loaf of sun-dried-tomato bread (60p). **The Cottage** (4 Castle St., tel. 071/45319) is a second-floor café/restaurant with a thatched roof and a vegetarian menu. They serve pizza, lasagna, quiche, and vegetarian curry with rice for £3.80, Monday–Saturday 9 AM–10 PM. The well-stocked **Quinnsworth** (O'Connell St., tel. 071/62788) is the place to go for groceries.

WORTH SEEING

Sligo's city center is small and walkable. From the intersection of O'Connell and Wine streets, head east down Stephen Street for Sligo's **County Museum, Municipal Art Gallery,** and **Yeats Museum,** all housed in the local library (Stephen St., tel. 071/42212). Admission is free, and the library is open Monday–Saturday 10–12:30 and 2:30–4:30 (shorter hrs in winter). The Yeats hall houses a comprehensive collection of Yeats's writings from 1889 to 1936, various editions of his plays and prose, and the Nobel Prize medal that was awarded to him in 1923. The penmanship is dreadful, but Yeats's letters to James Stephens and Oliver St. John Gogarty offer insight into Yeats's obsessive love for Sligo. Out the door and around the corner, the art gallery contains a respectably large collection of Irish and Anglo-Irish canvases. Of note are the oils and watercolors by Jack B. Yeats, Bill's brother.

On nearby Abbey Street, you'll find the ruins of Sligo's **Dominican Friary,** commonly known as "the Abbey." Founded in 1252 by Maurice FitzGerald, ancestor to the Earls of Kildare, the abbey was accidentally burned in 1414 and had to be completely rebuilt. In 1642, during the English Civil War, Sir Frederick Hamilton and a troop of Puritan soldiers sacked Sligo and once again demolished the abbey, an event described by Yeats in *The Curse of the Fires and the Shadow.* Today the abbey consists of a ruined nave, aisle, transept, and tower. It's the sort of isolated hideaway popular with Sunday lovers and wild dogs. The ruins are open daily 9:30–6:30, mid-June–mid-September, and admission is £1.50.

Back in town, the **Yeats Memorial Building** (Hyde Bridge, at O'Connell St., tel. 071/45847) houses a tiny art gallery, open Monday–Saturday 10–5:30, and the headquarters of the **Yeats Society** (tel. 071/42693). During the Yeats Summer School in the first two weeks of August, the society organizes lectures and Yeatsian theatrical performances, some of which are open to the public; call for current listings. You can also sit in on a lecture for £5. Across the street is a photo-worthy sculpture of the poet himself, draped in a flowing coat overlaid with poetic excerpts. It was unveiled in 1989 by Michael Yeats, W. B.'s son, in commemoration of the 50th anniversary of his father's death.

AFTER DARK

Sligo's most famous pub is **Hargadon's** (4–5 O'Connell St., tel. 071/70933), a dark, old-style public house filled with sepia photographs, antique whiskey jugs, and a maze of private oak-lined snugs. Top-rate grub is available Monday–Saturday for less than £3. Otherwise, the dilapidated **Cullen's Bar** and **Thomas Connolly,** both on Markievicz Road near the White House Hostel, are good for quiet pints in the company of rough-hewn locals. For a concert-volume dose of Hendrix and Bach, **Shoot the Crows** (Grattan St., no phone) is another solid choice. Traditional music is most common during the summer season; pick up a copy of the weekly *Sligo Champion* (75p), or the *Weekender,* a free weekly available at all newsagents, to see who's playing where and when. There's also a rather run-down looking, four-screen luxury cinema on Wine Street called the **Gaiety,** which you can escape into.

DONEGAL TOWN

Donegal Town is a small outpost of pubs and shops overlooking the River Eske. The entire village can be walked in 10 minutes, and nearly everything of interest is centered around the **Diamond,** which was once a marketplace but is now used as a parking lot. The town was founded in 1200 by the O'Donnell clan. Its Gaelic name, Dun na nGall (Fort of the Foreigners), pays tribute to the Norse raiders who first settled in County Donegal during the 9th century. In 1474, Red Hugh O'Donnell commissioned a castle (now destroyed) and the **Donegal Monastery,** on the riverbank south of the Diamond. The ivy-covered ruins are impressive, considering that the complex was burned to the ground in 1593, razed by the English in 1601, and ransacked again in 1607, at which time the monastery was abandoned. Prior to leaving, however, the monks had time to copy down a series of Old Irish legends in what they called *The Annals of the Four Masters.* For their efforts, the monks are remembered by a 20-foot obelisk (1937) in the Diamond's busy parking lot. Donegal's other prime attraction is **Donegal Castle,** half a block southwest of the Diamond. The castle was built in 1474 by Red Hugh the Younger. Restored in a tastefully simple manner in the mid-1990s, the castle harbors the so called "chimney piece," a gargantuan, sandstone fireplace wrought with minute reliefs. The castle is open June–October, daily 9:30–6, and admission is £2.

Despite the fact that it is not served by Irish Rail, Donegal Town is still a popular stop with day-trippers from Sligo. Throughout July and August, the town feels like a tacky amusement park, and most establishments charge outrageous prices to match. There are three youth hostels in town, however, and a handful of decent pubs, so don't fret if you get stuck here. If you're in the mood for a pint, try **Charlie's Star Bar** (Main St., tel. 073/21158) or **McGroarty's** (The Diamond, tel. 073/21049), which, between the two, have live traditional music most summer nights. Two other colorful pubs are **Tirconnail** (The Diamond, tel. 073/22188) and the **Scotsman** (Bridge St., tel. 073/22470). The Scotsman occasionally hosts low-key music sessions on summer weekends.

BASICS

The **tourist office** (Quay St., tel. 073/21148) overlooks the water south of the Diamond. It has maps, a list of B&Bs, and info on guided tours of the Donegal coast. It's open weedays 9–1 and 2–5, Saturday 9–1 (June–Aug., Mon.–Sat. until 8 and Sun. 10–1 and 2–5). The **Bank of Ireland** and **AIB** are both on the Diamond, open weekdays 10–4, and have ATMs that accept Plus, Cirrus, Visa, and MasterCard. To change money on weekends, try one of the large hotels or tourist shops on the Diamond, all of which offer dreary rates made worse by hefty 2%–5% commissions. Both **Doherty's Fishing Tackle** (Main St., tel. 073/21119) and the **Bike Shop** (Waterloo Pl., tel. 073/22515) rent mountain bikes for £6 per day.

COMING AND GOING

Lacking an official bus depot, all **Bus Éireann** coaches arrive and depart from the Diamond, outside the Abbey Hotel, where a small schedule lists common departure times. The Quay Street tourist office also provides information for all departures. Destinations from Donegal Town include Derry (6 per day, £7.70), Sligo (5 per day, £6), Letterkenny (6 per day, £5.90), Galway (4 per day, £10), Dublin (5 per day, £10), and Glencolumbkille (2 per day in summer, 1 per day in winter; £7). **McGeehan Coaches** (tel. 075/46101 or 075/46150) also runs buses to Dublin (£10) and day trips to Glencolumbkille (£3) and other nearby towns twice daily late-June–September.

WHERE TO SLEEP

B&B accommodations are easy to come by. **Riverside House** (tel. 073/21083) has beds for £16, and **Castle View** (tel. 073/22100) provides spacious private rooms for about £14 per person. Both are a three-minute walk south of the Diamond, on Waterloo Place just off Bridge Street, and overlook the River Eske. Larger and more modern is **Windemere House** (Quay St., tel. 073/21323), near the tourist office. The rooms (from £13.50 per person) are comfortable and spotless, and Mr. Ryle's breakfasts are unbeatable.

The IHH **Donegal Town Independent Hostel** (Killybegs Rd., tel. 073/22805), has 44 beds (£6) spread generously about a large, whitewashed house. The dorm rooms are well kept, and the cozy kitchen has all the amenities. You can also camp (£3.75 per person) on the lawn surrounding the hostel, which is 1 km (¾ mi) from the Diamond on the road to Killybegs. Closer to the center of town and in pristine condition is **Cliffview Budget Accommodation** (tel. 073/21684), on the Coast Road as it heads out of town toward Killybegs. The modern, well-designed accommodation costs from £7.50 for a dorm bed to £15 for a single. The price includes a simple breakfast. A proper "fry up" is £2 extra. You can also take the bus or hike 5 km (3 mi) to An Óige's **Ball Hill Hostel** (tel. 073/21174), where beds are £5.50–£6. From town, follow the Killybegs road for 2½ km (1½ mi), then turn left at the sign; or take any Bus Éireann coach toward Killybegs and ask to be let off near Ball Hill. The peaceful hostel is housed in a former coast-guard station and is within a stone's throw of the beach.

FOOD

Donegal's small size means budget travelers can expect little more than pub grub and greasy bags of chips. There are a few upscale restaurants in town, notably in the Abbey and Hyland hotels, but expect generic atmosphere and the din of tourists comparing their new sweaters. **Atlantic Hotel Café** (Main St., tel. 073/21080) does reasonable lunches and dinners for less than £8—mostly steaks, fish, and pastas—and is surprisingly cozy, considering the number of tourists ushered through. Cheaper and less crowded is **McGinty's No. 11 Café** (Main St., tel. 073/22416), a self-service sandwich shop with good sandwiches (£2) and burgers (£2.70). Otherwise, the best budget meals are done by **The Blueberry Tea Room** (Castle St., off the Diamond, tel. 073/22933). This second-floor restaurant and café serves excellent (and excellently priced) specials ranging from roast chicken (£4.50) to a bacon-and-broccoli quiche (£3.25). Although **Just Williams** (in the Hyland Central Hotel, the Diamond, tel. 073/21027) seems geared toward the tour-bus crowd, it serves heaping lunch specials, like lamb curry and a seafood pancake, for £5. **Foodland** (The Diamond, tel. 073/21006), open Monday–Saturday 9–7, is a well-stocked market smack in the center of town. For a trustworthy greasy chip shop, try **Beavers** on Main Street, which offers good cod in batter with chips for £2.80. The **Harbour Restaurant,** opposite the tourist office, has an excellent fish menu (£3.50–£8).

NEAR DONEGAL TOWN

KILCAR, DERRYLAHAN, AND SLIEVE LEAGUE

The village of Kilcar would probably be forgotten were it not for its proximity to IHH's Derrylahan Hostel (*see below*), one of the most popular hostels in Ireland. In fact, pretty much the only time people venture into Kilcar is to catch a bus or have a few pints in one of Kilcar's lively pubs. **Piper's Rest** (Main St., tel. 073/38205), probably the most attractive pub in town, serves up decent food and usually hosts music sessions on Wednesdays and weekends, as does **John Joe's Pub** (Main St., tel. 073/31093), a few doors away.

Most visitors, however, spend their day at the isolated hostel, which provides access to some of the best hiking in northwest Ireland. Within 3 km (2 mi) of the Derrylahan Hostel are trailheads to both **Slieve League** (2,972 feet) and the **Bunglass Cliffs,** the highest sea cliffs in the country. Slieve League (Sliabh Liec, or Mountain of the Pillars) is a ragged, razor-backed rise bordered by the River Glen and, at its foot, the village of Teelin. The mountain looks deceptively climbable from the back (the inaccessible front side borders the Atlantic Ocean), but once the fog rolls in, the footing can be perilous. At some points, the jagged trails wind within a foot of the cliff's edge, and the green heather that somehow thrives in the rocky soil is always slippery.

To access the mountain yourself, hitch or hike from the hostel to **Carrick,** a small two-pub town 5 km (3 mi) northwest. Walk just under a mile south on the road for Teelin and turn right at the sign for Bunglass. The hike to Bunglass is fairly easy, and the views are nothing short of incredible. Continue past Bunglass and head for the summit of Slieve League. On the way, you'll traverse trails with names like "Fog Ridge" and the aptly named "One Man's Pass." Be extra careful on windy days here—inexperienced hikers have been blown off the ridge by 50-mph gusts. Once you reach the summit, take a well-anchored peep over the cliff's edge. Almost 2,000 feet below, the pounding waves and white-water spray seem to move in slow motion, soundlessly. After you've humbled yourself before ocean, cliff, and sky, take the alternative route down, heading south for Cappagh and Teelin (follow the occasional weathered sign). Here you can grab lunch at **Rusty Mackerel Pub** (Teelin, tel. 073/39101), a hideaway filled with pipe-smoking fisherfolk. The entire circuit, from Carrick to Slieve League to Teelin, takes roughly five hours of medium-paced hiking, slightly more when heavy fog calls for extra vigilance.

BASICS • Both **Bus Éireann** and **McGeehan Coaches** (tel. 075/46101) stop outside John Joe's Pub in the center of Kilcar. There's no staffed bus depot or tourist office in town, but most shop owners have a sense of which bus leaves when for where. The town doesn't have an official bank, so change your foreign currency in one of Main Street's grocery stores. Most are open Monday–Saturday 9–6, and all offer equally poor rates.

WHERE TO SLEEP • The centrally located **Molloy's/Kilcar Lodge** (Main St., tel. 073/38156) is open March–October and offers comfortable private rooms from £13.50 per person, but anyone with good sense will head straight for the IHH **Derrylahan Hostel** (Carrick Rd., tel. 073/38079). Dorm beds are £6, double rooms £16, and tent sites £3. The 32-bed hostel is a steep 3 km (2 mi) north of Kilcar on the road to Carrick and overlooks Teelin Bay and the mountains. If you call from Kilcar or Carrick, one of the staff will come to get you. The hostel's well-stocked food shop sells enough to make a half-dozen different meals, the reception desk is open all day, and all guests are treated to biscuits and tea.

GLENCOLUMBKILLE

Glencolumbkille (pronounced glen-colm-KEEL) lies on the coast 13 km (8 mi) northwest of Kilcar. Although tiny even by Irish standards, Glencolumbkille manages to balance rural solitude with the occasional crafts shop and, best of all, a lively pub scene. It has yet to be "discovered" by mass tourism, but each year there's increased interest in this remote village. Part of the reason is that Glencolumbkille is at the heart of County Donegal's shrinking Gaeltacht. This gives the Glen a strong, rural Irish flavor, as do its affable country pubs and brightly painted row houses.

For a good overview, start at the beachfront **Folk Museum** (tel. 073/30017), where you can explore thatched-roof buildings on your own, or take one of the guided tours (£1.50) that start every half-hour daily, 10 to 6, mid-April–September (Sun. from noon). Then cross the strand and climb up to Glen Head (769 feet). Along the way, you'll pass a series of stunning cliffs studded with ancient hermit cells. Also of note is yet another squat **Martello Tower,** built by the British in 1804 to protect against an anticipated French invasion that never happened. Another good walk is the 8 km (5-mi) trek to **Malinbeg,** reached by following the coast road past both Doon Point and the Glencolumbkille Hotel. Look for the ruins of no less than five burial cairns, a ring fort, a second Martello Tower, and one of the best beaches in Ireland (renowned for its calm waters, dramatic scenery, and lovely golden sand).

BASICS • The **tourist office** (Main St., tel. 073/30116) is open mid-April–mid-October, Monday–Saturday 10–6. It has maps, walking guides, and a bureau de change open July–August. The **post office** (near Biddy's pub, tel. 073/30001), open weekdays 9–1 and 2–5, also has a bureau de change. Both **Bus Éireann** and **McGeehan's Coaches** (tel. 075/46101) stop three blocks from the tourist office. During summer, they both offer twice-daily service to Kilcar (£1.40), Killybegs (£1.80), and Donegal Town (£3.20).

WHERE TO SLEEP • Dooey Hostel (tel. 073/30130) has fantastic views of the Glen Head cliffs and beach. One side of the hostel is, quite literally, carved right out of the hillside, complete with jutting rocks and cascading plants. When it rains (and it *will* rain), water trickles through the rock formation and gurgles quietly by the dorm rooms. Dorm beds are £5.50, private rooms £6.50, and tent sites in the beautiful camping area cost £3.50. The hostel is a 1½-km (1-mi) walk from the tourist office (head west toward the beach and follow the signs), so stock up on groceries first. Otherwise, both **Mary Cunningham's** (Brackendale House, tel. 073/30038) and **Mrs. Byrne's** (Corner House, tel. 073/30021) offer standard B&B accommodations for around £14 per person; the latter is open April–September only. Look for them on the road to Carrick, 1 km (½ mi) outside Glencolumbkille. There are also a bunch of B&Bs near the folk museum and on the road to Malinbeg. If you're looking for a camping spot, the friendly owners of **Bridget McShane "Biddy's"** pub (Cashel St., tel. 073/30016) might let you pitch your tent for free in the grassy field behind the pub if you ask nicely.

LETTERKENNY

If nothing else, Letterkenny is a useful hub for those headed deeper into northern County Donegal. Both Bus Éireann and Lough Swilly Buses offer a variety of routes from here north to the beautiful Inishowen Peninsula and Fanad Head. If you're coming from Northern Ireland, particularly from Derry, Letterkenny is the last large town you'll come across for miles. For this reason, Letterkenny's restaurants, pubs, and two hostels are popular with backpackers and cyclists looking to rest and stock up on supplies (or those ravenously hungry after a week on the remote coast). Letterkenny gets most active during early August's **International Folk Festival,** which brings together musicians from all over Ireland and the world. For details on performances, contact the festival office (52 Main St., tel. 074/21754). If you're suffering from electronic-image withdrawal symptoms, there's an up-to-date, four-screen cinema on the main street where you can get a fix.

BASICS

The **tourist office** (Derry Rd., tel. 074/21160) is 1 km (¾ mi) outside of town on Derry Road. Letterkenny is small enough to navigate without a map, so the only reason to walk out here is for Saturday currency exchange and B&B information. Weekday exchanges can be made more conveniently at the **AIB** (61 Upper Main St., tel. 074/22877), open 10–4. **Church St. Cycles** (11 Church St., off Main St., tel. 074/26204) rents bikes for £7 per day, £30 per week, plus a £40 deposit.

COMING AND GOING

The **bus station** (Port Rd., tel. 074/21309) is a five-minute walk from the city center; turn left out of the depot, cross to the far side of the roundabout and follow the CITY CENTER signs. From here, **Bus Éireann**

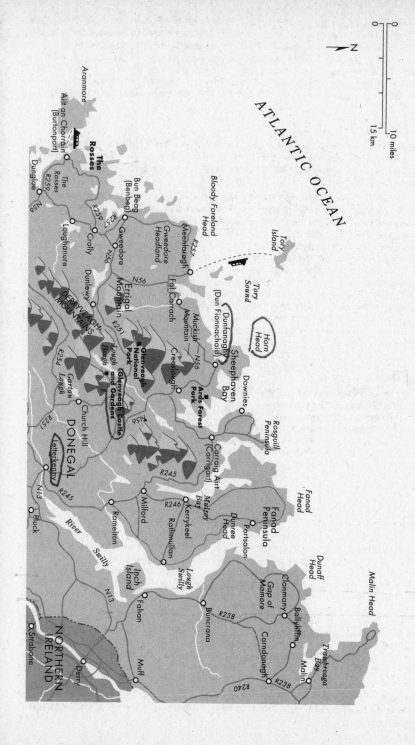

THE NORTHERN PENINSULAS

ATLANTIC OCEAN

10 miles
15 km
N

Aranmore
Ailt an Chorráin
(Burtonport)
Dungloe
N56
The Rosses
R259
The Rosses
Loughanure
Crolly
N56
Dunlewy
R257
R251
Bun Beag
(Bunbeg)
Gweedore
Gweedore Headland
Meenlaragh
Bloody Foreland Head
Tory Island
Tory Sound
Dunfanaghy
(Dún Fionnachaidh)
Horn Head
Sheephaven Bay
Downies
Rosguill Peninsula
Fanad Head
Dunaff Head
Malin Head
Trawbreaga Bay
Malin
Ballyliffin
Cloonmany
R238
Gap of Mamore
Carndonagh
R240
R238
Dunree Head
Fanad Peninsula
Portsalon
Mulroy Bay
Kerrykeel
Rathmullan
Buncrana
R238
Lough Swilly
Inch Island
Fahan
Muff
Derry
Strabane
NORTHERN IRELAND
N13
River Swilly
Ramelton
Milford
R246
R245
Letterkenny
R245
Pluck
N13
Church Hill
Gartan Lough
R251
DONEGAL
R254
DERRYVEAGH MOUNTAINS
Glenveagh National Park
Glenveagh Castle and Gardens
Lough Beagh
R251
Errigal Mountain
Meenbanad
Muckish Mountain
Creeslough
Ards Forest Park
Carraig Airt (Carrigart)
N56
Fál Carrach
N56

·123·

serves Derry (3 per day, £4.40), Sligo (3 per day; £9, or £6 for the first bus of the day), Galway (3 per day, £14), and Dublin (4 per day, £10). Most of northern Donegal is served by the **Lough Swilly Bus Co.** (tel. 074/22863), which also operates out of the Port Road Station. They provide an excellent means to explore the Northern Donegal coastline, with services running to Dungloe, via Creeslough, Dunfanaghy, Falcarragh, Gweedore, and Crolly, to name a few of the towns. There are four buses a day (£8 to Dungloe), two of which go via the Bloody Foreland. a trip highly recommended for its scenic beauty. Pick up a free timetable at the bus station. If you show them an ISIC card, they'll take 50% off the regular fare.

WHERE TO SLEEP

There are a number of B&Bs outside town on the roads to Sligo and Derry. Of them, **Ard na Greine** (Sentry Hill, tel. 074/21383) has rooms from £15. Closer to the bus station is **Covehill House** (Port Rd., tel. 074/21038), closed late-December–January, a comfortable five-room guest house with similar rates and excellent fried breakfasts.

Letterkenny has three hostels. The most spacious and best equipped is IHH's **The Manse Hostel** (High Rd., tel. 074/25238), set atop a hill and surrounded by a pleasant, sloping lawn. Dorm rooms (beds £6–£7) are airy and clean. From the bus station, walk down Port Road toward the town center and make a sharp right on High Road. One block from the center of town is **Rosemount Hostel** (3 Rosemount Terr., tel. 074/21181), which has beds for £5.50 and is open only June–September. The dorm rooms and kitchen can get cramped, but the facilities are clean and homey. From the bus station, walk down Port Road to Main Street; continue down Main Street for three blocks and turn left on Rosemount Terrace. The smallest of the three is the run-down **Port Hostel** (24 Port Rd., tel. 074/26288). Dark dorm rooms contain £5.75–£8.50 beds and musty odors. On the upside, the bedding is clean, and you can get a small discount at the adjoining **Café 24.** The owner also often lets people camp on the land around her house, just a few minutes away from the hostel (£2 per tent). You can also camp around Letterkenny's **Leisure Centre** (High Rd., tel. 074/25251) for free—just inquire at the center before pitching your tent. Showers cost £1, though.

FOOD

The most popular restaurant in town is **Pat's Pizza** (9 Market Sq., tel. 074/21761), where a 9-inch pizza with five toppings costs £5. You'll be privy to all the hot gossip around town, as the seating arrangements will have you elbow to elbow with Letterkenny's youth. The sign outside **Bakersville** (10 Church St., tel. 074/21887) promises "damn fine coffee," which they deliver along with piping-hot baked goods. Letterkenny is also well endowed with pubs. **Peadar McGeehin** (46 Main St., tel. 074/29564) has a quiet, mostly local crowd, while **The Orchard** (High Rd., tel. 074/21615) and **The Cottage** (25 Main St., tel. 074/21338) have livelier atmospheres. **Pulse** (Port Rd., tel. 074/24966) is the hottest club in town, occasionally featuring live bands.

NEAR LETTERKENNY

Head west and north out of Letterkenny, and you'll be entering an area that is perhaps the least developed and populated of all the scenic glories of Ireland. This may make the area difficult to explore without independent transport, but don't be put off; some buses do brave the region (*see below*), and you will be richly rewarded by the wild and rugged landscape that typifies northwest Donegal. Head for **Dunfanaghy,** a small seaside resort that overlooks the impressive Sheephaven Bay. The town itself is heavily frequented in summer by tourists from Derry, but it's a good spot to stock up on provisions. **Horn Head,** with its impressive cliffs and view of the surrounding coastline is a must see, and some distance away (bicycling is probably the best way to cover the 16-km/10-mi trip) are **Doe Castle** and **Lackagh Bridge.** At Lackagh Bridge, looking upriver, you can see distinctive Muckish Mountain, and downriver is the beginning of Sheephaven Bay, with Doe Castle perched on its low promontory fringed by a white sandy beach. In 1544, Doe Castle was the focus of internecine wars between the sons of McSweeney Doe, and in the 17th century it was the scene of bloody conflict between the Irish princes and the Crown, changing hands many times.

The **Screag An Iolair** hostel is set right in the middle of the mountains of Glenveigh National Park and makes a perfect base from which to set out on some serious and spectacular walks. **Mt. Errigal** is only a three-hour walk away.

COMING AND GOING

Some private bus services run to the more inaccessible areas in the high season. Try **McGeehan Coaches** for coaches from Donegal Town northward (tel. 075/46150 or 075/46101). **O'Donnell's Trans-Ulster Express** (tel. 075/48356) runs once-daily service from Belfast, Derry, and Donegal Town. This service passes through Letterkenny, Dunfanaghy, and Crolly, and other towns.

WHERE TO SLEEP

The roads leading to Dunfanaghy are full of B&Bs; the closest to town is **The Willows** (tel. 074/36446). Clean but small, with only six beds (£15 a person), it's open year-round and is on the main street. About 2 km (1 mi) on the road west is a hostel that's an attraction in itself; **Creggan Mill Hostel** (tel. 074/36507 or 36409) set alone amongst lush greenery. You can sleep in either the beautiful rustic old kiln house, where dorm beds cost £6–£8, or in the newly installed, 120-year-old railway carriage, which has romantic doubles for £10 a person or dorm beds from £8–£10. The hostel also has a camping site with good facilities for £4 per person. The hostel and garden are littered with quirky objects, and there is a very special feel to the place. Laundry facilities are available and cost £2. The hostel also arranges trips to Tory Island and other local sites. Be sure to arrive well stocked, as there are no shops nearby—or anything else, for that matter.

Near the tiny village of **Crolly,** you'll find the isolated **Screag An Iolair (Eagle's Nest) Hostel** (tel. 075/48593). Eammon, who runs the hostel, will have instant respect for you if you've conquered the one-hour uphill walk, past wild bog land, rushing streams, and a beautiful mountain lake to get to his hostel. If you're not in the mood to hike, he'll pick you up or you can take a taxi (£3). The hostel has a spartan, rustic feel, but it's very cozy. It also has a peculiar meditation room, with the naked torso of a young woman carved out of wood and placed in a Buddha-type position in the corner. Eammon's explanation is that this is a shrine to the Celtic goddess Brid (the goddess of fertility and young women). Beds are £6–£8, while laundry is £3; be sure to buy food in the village before you head up. The only problem is that the nearest pub is 5 km (3 mi) away, an Irish nightmare.

NORTHERN IRELAND

CALE SILER AND LAURENCE BELGRAVE

N orthern Ireland is small—about half the size of Delaware and less than one-fifth the size of the Republic of Ireland, its neighbor to the south. Because of its size, and because it wasn't a separate country prior to 1921, Northern Ireland is often lumped together with the Irish Republic. Both countries, after all, share more than just a similar climate and heritage. Both are dominated by rolling pastureland, craggy coasts, meandering stone fences, and isolated farm villages. The Irish traditions of hospitality and artful conversation also prevail in Northern Ireland.

The similarities, however, generally stop here. Politically speaking, Northern Ireland is administered and governed by England, much like Scotland and Wales. Northern Ireland, which nowadays includes six of Ulster's nine counties (the other three—Donegal, Monaghan, and Cavan—lie in the Republic), thus derives its social, economic, and political orientation from the British, who have maintained some presence in Ulster since the late 12th century. Over the past 20 years, in fact, Britain has spent millions of pounds in support of the province, mostly to sustain its heavily armed security forces, but also to install better roads and a dependable phone system. The English presence also accounts for Northern Ireland's currency (the British pound), its bright red post boxes (they're lime-green in the Republic), and the preponderance of some very un-Irish names like William Smyth and Victoria Browne.

At its closest point, Northern Ireland is only 27 km (17 mi) from Scotland, so there's always been a strong Scottish influence here. Ulster's Scottish connection meant that when England underwent its 16th-century conversion to Protestantism (thanks to Henry VIII), so did the majority of Ulster. And when James VI of Scotland was crowned James I of England, whole parts of Ulster were opened up for settlement by Protestant immigrants (read: confiscated by the Crown). These were generally farmers and merchants who competed with the native Irish for everything from grazing land to political favor. Being Protestant, of course, gave you certain advantages when dealing with Ulster's English administrators. Simply put, Protestants received free lands and Catholics didn't. English became Ulster's "first" language, replacing Irish, and the Gaelic culture was systematically repressed. As discriminatory practices became enshrined in law, Catholics rightly felt excluded, disenfranchised, and persecuted.

In terms of Catholic–Protestant relations, the pivotal event was the 1649 arrival in Ireland of Oliver Cromwell, a staunch Protestant who unseated (and beheaded) the pro-Catholic Charles I during the English Civil War. Cromwell was a despot who earned the everlasting hate of Catholic Ireland with his 1653 Act of Settlement, which stipulated that all Catholics were to relocate west of Ireland's Shannon River. Thousands were forcibly removed to Ireland's barren extremes, while the English nobility granted itself vast tracts of land throughout the country; later, they would rent the very same soil back to locals at extortionate rates.

England eventually relented in its policies, but the damage had already been done. Catholics understandably viewed England—and, by extension, most Protestants—as exploitative in the extreme. After Ireland gained its independence in 1921, England was left with a troublesome problem. Roughly 85% of Ulster was Protestant, but the newly created Republic of Ireland was emphatically Catholic. In the 1918 Parliamentary elections most southerners voted for Sinn Féin, or "We, Ourselves," the Nationalist pro-Catholic party. Ulster, on the other hand, voted to remain a part of the United Kingdom. Even though people saw themselves as Irish first and foremost, Ulster's Protestants feared they would be mistreated by the new countrywide Catholic majority. The solution: The creation on June 22, 1921, of Northern Ireland, a political entity governed and safeguarded by the British Crown and a country where Protestants far outnumbered Catholics. Needless to say, this solution opened a Pandora's box of problems.

For a small country, Northern Ireland has received more than its fair share of international press coverage in the last few decades—mostly along the lines of ". . . the IRA claimed responsibility today for a bombing that has left three dead and dozens wounded." This new wave of sectarian violence began in the late 1960s, after two decades of relative peace. The northern state had for years denied Catholics basic civil rights, and in the spirit of the '60s, a radical but peaceful movement for social justice sprang up all across the province. The government tried to suppress this movement and violence soon erupted. The participants were mainly the reborn IRA (Irish Republican Army), the RUC (Royal Ulster Constabulary, the province's police force), and Ulster's numerous Loyalist paramilitary factions (those who support British rule in Northern Ireland are often called Loyalists or Unionists). Particularly hard hit was Derry, Northern Ireland's second-largest city. On August 13, 1969, following a march by Derry Protestants through mostly Catholic ghettos, rioting forced Britain to dispatch an armed regiment. This was the first time in modern history that England had assumed an active military role in Ulster. At first, the presence of troops had a calming effect, as they protected Catholics who were being burned out of their homes by Protestant mobs with the tacit and sometimes active support of the police. But in time the IRA became angered by the sight of British troops on Irish soil and by the continuing biased actions of the government, and, intent on driving the British out, they initiated a ruthless bombing campaign in Belfast. To combat the rise in violence, the Northern Irish Prime Minister, Brian Faulkner, instituted an emergency power known as "internment without trial." In the climate of resentment that followed, the IRA stepped up its bombing attacks in Belfast and Derry. On the Protestant side, two new paramilitary organizations were born, the Ulster Volunteer Force (UVF) and the Ulster Defense Association (UDA), both outlawed Loyalist groups committed to Ulster's union with Britain.

Like the modern state of Israel, Northern Ireland is a political entity that draws its mandate from religion and history—a country where God and politics are tightly interwoven and where ancient quarrels still affect the tone of everyday life.

These developments simply provided fuel for the watershed event in Northern Irish history, the civil rights march in Derry on January 30, 1972—better known as Bloody Sunday. The British have their own story of what happened on that day, but the generally accepted version is that 13 unarmed Catholic civilians were shot dead by British paratroopers during the march. Countrywide protests ensued, as did a surge of sectarian tit-for-tat violence. On July 21, known as "Bloody Friday," 20 IRA bombs exploded within hours of one another in Belfast. The UVF responded with the beating and execution of Catholic civilians. Recognizing that the situation in Northern Ireland was about to degenerate into full-scale civil war, Britain took control on March 24, 1973 by establishing direct rule over the north and dispatching troops to occupy several "no-go" areas in Belfast. By the end of 1973, more than 800 people had been killed as a direct result of the Troubles, as they became known.

On August 31, 1994, after 25 years of political and sectarian conflict, the IRA declared a cease-fire and committed itself to the creation of a lasting peace and the reunification of Ireland. On October 12, 1994, the Loyalist paramilitary groups also declared a cease-fire. Sinn Féin (acting as the IRA's political wing) and the British government then began to wage a verbal war in the courtrooms over such issues as decommissioning of arms, withdrawing British troops, and disbanding the Protestant police force. For a time the citizens of Northern Ireland were able to experience what many of us take for granted: living without the constant fear of bombs, bullets, and terrorist threats. Tourism in Northern Ireland exploded, new businesses opened in anticipation of a lasting peace, and a new wave of optimism swept the island as the world community waited and hoped.

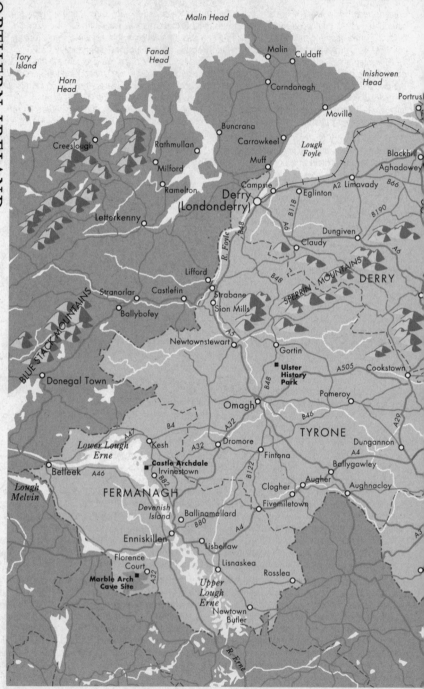

Kintyre
(Scotland)

e Giant's
useway

ce
tle

Rathlin
Island

Bull Pt.

Ballintoy

Ballycastle

Rue Pt.

Carrick
-a-rede

Ballintoy

A2

B15

Bushmills

ewart

eraine

Armoy

Cushendun

North Channel

Cushendall

Red Bay

Ballymoney

Glenariff

A2

ANTRIM MOUNTAINS

Glens of
Antrim

Carnlough Bay

R. Bann

ANTRIM

Carnlough

A26

A43

A42

TO STRANRAER,
CAIRNRYAN,
SCOTLAND

Ballymena

A36

Larne
Harbour

gh

rea

Ballygally

Larne

ghera

A8

A26

Ballyclare

TO STRANRAER,
ISLE OF MAN

more

Toome

Randalstown

Magherafelt

Whitehead

Antrim

Eden

Carrickfergus

Newtownabbey

Belfast Lough

Bangor

Belfast
International
Airport

A52

Lough
Neagh

Crumlin

Belfast

A20

Newtownards

Belfast
City
Airport

Ardboe

wartstown

Comber

Greyabbey

Ards
Peninsula

Lisburne

Strangford
Lough

Portadown

Hillsborough

Saintfield

A22

A20

Lurgan

Cragavon

A26

A24

Killyleagh

A3

A1

Ballynahinch

Strangford

Portaferry

Armagh

Banbridge

DOWN

Car Ferry

arkethill

R. Bann

A25

Downpatrick

y

Castlewellan

Dundrum

Ardglass

ARMAGH

A28

A25

A2

Bessbrook

B133

Dundrum Bay

N

Camlough

Newry

Newcastle

MOUNTAINS OF MOURNE

Slieve Donard
Mountain

KEY

Warrenpoint

A2

Rail Lines

Carlingford Lough

Kilkeel

Ferry Lines

0   10 miles

0   15 km

AN UNPRECEDENTED RETURN TO VIOLENCE

In 1996, the IRA began a full-scale campaign of terror in both Northern Ireland and the Republic of Ireland. The bombs in London's Canary Wharf and Manchester (which killed two, injured hundreds, and caused millions of dollars in damage) and the bizarre murder of Irish policeman Jerry McCabe were but a prelude to the worst violence in decades. The critical incident was the so-called "Siege of Drumcree." Essentially, the Orange Order (a Protestant group) decided to reroute its annual march through a Catholic neighborhood—knowing full well it would incite the wrath of the residents as well as Nationalists across the province. To prevent violence, the RUC, the Northern Irish police force, blocked the marchers, and a three-day standoff ensued. Protestants from all over the province poured into the city to support the Orangemen, and the RUC reversed its decision and allowed the Orangemen to march. Watching the peaceful Nationalist protesters get forcibly yanked from the roads and Catholic residents forced from their neighborhood to clear a way for the marchers enraged the Catholic community and unleashed the most violence—in virtually every Northern Irish city—seen since the late 1960s. Belfast and Derry were particularly hard hit: Dozens of cars were hijacked and set afire, stores were ransacked, and for a week the world had the chilling experience of watching Nationalist mobs and police exchange plastic bullets and gasoline bombs in almost nightly battles (one man was killed). At press time, summer 1997, Northern Ireland citizens were again bracing themselves for another summer of civil violence as the marching season approached. Four RUC men and several Catholic and Protestant civilians died during a resurgence of tit-for-tat killings, while talks between the Orange Order and the Nationalists broke down due to Unionist opposition.

However, the results of the British general election have brought about a growing sense of optimism for future peace in Northern Ireland. New Labour, under party leader Tony Blair, has discussed re-opening talks with Sinn Féin with the view of having them included in the all-party peace talks due to resume in September, 1997. And with Sinn Féin winning two seats at Westminster and one in the Dáil (the Republic's parliament), there are hopes of a new and lasting IRA cease-fire within a few months. It is generally agreed, however, that cease-fires on either side are unlikely until after the end of the potentially fraught marching season.

After a year and a half of delays by the British government, coupled with a continuing refusal to talk directly with Sinn Féin, a bomb exploded in London's Canary Wharf in February of 1996, heralding the renewal of the IRA's bloody campaign to reunite Northern Ireland with the Republic. Months later the Troubles-related violence reached a crescendo in the aftermath of the so-called "Siege of Drumcree" (*see* box, *above*). As we go to print, in summer 1997, the situation seems to be deteriorating: "All party" talks have stalled, and with Sinn Féin barred from the discussions, many question the effectiveness of the talks. To their credit, as of press time, the Unionist paramilitary groups have kept their cease-fire in spite of the IRA's bomb attacks.

Northern Ireland's sporadic bursts of violence, armored troop carriers, and fortress-like police stations definitely cast a pall over the province but should not deter you from visiting. Northern Ireland has the lowest crime rate in the United Kingdom and Ireland, and you are far more likely to be mugged in Dublin or Cork than affected by terrorist activity in Belfast or Derry. Tourists are rarely ever harmed or affected by the Troubles. But be smart: If there seems to be a lot of civil unrest going on (such as in July, prime marching season for the Orangemen), it may be best to stay out of the province or, at the very least, to avoid the staunchly Catholic or Protestant areas after dark. Otherwise, when there's little civil unrest (i.e., 99% of the time), Northern Ireland can be a pleasant and intriguing place to visit: The country is beautiful and the people extremely hospitable. Particularly worthwhile is the Causeway Coast, with the celebrated Giant's Causeway, and the lush lake land around Enniskillen and Lough Erne. Derry and Belfast are also most worthwhile stops—Belfast for its architecture and art scene, Derry for its fortified city center and reasonably bacchanalian pub scene (Derry also makes a good base for exploring County Fermanagh and, in the Republic, County Donegal).

Strange as it may seem, Northern Ireland is actually one of the safest places in Ireland for a tourist. With so many soldiers and police about, crime is not really a problem.

BASICS

PHONES

Country code: 011. British Telecom provides phone service in Northern Ireland. BT pay phones are easy to find throughout the province; the ones with a red stripe around them accept standard British coins, while phones with a green stripe require the use of a phone card, available at newsagents, train and bus stations, tourist information centers, and numerous other locations. Look for signs saying PHONECARDS SOLD HERE. Phone cards come with a fixed number of units (10, 20, 50, 100), each valued at 10p. You cannot use Telecom Éireann phone cards in the North, just as you cannot use British Telecom cards in the Republic. Dial 192 for general inquiries, 153 for international inquiries, and 155 for an international operator. To call the Republic from the North, dial 00353, followed by the area code without the initial "0," followed by the remainder of the number. For emergencies dial 999.

VISITOR INFORMATION

Northern Irish Tourist Information Centres are sprinkled throughout the country. Besides their requisite stock of maps and brochures, they also make lodging reservations for a £1–£3 fee. If you're planning an extended stay in Northern Ireland, consider purchasing their excellent pocket-size guides, *Where to Stay in Northern Ireland* (£4) and *Where to Eat in Northern Ireland* (£3). In general, Northern Irish tourist centers are open weekdays 9–5 with extended weekday and weekend hours in the summer. Offices in large cities are usually open on Saturday afternoons and Sunday mornings.

For other basic information *see* Chapter 1.

COMING AND GOING

BY BUS

Northern Ireland's bus company, **Ulsterbus** (tel. 01232/333–000), crosses the border to connect with Bus Éireann routes. The journey from Belfast to Dublin takes about 2¾ hours, with a change at Monaghan, and costs £10.

BY FERRY

The most convenient way to travel to Northern Ireland from the United Kingdom is via ferry. **SeaCat** (Donegall Quay, tel. 01232/313–543 from the Republic of Ireland, or 0345/523–523 from the North) ferries depart three to four times per day from Belfast's Donegall Quay to Stranraer, Scotland (90 min, £22–£25). **Stena Line** (tel. 0990/707–076 or 01233/647–047) sends four to eight ferries per day between Belfast Harbour and Stranraer. Tickets cost £22–£26 (£30–£38 round-trip). **P&O** (Fleet St. Terminal, Larne Harbour, tel. 0990/980–0888 or 01574/274–321) offers daily service from Larne Harbour, 32 km (20 mi) north of Belfast, to Cairnryan, Scotland. **Isle of Man Steam Packet Co.** (Donegall Quay, Belfast, tel. 01232/351–009) offers direct service from Belfast Harbour to the Isle of Man. Ferries sail from Belfast twice per week mid-April through September only, and tickets cost £25–£30. Students and Eurail and InterRail pass holders receive substantial discounts on most ferries, and bicycles are transported free on most routes. For more ferry information, *see* Coming and Going *in* Belfast, *below*.

BY PLANE

Northern Ireland's principal airport is **Belfast International Airport** (Crumlin, tel. 01849/422–888), 30 km (19 mi) northwest of the city, offering skeletal service to a handful of international destinations; call **Air UK** (tel. 01345/666–777) or **British Airways** (tel. 01345/222–111) for reservations. **Belfast City Airport** (Syndenham, tel. 01232/457–745), 6½ km (4 mi) northeast of town, handles U.K. flights only. **Aer Lingus** (tel. 01232/314–844) offers flights to Dublin, Shannon, and London; **British Airways** (tel. 0345/222–111) flies to most major cities in the United Kingdom; **Delta** (tel. 01232/480–526) goes to Dublin, London, and Manchester. Eight kilometers (5 miles) from Derry, **Eglantin Airport** (tel. 01504/810–784) is served by British Airways, with flights to Scotland and England.

BY TRAIN

The only train arrivals at Belfast Central Station from the Republic are from Dublin (12–18 per day). The trip takes roughly 2½ hours and costs £15. There is no direct train service between Derry and the Republic of Ireland.

GETTING AROUND

Since Northern Ireland is rather small and trains and buses are relatively cheap, most discount passes aren't such a great deal. In 1996, **Northern Irish Railways** had the fantastic policy of offering a day of unlimited rail travel for £5 Monday through Saturday. On Sundays NI Railways' Tracker ticket offers unlimited travel for £3, students £1.50; and Ulsterbus offers the Sunday Rambler with unlimited travel for £5, students £2.50. Ask at any station for details. One last note: The Republic-issued Travelsave stamp is good for the Dublin–Belfast trip, but not elsewhere in the North. The Youth Hostel Association of Northern Ireland (YHANI) and Translink offer a "Go As You Please" package for £69, which gives you seven days' unlimited travel by bus and rail and six nights' accommodation in any YHANI hostel. Contact YHANI (22 Donegall Rd., Belfast BT12 5JN, tel. 01232/324–733).

BY BICYCLE

If the weather is good—and most of the year it isn't—touring Northern Ireland by bike is a great way to go. Stena Lines and the Isle of Man Steam Packet Co. ferries will transport your bike for free, while Sea-Cat charges £10. Taking your bike on the train or bus costs an extra 25% of your one-way fare (be sure to purchase a bike pass at the train station before getting on the train). Bus drivers are generally more lenient and will sometimes let you take your bike gratis if there is room. The **Raleigh Rent-A-Bike** scheme offers mountain bikes for £7 per day, £35 per week, with a £40 deposit.

BY BUS

Bus travel is both quick and fairly priced. The extensive bus network means it's easy to reach any town from a major hub like Belfast or Derry. The principal bus company is the state-owned **Ulsterbus** (tel. 01232/333–000), which has offices scattered throughout the country. Comprehensive timetables are available free at any depot. An Ulsterbus trip from Belfast to Dublin costs £10 one-way; from Belfast to Derry the fare is £5.10 one-way. Ulsterbus gives substantial student discounts (10%–40% off) to those with an ISIC card. Ulsterbus also offers a range of day tours from Belfast for £7.50 to £18.50. A long-distance trip leaves around 9 AM and returns between 8:45 and 11:30 PM, depending on the journey you take. A number of the day tours explore the wild scenery of the Donegal Highlands (Mt. Errigal, Sheephaven Bay and Glenveagh National Park), while others head directly north to the Giant's Causeway and the Bushmills distillery. Specific day tours leave on specific days so you'll need to pick up a booklet from a local Ulsterbus Depot or The Travel Centre (Europa Buscentre, Glengall St., tel. 01232/337–006).

HITCHING

Hitchhiking in the North is much more difficult than in the Republic. The threat of terrorism has made many Northern Irish suspicious of hitchhikers, so don't be surprised if you get stuck for hours on a Northern Irish highway, vainly proffering your thumb as hundreds of cars pass by without so much as a wave. This is particularly true around Belfast and Derry but less so in the rural countryside, where the odds of getting a ride are much better. It's not easy, or recommended, to hitch across the border. If you need to, however, your chances are better if you get a ride with someone going the whole way. If you get a ride to the border and then try to find a ride across the border, you may be waiting for a long, long, long time.

BY TRAIN

Northern Irish Railways (NIR), the Northern Irish train network, is sorely limited. In fact, there are only three main routes: Belfast–Derry via Coleraine, Belfast–Bangor along the shore of Belfast Lough, and Belfast–Dublin. If you're headed for the Causeway Coast and don't have your own vehicle, you'll definitely end up on a bus. On the plus side, Northern Ireland's trains are comfortable and efficient. Pick up free route maps and timetables at Northern Rail's main depot, **Belfast Central** (E. Bridge St., tel. 01232/899–411).

WHERE TO SLEEP

By far, the cheapest beds in Northern Ireland can be found in youth hostels. But hostels fill up fast, especially during the summer, so be sure to book ahead. The best hostels are those run by **Independent Holiday Hostels (IHH),** a Republic-based operation with about 10 hostels scattered through Northern Ireland, and more popping up all the time. IHH hostels are cheap, with beds for £5–£7, and regulations are practically nil. A list of IHH hostels is available from tourist offices and member hostels.

If you plan to camp, pick up the "Guide to Caravan and Camping in Northern Ireland" (30p) or the "Caravan and Camping Guide" 1998 (£1.50). Both are available at Northern Ireland tourist offices.

Other hostels are operated by the **Youth Hostel Association of Northern Ireland (YHANI).** Currently there are eight, and the association plans to open more in the next few years. At YHANI hostels curfews and daytime lockouts are common, and check-in hours are generally 8–10 in the morning and 5–10 at night. Other annoying features include spineless bunk beds, noisy dorm rooms, and an early wake-up call. It costs £7–£9.50 to stay in a YHANI hostel, plus an additional one-time fee of £7.50 for a membership card (available at any hostel). The fee is unnecessary if you already have an An Óige or HI membership. Stop by any Northern Irish Tourist Information Centre or YHANI's Belfast office for a map and detailed list of member hostels. *22 Donegal Rd., Belfast, tel. 01232/324–733, fax 01232/439–699. Open weekdays 9–5.*

More comfortable and private are Northern Ireland's numerous bed-and-breakfasts (B&Bs), which generally charge £12–£19 per person. A standard Northern Irish breakfast (called, appropriately enough, an Ulsterfry) consists of fried eggs, fried bacon, cornflakes, juice, fried bread or potato, and coffee. Purchase the *Where to Stay in Northern Ireland* (£4) from any tourist office for a comprehensive list of B&Bs.

BELFAST

Northern Ireland's capital and largest city has been called everything from a well-armed wasteland to "Little Beirut." Yet take a stroll through the city center and you might wonder where the war-torn Belfast that you've seen on CNN is. With a well-respected university, a solid collection of performing-arts troupes, intriguing museums, and bustling industry, Belfast seems like any other vibrant, cosmopolitan capital—until an armored troop carrier rolls by. These tanklike vehicles are the main components of Northern Ireland's police force and are the most visible reminder that Belfast remains the traditional flash point for Northern Ireland's religious violence. Though 8,500 soldiers were sent to the city, in 1993 alone more than 125 residents were killed and at least 300 were wounded as a result of the Troubles. Some victims were targeted by the IRA, some by Protestant paramilitary groups, some even by the RUC and UDR, the province's ostensible peacekeepers.

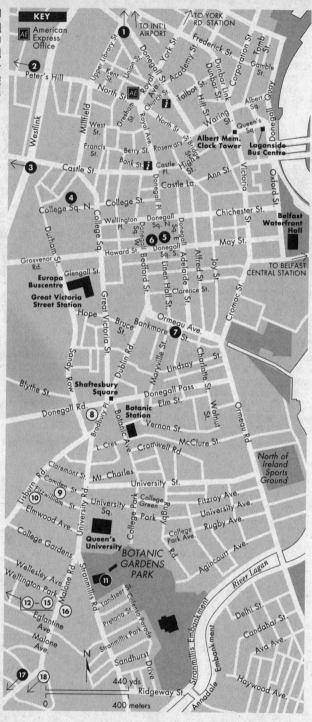

BELFAST

KEY

| AE | American Express Office |

Sights ●

Belfast Zoo, **1**
City Hall, **5**
Falls District, **3**
Linenhall Library, **6**
Malone House, **17**
Old Museum
Arts Centre, **4**
Ormeau Baths
Gallery, **7**
Shankill District, **2**
Ulster Museum, **11**

Lodging ○

Arnie's Backpacker
Hostel (IHH), **9**
Belfast YHANI, **8**
Eglantine Guest
House, **13**
The George Guest
House, **15**
Liserin Guest
House, **14**
The Marine
House, **12**
Peare Court Guest
House, **16**
Queen Mary's
YWCA, **10**
Queen's Elms Halls
of Residence, **18**

Belfast greatly changed after the cease-fire of 1994. A spirit of optimism pervaded the city, as English troops were sent home, streets in "sensitive" areas and strategic points along the Peace Line—a 15-foot wall built by the military in the mid-1970s to separate the Shankhill and Falls Road communities—were opened, and citizens opened new businesses to meet the growing tourist industry. This optimism and the progress of the all-party talks on Northern Ireland's future were dealt a harsh blow by the bombings in London and Manchester. In July of 1996, Belfast was rocked by some of the worst violence in the history of the Troubles in the wake of the Protestant Orange Order being allowed to march through a staunchly Catholic neighborhood in Portadown, south of Belfast in County Armagh. The present city climate is uncertain but more stable. If you visit the city in the hope of witnessing an incident or seeing any of the scars of its troubled history, you will be disappointed. For the time you are there, you might not even see a soldier or a roadblock. The Shankhill and Falls Road will probably strike you as tiny in comparison to the giants that the world media has transformed them into, but the bright, political murals on many of the walls and the atmosphere on those streets will remind the casual visitor that a huge divide separates the community. To understand the extent of this divide will take more than a casual visit and a few mural photographs.

Despite all its troubles, Belfast is a cultured and cosmopolitan capital. Helping to reinforce this image is the city center's vast, pedestrianized shopping district, and its handful of galleries, theaters, and museums. Like Edinburgh and Glasgow, Belfast has bolstered its reputation as "The City of the Arts" with an impressive list of events: the Belfast Music Festival (March), the Guinness Jazz & Blues Festival (mid-June), the Royal Ulster Arts Exhibition (August), the Belfast Folk Festival (early September), and the Belfast Arts & Drama Festival at Queen's (mid-November).

Belfast's location is striking: The city is nestled on the coast, buffered by green water on one side and by heath-covered hills on the other.

Considering the province's small size, the capital also makes a good base for exploring the Antrim Coast or County Derry, both of which are frequently served from Belfast by Northern Irish Railways and Ulsterbus. Even if you're short on time, Belfast is close enough to Dublin—2½ hours by train—to merit at least a day trip. This holds doubly true if your impression of the city has been gleaned from the world press. Although remnants of the grim, Orwellian reality of Belfast strike people in different ways, the bottom line is best summed up by a Northern Irish tourist brochure: "Despite what you've probably heard, Belfast is not what you expect."

BASICS

AMERICAN EXPRESS • This office offers currency exchange, helps with lost or stolen cards and checks, and cashes personal checks for AmEx cardholders only. The office does not hold mail. *108–112 Royal Ave., off North St., BT1 1DP, tel. 01232/242–341 or 0181/667–1111 for 24 hr emergency info. Open weekdays 9–5:30.*

BUREAU DE CHANGE • Tons of banks litter Donegall Square and Donegall Place. The **post office** (*see below*) also provides currency exchange and has an ATM outside that accepts Visa, MasterCard, Cirrus, and PLUS.

DISCOUNT TRAVEL AGENCY • USIT is Ireland's student travel center, where experts diligently find the cheapest domestic and international air, bus, train, and ferry deals available. *2 locations: Fountain Centre, College St., 1 block NW of Donegall Sq., tel. 01232/324–073; open weekdays 9:30–5:30 (Tues. from 10), Sat. 10–1. Queen's University, Student Union Bldg., University Rd., tel. 01232/241–830; open weekdays 9:30–5:30 (Wed. from 10).*

EMBASSY • United States Consulate. *Queen St., Belfast, tel. 01232/328–239. Open weekdays 1–5.*

LAUNDRY • The cheapest place to wash clothes is the launderette in **Queen's University Student Union Building** (University Rd., no phone). A load of wash costs £1, a spin in the dryer, 20p.

MAIL • Belfast's **General Post Office** provides the usual array of services and has a bureau de change. *25 Castle Pl., BT1 1BB, tel. 01232/323–740. Open weekdays 9–5:30, Sat. 9–7.*

VISITOR INFORMATION • The **Northern Irish Tourist Information Centre** stocks walking guides, maps, bus and train info, and extensive accommodations listings for the province. Particularly useful are their pocket-size lodging and restaurant guides (£3–£4). They also have a bureau de change and will book a room anywhere in the United Kingdom for £2.50. From July to August, they offer a toll-free information and reservation line open 7 PM–10 PM; dial 0800/404–050. *59 North St., tel. 01232/246–609.*

From Donegall Sq., walk north on Donegall Pl., turn right on North St. Open July–Aug., Mon.–Sat. 9–7, Sun. 10–4; Sept.–June, weekdays 9–5:15.

Bord Fáilte, the Irish Republic's national tourist office, has volumes of Republic-related information, from festival and transit schedules to maps, historical guides, and accommodations brochures. *53 Castle St., tel. 01232/327–888. From Donegall Sq., walk north on Donegall Pl., turn left on College St. Open weekdays 9–5 (Mar.–Sept., also Sat. 9–12:30).*

COMING AND GOING

BY BUS • The very modern **Europa Bus Centre** (Glengall St., off Great Victoria St., tel. 01232/333–000) provides service to Counties Tyrone, Fermanagh, Down, and all Irish Republic destinations. Buses depart from here to Omagh (10 per day, £5.80), Enniskillen (11 per day, £6.10), Derry (15 per day, £6.10 single), Newcastle (19 per day, £10.70), and Dublin (7 per day, 4 on Sun., £10), among other destinations. The station has an info desk staffed weekdays 9–6 and Saturday 10–6. To reach Donegall Square and the city center, turn right out of the station, left on Great Victoria Street, and right on Howard Street—an easy 5- to 10-minute walk.

The new **Laganside Bus Centre** serves Antrim (i.e., the Causeway Coast and the Glens of Antrim), the area immediately surrounding Belfast, and parts of County Down. Six to eight buses per day travel to Portrush and Ballycastle (both £5.60) and Cushendall via Ballymena or Larne (£4.50). The station's info counter (tel. 01232/320–011) is open Monday–Saturday 8:30–6. To get to Donegall Square, exit left on Albert Square, turn left on Victoria Street, and turn right on Chichester Street.

BY FERRY • Several companies sail directly from Belfast's **Donegall Quay Terminal,** on the north side of town near the York Street train station. **SeaCat** (tel. 0345/523–523) runs daily ferries (5 per day in summer) to Stranraer, Scotland. Fares are £23–£26 (£16–£17 students). **Stena Line** (tel. 0990/707–070 or 01232/615–950) also offers daily ferry service (8 per day in summer) to Stranraer. Tickets cost £22–£26, and Stena Line offers a 50% discount to Eurail and BritRail pass holders. The **Isle of Man Steam Packet Co.** (tel. 01232/351–009) offers service to the nearby Isle of Man; tickets are £25–£30. Ferries depart on Mondays and Fridays from mid-April to September. To reach Donegall Quay, take Bus 78 (£1.05) from Donegall Square or splurge on a cab (£2–£3.50). The terminal has no information line, so call the ferry companies directly or try the tourist office.

From Larne Harbour, 32 km (20 mi) north of Belfast, **P&O Ferries** (tel. 01574/274–321) offers daily service to Cairnryan, Scotland. The 2½-hour crossing costs £21–£25 (students receive discounts of up to 50%). There is convenient rail service from Belfast Central to Larne Harbour's train depot (£2.90), adjacent to the **Fleet Street Ferry Terminal** (tel. 01574/274–321).

BY PLANE • **Belfast International Airport** (Crumlin, tel. 018494/22888), 30 km (19 mi) northwest of town, offers service to a handful of international destinations—mainly Paris and Frankfurt. Airport shuttle buses (£3.70) leave Monday–Saturday every half hour (hourly on Sun.) from both the Europa Bus Centre and the airport, between 6 AM and 11:30 PM. **Belfast City Airport** (Syndenham, tel. 01232/457–745), with U.K. flights only, is 6½ km (4 mi) outside town. To reach it, take Bus 21 (78p) from Donegall Square or a train (£1.50) from Central Station to Sydenham Halt, an easy 10-minute walk from the airport. For more information about airlines serving both airports, *see* Coming and Going, *above.*

BY TRAIN • Belfast has two main rail stations, Belfast Central and (ironically) the more central Great Victorian Street Station, as well as a handful of other depots convenient for intra-Belfast travel. Free red-and-white **Rail-Link** (tel. 01232/246–485) shuttle buses travel between Belfast Central, the bus stations, Donegall Square, High Street, Oxford Street, Donegall Place, and the York Road depot. Outside each station—and along the streets—are shuttle stops marked RAIL-LINK; shuttles run every 10 minutes or so, Monday–Saturday only.

Northern Irish Railway's main depot, **Belfast Central** (E. Bridge St., tel. 01232/899–411) is 1 km (½ mi) east of the city center; to get to Donegall Square take a Rail-Link shuttle, a city bus, or exit left on East Bridge Street, turn right on Oxford Street, and turn left on May Street. Trains leave frequently for Dublin's Connolly (£15 single), Derry (£6.10 single), and Portrush (£5.15 single). If you're traveling to Scotland or England by ferry, a new rail link also provides direct service to Larne Harbour (17 per day, £3.10 single). Free train schedules are available at the ticket windows. The information counter is staffed Monday–Saturday 6:30 AM–11 PM, Sunday 9:15 AM–9:45 PM.

The shiny new **Great Victoria Street Station** is adjacent to the Europa Bus Centre (*see below*) and conveniently located in the city center. All trains traveling to or from Belfast Central also stop here, except trains on the Belfast–Dublin line, which only stop at Belfast Central.

GETTING AROUND

Belfast's principal sights are grouped around **Donegall Square,** the city's official center. North of Donegall Square is **Donegall Place,** Belfast's minimall mecca, where the streets bristle with Victorian shop fronts and Georgian office blocks. Until two years ago, Donegall Place and its tributaries—College Street, Castle Lane, Castle Place, and North Street—were off-limits to unauthorized vehicles and littered with RUC checkpoints and crowd barriers that helped ensure only peaceful pedestrians got through. From Donegall Square, walk south on Bedford Street (which becomes Dublin Road) to reach Shaftesbury Square and Queen's University (about a 10-minute walk), or take Bus 70 or 71. These areas are liberally sprinkled with pubs, cafés, and B&Bs.

BY BIKE • McConvey's (Pottinger's Entry, off High St., tel. 01232/330–322) rents mountain bikes on the Raleigh Rent-A-Bike plan for £7 per day or £40 per week, with £30 deposit.

BY BUS • Bus fares within Belfast range from 78p to £1.05, depending on the distance. Tickets can be purchased on board, at newsagents displaying a CITYBUS sign, or at the **Citybus Kiosk** (Donegall Sq. W, tel. 01232/246–485), which is open weekdays 8–5:30, Saturday 9–5:30. Nearly all local buses start or end their journeys at Donegall Square, the first at 6 AM and the last at 11 PM. Timetables and route maps are available from the Citybus Kiosk.

BY TRAIN • The **intercity train,** used mainly by suburban commuters, leaves Belfast Central every 10–15 minutes on its way toward **Botanic Station** and the new **Great Victoria Street Station,** conveniently located near Donegall Square. Botanic Avenue is lined with some of Belfast's best pubs and restaurants, and if you turn right from the depot you'll quickly be funneled onto Shaftesbury Square.

WHERE TO SLEEP

All of Belfast's best budget accommodations (including the hostels, YWCA, student residences, and B&Bs) are in the University neighborhood in South Belfast, generally considered the safest, most neutral section of the city. Most B&Bs are found on Eglantine Avenue and Wellington Park, off Lisburn and Malone roads. On Eglantine Avenue, you'll find five similarly priced B&Bs. At **The Marine House** (30 Eglantine Ave., tel. 01232/662–828), £19 will get you a night in a large, fluffy bed and an enormous fried breakfast. Across the street are **Eglantine Guest House** (21 Eglantine Ave., tel. 01232/667–585), with beds from £17–£19 (Louie, the owner, will also negotiate with the completely impoverished and desperate), and **Liserin Guest House** (17 Eglantine Ave., tel. 01232/660–769), with lovely, clean rooms for £19 per person. The **George Guest House** (9 Eglantine Ave., tel. 01232/683–212) offers spacious rooms for £19–£21 per person. **Pearl Court Guest House** (11 Malone Rd., Belfast BT9 6RT, tel. 01232/666–145) is a cut above the rest, with a smart, plush lounge and breakfast room, and beds for £20.50–£23.50.

HOSTELS • Arnie's Backpackers Hostel (IHH). This homey place has comfortable dorm beds (£7.50), an open fireplace and TV in the common room, and a clean kitchen. It's just down the street from Queen's University and near a number of watering holes. _63 Fitzwilliam St., tel. 01232/242–867. From Donegall Sq., take Bus 59 or walk south on Bedford St. past Shaftesbury Sq., veer right on Lisburn Rd., turn left on Fitzwilliam St. 19 beds. Laundry._

Belfast YHANI. This large, institutional complex has dorm beds for £9 and singles for £15. Unfortunately there's no kitchen, but the hostel cafeteria, which doubles as a common room, serves reasonably priced meals. They also give out maps and sell discount train tickets to Dublin. _22–32 Donegall Rd., tel. 01232/315–435. From Donegall Sq., walk south on Bedford St., turn right on Donegall Rd. 124 beds. Laundry, luggage storage._

Queen Mary's YWCA. This coed YWCA has two- and three-bed dorm rooms (beds £9) available June–August. _70 Fitzwilliam St., tel. 01232/240–439. Follow directions to Arnie's Backpackers Hostel (see above). 25 beds. Laundry, sheet rental (£2)._

STUDENT HOUSING • Queen's Elms Halls of Residence. These massive student high-rises are 1½ km (1 mi) from Queen's University. You can stay in a single (£12.80) or double (£10.10 per person) room equipped with desk and sink. If you have an ISIC card, you pay only £9.40 for either option. _78 Malone Rd., tel. 01232/381–608. From Donegall Sq. E, take Bus 71. Closed Sept. 7–mid-June (open Christmas and Easter holidays)._

FOOD

Belfast's city center is littered with chippies, fast-food chains, and a number of pubs, as well as a few pricey hotel restaurants. A better option is to head for the **Golden Mile,** a triangular area famed for its variety of restaurants. The Golden Mile is bounded by Howard Street, Great Victoria Street, and Dublin

THE ABCS OF NORTHERN IRISH GROUPS

INLA: The Irish National Liberation Army, a splinter group of the IRA. IRA–INLA infighting was responsible for numerous murders in the 1980s.

IRA: The Irish Republican Army, an illegal paramilitary outfit whose ultimate goal is the reunification of Northern Ireland with the Republic. Staunchly anti-Brit. Responsible for hundreds of murders and bombings, including the 1996 bombs in Manchester and London's Canary Wharf.

IRISH REGIMENT: Formerly known as the Ulster Defense Regiment, this army unit—drawn from the local Protestant population—is responsible for keeping the peace in Northern Ireland. Set up by the British Crown when a group of paratroopers was accused of killing 13 unarmed Catholic civilians in the 1972 Bloody Sunday massacre in Derry.

LOYALIST: Anyone pro-British in outlook, generally also Protestant.

ORANGEMEN: A legal Loyalist group, named after the Protestant William of Orange, conqueror of the Catholic James II at the Battle of the Boyne in 1690.

REPUBLICAN: Anyone who supports Northern Ireland's union with the Dublin-based Republic, or, more specifically, a supporter of Sinn Féin.

RUC: Royal Ulster Constabulary, general name for the Northern Irish police force.

SINN FÉIN: Republican political party. Commonly assumed to be the IRA's political wing.

THE TROUBLES: Generic term for Northern Ireland's current Catholic–Protestant turmoil.

UFF: Ulster Freedom Fighters, an illegal Loyalist group often linked to the larger UDA (Ulster Defense Association). When the UDA was legal, the UFF was the group named responsible for the hundreds of sectarian murders commonly assumed to have been committed by the UDA.

ULSTER: Historic name of the northern province of Ireland. Used today to denote the six counties still governed by Britain.

UVF: Ulster Volunteer Force, another illegal pro-Brit paramilitary group.

Road (which becomes Bedford Street). If nothing here strikes your fancy, continue south from Shaftesbury Square down either Botanic Avenue or Bradbury Place (which turns into University Road), two student quarters peppered with good restaurants and cafés. Nearby Lisburn Road has a variety of ethnic eateries. For fresh produce, a small **farmers market** is held daily on Castle Street near the Bord Fáilte office.

CITY CENTER • The city center's most famous restaurant is **Nick's Warehouse** (35 Hill St., off Warring St., tel. 0232/439–690). Although it looks frighteningly posh (and has prices to match), Nick's potato-herb soup is first-rate, as is the smoked haddock-and-salmon pasta. A full meal runs upward of £12, and closer to £20 with wine. Both **Kelly's Cellars** (30 Bank St., off Donegall Pl., tel. 01232/324–835) and **Deer's Head** (76 North St., tel. 01232/239–163) are renowned for their home-style pub grub. The Deer's Head even has vegetarian options, such as a veggie stir-fry (£4) and veggie burgers (£4). Another good place for pub grub is **White's Tavern** (High St., off Castle Pl., tel. 01232/243–080), reputedly the oldest pub in Belfast (established in 1630). Try the chicken-and-corn crepes (£3) or roast pork with chips (£4.50).

THE GOLDEN MILE • The Golden Mile's most famous landmark is **Crown Liquor Saloon** (46 Great Victoria St., tel. 01232/249–476). This Victorian-era pub is famous for its carved-oak ceiling and cozy, private snugs. A common call here is "pint of Guinness, bowl of stew, please," but also try the beef-and-Cafferty's pie (£4) or the steak, pea, and chip plate (£3.50). **Ho Ho Chinese Restaurant and Takeaway** (71 Dublin Rd., tel. 01232/237–811) has a huge selection of entrées for about £4 and is open until midnight most nights. The popular **Harvey's** (95 Great Victoria St., tel. 01232/233–433) serves a variety of tasty pizzas (£5), chili (£2.55), and vegetarian dishes (5.35). If you don't mind spending £12–£15 on a meal, head to **La Belle Epoque** (61 Dublin Rd., tel. 01232/323–244). This elegant place specializes in fresh game and fish complemented by an extensive wine list. The less well-off can still dine on a three-course lunch for £7. Much cheaper is **Speranza** (16 Shaftesbury Sq., tel. 01232/230–213), a family-run Italian restaurant that does pizza and pasta in the £5–£9 range.

UNIVERSITY AREA • South of Shaftesbury Square, on Botanic Avenue and University Road, you'll find a good collection of budget restaurants. At the upper end of the scale is **Saints & Scholars** (3 University Sq., off University Rd., tel. 01232/325–137), the sort of place students like to take their visiting parents. Choose from its generous appetizer menu (£2.50–£5), or try the duck confit (£8). More accessible is **Empire** (42 Botanic Ave., tel. 01232/328–110), a lively pub that offers deals like a burger and chips or a 10-inch pizza for £2, and the ever popular pizza-and-pint special (£4). The most famous chippy around is **Bishops** (34 Bradbury Pl., tel. 01232/311–827), which serves exceptional fish-and-chips for £3. **Jharna Tandoori** (133 Lisburn Rd., tel. 01232/381–299) serves tasty, spicy Indian entrées for £7–£9.50. **Eatwell Health Food Delicatessen** (413 Lisburn Rd., tel. 01232/664–362) has all sorts of good things to take on a picnic, such as vegetarian spring rolls (60p) and pita sandwiches (£1.20–£1.60).

WORTH SEEING

The Northern Irish Tourist Information Centre (*see above*) stocks free "Belfast Civic Trail" brochures, which provide a series of five highly detailed, self-guided walking tours. Each covers roughly a mile of the city center and takes about an hour to complete—strongly recommended for those with an eye for history. If you have a love of walking and drinking, check out the guided **Belfast Pub Walking Tours** (tel. 01232/658–337), which depart from the Northern Irish Tourist Information Centre every Saturday at 2 PM. The cost is £5—not including drinks. **Citybus** (tel. 01232/458–484) offers a 3½-hour "Belfast City Tour," which takes in Belfast Lough, the docks (where the Titanic was built), various Parliament buildings, and the Belfast Zoo. The tour costs £7, including tea and scones, and runs from June to August; call Citybus for current schedules and details on other tours to North Down and East Antrim.

BELFAST ZOO • This place is fairly standard as far as zoos go. Its biggest draw isn't its collection of animals—though the underwater viewing room that looks out at sea lions, penguins, and seals is pretty cool—but rather its location: high above the city in a vast mountainside park, which is free and always open. Climb up nearby Cave Hill for an unbeatable view of Belfast Lough and the city center. **Belfast Castle** (tel. 01232/776–925), on the wooded slopes adjacent to the zoo, is now an upscale restaurant open Monday–Saturday 9:30 AM–11:30 PM. *Antrim Rd., 6 mi north of city center, tel. 01232/776–277. From Donegall Sq. W, take Bus 5, 10, or 45. Admission: £4.50 in summer, £3.50 rest of year. Open Apr.–Sept., daily 10–5; Oct.–Mar., Sun.–Thurs. 10–3:30, Fri. 10–2:30.*

BOTANIC GARDENS • Popular with students and families on the weekends, the Botanic Gardens is a well-kept city park with plenty of grass, trees, and wrought-iron benches. In the park are **The Palm House,** a cast-iron and glass house built in 1839 by the Marquis of Donegall, with tropical palms and flowers in the humid east wing and colorful blossoms in the west wing. The nearby **Tropical Ravine** houses jungle plants. Farther into the park, near Queen's University's Physical Education building, is the sweet-smelling rose garden, with rows of blooming bushes. *Stranmills Rd., just past Queen's University. Admission free. From Donegall Sq. E, take Bus 69 or 71. Gardens open daily until sunset. Palm House and Tropical Ravine open weekdays 10–noon and 1–4, weekends 1–4 (Apr.–Sept., daily until 5).*

CITY HALL • Belfast's city center is dominated by its Renaissance-style City Hall, built between 1898 and 1906. Its most impressive feature is the 173-foot Great Dome, which dominates Donegall Square and the city center. Inside, look for the oak-and-marble Grand Stairway and, off the second-floor landing, the Council Chamber, Banquet Hall, and Great Hall. The Great Hall was destroyed by German bombers during World War II and has since been meticulously restored. Of interest in the Council Chamber are the ornate chairs used by King George V and Queen Mary at the opening of Northern Ireland's first parliament on June 22, 1921. Be sure to catch the 30-minute guided tour, given weekdays at 10:30 and 2:30 PM mid-June–September, and Wednesdays at 10:30 October–mid-April. *Donegall Sq., tel. 01232/320–202, ext. 2346. Admission free.*

FALLS AND SHANKILL DISTRICTS • Belfast is littered with grim reminders of the Troubles. West Belfast is where the majority of violence occurred, specifically in **Shankill,** a Protestant enclave, and **Falls Road,** Shankill's Catholic counterpart. Though these neighborhoods used to be patrolled 24 hours a day by the RUC and UDR—impartial forces in theory, more supportive of the Protestant (and illegal) UVF in practice—unescorted forays are reasonably safe. Though it's unlikely you'll be affected by religious unrest in either neighborhood, they're not the nicest of 'hoods and petty crime is a possibility. Previously, the only way to explore these areas was on a taxi tour, unofficially restricted to the Catholic or Protestant district depending upon the religion of the driver. It's still not a bad way to learn about the areas; cabdrivers line up along Castle Street (west of Donegall Place), and most are well versed in the area's history (it's a simple fact of life that most will know someone who has died as a result of partisan violence). Fares for these informal tours vary from £6 to £15, depending on the driver's interest and your ability to barter. Citybus (tel. 01232/458–484) also offers a comprehensive "Living History Tour" (£7), which offers an in-depth look at Belfast's history and includes most Troubles-related sites. Highlights include Fort Jericho (the most bombed and shot-at building in Northern Ireland), the murals throughout the city, and, strangely enough, tea and scones at the Europa Bus Station halfway through. Tours depart from the General Post Office (*see* Basics, *above*) June–August, Tuesday, Thursday, and Sunday at 9:30 and 2.

A highlight of any tour is **Milltown Cemetery,** the IRA's principal burial ground. Interspersed among the tombstones and makeshift memorials is a vast collection of pro-Republican murals. Along with the standard "We Will Never Surrender" and "Our Day Will Come" slogans, also note the IRA and Native American mural (a reference to the worldwide struggle against imperialism) and the faded handful of memorials depicting black-masked gunmen squashing the British Crown. Another hot spot for murals, this time pro-Brit, is along **Donegall** and **Crumlin Roads.** Popular cries here range from "One People, One Country, One Crown" and "Ulster welcomes the UDR" to the more inflammatory "God Bless the UVF." Other murals can be found on back streets and tenement walls just off Falls and Shankhill roads, but many are being voluntarily whitewashed to help heal old wounds.

LINENHALL LIBRARY • Belfast's oldest library was founded in 1788 by Wolfe Tone, legendary Irish revolutionary leader and staunch advocate for the freedom of speech. Since then, the staff has diligently collected virtually every scrap of Troubles-related propaganda and political commentary, no matter how inflammatory. This small but extremely intriguing library contains original underground newspapers, minuscule IRA messages smuggled into and out of prison (via various baked goods), threatening UFF calendars sent to Catholic "targets" as a vivid reminder that their days were numbered, and trinkets and posters crammed into every nook. As this is a place of research, access to the library is limited; call in the morning to try and arrange an afternoon viewing. *Donegall Sq. N, across from City Hall, tel. 01232/ 321–707. Open by appt. only weekdays 9:30–5.*

SINCLAIR SEAMEN'S PRESBYTERIAN CHURCH • Somewhat off the beaten track beside a highway overpass lies this little gem of a church. The exterior is nothing special, but inside it's littered with objects from old ships, each with a story of its own to tell. The organ has port, starboard, and mast lights from an old Guinness boat that used to work the River Liffey in Dublin. There's a bell from *H.M.S. Hood,* sunk to protect Portsmouth Harbour during the second World War. The bell is struck six times for the 7 PM service, just as it would be on a ship to call the watch. There is also an old brass wheel that faces the congregation and a brass binnacle (compass) that was used as a baptismal font, both of which were salvaged from a ship built in Detroit that sunk off the Northern Irish coast. The church was first set up in 1832 by an organization known as The Seamen's Friend Society, whose object was the religious improvement of seamen frequenting the port of Belfast. In those days Belfast was flourishing as a shipping port, and the church apparently proved very successful. It is normally open only Wednesday 2–5 PM, but if you give Ailsa Campbell a ring, she'll be happy to open it up for you, and if you're lucky, you'll be offered tea and scones and be given a personal tour of every fascinating object. *Corporation Sq., tel. 01232/715–997. Head north up Victoria Street–Dunbar Link and then right up Corporation Street. Admission free.*

BELFAST WATERFRONT HALL • This pristine, new conference and concert center was completed in January 1997, and if the cease-fire had held, it might have served as an testament to a new era. It does, nevertheless, inspire hope in the future of Belfast. It's worth a visit just to look at its ornate exterior and walk around its vast interior. It has been compared to a very modern version of London's Albert Hall. Outside the front door, you can stroll along the River Lagan and enjoy a cup of coffee at the Terrace Café. *Oxford St., tel. 01232/334–400.*

MALONE HOUSE • Malone House, 6½ km (4 mi) south of the city center, was built in the late 19th century to house Northern Ireland's growing national art collection and to serve as a high-class reception hall for visiting dignitaries. Although its prestigious art holdings have since been redistributed within the United Kingdom, it does contain a few historical portraits—mostly of long-forgotten dukes and earls—as well as a permanent exhibition on Belfast's city parks. More inspiring are Malone House's lush grounds, considered the best example of Victorian horticulture in the province. *Barnett Park, Upper Malone Rd., tel. 01232/681–246. From Donegall Sq. W, take Bus 71 or 72. Admission free. Open Mon.–Sat. 9:30–6. Park open 24 hrs.*

OLD MUSEUM ARTS CENTRE (OMAC) • This excellent center has helped put Belfast on the world art map. Although it doesn't have a permanent collection, the OMAC is committed to the best in modern art and performance, both Irish and international. Events range from classical drama to controversial sculpture and photography installations. Shows generally change on a weekly basis, so call for current schedules. Admission varies with each event. *7 College Sq. N, tel. 01232/235–053. From Donegall Sq. N, walk west to College Sq., turn right, then left on College Sq. N. Open Mon.–Sat. 10–5:30.*

ORMEAU BATHS GALLERY • Owned and operated by the city, this informal gallery hosts exhibitions of modern Irish and international art, and strives to present innovative and contemporary installations. In 1997, exhibits will include works by Jack B. Yeats, Will's brother. *18A Ormeau Ave., tel. 01232/321–402. Admission free. Open Tues.–Sat. 10–6.*

QUEEN'S UNIVERSITY • Dominating University Road is Queen's University itself. Most impressive is the Lanyon building, built in 1849, and the eye-catching, early-Victorian University Square that surrounds it. The university was originally established as a college in 1845 by Queen Victoria, and it achieved full university status in 1908. Today, roughly 9,000 students, most from Northern Ireland, attend school here. The University's most recent claim to fame is alumnus Seamus Heaney, 1995 Nobel Prize winner for Literature. Inside the Lanyon Building is a **visitor center** (tel. 01232/335–252) that can give you loads of info on the university. Free public lectures—more often than not dealing with some aspect of Northern Irish politics—are often given in summer by staff and visiting professors. *University Rd., south of Shaftesbury Sq., tel. 01232/245–133.*

ULSTER MUSEUM • Belfast's biggest and most comprehensive museum, the Ulster Museum is definitely worth a few hours of your time. Located in the Botanic Gardens (*see above*) opposite Queen's University, it is a massive four-level complex with a host of permanent and temporary exhibits on subjects including Ulster history since the 1600s, a history of the post office in Ireland, Irish archaeology, local flora and fauna, and much, much more. Especially noteworthy are David West's "Venice Chair," the incredible Miervaldis Polis's "Self Portrait," the biggest ant farm you've ever seen, and a collection of artifacts pilfered from Egypt and the Middle East during England's imperial tenure. The top floor is dedicated to a rather small collection of Irish art and 20th-century painting and sculpture. If you're in Belfast for a while, you may want to tackle the museum in smaller doses and make several trips here, especially since the admission is free. *Botanic Gardens, tel. 01232/383–000. Admission free. Open weekdays 10–5, Sat. 1–5, Sun. 2–5.*

AFTER DARK

Though the city center dies shortly after dark, Belfast still has a pretty lively nightlife. Head to the area between Shaftesbury Square and Queen's University, which is well endowed with pubs, movie theaters, and late-night coffeehouses. **Old Museum Arts Centre** (*see above*), **Grand Opera House** (Great Victoria

St., tel. 01232/241–919), **Crescent Arts Centre** (01232/242–338), and **Lyric Players Theatre** (55 Ridgeway St., tel. 01232/381–081) offer live entertainment ranging from opera and drama to dance and classical music. Tickets cost £4–£30, and student discounts of up to 50% are available. For more information on local goings-on, pick up the daily *Belfast Telegraph* (28p), the free biweekly *That's Entertainment,* or the monthly *Arts Link,* available at the tourist office and local newsagents.

PUBS • Finding a solid pint in Belfast's city center is annoyingly difficult, especially if you want to avoid the yuppie crowd. One of your best options is **Kelly's Cellars** (30 Bank St., off Donegall Pl., tel. 01232/324–835), but even here there's a thick suit-and-tie contingent. On the plus side, it does have blues, folk, and even the odd traditional session on weekend nights. **Katy Daly's** (17 Ormeau Ave., tel. 01232/325–968) hosts live music almost every night. The Victorian **Crown Liquor Saloon** (46 Great Victoria St., tel. 01232/249–467) is spectacular to look at but is plagued by a dull clientele. Try instead **Lavery's Gin House** (12 Bradbury Pl., off Shaftesbury Sq., tel. 01232/327–159), a motorcycle-friendly pub with lots of Dickensian charm. Downstairs there's a straitlaced bar and lounge, upstairs a more youthful drinking hall and Metallica-blasting jukebox. Lavery's also hosts a disco 9 PM–1 AM Monday–Saturday. The warehouse-size **Empire** (42 Botanic Ave., tel. 01232/228–110) is popular with students for its international beers. Some nights it also hosts live music, generally rock and metal. Closer to Queen's University are **Eglantine** (32 Malone Rd., tel. 01232/381–994) and **Botanic Inn** (23 Malone Rd., tel. 01232/660–460), known respectively as the "Egg" and "Bot." Two popular gay pubs are **Crow's Nest** (Skipper St., tel. 01232/325–491) and **Parliament Bar** (Dunbar Link, tel. 01232/234–520).

MUSIC • **Belfast Waterfront Hall** (Oxford St., tel. 01232/334–400) has a whole range of concerts and events throughout the year, from classical to Irish traditional and pop. Tickets range from £7.50–£22.50. You can purchase them at the box office or over the phone (tel. 01232/334–455). There's also a quiet café-restaurant called **The Terrace Café** (01232/244–966) that looks out over the River Lagan. It's open from 10 AM to 8 PM and offers sandwiches (£3.50) and a two-course lunch (£7.95) with a good wine list, if you're feeling in the mood. To get there from the center, head down May Street toward the river and Belfast Central Station, and you can't miss it unless you're walking in thick fog. The nearest bus station is Laganside.

THE CAUSEWAY COAST

Stretching for 80 km (50 mi) along Northern Ireland's Atlantic shore, the Causeway Coast holds most of the province's "don't miss" attractions. Besides Belfast, the Causeway Coast is the most heavily visited region in the north and the focus of innumerable package and day-trip tours that depart from Belfast. These guided tours are an efficient way to take in the Causeway's sights—from **Dunluce Castle** and the world-famous **Giant's Causeway** to the endless string of whitewashed fishing villages along the coast—but consider staying longer if at all possible. Between Cushendall and Portrush, there's enough here to merit at least three or four days of exploration. Northern Ireland's train and bus network hits the important towns, but a mountain bike is ideal for the Causeway's flat terrain. Hitching is also a relatively safe way to travel (though agonizingly slow), and you can always flag a bus down if the inevitable downpour occurs.

GLENS OF ANTRIM

BASICS

Glenariff Park Visitor Center (tel. 012667/58232) is nothing more than a coffee/gift shop with a small unstaffed exhibit on the park. So take your questions to the **Cushendall Tourist Office** (24 Mill St., tel. 012667/71180) before you trek to the park. It has a small stock of hiking guides and maps (for Glenariff and all nine glens) and can help you find a B&B. It's open January–September weekdays 10–1 (also June–Aug., weekdays 2:30–5 and Sat. 10–1). The tourist office doesn't exchange money, so try **Northern Bank** (5 Shore St., tel. 012667/71243), open weekdays 10–12:30 and 1:30–3:30.

COMING AND GOING

Buses depart from the Mill Street post office to Belfast (£4.50), stopping at the gates of Glenariff Park (£1.30) four times a day weekdays and three times on Saturday, with additional buses in July and

August. Two buses per day also run to Ballycastle (£2.50) July–August. Departure times are posted in the window of Cushendall's **post office** on Mill Street. It's possible to walk the scenic 10-km (6½-mi) road to the park, but be warned that this is an extremely steep trek.

WHERE TO SLEEP

The **Riverside Guest House** (14 Mill St., tel. 012667/71655) has three sumptuous, immaculate rooms for £15 per person, including Mrs. McKeegan's morning Ulsterfry. **Ryans** (9 Shore St., tel. 012667/71583) and **Glendale House** (46 Coast Rd., tel. 012667/71595) both have rooms from £13–£17. The YHANI **Cushendall Hostel** (42 Layde Rd., off Shore St., tel. 012667/71344), closed from late-December to January, is 1½ km (1 mi) north of town. A recent renovation has given a little life to what is basically an institutional and charmless abode. This is one of the few hostels on the Causeway Coast and attracts cyclists, backpackers, and wayward crazies. Dorm beds cost £6.50, and bikes rent for £6. From the town center, head north on Shore Street and follow the signs.

Sleeping in Glenariff Park is forbidden, but there is an excellent campground adjacent to the park's upper gate. **Glenariff Forest Park** (98 Glenariff Rd., tel. 012667/58232) sprawls over 5 acres and provides access to the park's signposted hiking trails, as well as showers. Its 40 tent sites (£8, including admission to the park) are hidden among trees and wildflowers. In Cushendall itself, **Cushendall Caravan Park** (62 Coast Rd., tel. 012667/71699), open April–October, has 20 tent sites (£4.50, £7.50 in summer), all within an easy walk of the village's pubs and chip shops.

WORTH SEEING

The nine glens (or forests) of Antrim are steeped in Irish mythology. Hugging the coast in isolated pockets between Larne and Ballycastle, the glens were inhabited by small bands of Irish monks as early as AD 700. Since then, these peaceful old-growth forests have become synonymous with Irishness. Pro-Republicans proudly note that Ossian, one of the greatest Celtic poets, is supposedly buried near Glenaan, and that Moira O'Neill, Celtic poetess and mystic, was born in the village of Cushendun. After a few pints, some locals reminisce incoherently about these two Irish cultural heroes while simultaneously lamenting the Glens' popularity with British tourists.

The Glens of Antrim are well worth several days of serious exploration. Marked trails stretch from Larne in the south to Ballycastle in the north, meandering at times through each of the nine unconnected glens. You'll need a full week and a rainproof tent to complete the nine-glen circuit, or you can stop for the day in **Glenariff Park,** the largest and most accessible of Antrim's glens. The park is open daily 8–8, and admission is £1. Inside are several easy hikes, including the **Waterfalls Trail** (follow the blue arrows), a 2½-km (1½-mi) path past rain-forest-like waterfalls along wooden gangways. Sadly, this, the most lush of Glenariff's trails, is often clogged with summer tourists. Brave them and then flee to the longer and slightly more strenuous **Scenic Hike** (follow the red arrows), which gives views of the entire glen. Additional hikes from both Glenariff and Cushendall are described in the "Guide to the Glens" (£1), available at the Cushendall tourist office (*see above*).

To reach Glenariff Park, head for the nearby village of **Cushendall,** which has regular bus service to the park. Only three blocks long and quaintly dull, Cushendall is built over a scenic stretch of the Glenariff River and has a hostel and some good pubs. From the village's red Curfew Tower (closed to the public), head left down Mill Street for sweater shops and chippies, or right down Shore Street for banks, grocers, and the youth hostel. Cushendall's best pint is poured at the atmospheric **McCullum's** (Mill St., tel. 01266/71330), but for lunchtime grub (summer only) and spontaneous traditional music, head next door to **Lurig Inn** (tel. 012667/71293). The best restaurant in town is **Harry's** (Mill St., tel. 012667/71022), which features dishes like tasty teriyaki chicken salad (£3.75) and vegetarian burritos (£7). Less expensive (and appetizing) is **Gillin's Coffee Shop** (Mill St., tel. 012267/71404). They serve good bread, decent sandwiches, simple salads, and a lot of fried stuff.

BALLYCASTLE

BASICS

Ballycastle's **tourist office** (Sheskburn House, 7 Mary St., tel. 012657/62024) is near the docks; from Quay Road, turn right on Mary Street and continue straight. This office has maps and brochures, can help you find a B&B, and will organize a Causeway Coast day trip. For currency exchange, head to one of the banks along Quay Road, Ann Street, or the Diamond. The **post office** (3 Ann St., tel. 012657/

62519) is open Monday–Saturday 9–1 and 2–5:30 (Wed. and Sat. until 12:30). You can rent bikes from **Stewarts** (30 Ann St., tel. 012657/62491).

COMING AND GOING

Ballycastle's unstaffed **bus depot** is behind the Diamond on the west end of town. If you're staying at the hostel, a closer bus stop is near the intersection of Quay Road and Mary Street, opposite the Marine Hotel. Ballycastle is well connected by bus to most of Northern Ireland, including routes to Belfast (£5.50), Cushendall (£2.40), Larne (£4.50), Ballintoy (£1.30), the Giant's Causeway (£2), Bushmills (£2.20), and Portrush (£2.90). There is no rail service to Ballycastle.

WHERE TO SLEEP

For the best breakfast on the island (with lots of fruit, yogurt, and cereal), stay at the superb **Glenluce Guest House** (42 Quay Rd., tel. 012657/62914) for £17.50 per person. At the other end of the spectrum is **Fair Head View,** which has plain doubles and a Continental breakfast for a mere £11 per person (£14 with full Irish breakfast).

The cheapest beds (£6) in town are at the comfortable IHH **Castle Hostel** (62 Quay Rd., tel. 012657/62337), on the east side of town near the pier and a five-minute walk from the center of town. They'll also let you camp in the backyard for £3 per person, which includes the use of all hostel facilities. If they're full, pitch your tent in one of the fields to the south of town (beyond Main St.) because the only other place in town is **Silver Cliffs Holiday Park** (tel. 012657/62550), which charges a scandalous £12 per site. Right by the harbor, **Ballycastle Backpackers** (4 North St., tel. 012657/63612) offers depressing dorm beds (£6) and free use of their washer.

FOOD

Try the popular **Wysner's Restaurant** (Ann St., tel. 012657/62372), a family-run bakery and coffee shop. **The Cellar Pizzeria** (The Diamond, tel. 01265/63037) squeezes wooden booths, pizza (£6–£7), and '80s rock into a tiny whitewashed basement. **Strand Restaurant** (The Strand, tel. 012657/62349) is a casual restaurant serving dishes like barbecued ribs (£4.80), pastas (£5), burgers (£3.50), and amazing ice cream and crepes (£2).

WORTH SEEING

Ballycastle, from the Irish Baile Caisleain (City of the Castle), lost its namesake ages ago, along with the staunch walls that once protected this seaside village from Norman and Viking raiders. Although the town's hostel draws crowds of backpackers and cyclists, tourists have largely ignored Ballycastle, despite the beautifully aged shops and pubs that line its Castle, Diamond, and Main streets.

Ballycastle is shaped like an hourglass, with its beach and dock at one end, its pubs and chippies at the other, and the 1-km-long (½-mi-long) Quay Road in between. There's not much to do here except gawk at old photographs and tarnished farm tools in the small, free **Ballycastle Museum** (59 Castle St., tel. 012657/62942), open Monday–Saturday noon–6. The local strand, accessed via a footbridge behind Mary Street, is popular when the weather's good, as is the footpath that meanders east along the coast. You can also stick around for a day trip to **Rathlin Island** or Ballintoy's **Carrick-a-Rede** (*see* Near Ballycastle, *below*), or for an after-dark crawl to one of Ballycastle's musty pubs. Just outside of town you'll find the ruins of the ancient **Bonamargy Friary.** Bushmills and Dunluce Castle (*see below*) are also day-trip possibilities, though they're slightly easier to get to from Portrush. In mid-June, the town's two-day **Fleadh Amhrán agus Rince,** one of Northern Ireland's best dance and traditional-music festivals, draws performers from all over. The **Ould Lammus Fair** in the last week of August is the oldest fair in Ireland and fills the town with traditional music and amusement-park rides. Venues change yearly, but there's inevitably a session or two held at the **House of McDonnell** (Castle St., tel. 012657/62975). Try **McCarroll's** (Quay Rd., tel. 012657/62123) or the **Boyd Arms** (4 The Diamond, tel. 012657/62364) for a quiet pint.

NEAR BALLYCASTLE

RATHLIN ISLAND

Rathlin Island lies in the middle of the treacherous North Channel, 9½ km (6 mi) north of Ballycastle and only 22 km (14 mi) from the Mull of Kintyre, Scotland. Lacking industry and agriculture, the islanders depend exclusively on the sea for their livelihood, evidenced by the number of scrawny fishing trawlers anchored in Rathlin's harbor. Rathlin's main attraction is its government-owned bird sanctuary—home to razorbills, fulmars, kittiwakes, puffins, buzzards, curlews, and peregrine falcons. The island provides a good sampling of Northern Ireland's terrain, with cliffs and boulders on the island's west end, circular sandy beaches near the harbor, and velvet green, rolling hills traversed by stone hedges in between. However, if you have already seen Inishbofin or the Aran Islands, and you are not a big fan of birds, the scenery may prove disappointing.

Bird-watching and hiking are Rathlin's main activities. At the west end of the island, **Bull Point,** with its **Western Lighthouse,** has the best cliff hiking, and premier views of the bird-covered rocks below (bring binoculars). If you don't feel like forking out £3 for a round-trip bus ticket, you can walk from the harbor to the lighthouse in about an hour. A 3-km (2-mi) circuit to **Bruce's Cave** on the east coast takes you by the island's Catholic and Protestant churches and their shared graveyard. The cave—accessible only by boat and only when the weather cooperates—is where Scotland's Robert the Bruce lived in exile after being defeated by Edward I in 1306. During summer, competing islanders meet all incoming ferries and offer minibus tours of the island (£3). Also during summer, weather permitting, Mr. Tom Cecil (tel. 012657/63915) leads full-day **scuba-diving trips** to any of the dozen shipwrecks that litter Church Bay, the island's principal port. Trips cost £45 (including all gear); proof of certification is required. Accommodation is provided by **Rathlin Guesthouse** (The Quay, tel. 012657/63917), within two minutes of the docks. It is open April–September and has four rooms at £15 per person; guests can also arrange for light meals. With permission, you can camp for free in the adjacent campground. The lone pub **McCuaig's** (The Harbour, tel. 012657/63974) serves a small selection of meals, but your only other dining option is a glorified snack bar charging outrageous prices, so bring your own food.

Rathlin Ferry Service (tel. 012657/63915) runs boats to Rathlin Island (45 min, £5.70 round-trip) year-round. From July to August, they depart Ballycastle Harbour daily at 10:30 AM and 12:15 PM and return from Rathlin at 9 AM, 11:15 AM, 4 PM, and 6 PM; January–March and November–December, they depart Ballycastle at 10:30 AM and 4 PM and return from Rathlin at 9 AM and 3 PM; April–June and September–October, they depart at 10:30 AM and 5 PM and return at 9 AM and 4 PM.

CARRICK-A-REDE

Between April and September every year, you can brave the Carrick-a-Rede rope bridge, which spans a 60-foot gap between the mainland and Carrick-a-Rede Island, off the coast 8 km (5 mi) west of Ballycastle. Carrick-a-Rede means "rock in the road" and refers to the island (the rock) that stands in the path of the salmon who follow the coast as they migrate to their home rivers to spawn. Salmon fishermen have set up this rope bridge in late April for the past 350 years, taking it down again after the salmon season ends. Crossing over to the rocky outcrop, they cast nets in the frothy water and catch throngs of salmon as they rush by. The creaky bridge is open to the public April–September 10–6 (June–Aug., until 8) and offers heart-stopping views of the crashing waves below. On Carrick-a-Rede itself, you can climb around the precarious terrain and revel in views of the stunning coastal cliffs and plenty of tourists. Be sure to look for the black-and-white razorbills on the cliff to your left as you cross the bridge. There's a tea shop next to the parking lot, which has a small exhibit on the bridge and the cliffs and serves soups and sandwiches. Ulsterbus passes the bridge on its route between Portrush to Ballycastle; ask the driver to let you off at the entrance.

GIANT'S CAUSEWAY

The Giant's Causeway is Northern Ireland's premier tourist attraction. Spanning the coast for some 3 km (2 mi), the Giant's Causeway and its 40,000 basalt blocks are truly impressive. Geologists say these interlocking six- and seven-sided basalt columns, ranging from 4 inches to 6 feet long, were formed by cooling lava 2 million years ago. Others claim the Causeway was built by the mythic Irish figure Finn MacCool, who constructed the Causeway to do battle with Bennandonnar, Scotland's legendary *Übermensch.* To reach the Giant's Causeway, 3 km (2 mi) north of Bushmills on the B146, take Ulsterbus's Portrush–Bushmills–Ballycastle bus (Bus 172), which stops at the visitor center's front gate. Buses go from Portrush to the Causeway (£2.60 round-trip) four times per day Monday–Saturday (9 per day July–Aug.). Buses also go from Ballycastle to the Causeway four times per day (except Sun.) and cost about the same. From the distillery, it's also an easy cycle or 30-minute walk.

One kilometer (½ mile) from the Causeway is a thoroughly modern **visitor center** (44 Causeway Rd., tel. 012657/31855), open daily 10–5 (slightly longer hrs in summer). The center runs a surprisingly good 25-minute audiovisual show (£1) dedicated to the site's geological and legendary history, has a tea shop (open mid-Mar.–Oct.) and a competitive bureau de change, and sells the best guide to walks in the area (50p). They also run a bus to the Causeway itself every 15 minutes (70p).

BLOODY SUNDAY

Bloody Sunday commemorates January 30, 1972, when British paratroopers opened fire on people participating in a nonviolent protest against the British policy of internment without trial. When the smoke cleared, 13 people, all Catholic and unarmed, had been killed. For the past 24 years, many have rallied in support of the victims, who were accused by the British Army of handling weapons. Known as the Bloody Sunday Justice Campaign, the supporters attained some success when the British government finally admitted that the victims were "innocent." Derry is filled with murals and memorials that serve as constant reminders of the struggle for justice, including the memorial at Free Derry Corner on Rossville Street carved with the inscription, "their epitaph is in the continuing struggle for democracy."

The adjacent **Causeway School Museum** (tel. 012657/31777), open daily 11–5 July–August only, shows a video documenting the rigors of 1920s school life. Visitors are also encouraged to try their hand at copperplate handwriting or "whipping a pirie," a curiously enjoyable punishment. Admission to the school is 75p. Afterward, walk or take the shuttle bus (80p round-trip) down to the Causeway itself. For excellent—and generally deserted—hiking, check the sign behind the visitor center. It outlines a half dozen easy hikes that skirt the pristine coastline and are unquestionably worth a few hours' exploration. The 5-km (3-mi) walk to Dunseverick Castle is one of the best as long as your interest lies with spectacular landscape—the one-tower "castle" isn't nearly as impressive as the land surrounding it.

PORTRUSH

BASICS

The **tourist office** (Dunluce Centre, Dunluce Ave., tel. 01265/823–333), open daily 9–8 April–October, is adjacent to the bus station. Inside you'll find brochures, maps, and a helpful staff that can book you into a B&B or on a guided tour of the Causeway Coast and change your money. Twenty-four-hour computerized information is available outside. For **currency exchange,** head to any one of the banks that line Eglinton and Main streets, or, on weekends, to the tourist office. **Bicycle Doctor** (104 Lower Main St., tel. 01265/824–340) rents bikes for £7 per day, £40 per week, with a £10 deposit. If you're staying at Macool's Hostel (*see below*), you'll only pay £5 per day or £30 per week.

COMING AND GOING

BY TRAIN • Portrush's **train station** (Eglinton St., tel. 01265/822–395) is within a five-minute walk of the town center; turn left from the station and keep straight. Except for its information counter (staffed June–Aug., Mon.–Sat. 11:12–1:40 and 2:40–8; Sept.–May, Mon.–Sat. 8:12–1:40 and 2:40–4:40), the station offers few comforts. Trains depart for Belfast (£5.90), Derry (£5 via Coleraine), and Lisburn (£5).

BY BUS • Portrush is well connected by bus to most destinations in Northern Ireland. The unstaffed **Ulsterbus depot** is near the traffic circle on Dunluce Avenue, across from the tourist office. An Ulsterbus representative can be found within the tourist office on weekdays for help with bus schedules. There's also an auxiliary stop adjacent to the rail station. If you're planning a Causeway Coast day trip, Bus 172 (Bushmills "Open Topper") is your best option. It leaves Portrush four times daily Monday–Saturday (9 times daily, July–Aug.) and has scheduled stops at Bushmills and the Giant's Causeway visitor center. A ticket costs £2.60 round-trip. The first bus departs Portrush at 7:25 AM; the last returns from the Giant's Causeway at 6:35 PM. Other destinations from Portrush include Portstewart (85p), Belfast (£5.60), and Derry (£4.80).

WHERE TO SLEEP

Portrush has two reasonably priced, outstanding B&Bs, both with excellent views of the beach. The first is **The Clarence** (7 Bath Terr., tel. 01265/823–575), an aged Georgian flat with 20 rooms (£12 per person) and a common lounge with truly knockout views of the ocean. To find it, turn left from the train depot and right on Bath Street. Next door is **The Rest-A-While** (6 Bath Terr., tel. 01265/822–827), a similarly old and brightly colored Georgian relic with rooms for £13 per person. For an extra £5, they'll provide lunch and dinner in addition to breakfast. More formal is **Seamara** (26 Mark St., tel. 01265/822–541), a prim family-run house that caters to a wealthier crowd and charges £15 per person. From the tourist office, continue straight down Mark Street to reach Seamara.

The comfy **Macool's Hostel** (5 Causeway View Terr., tel. 01265/824–845) is perched at the end of Portrush's main street and has great views of the nearby coastline. There are 20 fluffy-quilted dorm beds (£6), and hostel residency earns you small discounts at Skerries Pantry (*see below*) and the Bicycle Doctor (*see above*) around the corner. Coffee is free and they have a laundry (£2).

FOOD

Portrush teems with greasy chippies, kebab shops, and four-star tourist hotels with grossly overpriced dining rooms. There's hardly a decent meal to be found, and though the better of the rotten lot are reviewed below, they are mediocre at best. For a reasonable sit-down meal, try **Skerries Pantry** (Bath St., tel. 01265/822–248) or **Singing Kettle Café** (3 Atlantic Ave., tel. 01265/823–068). Both offer sandwiches, burgers, lasagnas, shakes, and soups for less than £4. The Singing Kettle's veggie Ulsterfry is only £3. More elegant is

The southeast tower of Dunluce Castle is haunted by Peter Carey, who was hung for three days over the cliffs in the 17th century.

Rowland's (92 Main St., tel. 01265/822–063), which serves French onion soup (£2) and entrées such as peppered chicken breast (£6.35), best topped off with a bottle of reasonably priced wine. **Dionysus** (53 Eglinton St, tel. 01265/823–855) is a Greek restaurant with a huge selection of vegetarian and vegan entrées in the £5–£6 range.

WORTH SEEING

Portrush may be the smarmiest, cheesiest, most touristy place in the British Isles. On summer weekends the town's gorgeous beaches and quaint harbor are framed by a seemingly endless array of grimy video arcades, tacky amusement-park rides, and throngs of fortysomethings with their shrieking entourage of children. The prime reason to come here is the town's proximity to Dunluce Castle, Bushmills, and the Giant's Causeway. All are within 11 km (7 mi) of Portrush and easily reached by bike or bus. If you're stuck here on a rainy day, you may want to visit the infamous **Waterworld** (The Harbour, tel. 01265/822–001), a massive complex filled with indoor swimming pools, diving boards, water slides, "Swedish" saunas, and an army of overeager preteens. Open June–September, Waterworld is yours for a day for £3.75 (£2.50 in Sept.).

Portrush is small and can comfortably be walked in less than 25 minutes. Most of the cafés, restaurants, and gift shops are between the Eglinton Street train station and the tip of Ramore Head. To the east are Strand Road's Georgian flats and crescent-shaped public beach. Both Eglinton and Causeway streets, Portrush's principal commercial avenues, funnel into Main Street, forming a wishbone of sorts. At the northern end of Main Street, look for Waterworld and the town's harbor. Celebrate your day trip to Portrush's nearby sights at **Atlantic Bar/MacNally's,** essentially one massive multilevel bar in the **Londonderry Hotel** (Main St., tel. 01265/823–693). More informal and comfortably cramped is **Harbour Bar** (tel. 01265/822–430), next to Waterworld.

NEAR PORTRUSH

DUNLUCE CASTLE

Halfway between Portrush and the Giant's Causeway, Dunluce Castle is one of Northern Ireland's most evocative ruins. Built by the MacDonnell clan in 1550, it perches on the edge of a ragged cliff with a commanding view of the Atlantic coast. Most of its towers and battlements were destroyed centuries ago, and over the years cliff erosion has played havoc with what's left of this 3-acre complex. Still, Dunluce's surviving patchwork of walls and round towers remains intensely beautiful, especially at sunset or on a foggy, gray day. Guarding the castle entrance is a **visitor center** (tel. 012657/31938) where you can see a slide show or join a guided tour. Directly underneath the castle is a sea cave where the family hid their ship. The cave is definitely worth a look but is accessed (at your own risk) via a steep and slippery trail to the right of the castle entrance. The castle is open April–September, Monday–Saturday 10–7 and Sunday 2–7 (Oct.–Mar. until 4 PM) and costs £1.50. Call 01265/824–444 for information.

Though Dunluce isn't officially served by public transportation, Ulsterbus's Causeway Coast Express drives right past it, and if you ask the driver, he or she will probably let you off at the castle entrance. Otherwise, you'll probably need to cycle the 5 km (3 mi) from Portrush to Dunluce along the A2 highway or hike for one hour from Portrush along the beach.

BUSHMILLS

Bushmills, the oldest licensed distillery in the world, was first granted a charter by King James I in 1608, although historical records refer to a distillery here as early as 1276. Today, Bushmills is one of the busiest and most respected distillers in Ireland, even more so after its low-key merger with the Republic's own distillery, Jameson of County Cork. Bushmills's greatest appeal to the whiskey drinker, however, is its guided tour, topped off with a complimentary shot of *uisce beatha,* the "water of life." Tours begin in the mashing and fermentation room, then proceed to the maturing and bottling warehouse. After this brief but informative tour, all visitors are led to the visitor center–cum–gift shop for their free sample of either Black Bush, Old Bushmills, or Bushmills Malt, the three flagship spirits. To reach the distillery, take any Causeway Coast Ulsterbus between Ballycastle and Portrush; all stop in the center of Bushmills Town. From here, follow the signs to the distillery gate. *Tel. 012657/31521. Admission: £2.50. Open June–Oct., daily 9–4; Nov.–May, Mon.–Thurs. 9–4 , Fri. 9–noon. Tours leave approximately every 15 min.*

DERRY

What you call this city is more of a political issue than one of simple custom: While Republicans call it Derry, its official name, Londonderry is used by those in favor of British rule. But whatever you choose to call it, it's still one of Northern Ireland's most underrated towns. Despite the factories and low-income tenements along the banks of the River Foyle, the city is full of cultural artifacts and historic beauty. This is particularly noticeable in the streets and alleys that fan outward from the Diamond—the historic center of Derry where St. Colomb founded his first monastery in 546 at the present-day site of Long Tower Church. Here, encircled by Derry's 20-foot-tall, 17th-century walls, fine examples of Georgian and Victorian architecture rub shoulders with a handful of old-style pubs, cathedrals, museums, and unpretentious shopping malls. Like many Northern Irish cities, Derry has a long, gruesome history of Troubles-related violence. Outside the city walls, a depressing collection of slums, barbed wire, and security-conscious suburbanites attest to the hard times. But inside the walls, Derry is relaxed and confident and filled with quaint Georgian and Victorian town houses, geographically and symbolically above the violence and riots that rocked the city in July of 1996 (*see box* An Unprecedented Return to Violence, *above*). Derry's cultured air can be sampled at **Orchard Street Gallery** (Orchard St., tel. 01504/269–675), **Gordon Gallery** (7 London St., tel. 01504/374–044), and **Foyle Arts Centre** (Lawrence Hill, tel. 01504/266–657). All have secured solid reputations by showcasing the best in local and national art.

Derry boasts one of the largest college-age populations in Ireland, so the pub scene here is a pleasant change from the sterile sobriety of Northern Ireland's smaller towns. In mid-August, another good reason to come is the annual **Busking Festival.** With cash prizes topping £1,000, this bacchanalian event attracts some of the most bizarre and talented street musicians from the United Kingdom and Ireland.

BASICS

The **tourist office** houses both the Northern Irish and Irish Republic tourist boards and is a treasure trove of information. Besides free city maps, this office has heaps of brochures with details about B&Bs, trains, buses, and theater and art happenings. Pick up a copy of the free and helpful *Derry Tourist Guide.* They also organize guided walks and bus tours of the city. *8 Bishop St., 1 block west of the Diamond, tel. 01504/267–284. Open July–Aug., Mon.–Sat. 9–8, Sun. 10–6; Sept.–June, weekdays 9–5:15.*

Derry's student-run **USIT Travel Center** (33 Ferryquay St., tel. 01504/371–888) is two blocks south of the Diamond. Come here for budget fares and tips on traveling cheaply. For a small fee, they can reschedule most airline tickets. The main **post office** (3 Customs House Quay, BT48 6TT, tel. 01504/362–274) is on the River Foyle's west bank, just outside the city walls, and offers Saturday currency exchange (9–12:30). During the week, head to any of the 20 banks that line Shipquay Street and the Diamond.

COMING AND GOING

The symbolic heart of Derry is the **Diamond,** a small square inside the 17th-century city walls. Most of Derry's sights and nearly all of the pubs and eating establishments lie in or around the city walls, primarily on Strand Road and Shipquay Street.

BY BUS • Derry is well connected with Northern Ireland's major and minor towns. The **Foyle Street depot** (Foyle St., tel. 01504/262–261) is on the River Foyle's western shore; here you can pick up a free route map and schedule booklet. A staffed info counter is open weekdays 6–5:30, Saturday 8–5:30, and for bus arrivals on Sunday. To reach the city center and the Diamond, turn right from the depot and immediately left on Shipquay Street. Ulsterbus destinations include Belfast (1 per hr, £5.90), Portrush (every 2 hrs, £4.80), Portstewart (every 2 hrs, £4.50), and Omagh (11 per day, £4). Republic destinations include Dublin (5 per day, £10), Letterkenny (6 per day, £4.30), and Donegal Town (6 per day, £7.70).

If you're Donegal-bound, the independent **Lough Swilly Bus Co.** (Foyle St., tel. 01504/262–017) offers more frequent service than Ulsterbus to the Republic's northwest corner. Pick up a free booklet with fares and timetables from their office on the second floor of the bus station. All buses leave from the Foyle Street offices, down the road from Ulsterbus. Generally, destinations include Letterkenny, Fanad Head, and the Inishowen Peninsula; all fares are less than £10 one-way, and you get half off with an ISIC card.

On Halloween in Derry, the whole city turns out decked in their wildest homemade costumes. They have good reason: No pub will serve you a drink without one.

BY TRAIN • **Derry Station** (Duke St., tel. 01504/42228) is on the River Foyle's eastern bank, across the water from Derry's walled city center. An information counter is open Monday–Saturday 9–5:30. A free shuttle whisks people across the river to the bus station after all major train arrivals. If you're heading to the train station, buses marked N.I.R. depart from the Ulsterbus station (*see below*) 20 minutes before most major train departures. **Northern Irish Railway** trains leave for Portrush (7 per day, £4.75), Lisburn (7 per day, £5.85), Belfast (7 per day, £5.85), and Dublin Connolly via Newry (4 per day, £17.30 single).

GETTING AROUND

Derry's old walls surround all of the main tourist areas except the Waterloo district, north of the walls, which is popular with shoppers. The **Diamond** is the main town square and streets fan out from it to all sections of downtown. The famous republican **Bogside** district is to the west of the walls, and the loyalist **Waterside** is on the east side of the River Foyle.

BY BIKE • The **YHANI** hostel (*see below*) rents mountain bikes on the Raleigh Rent-A-Bike plan for £7 per day or £40 per week, with £30 deposit.

BY BUS • Bus fares within Derry range from 78p to £1.05, depending on the distance. Tickets can be purchased on board and at newsagents displaying a CITYBUS sign. Nearly all local buses start or end their journeys at the Diamond, the first at 6 AM and the last at 11 PM.

WHERE TO SLEEP

The cheapest B&Bs in town are **Mrs. Cassidy's** (86 Duncreggan Rd., tel. 01504/374–551) and **Groarty House** (62 Groarty Rd., tel. 01504/261–403), which both have rooms from £13.50 per person, and **Mrs. Wiley's** (153 Culmore Rd., tel. 01504/352–932), which has slightly grimmer rooms from £11 per person. **Florence House** (16 Northland Rd., tel. 01504/268–093), near the university, is a cozy five-room B&B with rooms for £15 per person.

YHANI's **Oakgrove Manor** (4–6 Magazine St., tel. 01504/372–273) is a big, modern complex located within the city walls. Its dorm rooms (beds £7.50–9) and kitchen are institutional and bland but super-clean. They also have singles (£15) and doubles (£28) with shower and breakfast. The hostel has laundry facilities and a 2 AM curfew and is a short, well-signposted walk from the bus station. A much better choice is **Aberfoyle Independent Hostel** (29 Aberfoyle Terr., tel. 01504/370–011), which occupies a brick Victorian town house. Beds in singles, doubles, and dorms all go for £7.50. Be sure and call ahead to snag the cheapest double on the island. Your charming host, Tina, provides tea, coffee, milk, and bread in the handsome kitchen. To get here, exit right from the bus station, walk down Strand Road for 10 minutes, and keep a sharp eye out for the hostel on your left. **Magee College** (Northland Rd., tel. 01504/265–621) rents 150 spartan rooms June–September for £12 per person. The coed **YMCA** (51 Glenshane Rd., tel. 01504/301–662), on the east side of the Foyle River (20 minutes away by bus), offers basic, clean accommodations for £5 per dorm bed from May to September. To get here from Ulsterbus's Foyle Street depot, take any bus going to Dungiven or Claudy to Glenshane Road.

THE BEST HOSTEL IN IRELAND

Situated in sheep country, 5 km (3 mi) outside Dungiven (southeast of Derry), the IHH Flax Mill Hostel (Mill Ln., Derrylane, Co. Derry, tel. 01504/742–655) is a musty, 18th-century Irish cottage with no electricity. Conversations are held by candlelight and gas lamp within the gorgeously aged stone walls of the family room. There are 20 beds (£5 each), and tent sites go for £3. An amazing breakfast is only £1.50 extra and includes fresh eggs from the henhouse and homemade bread and rhubarb jam. The local pub—a five-minute walk—will pour your pint to go. Owned by a German-Irish couple who speak both languages fluently, the Flax Mill draws large crowds of backpackers during the summer, many on return trips specifically to this hostel. Reservations are advised. To get here, take one of Ulsterbus's six daily buses from Derry to Dungiven (£3). Once you arrive, give the hostel a call and they will pick you up. But be forewarned: You may end up staying for weeks rather than the day or two you planned.

FOOD

Derry's budget eateries are clustered around Shipquay and Strand streets. At **Piemonte Pizzeria** (Clarendon Rd., off Strand St., tel. 01504/266–828), open for dinner nightly and until 2:30 AM on weekends, an ultra-friendly wait staff serves excellent pastas (£4) and pizzas (£3–£4) beneath a gaggle of plastic sea creatures clinging to a huge net. **Glue Pot** (36 Shipquay St., tel. 01504/367–463) is a quiet, family-run pub with soup-and-sandwich combinations and lasagna for less than £4. Derry's best Chinese restaurant is **Mandarin Palace** (134 Strand Rd., tel. 01504/264–613), where most dishes cost less than £6. At either branch of **The Sandwich Co.** (The Diamond, tel. 01504/372–500; and 61 Strand Rd., tel. 01504/266–771), you can choose from a creative list of sandwiches or design your own for £1.50 to £2.75. The best place for good, cheap eats is **Boston Tea Party** (In the Craft Village, tel. 01504/264–568), which serves dishes like lasagna with a side salad (£2), quiche (£1.75), and chicken curry with a baked potato (£1.50).

WORTH SEEING

Most of Derry's attractions lie within its well-preserved city walls, which stretch for 1½ km (1 mi) from Foyle and Magazine streets in the north to Artillery and Market streets in the south. The walls were closed to the public until 1995, and though there is still a military presence in the northwest corner (video cameras and barbed wire), the walls now make a very pleasant walk, providing good views of the surrounding neighborhoods, along with descriptive plaques and informative markers. It's an area ideal for aimless, impromptu rambles.

The **Tower Museum** (Union Hall Pl., tel. 01504/372–411), open Tuesday–Saturday 10–5 (also July–August, Mon. 10–5 and Sun. 2–5) is partially housed in the reconstructed O'Doherty Tower, which was built in 1615 by the O'Dohertys for their overlords (the O'Donnells) in lieu of tax payments. The intricate, well-planned "Story of Derry" exhibit takes you from the city's prehistoric origins to the present, hitting all the big events along the way, with loads of high-tech audiovisual displays. Admission is £3. To the south, **Derry Craft Village** (Shipquay St., tel. 01504/260–329), open daily 9–5:30, offers a novel shopping experience. Instead of the standard minimall format, it combines retail establishments, workshops, and residential apartments in a medieval setting. **St. Columb's Cathedral** (off Bishop St., by courthouse, tel. 01504/267–313), is one of the first Protestant cathedrals built in the United Kingdom after the Reformation. In addition to its intricate corbeled roof and austere spire, the church contains the oldest and largest bells in Ireland (dating from the 1620s). Notice the colorful procession of banners in the nave, a proud statement of pro-British sentiments. The £1 cathedral admission will also get you into the one-room, chock-full-of-history **Chapter House Museum,** which displays a few 16th-century Bibles and the oldest surviving map of Derry (from 1600). The museum is open Monday–Saturday 9–5. Outside the walls, on Foyle Street, near Shipquay Gate, the redbrick **Guildhall** (Foyle St., tel. 01504/365–151), originally built in 1890, is worth a visit for its impressive stained-glass windows; admission is free. Nearby, at the **Foyle Valley Railway Centre** (Foyle Rd. Station, tel. 01504/265–234), you'll see mothballed locomotives, antique signal levers, and lots of railroad paraphernalia. The museum is open Tuesday–Saturday 10–4:30 (also May–Sept., Sun. 2–5:30). Admission is free, but the short train ride along the waterfront costs £2.

If you want a glimpse of Derry's ugly but fascinating underside, consider a trip to the **Fountain** and **Bog-side** districts. The Fountain, a fiercely Protestant enclave, is best seen along Fountain Road; exit the city walls through the Bishop Street gate. Here you'll find smatterings of pro-British graffiti; red, white, and blue curbs and light posts; and lots of Union Jacks, all harsh reminders of the troubles. To see the flip side of the coin, head north from the Diamond along Butcher Street, and veer left outside the city walls to reach the Bogside district, also known as Free Derry—a carryover from the days when this Rossville Street neigh-borhood was an IRA stronghold studiously avoided by the RUC. The Bogside (and some of the city center) saw horrendous riot-ing in July of 1996 in response to the so-called "Siege of Dum-cree": dozens of cars were hijacked and burned, and hundreds of plastic bullets and Molotov cocktails were exchanged between Nationalists and the RUC. Since then the area has been relatively quiet. The Bogside has more striking murals than the Fountain, some of which can be seen at a distance from the city walls.

In 1972, the Guildhall was partially destroyed by an IRA bomber who was later elected to an influential Derry city council.

AFTER DARK

Derry has a surprisingly hopping after-dark scene. Pub aficionados should head directly for Waterloo Street, off Strand Street. Some eight pubs line this alley—**Bound for Boston, Michael Tracy's,** and **Peader O'Donnells** are filled with locals nightly. Come midnight, when all the pubs have closed, drunken mobs spill out onto Waterloo Street, where they linger and chat for hours. **Derby** (63 Great James St., tel. 01504/361–635), Magee University's student pub, is good for brainy chitchat, though some nights student ID is required at the door. **Metro** (3 Bank Pl., tel. 01504/267–401) has the old-fashioned good looks of a quiet country bar, despite the fact that its young crowd is dead drunk most nights. Not only is **Strand Bar** (Strand Rd., tel. 01504/260–494) a great pub in its own right, but there's free live jazz or traditional music in the basement a few nights a week, and a disco (cover £3–£6) upstairs on the weekends. The most popular music clubs around are **Squires Nightclub** (33 Shipquay St., tel. 01504/266–017), in the center of town, and the upstairs club at **Carraig Bar** (113–121 Strand Rd., tel. 01504/267–529), near the university. Both feature mostly pop-rock at deafening levels. **Foyle Arts Centre** (Lawrence Hill, tel. 01504/266–657) puts on a grab bag of local and international theatrical, dance, and symphonic performances. For entertainment listings, pick up the biweekly *Derry Journal* (50p) or the weekly *Londonderry Sentinel* (55p).

TYRONE AND FERMANAGH

South of County Londonderry, the counties of Tyrone and Fermanagh constitute the bulk of Northern Ireland's unheralded southern extreme. Despite the region's natural beauty, backpackers and budget travelers are rare here. Tyrone and Fermanagh boast few well-known tourist sites, have only a single hostel (*see* Enniskillen, *below*), and are completely ignored by Northern Irish Railway's train network. Cyclists may find this a boon rather than a drawback, since the region's uncrowded rural roads allow for some excellent sightseeing. Otherwise, unless you're forced to stop on the way to or from Donegal, stick with Northern Ireland's more traditional haunts. The only exception may be Enniskillen, a scenic village perched on the edge of the impressive Lough Erne.

OMAGH

COMING AND GOING

From Omagh's Mountjoy Road station, **Ulsterbus** runs buses to Derry (hourly, £4), Enniskillen (8 per day, £3.70), Belfast (9 per day, £5.60), and Dublin (6 per day, £9 single). If you're cycling between Derry and Omagh, take the scenic B48 rather than the congested A5. Hitchers, on the other hand, should stick to the busier A5.

WORTH SEEING

Omagh, one of County Tyrone's largest commercial centers, sits in the Clogher Valley, 53 km (33 mi) south of Derry. Omagh is easily reached by bus from Derry, but it tends to attract a wealthy, rental-car breed of tourists. You'll find few worthwhile attractions in Omagh proper, and even fewer budget amenities to cushion the blow—no youth hostel or cheap cafés, no hip hangouts or adventurous nighttime diversions.

Omagh's main attractions are the historically themed **Ulster-American Folk Park** (Mellon Rd., Castletown, 3 mi north of Omagh on A5, tel. 01662/243–292) and **Ulster History Park** (Gortin Glen, 17 mi north of Omagh on B48, tel. 01662/648–188). The first is dedicated to Northern Irish emigrants who resettled in America during the 18th and 19th centuries. Exhibits include full-scale replicas of Irish peasant cottages, Pennsylvania farmhouses, and immigrant transport ships. Admission is £3.50 and the park is open Monday–Saturday 11–6:30, Sunday 11:30–7 (Oct.–Easter, weekdays 10:30–5). The latter, another open-air museum dominated by full-scale models, documents Irish history from the first known settlers to the 12th-century arrival of the Normans. Admission is £3. It's open April–September, Monday–Saturday 10:30–6:30, Sunday 11–7; and October–March, weekdays 10:30–5. Both are worthwhile if you happen to be in the neighborhood, but don't make a special trip to get here. For the Ulster-American Park, Ulsterbus's Omagh–Derry service stops outside the front gate 10 times daily; for the Ulster History Park, take one of Ulsterbus's twice-daily Omagh–Gortin coaches (£2.30 round-trip). The last admission to both parks is 1½ hours before closing.

Omagh's **tourist office** (1 Market St., tel. 01662/247–831), open weekdays 9–5 (Apr.–Sept., also Sat. 9–5), is in the easily navigated city center. Across the street, **Conway's Cycles** (Market St., tel. 01662/246–195) rents bikes on the Raleigh scheme for £7 per day, £35 per week, plus a £40 deposit. The **bus station** (Mountjoy Rd., tel. 01662/242–711), adjacent to the River Camowen, has an info desk open weekdays 9–5:45. In between lie Omagh's shopping malls, RUC barracks, and lifeless run-of-the-mill pubs. Two exceptions to the latter are **Gallagher's** (39 High St., tel. 01662/242–698) and the wonderfully musty **Bogan's** (20 High St., tel. 01662/242–991). For food, try **Libbi's** (52 Market St., tel. 01662/242–969), a cheap and wholesome sandwich shop, or **Pink Elephant** (19 High St., tel. 01662/249–805), a reasonably priced greasy spoon. The quiet **Glenhordial Hostel** (9A Waterworks Rd., Glenhordial, tel. 01662/241–973) is 4 km (2½ mi) from Omagh and offers free shuttle service (call Marella when you get into town). Comfy dorm beds are £6. Otherwise, the only budget-friendly B&B in town is **Ardmore** (12 Tamlaght Rd., tel. 01662/243–381), which charges £15 per person.

ENNISKILLEN

COMING AND GOING

Enniskillen's **bus station** (Wellington Rd., tel. 01365/322–633) has an info desk open weekdays 9–5:30. To reach the city center from here, turn right out of the station and cross Wellington Road; High and Townhall streets are two blocks ahead. Buses leave Enniskillen for Omagh (8 per day, £3.70), Derry (7 per day, £5.60), Belfast (10 per day, £5.90), and Dublin (4 per day, £9.70).

WHERE TO SLEEP AND EAT

The closest thing to a hostel in town is **Lakeland Canoe Centre** (Castle Island, tel. 01365/324–250), with dorm beds for £9 and camping for £4. The Lakeland is, quite literally, in the middle of the lough, but they'll come pick you up if you call. They rent pedal boats and tandem bikes and offer the occasional water-sports class. Otherwise, from February through November, try **Carraig Aonrai** (19 Sligo Rd., tel. 01365/324–889), where dorm accommodations cost £10.50, or **Rossole Guesthouse** (85 Sligo Rd, tel. 01365/323–462), a modern town house on the banks of Rossole Lake, with rooms from £15. The nearest YHANI hostel is **Castle Archdale Country Park** (tel. 01365/328118), 14 km (9 mi) north of

Enniskillen on the eastern shore of Lough Erne, where beds are £6.50 and tent sites are £5. To get here, take Ulsterbus 194 (£2) and ask the driver to let you out at the entrance to the Castle Archdale Park (one stop before Lisnarick). In the summer, buses often don't stop at the Castle Archdale Park at all; get off at Lisnarick, the next closest stop, and the hostel staff will pick you up if you call.

The best restaurant for miles is **Oscar's** (29 Belmore St., tel. 01365/327–037), open after 5 PM, a subdued place with lots of Oscar Wilde paraphernalia. Soups and sandwiches start at a reasonable £2, but splurge and try the seafood omelets (£6) or the chicken Kiev (£7). Slightly cheaper is **Golden Arrow** (23 Townhall St., tel. 01365/322–259), which serves chicken pie and chips (£2.25) and sandwiches (£1.30). **Franco's Pizzeria and Seafood Bar** (Queen Elizabeth Rd., tel. 01365/324–424) is a cozy place featuring pizza and pastas for around £6, in addition to a variety of reasonably priced fish dishes.

WORTH SEEING

Built on an island on the fringe of Lough Erne, Enniskillen is a pleasantly small and smart-looking town. The principal thoroughfares, Townhall and High Streets, are crowded with old-style pubs and rows of redbrick Georgian flats, and the waterfront **Enniskillen Castle** (Wellington Rd., tel. 01365/325–000) is one of the best-preserved monuments in Northern Ireland. This ancient stronghold, built by the Maguire clan in 1670, houses the Fermanagh County and Fusiliers Regimental Museum, as well as temporary exhibits. It's open May–September, Tuesday–Friday 10–5, Monday and Saturday 2–5 (also July–Aug., Sun. 2–5), and admission is £2.

Nearby, look for the daunting **St. Michael's** and **St. MacArtin's** cathedrals, both on Church Street. Continue west down Church Street for High Street's pubs and restaurants. Farther west on Belmore Street, in another pocket of pubs and chippies, are **McCartney's** (17 Belmore St., tel. 01365/322–012) and **McGee's Spirit Shop** (25 Belmore St., tel. 01365/324–996), the city's best watering holes. **Bush Bar and Lounge** (26 Townhall St, tel. 01365/325–210) often hosts live music.

Another good reason to visit Enniskillen is its location, nestled on the banks of Lough Erne in the heart of Fermanagh's stunning lake district. Cyclists in particular could spend a day or two exploring the lough's picture-perfect, 72-km (45-mi) shoreline. The rural A46/Bundoran road meanders along its pristine southern bank, and the equally scenic B82/Lisnarick road keeps to the east and passes the region's only youth hostel (*see* Where to Sleep and Eat, *above*). Another good day trip is to **Devenish Island,** 3 km (2 mi) north of Enniskillen, which boasts a well-preserved medieval monastic settlement with a ruined abbey and an 82-foot-tall round tower. The **M.V. Kestrel** (Brook Park, tel. 01365/322–882) runs 1¾-hour boat tours (£5) of Lough Erne that include a stop on Devenish Island. Enniskillen's **tourist office** (Wellington Rd., tel. 01365/323–110), adjacent to the Ulsterbus depot, has a bureau de change, books B&B accommodations (£1 fee), and will load you down with glossy brochures and information on transportation to Lough Erne and Devenish Island.

Also consider a day trip to the **Marble Arch Caves** (Marlbank Scenic Loop, Florence Ct., tel. 01365/348–855), the region's most popular tourist attraction. Inside the vast underground complex are subterranean rivers, waterfalls, and eerie passageways, all studded with the usual stalactite/stalagmite cave formations. You actually take a boat on an underground river for part of the tour. The Marble Arch Caves are 30 km (19 mi) south of Enniskillen on the A32, a short but semisteep cycle from town, and they're open late March–June and September, daily 10–4:30. Admission is £5. Apart from hitching, you can get a ride with **County Cabs** (tel. 01365/328–888) or **Cleenish Taxi Service** (tel. 0365/322–255), both of which run daily service to the caves for £8 one-way (make some new cave-loving friends to split the fare).

IRELAND AT A GLANCE:
A CHRONOLOGY

CA. 6000 BC • Mesolithic (middle Stone Age) hunter-gatherers migrate from Scotland to the northeastern Irish coast.

CA. 3500 BC • Neolithic (new Stone Age) settlers (origins uncertain) bring agriculture, pottery, and weaving. They also build massive megaliths—stone monuments with counterparts in England (Stonehenge), Brittany (Carnac), and elsewhere in Europe.

CA. 700 BC • Celtic tribes begin to arrive via Britain and France; they divide Ireland into "fifths" or provinces, including Ulster, Leinster, Connaught, Meath, and Munster.

CA. AD 100 • Ireland becomes the center of Celtic culture and trade without being settled by the Romans.

432 • Traditional date for the arrival of St. Patrick and Christianity; in fact, Irish conversion to Christianity began at least a century earlier.

CA. 500–800 • Golden Age of Irish monasticism; as many as 3,000 study at Clonard (Meath). Irish missionaries carry the faith to barbarian Europe; art (exemplified by the *Book of Kells,* ca. 700) and Gaelic poetry flourish.

795 • First Scandinavian Viking invasion; raids continue for the next 200 years. Viking towns founded, include Dublin, Waterford, Wexford, Cork, and Limerick.

1014 • Vikings decisively defeated at Clontarf by Irish troops under King Brian Boru of Munster. His murder cuts short hopes of a unified Ireland.

1066 • Normans (French descendants of Viking invaders) conquer England and set their sights on Ireland as well.

1169 • Dermot MacMurrough, exiled king of Munster, invites the Anglo-Norman adventurer Richard FitzGilbert de Clare ("Strongbow") to help him regain his throne, beginning a pattern of English opportunism and bad decisions by the Irish.

1172 • Pope Alexander III confirms Henry II, king of England, as feudal lord of Ireland. Over the next two centuries, Anglo-Norman nobles establish estates, intermarry with the native population, and act in a manner similar to the neighboring Celtic chieftains. Actual control by the English crown is confined to a small area known as "the land of peace" or "the Pale" around Dublin.

1366 • Statutes of Kilkenny attempt belatedly to enforce ethnic divisions by prohibiting the expression of Irish language and culture and intermarriage between the Irish and English, but Gaelic culture prevails, and the Pale continues to contract. Constant warfare among the great landowners keeps Ireland poor, divided, and isolated from the rest of Europe.

1477–1513 • Garret Mor ("Gerald the Great") FitzGerald, eighth earl of Kildare, dominates Irish affairs as lord deputy (the representative of the English crown).

1494 • Henry VII removes Kildare from office (he is soon reinstated), and initiates Statute of Drogheda (Poyning's Law), which is in force until 1782—Irish Parliament can only meet by consent of the king of England.

1534–40 • Henry VIII's break with the Catholic Church leads to insurrection in Ireland, led by Garret Mor's grandson Lord Offaly ("Silken Thomas"). He is executed with five of his brothers.

1541 • Parliament proclaims Henry VIII king of Ireland (his previous status was merely a feudal lord). Irish magnates reluctantly surrender their lands to him as their overlord. Hereafter, a constant English presence is required to keep the peace; no single Irish family replaces the FitzGeralds.

1558–1603 • Reign of Queen Elizabeth I; her fear of Irish intrigue with Catholic enemies of England leads to expansion of English power, including the Munster "plantation" (colony) scheme and the division of Ireland into English-style counties.

1580–88 • Edmund Spenser, an administrator for the Crown in Ireland, writes *The Faerie Queene.*

1591 • Trinity College, Dublin, is founded.

1595–1603 • Rebellion of Hugh O'Neill, earl of Tyrone (Ulster). Defeats England at Yellow Ford (1598), but assistance from Spain is inadequate; Tyrone surrenders at Mellifont six days after Queen Elizabeth's death.

1607 • The Flight of the Earls, and the beginning of "the Troubles." The earl of Tyrone and his ally Tyrconnell flee to Rome; their lands in Ulster are confiscated and opened to Protestant settlers, mostly Scots.

1641 • Charles I's policies provoke insurrection in Ulster and, soon after, civil war in England.

1649 • August: British leader Oliver Cromwell, having defeated Charles and witnessed his execution, invades Ireland, determined to crush Catholic opposition. Massacres at Drogheda and Wexford.

1652 • Act of Settlement—lands of Cromwell's opponents are confiscated, and owners are forced across the Shannon to Connaught. Never fully carried out, this policy nonetheless establishes Protestant ascendancy.

1678 • In the wake of the Popish Plot to assassinate King Charles II, Catholics are barred from British parliaments.

1683 • Dublin Philosophical Society founded, modeled on the Royal Society of London.

1689 • Having attempted, among other things, to repeal the Act of Settlement, King James II (a Catholic) is deposed and flees to Ireland. His daughter Mary and her husband William of Orange assume the throne.

1690 • James is defeated by William III at the Battle of the Boyne.

1704 • First laws of the Penal Code are enacted, restricting Catholic landowning; later laws prohibited voting, education, and military service among the Catholics.

1775 • American War of Independence begins, precipitating Irish unrest. Henry Grattan (1746–1820), a Protestant barrister, enters the Irish Parliament.

1778 • Land clauses of Penal Code are repealed.

1782 • Grattan's Parliament—Grattan asserts independence of Irish Parliament from Britain. Britain agrees, but independence is easier to declare than to sustain.

1798 • Inspired by the French Revolution and dissatisfied with the slow progress of Parliament, Wolfe Tone's United Irishmen rebel but are defeated.

1800 • The Irish Parliament votes itself out of existence and agrees to union with Britain, effective January 1, 1801.

1823 • Daniel O'Connell (1775–1847), "the Liberator," founds the Catholic Association to campaign for Catholic Emancipation.

1828 • O'Connell's election to Parliament (illegal, because he was a Catholic) leads to passage of Catholic Emancipation Act in 1829; later, he works for repeal of the Union.

1845–48 • Failure of potato crop leads to famine; thousands die, others migrate.

1848 • "Young Ireland," a radical party, leads an abortive rebellion.

1856 • Birth of George Bernard Shaw, playwright (d. 1950).

1858 • Fenian Brotherhood founded in New York by Irish immigrants with the aim of overthrowing British rule. A revolt in 1867 fails, but it compels Gladstone, the British prime minister, to disestablish the Anglican Church (1869) and reform landholding (1870) in Ireland. The government also increases its powers of repression.

1865 • Birth of William Butler Yeats, the great Irish poet (d. 1939).

1871 • Isaac Butts founds parliamentary Home Rule Party, soon dominated by Charles Stewart Parnell (1846–91, descendant of English Protestants), who tries to force the issue by obstructing parliamentary business.

1881 • Gladstone's second Land Act opposed by Parnell, who leads a boycott (named for Captain Boycott, its first victim) of landlords.

1882 • Phoenix Park murders—British officials murdered by Fenians. Prevention of Crime bill that follows suspends trial by jury and increases police powers. Acts of terrorism increase. Parnell disavows all connection with Fenians. Birth of James Joyce, novelist (d. 1941).

1886 • Gladstone introduces his first Home Rule Bill, which is defeated. Ulster Protestants fear Catholic domination and revive Orange Order (named for William of Orange) to oppose Home Rule.

1890 • Parnell is named corespondent in the divorce case of Kitty O'Shea; his career is ruined.

1893 • Second Home Rule Bill passes Commons but is defeated by Lords. Subsequent policy is to "kill Home Rule with kindness" with land reform, but cultural nationalism revives with founding of Gaelic League to promote Irish language. Yeats, John Synge (1871–1909), and other writers find inspiration in Gaelic past.

1898 • On the anniversary of Wolfe Tone's rebellion, Arthur Griffith (1872–1922) founds the Dublin newspaper the *United Irishman,* preaching *sinn fein* ("we ourselves")—secession from Britain; Sinn Fein party founded 1905. Socialist James Connolly (executed 1916) founds the *Workers' Republic.*

1904 • Abbey Theatre opens in Dublin.

1912 • Third Home Rule Bill passes Commons but is rejected by Lords. Under new rules, however, Lords' veto is null after two years. Meanwhile, Ulster Protestants plan defiance; the Ulster Volunteers recruit 100,000. Radical Republicans such as Connolly, Patrick Pearse, and others of the Irish Republican Brotherhood (IRB) preach insurrection and recruit their own volunteers.

1914 • Outbreak of war postpones implementation of Home Rule until peace returns. Parliamentarians agree, but radicals plan revolt.

1916 • Easter Uprising—IRB stages insurrection in Dublin and declares independence; the uprising fails, but the execution of 15 leaders by the British turns public opinion in favor of the insurgents. Yeats writes "a terrible beauty is born."

1919 • January: Irish Parliamentarians meet as the Dail Éireann (Irish Assembly) and declare independence. September: Dail suppressed; Sinn Fein made illegal.

1920–21 • War breaks out between Britain and Ireland: the "Black and Tans" versus the Irish Republican Army (IRA). Government of Ireland Act declares separate parliaments for north and south and continued ties to Britain. Elections follow, but the Sinn Fein majority in the south again declare themselves the Dail Éireann under Eamonn de Valera (1882–1975), rejecting British authority. December 1921: Anglo-Irish Treaty grants the south dominion status as the Irish Free State, allowing the north to remain under Britain.

1922 • De Valera and his Republican followers reject the treaty; civil war results. The Irish Free State adopts a constitution; William T. Cosgrave becomes president. Michael Collins, chairman of the Irish Free State and Commander-in-Chief of the Army, is shot dead in his County Cork, not far from where he was born. In Paris, James Joyce's *Ulysses* is published.

1923 • De Valera is arrested and the civil war ends, but Republican agitation and terrorism continue. William Butler Yeats is the first Irish writer to be awarded the Nobel Prize in Literature.

1925 • George Bernard Shaw wins the Nobel Prize in Literature.

1932 • De Valera, who had founded the Fianna Fáil party in 1926, begins a 16-year term as Taioseach (Prime Minister).

1932–36 • Tariff war with Britain.

1938 • New constitution creates Republic of Ireland with no ties to Britain.

1947 • The statue of Queen Victoria is removed from the courtyard in front of the Irish Parliament in Dublin.

1969 • The annual Apprentice Boys' march in Derry, Northern Ireland, leads to rioting between Catholics and Protestants. British troops, called in to keep the peace, remain in Northern Ireland to this day. Samuel Beckett is awarded the Nobel Prize in Literature, but declines to travel to Oslo to receive it.

1972 • Republic of Ireland admitted to European Economic Community. Troubles continue in the north: In Derry on January 30, British troops shoot 13 unarmed demonstrators on "Bloody Sunday." Stormont (the Northern Parliament) is suspended and direct rule from London is imposed. Acts of terrorism on both sides leads to draconian law enforcement by the British.

1979 • Pope John Paul II visits Ireland and celebrates mass in Phoenix Park; more than a million people attend.

1986 • Anglo-Irish Agreement signed, giving the Republic of Ireland a stronger voice in northern affairs.

1988 • Dublin celebrates its millennium.

1991 • Mary Robinson becomes the first female President of the Republic of Ireland. Peace talks begin between the British and Irish governments and the main political parties of the North, excepting Sinn Féin.

1992 • Ireland approves European Union. Sixty-two percent of the Irish vote in a referendum in favor of allowing pregnant women to seek an abortion abroad.

1994 • The IRA, in response to advances made by the Irish, British, and U.S. governments, announces a complete cessation of activities. Protestant paramilitary groups follow suit one month later.

1995 • After 25 years, daylight troop patrols are discontinued in Belfast. Seamus Heaney receives the Nobel Prize in Literature, the fourth Irish writer in less than 75 years so honored.

1996 • The IRA, in frustration with the slow progress in the peace talks, explode bombs on the British mainland, throwing the whole peace process into doubt. But violence has not returned to the province, and all parties say they are committed to peace.

1997 • The Republic of Ireland legalizes divorce. Ireland is rated the fastest growing economy in the industrialized world. IRA declare new ceasefire and are admitted into all party talks.

IT'S ALL IN THE NAME

BY FIONN DAVENPORT

I n a small coffee shop outside of Galway Town, Seamus D., a young man from Dublin, sat eating a warm scone and drinking a hot cup of tea. He had driven that morning from home, crossing from coast to coast—from east to west—in a matter of hours, on a trip that brought him from the familiarity of Dublin to the excitement of what was to him, despite his Irishness, a foreign place. He had never been to this part of the country—was it possible that he was a foreigner here? The feeling in his stomach seemed to say so.

Along the journey he fought the notion that he was being irrational; he had listened to tapes of Irish traditional music and had recognized many of the tunes (though the names of the different jigs, reels, and laments meant nothing to him); he knew the history of the area as well as his own family past; he could imitate the gruff lilt of the Galway accent to the point where he might actually pass as a local, if only for a couple of minutes, in a crowded bar where conversation and the effects of the stout would surely dull a quick ear. But as he finished the rest of his snack, he felt slightly lost—and thrilled at the thought of what lay ahead.

His acquaintance with the west of Ireland, and Galway in particular, was that of a pen pal. His knowledge was secondhand and was locked in a cage of big-city ideas about "minor" towns. It was no accident that, as a rule, the Irish talked about trips to and from the capital as going up to Dublin and going down to the country. Dubliners have a tendency of looking at non-Dubliners as though they were a kind of ancient grandparents, to be loved—and sometimes hated—with a tinge of superiority that one usually feels toward the old and slightly out of touch. Dublin was the new Ireland, the rest of the country a land of verdant beauty and peculiar customs; it was where you could "get away from it all"; it was the greatest backyard in the world.

If it was a backyard, he had spent too long indoors. He settled into the driver's seat for the last leg of the journey, now less than an hour away. He was going to Kinvara, a small fishing port on the Atlantic coast that was home and final resting place of his paternal grandfather, a hamlet described in his guidebook as a "delightful village tucked away on the southeast corner of Galway Bay."

He had come in search of traces of his grandfather Seamus, a man in a grave not quite forgotten, but ignored. Perhaps the sight of their shared name—once proudly engraved in the elegant stone, now hidden by weeds and moss—would make everything seem less foreign to him and more a reminder of home and a past he knew little about.

His grandfather had died in the late fifties, and nobody had visited his grave since the day of the funeral, when a resigned widow and a puzzled boy—his father—buried a man they never really knew. His death brought little grief to wife or son, despite the fears of the woman and the tears of the child, now alone after so many years of being left alone by a man whose beds and favorite pubs were in faraway London, Chicago, New York, or wherever the creditors could be kept at bay. The widow and the son mourned respectfully but not excessively: the family had declared Seamus a "bad" man and his passing was met with stoic indifference.

In Kinvara, Seamus the younger was struck by the picturesque quality of the village: the houses were wrapped around a small bay used as a port by the local fishermen. Wooden longboats were run aground on the pebbled beach, idle through the long winter months when challenging the merciless sea would have been suicidal. On a small hill to one side of the bay was Kinvara's most famous landmark, Dungaire Castle, a stronghold of the O'Brien family before it was captured by the Tourist Board and turned into a curiosity, complete with a souvenir shop and nighttime medieval banquets. But sightseeing was not Seamus' priority, so he turned his attention to the matter at hand. He had to find the graveyard but needed directions. He decided to go to the pub.

The pub was a small terraced house, undistinguishable from the houses on either side except for the "Lynch's" sign over the door. Its pebble-dash front was painted in a pastel yellow that, along with the colored shades of the other houses, gave the whole town an almost fairy-tale look, as though it were an Irish version of a Lego village. He stepped inside and over to the bar. He waited a moment before the barman looked up from his newspaper to acknowledge his presence.

"A pint of plain, please."

The barman pulled a glass from beneath the bar and rested it under the tap. A flick of his wrist and the glass began to fill up with black, creamy liquid. When it was about three-quarters full he pushed the tap back and sat the glass on the bar. Within a couple of minutes the pint had settled and a thin white head had formed. He held it a second time under the tap and filled it to the rim, and once again the barman sat the pint on the bar. He did all of this without once stirring from his stool, only looking up from his newspaper to make sure that the glass didn't overflow.

"And a packet of peanuts, please. Oh, and could you be so kind as to tell me where the cemetery is?"

The barman raised his eyes. "What kind?" Seamus stared back, a little perplexed. The barman spoke again. "Salted or plain? Do you want salted peanuts or plain ones?"

"Plain, please." But what about the cemetery?

"Two, please," the barman said. Seamus took out a five-pound note from his wallet and left it on the bar.

"Which graveyard are you lookin' for? The new one or the old one?"

Ah, some information. "I don't know which one. I'm trying to find my grandfather's grave . . ."

"What was his name?"

"Seamus." The barman looked at him. "Seamus D."

"He can't be buried around here," the barman said firmly. "That's a Clare name, not a Galway name. Are you sure you have the right town?" The barman's tone bordered on the bored, which brought the risk of an end to the conversation and would leave him with no clue as to where to go.

"I knew Michael D. well." The voice came from behind Seamus and startled him. He turned around, and in the corner there was a small man dressed in a dark suit at a small table full of empty pint glasses. Seamus had not seen him against the dark walls when he came in. Perhaps this fellow had been a local for so long that his molecules had fused with those of the bar, and had become a rural version of Flann O'Brien's *The Third Policeman*.

"My grandfather's name was Seamus, not Michael," Seamus responded politely. Despite his visions of men who were half-human and half-pub, he feared that he was wasting his time. Ah, but big-city time and country time were two different things altogether.

"That's right," the man said, "but your great-grandfather was Michael. I knew him well and his son, too, that is, your grandfather," the man continued. "Julia's husband he was, at least before he died and she took her brood up to her people in Dublin." Seamus smiled at the man, but he ignored the gesture and continued talking. "He commanded a brigade in the war against the British, I remember. A tallish fellow, and he liked his pint. By God, he liked his pint. He once told me a story about how the Black and Tans were chasing him and he hid in a stream for three days and four nights so that their dogs wouldn't catch his scent." Seamus had heard this story from his own father, but in his version he had stayed in the stream only a couple of hours.

The barman listened intently, and then declared "Oh, I remember him now. He drank in here when Da was running things!" Seamus turned to the barman and was surprised to see a smile come across his face as he spoke. "He was a fine man, if I remember correctly." He was an awful man, Seamus thought to himself, but he who is fond of the drink will be one thing to the person serving him and another to his family. "Great with the stories, generous with friends, gracious with his enemies, and a bit of a charmer with the ladies." The barman looked at Seamus. "So, he was your grandfather, then?"

"He was."

"Well then, my young Dub, you've come home, haven't you?" He offered his hand. "You'll be needing a few and a bit of a rest before you tackle the cemetery. A grave and sullen place it is. The first pint is on me. Taidgh O Shaughnessy at your service."

IRISH FAMILY NAMES

Antrim
Lynch
McDonnell
McNeill
O'Hara
O'Neill
Quinn

Armagh
Hanlon
McCann

Carlow
Kinsella
Nolan
O'Neill

Cavan
Boylan
Lynch
McCabe
McGovern
McGowan
McNally
O'Reilly
Sheridan

Clare
Aherne
Boland
Clancy
Daly
Lynch
McGrath
McInerney
McMahon
McNamara
Molon(e)y
O'Brien
O'Dea
O'Grady
O'Halloran
O'Loughlin

Cork
Barry
Callaghan
Cullinane
Donovan
Driscoll
Flynn
Hennessey
Hogan
Lynch
McCarthy
McSweeney
Murphy
Nugent
O'Casey
O'Cullane
(Collins)

O'Keefe
O'Leary
O'Mahony
O'Riordan
Roche
Scanlon
Sheridan

Derry
Cahan
Hegarty
Kelly
McLaughlin

Donegal
Boyle
Clery
Doherty
Friel
Gallagher
Gormley
McGrath
McLoughlin
McSweeney
Mooney
O'Donnell

Down
Lynch
McGuinness
O'Neil
White

Dublin
Hennessey
O'Casey
Plunkett

Fermanagh
Cassidy
Connolly
Corrigan
Flanagan
Maguire
McManus

Galway
Blake
Burke
Clery
Fah(e)y
French
Jennings
Joyce
Kelly
Kenny
Kirwan
Lynch
Madden
Moran
O'Flaherty
O'Halloran

Kerry
Connor
Fitzgerald
Galvin
McCarthy
Moriarty
O'Connell
O'Donoghue
O'Shea
O'Sullivan

Kildare
Cullen
Fitzgerald
O'Byrne
White

Kilkenny
Butler
Fitzpatrick
O'Carroll
Tobin

Laois
Dempsey
Doran
Dunn(e)
Kelly
Moore

Leitrim
Clancy
O'Rourke

Limerick
Fitzgerald
Fitzgibbon
McKeough
O'Brien
O'Cullane
(Collins)
O'Grady
Woulfe

Longford
O'Farrell
Quinn

Louth
O'Carroll
Plunkett

Mayo
Burke
Costello
Dugan
Gormley
Horan
Jennings
Jordan
Kelly
Madden
O'Malley

Meath
Coffey
Connolly
Cusack
Dillon
Hayes
Hennessey
Plunkett
Quinlan

Monaghan
Boylan
Connolly
Hanratty
McKenna
McMahon
McNally

Offaly
Coghlan
Dempsey
Fallon
(Maher)
Malone
Meagher
Molloy
O'Carroll
Sheridan

Roscommon
Fallon
Flanagan
Flynn
Hanley
McDermot
McKeogh
McManus
Molloy
Murphy

Sligo
Boland
Higgins
McDonagh
O'Dowd
O'Hara
Rafferty

Tipperary
Butler
Fogarty
Kennedy
Lynch
Meagher
(Maher)
O'Carroll
O'Dwyer
O'Meara
Purcell
Ryan

Tyrone
Cahan
Donnelly
Gormley
Hagan
Murphy
O'Neill
Quinn

Waterford
Keane
McGrath
O'Brien
Phelan
Power

Westmeath
Coffey
Dalton
Daly
Dillon
Sheridan

Wexford
Doran
Doyle
Hartley
Kavanagh
Keating
Kinsella
McKeogh
Redmond
Walsh

Wicklow
Cullen
Kelly
McKeogh
O'Byrne
O'Toole

BOOKS AND VIDEOS

AUTOBIOGRAPHY

Since it was published in September 1996, *Angela's Ashes,* Frank McCourt's enormously affecting memoir of growing up desperately poor in Limerick, has garnered every major American literary accolade, from the Pulitzer Prize to the National Book Critics Circle Award, and has become a fixture at the top of American bestseller lists. In *An Only Child* and *My Father's Son* (1969), Frank O'Connor, known primarily for his fiction and short stories, recounts his years as an Irish revolutionary and later as an intellectual in Dublin during the 1920s. Christy Brown's *My Left Foot* is the autobiographical account of a Dublin artist stricken with cerebral palsy (*see* Movies and Videos, *below*).

GUIDEBOOKS AND TRAVEL LITERATURE

Exploring Ireland (2nd Ed.), also published by Fodor's, a full-color guide packed with photographs, is an excellent companion guide to this edition.

Peter Somerville-Large's *Dublin* is packed with anecdotes relating to the famed Irish city. *Georgian Dublin,* by Desmond Guinness, the founder of the Irish Georgian Society, explores the city's architecture, with photographs and plans of Dublin's most admirable buildings. The most up-to-date work on the Aran Islands is Tim Robinson's award-winning *The Stones of Aran: Pilgrimage.* Robinson has also written a long introduction to the Penguin edition of J. M. Synge's 1907 classic, *The Aran Islands.* Tomas Ó Crohán's *The Islandman* provides a good background on Dingle and the Blasket Islands.

In *Round Ireland in Low Gear* (1988), famed British travel writer Eric Newby writes breezily of his bicycle journey with his wife around the wet Emerald Isle. Fifty years older but no less fresh is H.V. Morton's *In Search of Ireland* (1938). Rebecca Solnit uses Ireland as a sounding board for her meditations on travel in *A Book of Migrations: Some Passages in Ireland* (1997).

HISTORY AND CURRENT AFFAIRS

For two intriguing studies of Irish culture and history, consult Constantine FitzGibbon's *The Irish in Ireland* and Sean O'Faolain's *The Irish: A Character Study,* which traces the history of Ireland from Celtic times. J. C. Beckett's *The Making of Modern Ireland,* a concise introduction to Irish history, covers the years between 1603 and 1923. *Modern Ireland,* by R. F. Foster, spans the years between 1600 and 1972. An up-to-date analysis of the making of modern Ireland can be found in *Ireland 1912–1985 Politics and Society,* by J. J. Lee. For an acclaimed history of Irish nationalism, try Robert Kee's *The Green Flag.* Peter De Rosa's *Rebels: The Irish Rising of 1916* is a popularly written, novelistic history of the defining event of modern Irish history. Irish country-house devotees should read *Aristocrats: Caroline, Emily, Louisa and Sarah Lennox, 1740–1832,* by Stella Tillyard; Louisa was the force behind Castletown House.

John Ardagh's *Ireland and the Irish: Portrait of a Changing Society* (1997) is the best current sociological and economic analysis of modern Ireland. *"We Wrecked the Place": Contemplating an End to the Northern Irish Troubles* (1996) by Belfast-based journalist Jonathan Stevenson is the best recent book on the subject. John Conroy's *Belfast Diary: War as a Way of Life* (1995) was reissued with a new afterword on the ceasefire. Neither Colm Toibin's *Bad Blood: A Walk Along the Irish Border* nor Carlo Gebler's *The Glass Curtain: Inside an Ulster Community* are published in the U.S., but both are worth tracking down.

Rosemary Mahoney, a young Irish-American writer, moved to Ireland, where she wrote *Whoredom in Kimmage: Irish Women Coming of Age* (1993), a collective portrait of Irish women *and* men in the early 1990s.

LITERARY BIOGRAPHY AND CRITICISM

Richard Ellman's *James Joyce* (1959) is recognized as the finest literary biography ever written, and is easily the best introduction to the man and his work. Ellman completed his second biographical masterpiece, *Oscar Wilde* (1988), shortly before his death, after more than 20 years of research. Ellman also wrote *Yeats: The Man and the Masks* (1978), although the first volume of Roy F. Foster's new biography, *W. B. Yeats: A Life—The Apprentice Mage 1865–1914, Vol. 1* (1997) has been welcomed as definitive, on the caliber of Ellman's Joyce and Wilde bios. Michael Holroyd's exhaustive, four-volume biography of George Bernard Shaw (1988, 1988, 1991 and 1993) will tell you everything you want to know about the larger-than-life, Nobel Prize–winning dramatist, critic, and social reformer. Samuel Beckett himself asked James Knowlson to write his biography; the result, *Damned to Fame: The Life of Samuel Beckett*, was published in 1996 and is widely regarded as the definitive life of the writer. William Trevor's *A Writer's Ireland: Landscape in Literature* (1984) explores the influence of Ireland's changing landscape on its writers. *Inventing Ireland: The Literature of Modern Nation* (1995) by Declan Kiberd is a major literary history of modern Ireland.

LITERATURE

Ulysses (1922) is the linguistically innovative masterpiece by James Joyce, one of the titans of 20th-century literature. Emulating the structure of *The Odyssey,* and using an unprecedented stream of consciousness technique, Joyce follows Leopold and Molly Bloom and Stephen Daedalus through the course of a single day—June 16, 1904—around Dublin. (Joyce set *Ulysses* on the day he and his future wife, Nora Barnacle, had their first date.) More accessible introductions to Joyce's writing include *A Portrait of the Artist as a Young Man* (1916) and *Dubliners* (1914), a collection of short stories (its most accomplished story, "The Dead," was made into a movie starring Angelica Huston in 1988). Joyce aficionados may want to tackle his final, gigantic work, *Finnegan's Wake* (1939), which takes the linguistic experimentation of *Ulysses* to an almost incomprehensible level. Arguably the greatest literary challenge of the 20th century, its pages include word plays and phonetic metaphors in over 100 languages. To prepare you for reading Joyce, you might seek out audio recordings in which he reads in his inimitable lilting tenor voice.

Samuel Beckett fills his story collection *More Pricks than Kicks* with Dublin characters; if you enjoy literary gamesmanship, you may also want to try Beckett's trilogy—*Molloy* (1951), *Malone Dies* (1951), and *The Unnamable* (1953).

If you're drawn to tales of unrequited love, turn to Elizabeth Bowen's stories and her novel, *The Last September* (1929), set in Ireland during the Irish Civil War. Coming-of-age novels include *Under the Eye of the Clock,* a somewhat autobiographical work by Christopher Nolan, which takes as its subject a handicapped youth discovering the pleasures of language, and *Fools of Fortune* (1983), by William Trevor, which treats the loss of an ideal childhood, brought about by a changing political climate. Trevor's *The Silence in the Garden* (1988) is also worth looking for.

If you prefer reading more magical novels, take a look at James Stephens's *A Crock of Gold* (1912), a charming and wise fairy tale written for adults, and Flann O'Brien's *At Swim-Two-Birds* (1939), a surrealistic tale full of Irish folklore.

One of Ireland's foremost fiction writers working today, Edna O'Brien began her career with the comic novel, *The Country Girls* (1960), and has published seventeen books since, most recently *House of Splendid Isolation* (1994) and *Down By the River* (1997). Like many of her compatriots, she is a superb short-story writer. Her collection, *A Fanatic Heart* (1985), is one of her best. Other superbly crafted story collections, full of acute observations of Ireland's social and political landscape, include Benedict Kiely's *The State of Ireland,* Mary Lavin's *Collected Stories,* Frank O'Connor's *Collected Stories* (1952), William Trevor's *Collected Stories* (1993), and John McGahern's *Collected Stories* (1993).

Thomas Flanagan's *The Year of the French* is a historical novel about the people of County Mayo, who revolted in 1798 with the help of French revolutionaries. *A Nest of Simple Folk,* by Sean O'Faolain, follows three generations of an Irish family between 1854 and 1916. Leon Uris's *Trinity* covers the years 1840–1916, as seen through the eyes of British, Irish Catholic, and Ulster Protestant families. In *No Country for Young Men,* Julia O'Faolain writes of two Irish families struggling to overcome the effects of the Irish Civil War. In John McGahern's prizewinning novel *Amongst Women,* modern-day Ireland attempts to reconcile itself to the upheavals of the early years of this century. For a more contemporary look at life in urban Ireland, try the phenomenally successful Roddy Doyle: His "Barrytown Trilogy"—*The Snapper, The Commitments,* and *The Van*—have all been made into films; *Paddy Clarke Ha Ha Ha,* another success, is sure to follow. Shortlisted for the Booker Prize, *Reading in the Dark* (1997) marks the novelistic debut of Seamus Deane, a poet, critic, and editor. It covers familiar territory—a family in 1920 Ireland riven by political strife—but does so with extraordinarily evocative language.

MOVIES AND VIDEOS

There has been a plethora of movies made in or about Ireland, and the number of Irish characters on screen is legion (the most numerous being priests, drunks, New York cops, and Old Mother Riley). *Juno and the Paycock* (known in the United States as *The Shame of Mary Boyle*) and *The Plough and the Stars* (1936), about the months leading up to the Easter Uprising, are early screen adaptations of Sean O'Casey's theatrical masterpieces. John Ford's superb *The Informer* (1935) is a full-blooded and highly stylized tale of an IRA leader's betrayal during the struggle for independence by a simpleminded hanger-on who wants to emigrate to the United States. Ford's boisterous comedy, *The Quiet Man* (1952) is an Irish-village version of *The Taming of the Shrew*, with John Wayne playing a box who returns to his ancestor's village in the West of Ireland to claim local beauty Maureen O'Hara, and Barry Fitzgerald. David Lean's epic, *Ryan's Daughter* (1970), is a four-hour pastoral melodrama of a village schoolmaster's wife falling for a British officer in the troubled Ireland of 1916; the film was a critical and commercial disaster for Lean, who didn't make another film for 14 years.

Daniel Day Lewis and Brenda Fricker give Oscar-winning performances in Jim Sheridan's *My Left Foot* (1989), a biography of Christy Brown, the Irish writer and painter crippled from birth by cerebral palsy. Alan Parker's *The Commitments* (1991), from Roddy Doyle's best-seller, humorously recounts the efforts of a group of young, working-class northside Dubliners trying to make it as a soul band. A made-for-TV version of another of Doyle's best-sellers, *The Snapper* (1993) is a touching, funny tale of a Dublin girl's struggles to be a single mother in the face of an orthodox and often unforgiving society. *The Van* (1997) completes the "Trilogy, as the books that were the basis of these three films are known. In *A Man of No Importance* (1994), Albert Finney plays a sexually repressed bus conductor whose passion for poetry leads him to stage Wilde's *Salomé*. John Sayles hooked up with acclaimed cinematographer Haskell Wexler to make *The Secret of Roan Inish* (1996), a magical realist fable about a Selkie—a creature from Celtic folkore who is a seal in the water and a woman on land—and the fisherman's family whose lives she changes.

Some of the best movies made in Ireland deal with the Troubles that have afflicted Northern Ireland. *Four Days in July* (1984), directed by Mike Leigh in classic *cinema verité* style, is a poignant and compelling portrayal of the sectarian divide in working-class Belfast. Based on actual events, Ken Loach's *Hidden Agenda* (1990) is a hard-hitting thriller about the murder of an American lawyer working for Amnesty International in the troubled North. As the plot unfolds, it becomes clear that the highest echelons of the British government and secret services are involved. Helen Mirrren stars as the widow of an executed Protestant policeman in *Cal* (1984), based on Bernard MacLaverty's masterful novel about the Troubles. Daniel Day Lewis was nominated for an Academy Award for his portrayal of Gerry Conlon, the wrongfully imprisoned Irish youth, in Jim Sheridan's *In the Name of the Father* (1993). Neil Jordan's *Michael Collins* (1996) depicts the turbulent life of the heroic Commander-in-Chief of the Irish Republican Army from the Easter Uprising in 1916, when Collins was 25, until his assassination in West Cork six years later; it went on to become the highest-grossing film ever in Ireland. Helen Mirren again plays a widow in *Some Mother's Son* (1997), set during the 1981 Maze Prison Hunger Strike that claimed Bobby Sands.

PERIODICAL

Billing itself as "A magazine for the Irish diaspora: An ongoing celebration of Ireland and the Irish around the world," *The World of Hibernia* (issued quarterly; US [$50], Canada [$60 U.S.], and rest of the world [$80 U.S.]: 340 Madison Ave., Suite 411, New York, NY 10164-2920; Ireland and Britain [£32]: 22 Crofton Rd., Dun Laoghaire, Co. Dublin) has savvy, solid editorial coverage. Its quality is also high (on par with the finest art magazines), making it a magazine you're likely to keep on your coffee table months after the issue date.

POETRY

The poems of William Butler Yeats, Ireland's most celebrated poet, often describe the Irish landscape, including the Sligo and Coole countryside. A favorite poet among the Irish is Patrick Kavanagh, whose distinguished career was devoted to writing exceptionally about ordinary lives. Winner of the *Irish Times–Aer Lingus* Literary prize in 1993, Derek Mahon is the author of *Selected Poems* (1992) and many other books. Northern Ireland serves as the setting for many of Seamus Heaney's poems. *Selected Poems 1996–1987* (1990) and *The Spirit Level* (1996), his first collection published since he won the Nobel Prize in Literature in 1995, are both highly recommended introductions to his work. Though not as well known outside Ireland as Heaney, Paul Muldoon is another major Irish poet. His *Selected Poems: 1968–1986* (1987) and his most recent volume, *The Annals of Chile* (1994) are both good places to start. Eavan Boland is widely regarded as among the top tier of Irish poets, and the finest woman writing poetry in Ireland today. *An Origin Like Water: Collected Poems 1957–1987* (1996) and *Object Lessons: The Life of the Woman and the Poet in Our Time* (1995) are two of her recent books.

THEATER

Ireland's playwrights are as distinguished as its novelists and short story writers. Samuel Beckett, who moved from Ireland to Paris and began writing in French, is the author of the comic modernist masterpiece *Waiting for Godot* (1952), among many other plays. Oscar Wilde's finest plays, *The Importance of Being Earnest* and *An Ideal Husband* (both 1895), were playing to packed audiences in London when he was charged by his lover's father as a somdomite [sic, setting in motion the trials that lead to his downfall. Among the many plays of George Bernard Shaw, who grew up in Dublin, are *Arms and the Man* (1894), *Major Barbara* (1905), *Pygmalion* (1913), and *Saint Joan* (1923).

The history of Irish theater includes a good number of controversial plays, such as J. M. Synge's *The Playboy of the Western World,* which was considered morally outrageous at the time of its opening in 1907 ("Playboy riots" took place in Dublin when the play was produced at the Abbey Theatre), but is appreciated today for its poetic language. Sean O'Casey wrote passionately about social injustice and working-class characters around the time of the Irish Civil War in such plays as *The Plough and the Stars* (1926) and *Juno and the Paycock* (1924). *The Quare Fellow* (1956), by Brendan Behan, challenged accepted mores in the 1950's and at the time could only be produced in London. Behan is also well known for his play *The Hostage* and for *Borstal Boy* (1958), his memoirs. Two more recently recognized playwrights are Hugh Leonard (*Da* and *A Life*) and Brian Friel (*Philadelphia, Here I Come!, The Faith Healer,* and *Dancing at Lughnasa*), whose work often illuminates Irish small-town life.

INDEX

WHEREVER
YOU TRAVEL,
*H*ELP IS NEVER
FAR AWAY.

From planning your trip to providing travel assistance along the way, American Express® Travel Service Offices are always there to help.

Ireland

American Express Travel Service
116 Grafton Street
Dublin
1/677-2874

American Express Travel Service
International Hotel
East Avenue Road
Killarney
64/35 722

do more AMERICAN EXPRESS®
Travel

http://www.americanexpress.com/travel